Africa

Africa: An Introduction invites you into Africa: a continent rich with culture and history, with diverse populations stretching from the dense tropical rain forest of the Congo basin, right up to the Sahara Desert in the north, and down to the Mediterranean climates of the far south.

Containing fifty-five countries, and covering over 20 percent of the world's landmass, Africa is the birthplace of humanity, yet the image of Africa in the West is often negative, that of a continent riddled with endemic problems. This accessible and engaging guide to the African continent guides the reader through the history, geography, and politics of Africa. It ranges from the impact of slavery and imperialism through to the rise of African nationalism and the achievement of independence, and up to the present moment. Key topics covered include literature, art, technology, religion, the condition of African women, health, education, and the mounting environmental concerns faced by African people.

As Africa moves beyond the painful legacies of slavery and imperialism, this book provides an engaging, uplifting, and accessible introduction to a rapidly modernizing and diverse continent. Suitable for high school and undergraduate students studying Africa, this book will also serve as the perfect introduction for anyone looking to understand the history of Africa and the Africa of today.

Eustace Palmer is Emeritus Professor of English and erstwhile Coordinator of Africana Studies at Georgia College and State University, USA. He was born in Sierra Leone, and taught at Fourah Bay College, the University of Sierra Leone, for several years, before relocating to the United States. He is one of the pioneer critics of African literature and is regarded as one of the world's leading authorities in that field.

Africa

An Introduction

Eustace Palmer

LONDON AND NEW YORK

First published 2022
by Routledge
2 Park Square, Milton Park, Abingdon, Oxon OX14 4RN

and by Routledge
605 Third Avenue, New York, NY 10158

Routledge is an imprint of the Taylor & Francis Group, an informa business

British Library Cataloguing-in-Publication Data
A catalogue record for this book is available from the British Library

Library of Congress Cataloging-in-Publication Data
Names: Palmer, Eustace, author.
Title: Africa : an introduction / Eustace Palmer.
Description: Abingdon, Oxon ; New York, NY : Routledge, 2021. |
Includes bibliographical references and index.
Identifiers: LCCN 2020057533 (print) | LCCN 2020057534 (ebook) |
ISBN 9780367629830 (hardback) | ISBN 9780367433734 (paperback) |
ISBN 9781003111733 (ebook)
Subjects: LCSH: Africa--History. | Africa--Social conditions. |
Africa--Economic conditions.
Classification: LCC DT20 .P35 2021 (print) | LCC DT20 (ebook) |
DDC 960--dc23
LC record available at https://lccn.loc.gov/2020057533
LC ebook record available at https://lccn.loc.gov/2020057534

ISBN: 978-0-367-62983-0 (hbk)
ISBN: 978-0-367-43373-4 (pbk)
ISBN: 978-1-003-11173-3 (ebk)

DOI: 10.4324/9781003111733

Typeset in Bembo
by Taylor & Francis Books

Contents

Illustrations

Figures

Tables

Acknowledgments

A work like this inevitably draws from several disciplines, and as I prepared for it over the years while teaching "Introduction to African Studies" and doing the necessary research, I had to consult several sources in those various disciplines and draw upon the scholarship of noted Africanists. These include experts like Ali Mazrui, Basil Davidson, J. D. Fage, Ajayi and Crowder, Henry Louis Gates, John Mbiti, Geoffrey Parrinder, Chrispin Matsika, Isidore Okpewho, Mario Azevedo, April Gordon, Donald Gordon, Oyekan Owomoyela, Kevin Shillington, Alpha Bah, Julius Nyang'oro, Ambrose Moyo, C.G.Baeta, Kwabena Nketia, Babs Fafunwa, Hunt Davis, and others. I apologize that I cannot list them all here, but I have made strenuous efforts to acknowledge my debt to them in the text and in the references and suggestions for further reading. I apologize if I have inadvertently left anyone out.

I would also like to express my gratitude to colleagues and students I interacted with over the years who helped sharpen my insights into African affairs. In particular, I would like to mention my fellow members of the University System of Georgia Africa Council (USAC), which is entrusted with the responsibility of promoting knowledge of Africa within the University System of Georgia and the state as a whole. Once every year since 1997, USAC has staged a simulation of the annual meeting of African Heads of State called the Southeast Model of the African Union. This is actually a conference bringing together students and faculty in the System for an extensive discussion of African affairs. The experience and the insights derived both from the preparation for the conference and the discussions at the conference itself were invaluable in guiding my judgments, and helped provide the motivation for this book. Thanks to you all!

Introduction

The rationale for African studies

The motivation for this work was the belief that people in the Western world in general, and those in the United States in particular, should, for various reasons, be informed about the African continent. This particularly applies to young people who, no matter how young they might be at the moment, will in the future be in a position to influence the nature of policy on Africa and other parts of the world. In order to influence their governments and others in authority they must be well informed. The need to be knowledgeable about Africa is, of course, not confined to young people; every thinking individual who will be in a position to influence policies and decisions in any way, even if that influence is as rudimentary as a vote, should ensure that their influence proceed from knowledge of the facts, the facts of history and culture, and the nature of current affairs on the continent. Sadly, however, we are bombarded every day with evidence of ignorance in the Western world about the facts of African history, African lifestyles and cultures, and the current state of affairs on this very important continent. The situation is less acute in Europe, probably because the exploration of the African continent by Europeans and the subsequent imperialist activity resulted in the involvement and interest of several groups of Europeans in Africa, from missionaries to merchants, to administrators to professors and teachers. The United States' involvement is rather more recent, and in spite of the recent advances made by Africanists in American universities since the seventies, the ignorance is still pervasive.

One of the most important reasons why it is necessary to promote knowledge of Africa in the United States is that there is so much misconception and, at times, deliberate misinformation about Africa in the West in general. This is, of course, not confined to the present time. It can be traced way back to the days of slavery and even earlier. As far as the Romans were concerned, Africans were only fit to be slaves or used as sex objects. One only has to read *The Satyricon* of Petronius Arbiter to realize this. Actually the Romans had some knowledge about Africa, but the only part they knew was Northern Africa: places like Egypt, Tunisia, and Morocco. As we will see, the whole of Northern Africa was involved with the rest of the Mediterranean world and participated in the dynamics of that area, but even so the Romans, while recognizing the importance of places like Egypt, always saw North Africa as a deadly threat that would, if permitted, enfeeble the majestic Roman Empire. North Africa therefore had to be conquered. As one of the Roman generals put it, "Carthage must be destroyed," and it was. And Egypt too was subsequently conquered. Fast-forwarding to the Renaissance and Elizabethan days we note the racial prejudice that tinged Europeans' attitudes towards Africa and the African. Shakespeare was, in fact, much more generous than some of his contemporaries towards Africa and the African. He can see the humanity in Othello in the play of that

DOI: 10.4324/9781003111733-1

name, but in the same play he reflects the Venetians' racial stereotypes. They refer to Othello as having "thick lips"; some see him as little better than a beast from a place with all kinds of strange creatures and strange practices. Slavery was partly caused by European attitudes towards Africa and Africans whom they saw as being no more than beasts living in a "dark" continent which was itself the home of evil. Imperialism was partly the result of Europeans seeing Africa as an inferior and barbaric place that they had the right to take over. Even later intellectuals like Hegel saw Africa as having made no meaningful contribution to world history and progress. So there have always been misconceptions about Africa.

Some of the current misconceptions are due to ignorance, but some are due to racism and deliberate manipulation of the truth for purposes of sensationalism, propaganda, or commercial success. A number of Westerners would claim that the black peoples of Africa are descendants of the Children of Ham who were cursed and should therefore be outside the circle of civilized peoples. This mistaken and repulsive view was used to justify slavery, as were Darwinian theories of evolution which located black people way down in the evolutionary scale as the humans most related to the apes from whom humans evolved. Such attitudes and views have been largely discredited, but it is amazing how widespread they still are in certain parts of the world including the United States, where some people, even in high places, could still refer to Africans as monkeys. These attitudes seem to have been locked in the unconscious of many. Some of the early travelers from the Western world to Africa, people who included anthropologists, missionaries, merchants, and even administrators, brought back highly sensationalized and blatantly false accounts of their travels and of the nature of the peoples of Africa. Their intention was not so much to convey the facts and the truth as to present their audience with vignettes of the sensational and reinforce the pervasive stereotypes. The activities of people like the novelist/sailor Joseph Conrad and the explorer Henry Morton Stanley are well known and will be discussed later. They and others brought back pictures of Africans as lazy, indulging in barbaric practices like cannibalism and human sacrifice, ignorant, incapable of rational thought and given over to emotionalism, predisposed to filth, dirty and unaware of the need for personal hygiene, completely untrustworthy, and so on. Most of these travelers operated from and returned to Europe, but some of them were associated with the United States. Henry Morton Stanley was a leading example. He was, in fact, supported in his travels by some leading American groups. The stereotypes that were reinforced by these travelers stuck. I recall that early in my American career when I was living in an apartment complex, a young boy remarked that his mother had told him that I ate people. It was a vicious thing to tell a child. The African had become the bogeyman that could be used to scare children or intimidate them into compliance.

Most Americans get their information about Africa through the media, but this information they get from the media is often inaccurate, sensational, or only one side of the picture at best. The media, as is generally known, is mostly interested in presenting the news, and the news it brings is generally bad news. Reports come from Africa only when there are wars, coups d'etat, military uprisings, starvation because of droughts, floods, election fraud, killing diseases, and so on. The news is never about the educational progress being made, the new infrastructure being created, legal advances especially on the condition of women, the success of the democratic experiment in certain countries, the achievements of inventors and successful business people, the increase in agricultural production, and the new publications by writers. By concentrating on the bad and the exotic, the media only serves to reinforce the stereotypes. There is no doubt that the news from Africa presented by the media is part of the African reality. There have been civil wars, genocide, starvation, violence, election fraud, illiteracy, and corruption in Africa. But there have also been thousands of graduates who got their degrees from universities, some of which are highly regarded throughout the world; great advances in economic management in some countries; and spectacular architectural successes. The World Bank Global Economics Prospects Data published in June 2019 suggested that two African countries were among the world's fastest growing economies in 2019: Ethiopia and Rwanda. The top ten include three other African countries: Côte d'Ivoire, Djibouti, and Senegal. For its part, the International Monetary Fund, in data published in October 2020 and based on information about 194 countries, suggested that three of the five fastest developing economies are in Africa: South Sudan, Egypt, Benin. The top ten include three other African countries: Rwanda, Ethiopia, Tanzania.

If one asks American children, say up to the age of 16, what image comes to their minds when Africa is mentioned or when they think of Africa, the following are among the results one will get. Many will certainly mention dirty, unkempt, and unwashed black Africans, including adults and children, moving about their compounds. Some of these, particularly the women, might have loads on their heads. The American children will mention this because this is the reality of what the media presents about Africa and Africans. These children would never have seen pictures of elegantly dressed Africans driving their cars or riding in trains or shopping in supermarkets. Africans are not dirty because they are black; in fact, Africans in the rural areas take delight in bathing in the streams to such an extent that in some areas the places where men and women should bathe are clearly demarcated. And yet, the notion that Africans are dirty is so prevalent that some Africans are given advice, on coming to the US, about the number of times a day they should have a shower. No doubt also, some Africans go barefoot and some women carry loads on their heads, but that is not the only reality.

Some of the children might well point to the fact that Africa is a place where there are continuing civil wars and say that the picture that most readily comes to mind is of half-naked corpses recently slaughtered in a massacre and littering the ground. Of course that too is part of the reality. There have been and still are civil wars in Africa, some of which have been extremely brutal. But that is, again, not the only reality. The children would obviously not have heard of the success stories in Africa in so far as political matters are concerned. Countries like Liberia and Nigeria have staged a remarkable comeback from brutal civil wars, and others like Ghana, Senegal, and Tanzania have never known civil wars and are shining examples of successful democratic experiments in Africa. Some of the children might well mention pictures of people suffering from the ravages of diseases like AIDS and Ebola and even suggest that they have been informed that some dreadful diseases come from Africa. Of course, dreadful diseases come from everywhere, and it is part of the agenda of some individuals and groups to suggest that they come from particular places. There are forces in the US at the moment out to brand the coronavirus as a Chinese virus. It is part of the reality that Africa has been ravaged by some diseases and that the healthcare infrastructure is one of the worst aspects of the current African situation. But that, too, is not the only reality. The children would not know, of course, about the devotion and dedication of the scanty medical staff in some areas who do their best for their patients, or of the remarkable alternative traditional system that delivers healthcare to millions of rural people, or of the successful experiments in highly respected medical schools and teaching hospitals in places like Ghana, Nigeria, and Tanzania. That too is part of the reality.

Apart from the need to dispel misconceptions, the reasons why the United States should be informed about Africa and African affairs are legion; they are strategic, political, social, and economic. For good or for ill, the United States has to play a very important role in world affairs which include African affairs. In spite of the recent isolationist trend in the country, recent events have clearly demonstrated that the United States cannot turn its back on what is going on in Africa and the rest of the world. It has now become a cliché which is true nonetheless, that recent technological advances have made the world a smaller place, and therefore events happening in one corner will inevitably have a marked effect on places thousands of miles away. Because of the ease of communication and air travel an Ebola crisis in Liberia and Central Africa could have a serious impact on the United States, and it would be in everyone's interest to know the nature of that disease and the places where it is most prevalent in order to get a handle on it and save lives all over the world. The United States has been and is still concerned about terrorists groups like al-Qaeda and others like ISIS, groups that have had and still could have a disastrous impact on the country. We must therefore inform ourselves about offshoots of these groups that operate in Africa like Boko Haram that recently abducted hundreds of schoolgirls in Nigeria. These groups have offshoots operating in other parts of Africa, some of them successfully. The terrorists and pirates operating in Somalia pose a threat to the Horn of Africa, the successful operation of the Suez Canal, and America's allies in the Middle East. We recently saw how lack of knowledge about the real situation on the ground in places like Libya and Somalia had disastrous consequences in those countries but also generated political repercussions at home in the USA.

The people of Africa might be individually poor, and there is no denying that some countries in Africa are among the poorest in the world. And yet Africa has such vast natural resources and such tremendous economic potential that Fareed Zacharia, in one of his Global Public Square programs on CNN, declared that Africa is to be considered the continent of the future. He came to this conclusion largely because of Africa's economic potential. It seems that the United States, especially in current circumstances, still has to discover this. President Barack Obama's understanding of this led him to call a summit of African leaders and American business leaders to consider economic and business cooperation between the United States and Africa. Predictably, the Trump administration was not interested. However, the Chinese are tremendously interested in Africa's economic potential and are inserting themselves in African economies in a very big way, with all kinds of implications for the global economy. The United States is, at the moment, so dependent on carbon fuel, that even though it produces a lot itself, it must import a fair amount of crude oil from outside. Most Americans do not know that Nigeria in Western Africa is one of the United States' most important suppliers of crude oil, and that the gas they might have put into their gas tanks over the weekend might have come from Nigeria. If there is political upheaval in that country, it might affect the flow of crude oil and therefore its price in the United States. Most African nations recently decided to adopt a common currency, and, while the European Union seems to be having all kinds of problems, African leaders have formed a common market which will include 1.2 billion people, the second largest market in the world. This will have far-reaching economic consequences. The United States had better pay attention to its economic relations with Africa.

Decisions on social matters, like abortion, female circumcision, and homosexuality, which are taken in Africa, can also have reverberations in the United States, particularly with regard to Africans from the relevant African countries who have relocated to the United States. However, they also concern American groups interested in these matters who also have connections with African countries. Recently, we heard about American fundamentalists trying to influence the Uganda government's legislation on homosexuality, and others have tried to influence decisions on female circumcision. Whatever their views might be, it is important that these groups inform themselves about the African historical, religious, and cultural situations before trying to influence policies. The current coronavirus gives a standing lesson about the need to be informed about what is going on in other continents. It is now quite clear that there was a shortage of accurate information about the situation in China and Europe, and this contributed to the virulence of the disease in the USA. However, the situation in Africa should also be carefully studied. Of all the continents, Africa seems to have been hit least hard. Why is that? Is it because of the nature of the African climate? Is it because Africans tend to travel less often by air than people on other continents? Does it have anything to do with the economic situations of Africans? Knowledge of all these issues might help in determining our responses to other pandemics.

It should be obvious, then, that people in the West should be better informed about Africa. The record needs to be set straight. Although there is regrettable ignorance about Africa among the general population in the West, particularly in the United States, the academic study of Africa in the US and elsewhere has proceeded since the end of World War II. This happened for several reasons. It was, of course, partly motivated by the need to have a clearer and more accurate picture of Africa than the sensationalized and distorted versions that had been put out by some nineteenth- and early twentieth-century travelers, anthropologists, imperialist administrators, and even missionaries. This was the period when several universities were established in Africa, universities like Ibadan and Nsukka in Nigeria, Legon in Ghana, and Dar es Salaam in Tanzania. These universities felt they had an obligation to conduct research into all aspects of African affairs. The period also coincided with the rise of African nationalism, and the drive towards independence. The heightened African consciousness and the increased awareness by Africans of their identity, their dignity, and their selfhood meant that they themselves were desirous to find out more about their own continent and to disseminate this information. It was to be the true and accurate information that some people in other parts of the world had not been interested in or had distorted. The new academic interest in African affairs was also strengthened by the rise in importance of the African American population in the United States and the burgeoning civil rights movement. African Americans would soon form a most important voting bloc, and their clamor for their rights went hand in hand with increased awareness of their genuine identity, an identity which had a lot to do with their origins in Africa. They wanted to know more about the places in Africa where they came from and this desire helped to bolster research.

The establishment of the United Nations after World War II was a ground-breaking event in several ways. It was certainly crucial for the intensification of research into African affairs. The United Nations consisted of several agencies like the World Health Organization (WHO) and the United Nations Educational, Social and Cultural Organization (UNESCO) which were very much involved in all areas of the world and, at times, gave loans or aid for certain projects. In order to do so properly and successfully, there had to be accurate information about what was going on in those areas. At this time Africa, because of the dawn of independence, was in a position to receive considerable aid from the UN which therefore needed to have accurate information.

Another factor which led to the intensification of research into African affairs and the involvement of the US in Africa was the Cold War which followed the end of World War II. This was the ideological rivalry between the US and its European allies, on the one hand, and the Soviet Union and its own allies, on the other. It was essentially a competition to see whether the communist or the democratic way of life would win. Each bloc looked for supporters all over the world, and the newly independent countries of Africa seemed to be rich pickings. The competition in Africa actually started after the independence of the Congo in 1960. The new Congolese leader, Patrice Lumumba, was Marxist in orientation and it therefore seemed as if he would make that vast country in the heart of Africa, with its vast and rich natural resources, lean towards the Soviet bloc. America, of course, was not prepared to allow this to happen. The consequence was a complicated set of intrigues resulting in the assassination of Lumumba, which was engineered by the CIA, the Belgians, and some political elements within the Congo. The internal conflict within the Congo continues to this day and from that time America's interest and involvement in Africa became even more pronounced. It included involvement in conflicts in Angola, Mozambique, and, more recently, Libya. This involvement in its turn led to more intensified academic study.

Finally, some would say that the main reason for this heightened academic and even political interest in Africa was the realization that this continent possesses vast untapped economic potential, more so than any other continent. All the various precious and valuable metals and minerals are here: rutile, uranium, iron, copper, diamonds, gold, titanium, and, of course, oil. The continent has tremendous agricultural potential, tremendous potential for tourism, and tremendous fisheries resources. It was recognized, even at that time, that this would be a continent to watch out for, and knowledge of it was therefore essential. All this led to the rise of African Studies. In the US it started in the 1950s and greatly expanded in the 1960s, and it has been growing ever since. There are now some notable schools of African Studies at universities such as Florida, Ohio State, and Wisconsin, and the African Studies Association is one of the most prestigious academic associations in the US.

If there is so much academic interest in African affairs in the US, there must be numerous books on the subject. Why is there a need for yet another book about Africa? There is always space for books with new insights on a topic, but this book was motivated by the need for one specifically directed at students in high school or the first two years of university, who want a concise and simple introduction to the subject. There are lots of excellent books on African affairs in general, on specific topics and on specific countries, but what is needed is a basic introduction for those students who know virtually nothing about the continent. Even as far as general accounts go, one could immediately think of two, at least. These are Mario Azevedo's *Africana Studies* and April and Donald Gordon's *Understanding Contemporary Africa*. Both are excellent works to which I am indebted, but *Africana Studies* is about both African and African American affairs, and students who want information on just African affairs might not wish to spend on a bulky book, half of which they would not use. April and Donald Gordon's *Understanding Contemporary Africa* is very detailed and well laid out, but it seems more suitable for upper-division and graduate students. This book is intended for freshmen and sophomores, and students in the higher years of high school. It deals with most of the important topics, although for obvious reasons it has had to leave out issues like sports, film, or business. After teaching "Introduction to African Studies" for over twenty years, I have felt the need for such a book. I hope that it will give students a clear idea of what has happened and is happening on the African continent and the extent of Africa's ingenuity, inventiveness, and contribution to world progress.

1 The geography of Africa and topics in African history

The first point to make is that Africa is a continent, not a country. Africa is, in fact, the second largest of the continents, second only to Asia, and it has more countries than any other continent—55, in fact. Some of these countries, like the Democratic Republic of the Congo and Algeria, are among the largest in the world. Others, like Nigeria, are among the most populous. The entire United States can fit into the continent of Africa three times, with something left over. The population of Africa has exceeded the one billion mark.

There is some justification in claiming that Africa is the most central of the continents. It is almost surrounded by three of the world's greatest waterways: the Atlantic Ocean to the west, the Indian Ocean to the east, and the Mediterranean Sea to the north. The Red Sea which joins the Gulf of Aden and the Arabian Sea, the northern parts of the Indian Ocean, borders Africa to the north-east, and it is only the existence of the tiny Isthmus of Suez that prevents it from being completely surrounded by water. Africa is the only one of the continents that is traversed by those three important latitudes: the Tropic of Cancer to the north, the Tropic of Capricorn to the south, and the Equator which cuts Africa almost in half. It passes through Gabon, Congo Brazzaville, the Democratic Republic of the Congo, Uganda, Kenya, and Somalia. The fact that Africa is traversed by both the Tropics of Capricorn and Cancer means that most of the continent is within the Tropics. This is why Africa is often referred to as "tropical Africa." One consequence of this is that most of Africa has very high temperatures throughout the year, with all kinds of further consequences for agriculture, the environment, and economic development in general. The only parts of the continent that can experience very low temperatures are the extreme north, the extreme south, and the high-altitude areas in the east in places like Kenya, where it can actually snow at certain times of the year.

High temperature can lead to air rising and then to condensation and rainfall. This is true of Africa as it is of other places. Because of the high temperatures in most of Africa, a curious phenomenon has occurred called the Intertropical Convergence Zone or ITCZ. It is the primary rain-making mechanism in tropical areas, particularly in Africa, where most countries are tropical or have tropical zones. Because of the high temperatures on the surface, the air is heated and it rises. But having risen it cools rapidly, and if water vapor is present it condenses and there is then precipitation, which is rain. This rain-making activity shifts, depending on the time of the year and the position of the sun, and it roughly correlates with the time the sun is overhead in any particular area. Thus, in Sierra Leone which is six and a half degrees north of the equator, the rain-making activity occurs when the sun is overhead in the northern hemisphere, and the rainy season lasts from about May to October. November to about the end of April are

DOI: 10.4324/9781003111733-2

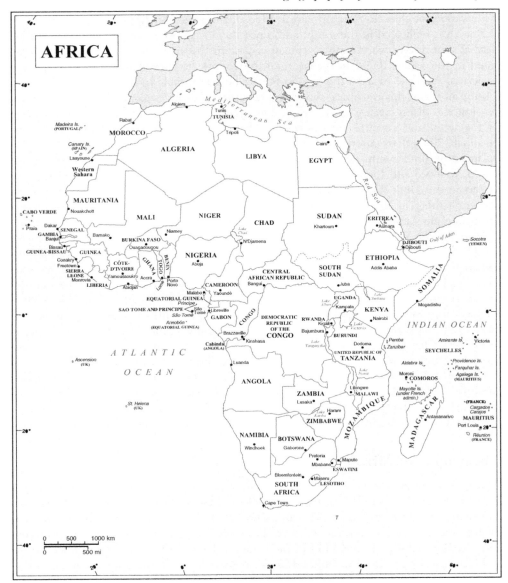

Figure 1.1 Map of Africa.
Source: Based on UN map 4045

dry months. In many parts of tropical Africa there are two main seasons, the rainy season and the dry season, and the time of the seasons is normally dependent on when and where the sun is overhead. The amount of rainfall is not evenly distributed. Some areas in the center of Africa have very heavy rainfall, while in others the rainfall is sparse. There are also variations from year to year. All this has serious consequences for agriculture and the rearing of animals and therefore for economic development.

The vastness of the continent, the fact that it is traversed by the equator, and also that some of it lies even beyond the Tropics of Cancer and Capricorn, mean that there is a wide variety of climatic zones in Africa. Indeed, almost every climatic zone that exists in the north is replicated in the south, and, since there is a correlation between climate and natural vegetation, every natural vegetation pattern that exists in the north is also replicated in the south. Right in the heart of the continent is the dense tropical rain forest associated with the basin of the Congo River and comparable to the Amazon rain forest. To the north of this is tropical woodland savannah and this is paralleled to the south by tropical woodland savannah. The tropical grassland savannah which is found to the north of the woodland savannah in the north is balanced in the south by tropical grassland savannah. Then there is semi-arid scrubland, or semi-desert, called the Sahel in the north, balanced by similar semi-desert in the south. The Sahara Desert, the largest desert in the world, follows, and this is replicated somewhat by the Namib Desert and the Kalahari Desert in the south. Finally, Mediterranean forest vegetation in the north is balanced by the same thing in the south. The only exception to this pattern is the mountain and temperate grassland area found in the highlands of Kenya and Ethiopia.

Many of the world's most remarkable physical features exist in Africa. Africa has the world's longest river, the Nile, which is over four thousand miles long and has played a remarkable role in the history of the world. It is the source of the fertility of Egypt and many other parts of the north and north-east and largely accounts for the fact that this area is regarded as one of the cradles of civilization. The Congo River in the heart of Africa is also one of the world's great rivers, helping to provide sustenance for the second largest rain forest in the world, a rain forest second only to the Amazon's. The Niger in West Africa has also nurtured formidable civilizations. So have the Zambesi and other rivers in Southern Africa. Africa also has some of the world's largest lakes; indeed, the continent can be said to have its own Great Lakes system. Some of the world's highest mountains are in Africa, namely Mount Kenya and Mount Kilimanjaro, in Kenya and Tanzania respectively. The world's largest desert, the Sahara Desert, is in Africa, as is arguably the world's most spectacular waterfall, the Victoria Falls in Southern Africa.

The peoples of Africa

The peoples of Africa speak thousands of languages and belong to three main groups. First, there are the so-called Caucasoid peoples. These are people of Arab ancestry who live mainly in the north and north-east. They are the descendants of Arab traders, merchants, and military adventurers who swept across North Africa from the seventh-century CE. But included in the ranks of the Caucasoid are the Berbers who also live in the north and are the original inhabitants of Northern Africa. All these people live north of the Sahara. Then there are the Negroid people who constitute over 70 percent of the African population and live largely in sub-Saharan Africa. In the extreme south are the Khoisan people who are distinguished by the clicks that occur in their languages. In the past, some scholars used to apply the derogatory names of Bushmen and Hottentots to these people, a practice which is largely discontinued. There are only a few hundred thousand of them left and they are mainly hunters and gatherers. There are also Europeans descended from European imperialist nations who settled in certain parts of Africa largely because the climate was conducive to European settlement. Some scholars include these among the Caucasoid peoples, because they are really descended from people who today are regarded as Caucasians, but because of their history and the areas they inhabit in Africa today, they are best treated separately. They inhabit Southern Africa in countries like Zimbabwe and South Africa, and the cooler highland regions such as Kenya in

East Africa. There are peoples of Indian descent whose ancestors were brought to East Africa by the British colonialists to work on the railways, and finally there are peoples of mixed racial origin.

Tectonic shift and its consequences

One of the most interesting theories about world geography relates to the great tectonic shift involving the movement of large masses of the earth's surface. The theory suggests that in the distant prehistoric past, about one hundred million years ago, all the world's continents formed just one enormous land mass called Pangea. The landmasses in the south were called Gondwana, with Africa being the centerpiece. Because of the great continental or tectonic shift, however, North and South America, Antarctica, Australia, and India moved away from Africa and were supposedly replaced by great masses of water. That the theory is plausible becomes apparent if one looks at the present shape of both South America and Africa. The north, north-eastern and eastern coasts of South America fit almost perfectly into Africa's western and south-western coasts. This theory also explains the nature of the African coast in general. When masses break away from each other the remaining edges are bound to be sharp and almost vertical. This is the nature of most of the African coast, which is characterized by steep, almost vertical edges, generally called the Great Escarpment. In many parts of Africa, the land rises steeply from the comparatively narrow coast until it reaches a broad plateau. Of course, the steepness varies from area to area. One major consequence of this is that in order to reach the ocean, rivers have to tumble over numerous waterfalls and rapids. This is the case with most of Africa's rivers, and it has other consequences for transportation and development in general. It means that African rivers are difficult to navigate from the ocean right up to the interior, because the rapids and waterfalls must be overcome. Once they are over-come, however, the rivers are navigable to their sources and transportation is much easier. This partly explains why the early European explorers of Africa, and even slavers, were unable to penetrate to the interior and confined their activities to the coast. The phenomenon also has interesting implications for the construction of roads and railways from the interior to the coast. These were only constructed where they were absolutely essential for the movement of produce and other resources. Harbors in Africa have to be constructed at great cost because there are few natural harbors. The phenomenon can also be said to have delayed colonialism, because it delayed entry into the interior by the explorers, merchants, and imperial administrators. It is also not surprising, some scholars claim, that the most influential and powerful of the early states, kingdoms, and empires in Africa were formed in the interior and not in the coastal areas.

Aspects of African history

Let us begin the discussion of aspects of African history with a look at some of the most misleading and derogatory statements of some Western scholars and historians about Africa and African history. Professor Hugh Trevor-Roper, one-time Regius Professor of Modern History at Oxford University, made the appalling statement that Africa has no history and that the African past was nothing but the unrewarding gyrations of barbarous tribes. In a BBC lecture he said, "Perhaps in the future there will be some African history to teach. But at present there is none. There is only the history of the Europeans in Africa" ("The Rise of Christian Europe," *The Listener*, November 28, 1963, p. 871).

Another famous British historian, Arnold Toynbee, and the German philosopher Georg Hegel made similar statements. If we assume that by history we mean the past of any people, a past that includes various aspects like actions, culture, lifestyle, and so on, then it must inevitably follow that every people must have a history, that they must have a past, whether attractive or unattractive. As a noted historian, Trevor-Roper must have been aware of this. His statement, therefore, can only be regarded as a racist attempt to denigrate Africa and Africans and has no connection with history as we know it. The second part of his statement, that the African past was nothing but the unrewarding gyrations of barbarous tribes, reinforces this, as does Toynbee's assertion that Africa had not contributed anything positive to any civilization. These evaluations are, of course, completely false, as this work will show. It is partly the intention of this work to show-case African ingenuity in the past and the present.

If one wanted to be generous to people like Trevor-Roper, one might say that their views stemmed, not merely from a jaundiced view of history, but from the limitations of the tools that were in use at the time to construct history; they stemmed, that is, from inadequate historical methodology. Up to the start of the twentieth century European historians believed that history could only be reconstructed from written records, largely official records, and that without official records there could be no history. I call this inadequate historical methodology because there could be lots of other sources of historical information. For instance, in Africa there is the oral tradition which is the source of historical information of many societies, because some of these societies were not literate. The people's historical record has therefore been kept in the collective consciousness through the generations. Even in the Western world there has been a reliance on oral information to reconstruct history.

Apart from the oral tradition, other sources could be used for historical information. We know that archaeology could give and has given lots of information about societies all over the world, and this now applies even to Africa. Even linguistics is being used in this regard. The presence of certain linguistic features in various places could tell us quite a lot about the movements of people or about societies influencing each other. All this means that attitudes towards African history and the nature of African historical methodology have changed drastically since the days of Trevor-Roper, Arnold Toynbee, and Georg Hegel. The change was partly motivated by the achievement of independence by African countries. Independence gave Africans a sense of pride and therefore a heightened desire to find out more about their past and set the record straight. African nationalism and the drive towards independence coincided, more or less, with the rise of African universities and therefore with the appearance on the scene of trained African historians dedicated to doing historical research in order to reconstruct their countries' histories. Quite often, they did this in collaboration with Western historians interested in Africa and scholars in the mushrooming Centers of African Studies in Britain, the USA, and Europe.

Historians like Trevor-Roper and Toynbee derived their judgments not just from official written records, but Western written records. They did not bother to investigate the existence of non-Western written records. However, as Kevin Shillington and others have shown, the kingdoms of Nubia and Meroe kept literate records from the sixth century BCE and the Ethiopians kept written records from at least the ninth century CE. Most interesting, perhaps, are the records kept by Arab travelers in Africa. After the establishment of Islam by Muhammad in the seventh century CE, the Arabs traveled extensively in Africa as traders, merchants, and warriors conducting jihads in the attempt to spread the Moslem religion. Some of them wrote detailed accounts of their experiences. Two noted names are Al Bakri, who lived in the eleventh century, and Al Idriss, who lived in the twelfth. In their accounts, which are written in Arabic, they tell us of splendid West African cities and empires like Mali, Songhay, and Ghana, centers of learning, and properly administered kingdoms. Archaeology has also contributed immensely in giving us information of the Nubians of Kush, and of Great Zimbabwe and a great African civilization in the south. In refutation, therefore, of those who claimed that Africa has no history, the reconstruction of African history is proceeding apace, led by the work of African scholars themselves. With new historical methodology such as the use of the oral tradition, linguistics, archaeology, and non-Western written records, they have been able to assemble compelling accounts of Africa's past.

Africa: the home of humankind

In refutation of those who hold derogatory views about Africa it is essential to stress that Africa is the home of humankind. According to Darwinian theory of evolution, the human species evolved over millions of years from our primate relatives, the apes. The assertion that Africa is the home of humankind is based not just on theory, but on demonstrable scientific fact, and is the result of scientific examination and dating of fossils discovered in Africa and other parts of the world. The evolution of the human species started between ten and fifteen million years ago when certain apes began to develop humanlike characteristics such as larger brains and the ability to walk upright on two legs. This phenomenon is thought to have occurred in Africa because of the favorable nature of the African environment. These apelike creatures with human characteristics are called hominins or "hominids," from the Latin word *homo*, which means "man." The researches of archaeologists, anthropologists, and paleoanthropologists revealed that these early hominins existed in the grasslands and woodlands of Eastern and Southern Africa and perfected the technique of walking on their hind legs because of the need to spot predators. It was these hominins that gradually evolved into human beings in several stages.

The next stage in the story of the evolution of the hominins into human beings was an apelike creature with human characteristics that was about 2.5 million years' old and named "Australopithecus." This creature could use tools such as sticks and stones. Next came a new species of hominins, discovered in 1964 by Mary and Louis Leakey in the Olduvai Gorge in Tanzania, that had the ability to make its own tools. The creature was therefore called *Homo habilis*, and the fossilized skull estimated to be 2.5 million years' old. The next stage in the process was the appearance of *Homo erectus* or upright man. This was a creature that could both walk and stand erect on two legs and not merely cut or chop off simple tools from rocks, like *Homo habilis*, but could also shape them to a predetermined plan. Most importantly, it was *Homo erectus* that started the movement of the hominins out of Africa. The reason for the movement out of Africa to the other continents might have been the environmental and climatic instability that obtained on the earth between 1 million and 500,000 years ago, but also to the fact that *Homo erectus* was better able to adapt to changing conditions, and conditions in other areas, than previous species of hominins. The next stage was the emergence in Africa, about 600,000 years ago, of another species, *Homo heidelbergensis*, with a brain the size of a modern human brain. While those members of *Homo heidelbergensis* who crossed over to Europe gave rise to species like *Homo neanderthalis*, *Homo heidelbergensis* in Africa gave way to *Homo sapiens*, the modern human being in other words, about 200,000 years ago. *Homo sapiens*, which was very much like modern humans, continued the move to other continents and spread throughout the world. Scientists have concluded, through the use of DNA, that all human beings everywhere in the world can be traced to a common woman ancestor, called "Eve," who lived in Africa, and whose descendants began to emigrate from Africa to other parts of the world between 180,000 and 90,000 years ago. They displaced other groups such as the Neanderthals, and eventually came to populate the whole world. As these descendants migrated, they adapted themselves to the climatic conditions they encountered. While those in Africa remained dark to protect them from the harmful effects of the direct sun, those in Europe and other places became paler so that they could absorb more of the rays of the less direct sunlight.

Bantu migrations

One of the most fascinating phenomena in African history is what has been referred to as the Bantu "migrations" or the Bantu expansion. This relates to the process whereby a group of African people originally inhabiting an area east of Nigeria, probably in what is now the country of Cameroon, spread across most of sub-Saharan Africa. It was once thought that this remarkable movement occurred in the recent past, starting at about 900 CE, and was done mostly through conquest, since other means would have required a longer time. However, more intensive archaeological research and the use of more advanced scientific research tools have led to the conclusion that the expansion was a more gradual process which started in the early centuries of the first millennium and stretched to about the eighteenth century. This is why some scholars think that the term "migration" is misleading and prefer the term "expansion." The reason for the development of this theory of expansion was the commonalities that exist among the myriad sub-Saharan African languages, of which there are more than a thousand. This is the reason why all these languages are sometimes referred to as the Bantu languages. In the early twentieth century scholars recognized that most African peoples from parts of Western Africa, eastward through Kenya, and southward along most of Africa right down to South Africa spoke languages that had a lot in common. For instance, most of them had the suffix "ntu," which means "person." To get the plural of a noun, the prefix "ba" is often added. For instance, in Lesotho a single individual is an msotho, but the people in general are the Basotho. The word Bantu therefore means people. Scholars have now largely come to the conclusion that about 3000 years ago large-scale settlements emerged in the West African savannah of Bantu-speaking peoples who were very skilled at farming and fishing. They soon became even more expert at farming, cultivating crops such as yams and oil palm, and raising goats. These people were more advanced and cultivated than other sub-Saharan Africans at the time, such as those who lived in the rain forest in Central Africa and further south. They made pottery and smelted iron to make spears, hoes, scythes, and axes. Inevitably the population of these comparatively prosperous people grew, which was one reason why some of them started to move outwards. Another reason was that changing climatic and environmental conditions, such as the drying desert, forced some of the Saharan and Sahel farmers to move south and put pressure on these Bantu farmers and fisher people, causing them to move in turn. They moved as far east as Kenya, crossing the rivers of Central Africa, and then as far south as the tip of South Africa. Because they were more advanced technologically than the people they met, they were able to subdue them in some cases, but in others they were able to mingle with them peacefully and introduce their more advanced agricultural techniques. They also learnt to cultivate Asian yams and bananas which had been introduced to Africa by Polynesian sailors who had arrived in Madagascar in the early centuries of the first millennium. They intermarried with the locals they found, and created new states, new kingdoms, and new languages. The consequence of this was that by 1100 CE most of Central, Eastern, and Southern Africa was populated by Bantu-speaking peoples who, in some cases, had completely replaced the original inhabitants like the Khoisan peoples.

Ancient Egypt

Egypt (largely ancient Egypt) in Northern Africa is one of the few African countries that one could be sure almost everyone in North America would have heard of; after all, it features prominently in the Old Testament and is therefore universally recognized as one of the major players in the ancient world. So strong, however, is the impulse in certain quarters to deny Africa the distinction of having made a substantial contribution to world history and world development that some people are prepared to assert that Egypt is not African at all, and that it has more in common with the Arabic-speaking peoples of South West Asia and the Arab world. They would claim that the Egyptians and some other North African peoples came originally form Arabia. Now it is clear that Egypt and some other North African countries such as Algeria, Morocco, Tunisia, and Libya have a lot in common with the Middle Eastern countries. These Arabic-speaking North African countries, which are collectively referred to as the Mahgreb, are united by the common language Arabic and the common religion Islam. It is also true that they share a lot in common with the Arab world and are sometimes regarded as being Middle Eastern. On the face of it, however, it is ridiculous to claim that countries that are geographically located in Africa are not African. Africa is not one vast monolithic entity; it has a variety of peoples, cultures and languages, and because of the movements of people and various influences throughout history it should not be surprising that people in one part of Africa may have connections with people on another continent. Fundamentally, however, we must be careful to make a distinction between the ancient Egyptians and most of the present inhabitants of Egypt and other parts of the Mahgreb. The majority of the present inhabitants of Egypt and the other Mahgreb countries are descendants of Arabic-speaking peoples who started moving to Africa no earlier than the seventh century CE after the establishment of Islam. Some of these people were merchants interested in trade, but many of them were interested in spreading Islam by war, conquest, and other means. The people who inhabited Egypt before this, the people who built the pyramids and were responsible for the remarkable contribution that ancient Egypt made to world development in several fields, the ancient Egyptians in other words, were indigenous Africans, not Arabs. Some of the wall paintings that we still have, and some of the sculptures in the great Cairo Museum, might even suggest that some of the ancient Egyptians were people of color, like their Nubian neighbors to the south.

Egypt's first major contribution to world development has often been asserted. Ancient Egypt, with the Nile valley, is incontestably one of the earliest places where civilization as we know it can be said to have started. It is now generally agreed that civilization can be said to have started when man moved from the hunter-gatherer stage to the stage of purposive cultivation of crops and herding of animals: the agricultural revolution, in other words. It is significant that this development took place along river valleys in places where water supply was abundant. About ten thousand years ago or so, humans, faced with expanding populations and the need for more food, realized that grains and other plants that were near water sources or were not surrounded by non-edible plants did rather better than others. Deliberately removing the noxious weeds or making sure that the plants had more water greatly increased productivity. Thus, there was a gradual move to the actual planting or cultivation of crops. Similarly, humans realized that animals that were not harassed by predators increased greatly in numbers; therefore, actually protecting these animals would lead to a more stable or even higher and better developed animal population, and consequently more food. Hence herding arose. The increase in food production, and the fact that humans no longer needed to move from place to place to gather or hunt their food, had some very interesting consequences for human development. It led to the rise of settlements or settled communities. Agricultural production necessarily demands settled communities.

Settlements led to the need to construct permanent housing rather than structures that would have to be demolished when it became necessary to move from one location to another in search of food. There was also the need to build structures to store food. This led to the development of tools that could be used for this purpose as well as other artifacts useful in settlements. Since people also now live in comparatively larger communities there is a need to regulate relationships among them, so social organization and laws emerge, and eventually certain leaders in society also emerge. Anyone, in fact, who has the ability to produce more or store more gradually assumes a leading role in the community. The need to keep a record of how much has been produced or how much was loaned out to another member of the community would lead to the development of a record-keeping system, and thus the development of writing. Agricultural activity also means dependence on the weather, the climate and other forces of nature and therefore a need to understand or be in a good relationship with those forces of nature; hence the rise of religion and some kind spiritual awareness. Finally, increased food production leads to surpluses. This in itself has two very important consequences. First, the surplus food can be exchanged for other commodities, such as tools or services, with other communities that need the food, by a simple system of barter or by other methods. Thus, trade emerges within communities and then among communities. Secondly, the food surplus means that not everyone has to be engaged in the actual production of food, so specialization emerges, and some people become carpenters, builders, weavers, and so on. A class system also emerges based on what one does and how much food one is able to obtain or to produce. The entire structure of a civilized society, then, is linked with the change to an agricultural society. How did this happen in Egypt and what were its consequences?

There is evidence that about seven thousand years ago crop cultivation and the herding of cattle existed in Egypt along the Nile valley. The herdsmen were semi-nomadic pastoralists who moved their cattle that had to be protected from predators from the savannah lands to the Nile valley where they could be sure of abundant water supply. Because of the changing climatic conditions they were dependent on the forces of nature, and religious awareness started to emerge together with social stratification. The waters of the Nile, bringing with them rich deposits of silt from the Ethiopian highlands and other places provided an environment remarkably suited to prosperous farming and many settlements emerged. With increased crop production trade with other communities along routes to both the East and the West emerged. With the inevitable population expansion that was one of the consequences of abundant food production, there was competition for grazing and arable land and therefore a need for the people to live in fortified settlements or cities under proven leaders. Hence the rise of urbanization and of what have been called "proto-states" as leaders vied with each other and sought to establish alliances for protection (Shillington, 33). Trade routes to Nubia to the south and to the Red Sea and even to Western Asia for gold, ebony, and ivory were developed and helped bolster the influence of some of the leaders. Quite obviously, there was a move towards the idea of kingship and a ruling class consisting of the leaders and their henchmen who controlled access to the trade routes and therefore the rich supplies of gold and other precious things. Eventually, these proto-states became consolidated into what became known as Upper Egypt and Lower Egypt. Upper Egypt was actually what would now be regarded as Southern Egypt and Lower Egypt was Northern Egypt, including the area around the Nile Delta, or the lower reaches of the Nile. The growing religious awareness caused the rulers of these proto-kingdoms and the ruling classes in general to think seriously of the after-life. They saw themselves as living the same kind of lavish and prosperous lifestyle they were accustomed to on earth and they started constructing tombs for themselves which were adorned with all the artifacts they felt they would need in a lavish life in the hereafter. Shillington suggests that it is clear that these rulers were not just thinking of the after-life, but were preparing to share it with the gods and to see themselves as supernatural beings on a par with the gods. One can see in this the beginnings not only of a gradual move towards the construction of the pyramids by the later Pharaohs, but the emergence of the concept of the ruler as a god.

The period in Egypt up to about 3100 BCE was one of turbulence with rival proto-kings competing for absolute leadership in both Upper and Lower Egypt. However, at this time, one leader gained the supremacy in Upper Egypt and then succeeded in moving his army northwards and conquering the whole of Lower Egypt. The whole of Egypt, right up to the first cataract, thus became unified under one ruler and the First Dynasty was established. Thus started the great age of the pharaohs which was to last for another three thousand years. This was the great age and the great civilization that was responsible for the construction of those remarkable objects of architecture and engineering, the pyramids; this was the civilization that invented and established one of the earliest writing systems in hieroglyphics. They also had a unique religion which saw the king as a god and they perfected the technique of mummification, preserving corpses that last to this day.

Even if the ancient Egyptians had done nothing else, the construction of the pyramids, collectively considered one of the wonders of the ancient world, would have been sufficient testament to their ingenuity and remarkable capacity for inventiveness, and to the ingenuity and inventiveness of Africans in general. As is well known, the pyramids were intended as burial tombs for the pharaohs. Each pharaoh constructed his tomb before his death. If engineering can be defined as the art of constructing edifices that remain standing, then the pyramids are marvels of engineering because these massive structures have stood the test of time for four thousand years and more.

As already indicated, the ancient Egyptians mastered a number of other arts and sciences. They were experts at astronomy, and they were the ones who developed the world's first annual 12-month calendar of 365 days, which is still in use today. Their expertise in astronomy has been partly attributed to the fact that the clear Egyptian skies make possible the concentrated observation and study of the heavens. With regard to mummification, this had been practiced even before the unification of Egypt. It is interesting to note that this skill was available not only in Egypt, but in several other parts of Africa, long before it became known in Europe and other places. In ancient

Figure 1.2 Giza Plateau: Great Sphinx with Pyramid of Khafra in background.
Source: By Daniel Mayer - Own work, CC BY-SA 4.0,
https://commons.wikimedia.org/w/index.php?curid=4672571

Egypt, the object of the mummification was not just preservation, but to demonstrate the god-like nature of the king who was destined for immortality with the other gods. It is significant that only the kings and their noble relations were mummified.

Ancient Egyptian history is normally divided into periods. The period up to 3200 BCE is usually called the Predynastic period. This is the period of political organization with rival leaders emerging and seeking to protect themselves and their territories by making alliances. This is followed by the Archaic period when there were two states, Lower Egypt and Upper Egypt, leading up to the unification, and it lasted from 3200 to 2900 BCE. This is the period when the emerging kings began to assume god-like characteristics and demonstrate god-like authority. With unification began the line of the pharaohs and the various dynasties, involving the establishment of what is known as the Old Kingdom (2900–2280 BCE). This was a period of tremendous prosperity, great stability, and manifest military power, with the god-like pharaohs in total control. The invention of hieroglyphics enabled them to maintain accurate records and thereby have mastery over the country's resources and the economy as a whole. This was the period of pharaohs like Djoser, who built the first pyramid; Khufu, who built the largest; Djedefra; and Khafra. It must be noted that Khafra, apart from building his own great pyramid to serve as his tomb, also built the great Sphynx nearby, which displays Khafra's face on the body of a huge lion with huge arms, claws, and body outstretched on the earth. Foreign trade helped to augment the wealth and power of the pharaohs, and there were also military expeditions as they attempted to extend their influence beyond the first cataract to Nubia.

The Old Kingdom was followed by the First Intermediate Period (2280–2060 BCE). This was a period of disorder, political and social anarchy, and civil wars as a decline of faith in the supposedly god-like monarch led local potentates to become increasingly recalcitrant. Nubia, which had been put under enormous pressure by the once-powerful Pharaohs, now took advantage of the Egyptian civil strife to regain lost territory and pushed back the Egyptians to the first cataract which was the original border.

The Middle Kingdom (2060–1785 BCE) saw the restoration of order and military might. A new pharaoh, Mentuhotep II, who originally came from Thebes, was able to subdue the rebellious regional overlords and reconquer Lower Egypt. Mentuhotep was not only a mighty military warrior, but also a brilliant and efficient administrator who completely reorganized the bureaucracy. During this period Mentuhotep's successors were able to move south and reconquer parts of Nubia up to the second cataract. Nubia, for all practical purposes, now became an integral part of Egypt and the Nubians became almost thoroughly Egyptianized. Foreign trade was reconsolidated, and the grandeur and power of Egypt was restored.

The Middle Kingdom was followed by the Second Intermediate Period. For the first time, parts of Egypt (Lower Egypt) were invaded by Asiatic peoples from Western Asia, called Hyksos, who crossed the Sinai Desert and occupied the Nile Delta area. The occupation was made even easier by the fact that the kings of Egypt had never kept a standing army, because they felt Egypt as a whole was protected by the desert to the west, desert and the Red Sea to the east, and cataracts to the south, thus giving a false sense of security. Moreover, the Hyksos had the advantage of the latest military technology and the latest weapon: horse-drawn chariots. The occupation of Lower Egypt dealt a blow to the Egyptians' sense of their own superiority, so they learnt the lessons of the invasion, organized a standing army, and eventually liberated Lower Egypt from the Hyksos whom they sent back to Asia.

The re-establishment of Egyptian power led to the New Kingdom (1580–1085 BCE), probably the most remarkable period in ancient Egyptian history. It was a period of great political and military expansion. With a standing army that had recently expelled the Hyksos, Egypt now became a major world power. Its armies moved into and conquered Lebanon and Syria to the north-east and Nubia as far as the fourth cataract to the south. Egypt, in fact, established an empire. Trade was greatly expanded. It included commodities such as gold, ivory, incense, and hardwood. It proceeded down the Red Sea, and it reached as far south as "the land of Punt," as the Egyptians called Northern Ethiopia. One of the ways in which the Egyptian pharaohs showed their might and their influence during this time was in building massive temples and statues. This was the period of the expansion of the great Karnak Temple Complex near Luxor, which is the largest religious building the world has ever seen. Imagine a religious building larger than St. Peter's in Rome or St. Paul's in London! They constructed another huge temple complex at Luxor and linked it to Karnak with a corridor of sphinxes. Like the earlier pharaohs, the pharaohs of this period built their tombs in advance of their deaths, but they did not build pyramids. Instead, they constructed ornate burial chambers carved in the hills to the west of Thebes, to which the royal capital had been moved from Memphis. It was in this area that the magnificent tomb of the young pharaoh Tutankhamun was uncovered in 1924. The magnificence of this tomb is a testament to the wealth and power of the pharaohs of this period. This was the period of the Pharaoh Ramesis II, the pharaoh who is reputed to have dueled with Moses and refused to let the Israelites go, although there are a few scholars who believe it was another pharaoh. However, Ramesis has other great claims to fame. He was the pharaoh who built the famous Abu-Simbel temples in lower Nubia around 1300 BCE. These huge temples were actually cut out of rocks. Ramesis II is reputed to have lived to the great age of 92 and to have fathered hundreds of children.

Finally, there is the post-1085 period. This is a period of turmoil and decline during which countries that had been conquered by Egypt asserted their independence and achieved liberation, and foreign invaders took over parts of Egypt or occupied the entire country. Palestine was liberated. Nubia not only broke free, it moved north and took over the throne of Egypt in 728 BCE, establishing a Kushite dynasty. By this time, Nubia had become thoroughly Egyptianized, so the occupation was made even easier. However, an Assyrian army invaded Egypt in 658 BCE, took over the country, and pushed the Kushites back to Nubia, which eventually became an expanded and flourishing state in its own right with its capital at Napata. The Assyrians were themselves expelled from Egypt with the help of mercenaries from Lydia and Greece who established another dynasty themselves. Persians then invaded and established another dynasty which was overthrown in its turn. An Egyptian dynasty then ruled Egypt for the next sixty years, but another Persian invasion and occupation followed in 341 BCE. Finally, all these events culminated in the invasion and conquest of Egypt by Alexander the Great in 332 BCE. This put an end to the 3000-year-old era of the pharaohs. It is significant that some of the pharaohs were actually women. Although some of them came to power by acting as regents for minors, it is also clear that some of them were monarchs in their own right. We could also grasp from all this is that the ancient Egyptians, the people who were responsible for all these remarkable achievements and made such major contributions to world history and world development, were not Arabs from another continent, but indigenous Africans.

Axum/Ethiopia

The country of Ethiopia on the Horn of Africa to the north-east provides one of the most remarkable examples of African resilience, ingenuity, and determination to resist the ravages of foreign occupation. It must also be regarded as one of the bastions of Christianity throughout the ages. Because of its proximity to the area where Christianity started, it was one of the earliest places to be converted to Christianity in the whole world. Some scholars believe that Christianity was brought to Ethiopia by one of the apostles as early as the first century. However that may be, it is certain that Ethiopia had become Christian in the early years of the fourth century CE, long before many European countries, and it has remained formidably Christian ever since. Ethiopia was highly regarded even in ancient times. It was generally referred to as Abyssinia and is mentioned in the Old Testament. The Queen of Sheba, who made a famous visit to King Solomon of Judea, was reputed to have been Queen of Abyssinia. Indeed, the product of the liaison between Solomon and Sheba is reputed to have been the founder of a famous royal dynasty whose successors, in one way or another, ruled Ethiopia until the overthrow of the monarchy in the later years of the twentieth century. In the pre-imperialist era European potentates, particularly the Portuguese, sought acquaintance and alliance with Ethiopia, particularly because of its strategic position with the then Muslim world which European states wanted to outdo in all spheres of world activity, and the

Ethiopians cleverly took advantage of this situation in a most masterful way. The Ethiopians were and still are very proud of their Christian heritage. Where, as we shall see, kings and emperors of the Western Sudanic states used Islam to justify and advance their dynastic aspirations, the Ethiopian monarchs used Christianity as the main justification for their hold on power and the strategy was highly successful. In 1977, during the magnificent African Festival of the Arts and Culture (FESTAC) held in Lagos, the then capital of Nigeria, the Ethiopians were designated as the host of the next FESTAC and therefore had to mount an exhibition to showcase their historical and cultural achievements as a preview of what Africa was to expect of them. The centerpiece of the magnificent exhibition they staged was their Christian heritage, going back more than fifteen hundred years. Unlike many states in Africa, the Ethiopians also had their own script, their own written language, and a comparatively high degree of literacy.

Right up to the Renaissance, Europeans used the term "Ethiope" to refer to black people, thus suggesting that the Ethiopians were black. Of course, the indigenous inhabitants of the area just south of Nubia, in what is now Northern Ethiopia, must have been black, although, because of the proximity to Asia, there might eventually have been infusions of Asiatic peoples leading to an Afro-Asiatic population speaking an Afro-Asiatic language. These people lived in small settlements and were generally farmers. They engaged in trade with ancient Egypt who referred to the land as the "Land of Punt." As from the sixth century BCE, immigrants from what is now known as Yemen, but was then called Saba, began to cross the Red Sea and settle in Northern Ethiopia, thus forming the state known as Axum. They were excellent farmers and competent traders, trading mostly in Ivory. They intermarried with the local population and extended their settlements into what would eventually become the country of Ethiopia. Axum could therefore be regarded as the ancestor of Ethiopia. Even before they came to Axum, the Sabaeans were already literate and had their own script. Eventually, a new language called Geez evolved out of the Sabaean language, and it was from this that Amharic, the language of modern Ethiopia, evolved. Largely because they were such successful farmers and traders who took advantage of the fertility of the soil, their own irrigation skills, and the potential of trade with ports along the Indian Ocean, the Geez-speaking Sabaeans were able to establish their own state of Axum by the first century BCE.

By the fourth century CE the people of Axum had achieved tremendous prosperity. They traded not only with their neighbors, but also with the Greeks and Romans. They imported goods like silver, gold, olive oil, and wine, and they exported ivory, frankincense, myrrh, and even slaves they had captured in skirmishes. They were able to mint their own coinage, and their craftsmen were able to make luxury goods out of glass crystal, brass, and copper that were highly valued by people like the Greeks, the Romans, and the Egyptians. Most important, however, was the nature of their architecture. The people of Axum were experts at constructing massive stone structures. The original Sabaean settlers had brought the expertise with them from Saba, but the Axumites now greatly improved on it. They built monuments like palaces, temples, and royal tombs. The most remarkable of their stone constructions were extremely tall solid stone structures with intricate carvings on them intended to indicate the burial places of some of their kings. Some of these stone structures, which are called "stelae," are still standing at the present day, thus demonstrating that they, like the pyramids, are marvels of engineering. Some of them rose to one hundred feet in height and more than 700 tons of rock were used in their construction.

Very impressive also were the manifestations of Axum's Christian culture. Axum was converted to Christianity in the fourth century CE when King Ezana (320–350 CE) was converted by Christian scholars from Alexandria in Egypt. The Coptic Church, of course, had already been in existence in Egypt from the first century CE. In the early centuries of the first millennium, therefore, Axum was ruled by a Christian king whose authority was sanctioned by Christianity and a generally supportive aristocracy consisting of chieftains and landowners and whose wealth derived largely from foreign trade. Over time, the kings gradually extended their influence southwards to include more of what is now known as Ethiopia. With the establishment of Islam in the first half of the seventh century CE, and the consequent shift in the patterns of trade in the Arabian Peninsula and the Fertile Crescent, the power and influence of Axum/Ethiopia declined somewhat. However, Ethiopian power recovered as demands for its most important products increased, and the recovery was reinforced by the emergence of a powerful new dynasty, the co-called "Zagwe" dynasty around 1150 CE. The Zagwe dynasty was actually launched by military leaders who were also part of the country's elite and it actually started when Mara Tekle Haimanot seized the throne in 1150 (Shillington, 123). Haimanot and his Zagwe successors claimed to have the sanction of the powerful Christian Church and sought to bolster their position by claiming descent from the biblical Moses. The kings in turn encouraged the spread and influence of Christianity. It was at this time that the establishment of the powerful monasteries, for which Ethiopia has become famous, was consolidated. Enjoying the sympathy and support of the Zagwe Kings, the Ethiopian Church became very powerful. It was so powerful, and Christianity was so important in this corner of North Eastern Africa, that scholars like Henry Louis Gates could call the area "The Holy Land." Ethiopians saw themselves as a very important bastion of the Christian Church. Ethiopia itself was regarded as part of the ancient Archdiocese of Alexandria in Egypt (Shillington, 124). However, the Ethiopian Church developed its own characteristics, and, with their own unique and influential monastic tradition, the Ethiopians became very proud of their church, whose position and influence they saw as deriving from the Old Testament, and they even saw themselves as the genuine descendants of the Children of Israel.

Perhaps the most remarkable illustration of the power and influence of Christianity and the Ethiopian Church during this period was the construction of some unique cathedral-like churches hewn out of solid rock in the mountainside. They were therefore as unique pieces of engineering and architecture as the stelae and the pyramids and are a further testament to African ingenuity and creativity. They were constructed during the reign of King Lalibela (1185–1225) and are a further testament to the relationship between the kings and the Church. Eleven of these churches were carved out in an area near the capital and the whole area was called Lalibela after the King. Some of the churches were named after important sites in the Bible such as Golgotha, which has led some scholars, like Dr. Sergew Sellasie, to suggest that the churches were an attempt to recreate Jerusalem in the mountains of Ethiopia (Shillington, 125).

A new dynasty came into being in 1270; it not only claimed biblical and Christian legitimacy, but also called itself the Solomonid dynasty because it claimed to be descended from King Solomon of Judea and the Queen of Sheba. The Solomonid dynasty expanded the kingdom to include further areas to the south by military conquest and by building new monasteries to convert their opponents to Christianity. This brought them into conflict with the Muslims who were penetrating from Egypt to the south and east. A state of almost perpetual war now existed between the Muslims, who even went as far as to gain ascendancy over the Somalis, and the Christian Ethiopians. At first the Ethiopians were extremely successful in these conflicts because of their highly efficient and organized army and the loyalty of the Ethiopian aristocracy to their king. Eventually, during the sixteenth century, the Muslims who had by now learnt their lesson and had created an efficient army, declared a holy war against Christian Ethiopia, a so-called "jihad." They did this precisely at a time when the reputed Ethiopian unity was showing signs of fracture and when the Muslims were now united by the fervor of a "jihad" and the need to destroy Christian Ethiopia and the threat it posed to Muslim expansion. Moreover, Ethiopia "unity" was really unity among the king, the royal family, and the aristocracy who menaced and plundered the ordinary peasants. The Muslim army also had the latest in military technology in the form of armaments they got from the Turks who had taken over Egypt. Therefore when the Muslim army of the Sultanate of Adal engaged the much larger Ethiopian army at the battle of Shimbra Kure in 1529, the Ethiopians were signally defeated and for the next few years the Muslims went on the rampage destroying much in Ethiopia.

And now a very interesting intervention occurred. For several centuries the Ethiopians, though building their country by their own exertions, had been in contact with Europe through Christianity. We have already seen that the Portuguese, in particular, had always wanted to establish contact with a reputed Ethiopian king as an ally against the Muslims. Portuguese ambassadors had existed at King Lebna Dengal's court since 1520, and the king, in his desperation, now appealed to the Portuguese, in particular, and Europe, in general, for support against the common enemy, the Muslims. So we have the interesting situation in which a sovereign African nation appeals to Europe for military support against other Africans. This would have all kinds of implications for the future. The Portuguese responded positively and sent a military force to Ethiopia, and the joint force of Portuguese and Ethiopian soldiers inflicted a tremendous defeat on the Muslim forces. The Muslim influence in this area of Africa disintegrated and Christian Ethiopia survived and did so for another 450 years. Some argue that in appealing to the Portuguese for help against the Muslims, many of whom were actually native Africans, Ethiopia was setting the stage or, at least, providing a pretext for imperialist intervention. Be that as it may, Ethiopia was able to survive all these attempts as will appear later.

The Almoravids and the rise of Islamic influence in Africa

Islam was established in the Middle East by the Prophet Muhammad around 633 CE. Since this area was very close to North East, North, and North Western Africa, and the Muslims believed in spreading their religion by trade and military conquest, it was inevitable that the new religion would eventually have a very powerful impact on the development of various states in the northern half of Africa. The original inhabitants of North Western Africa including the Western Sahara were the Berbers. They were farmers, traders, and nomadic pastoralists, moving, at times, with their herds in search of water and new grazing land. Engagement in trade had also brought them in contact with some of the people immediately south of the Sahara, in the area sometimes called the Western Sudan. The Western Sudan, which is a very large area in North Western Africa to the south of the Sahara, is not to be confused with the country called Sudan, much further to the east. The Berbers consisted of various clans or groups, one of the most important being the so-called Lamtuna Sanhaja Berbers. They traded with the people of the Western Sudan but were also often in conflict with some of them, particularly the

Soninke of the Ghana Empire. The Berbers were attracted to Islam by its comparatively simple theology, its acceptance of practices like polygamy, and its basic opposition to systems of caste and class. At this time, Islam had been largely brought over from the Middle East by Islamic merchants, though force would later play a major role.

One of the central pivots of Islam is that every Muslim who can afford to must make the pilgrimage to Mecca, the Muslim holy city, at least once. In 1036 an Islamic Sanhaja chieftain made the pilgrimage and was not only awed by the religious atmosphere, but also became strangely conscious of the inadequacies of his own Berber people as Muslims. He found them totally ignorant of the basic precepts of Islam and completely lacking in religious fervor. The problem was that the Berbers were mostly illiterate and most of them had not even read the Qur'an, the Muslim holy book. Like many of the early converts to Islam, and even to Christianity in Africa, some of them continued to practice their traditional, and in this case, non-Islamic rituals. On his way back from Mecca, the chieftain stopped at a place called Qayrawan and held conversations with Muslim scholars there, informing them of his reservations about his people's religious devotion. The result was that he was accompanied home by a scholar named Abdallah, whose purpose, apparently, was to straighten the religious consciousness of the Berbers.

Abdallah's own observation confirmed everything the chieftain had described. However, he was unable to do much with the Berbers. In despair he withdrew to a site in a remote area of Mauritania to indulge in a hermit-like existence. But he was also able to attract a group of loyal and very devoted Islamic supporters called "Al-Murabitun" or "The Almoravids." Thus, the Almoravid movement was born. It consisted, not of people of Arab descent, but of Berbers, indigenous inhabitants of North Africa. The Almoravid movement was therefore an Islamic movement that believed in strict adherence to Islamic principles. But it soon became much more than a strict religious movement; it became a political and even military movement determined to impose the Islamic religion and strict Islamic principles on "the infidels." It would soon have a very marked impact on Northern Africa and even South Western Europe. The new religious fervor of the Almoravids resonated with quite a few of the Berber clans, especially the Sanhaja Lamtuna, who recognized an opportunity to launch attacks and conduct a holy war against their traditional foes, the Soninke. The movement also grew to become a unifying force among the Sanhaja, many of whom were not only now converted to Islam but were staunch Almoravids. They soon became a very powerful and effective fighting force, a mass army that soon conquered Awdaghust, a prominent city of the Ghanaian Empire to the south; they took over large sections of Morocco; the capture of Awdaghust enabled them to gain control of the very important trans-Saharan gold trade, and so they became a very important economic player. They have even been credited with the conquest and fall of the ancient medieval Empire of Ghana in 1076 and its eventual conversion to Islam. However, some scholars believe that Ghana declined and came to an end through a process of gradual deterioration and voluntary conversion (Shillington, 104). It seems certain, however, that the activities of the Almoravids must have played a very important role in bringing down the Empire of Ghana, which included their traditional enemies the Soninke.

The Almoravids were also responsible for other notable, world-shattering feats. The Muslims had always had their eyes on nearby Southern Spain and longed to bring it under Muslim control. When it actually happened, it was the powerful Almoravid army that performed the feat and thus ensured the extension of Muslim culture to Southern Europe as can be seen in places like Granada in Spain. Thus, the influence of the

Almoravids was not only political, social, economic, and military, but also cultural, and this applies to the situation in Northern Africa. Although the Almoravids eventually began to deteriorate politically, their influence continued and some of their successors continued the work they had begun in extending Islamic culture and learning throughout the whole of Northern Africa. The complete conversion of all the Berbers to Islam must be regarded as one of the achievements of the Almoravids. This led to the introduction of the Arabic language and Arabic culture to this area of Africa, and to widespread literacy through the teaching of the Qur'an. Not only was literacy widespread, the mosques became centers of learning and it is even thought in some circles that what must have been the first university in the world actually started here with the community of very learned scholars who attracted students in various fields. The "university" of course declined. However, this part of Northern and North Western Africa, with its Almoravid influences and associations, was part of the vast Arab–Berber–Muslim world which made remarkable contributions to fields such as science and mathematics. It is to all these peoples that we owe the modern numeral system, counting from one to ten. It is to them that we owe algebra, the decimal point, and the number zero, as well as other developments in physics, chemistry, and astronomy. These parts of Northern and North Western Africa were part of the vast Muslim intellectual tradition that gave so much to the modern world (Shillington, 105).

The ancient West African empires: Ghana

Two major factors helped shape the development of the early West African empires, Ghana, Mali, and Songhay: the rise of Islam and the trans-Saharan trade in gold and salt. The trans-Saharan trade involved the movement of desert dwellers like the Berbers to the edge of the desert to the north or the south to exchange salt, which they had in abundance, for other products such as food items that they could get from the people of the Sahel to the south and others to the north. The desert dwellers were mostly nomadic pastoralists and the trade with others, particularly those on the southern edge of the desert, was originally a part-time activity to enable them to get food. There was abundance of salt beneath the surface of the desert and in some places it existed in huge slabs which were even used occasionally to construct houses. The selling of huge slabs of salt goes on in these North African areas even today, as the videos done by Henry Louis Gates have shown. Originally these desert traders used pack oxen as the means of transporting their goods across the desert, but there were severe limitations on the use of these animals, even though certain breeds became accustomed to traveling across the desert. There was a limit to the speed at which they could travel and the number of days they could travel without food and water.

   The introduction of the camel in the fourth century CE completely revolutionized the trans-Saharan trade. It was a revolution that was as drastic as the introduction of railway transport in more modern times. Several characteristics of the camel contributed to this. Although each camel could carry no more than a good pack ox, it could travel at a much steadier pace, covering 25 to 30 kilometers a day. It could also go for up to ten days without fresh supplies of water, making use of the water stored in its gut and the fat in its hump. It could withstand the rapid changes of temperature in the desert: extreme heat during the day alternating with very low temperatures at night. Its splayed feet were much more attuned to walking on the sand than those of other animals. The use of the camel enabled the desert peoples to travel much further and to engage more distant peoples in their trade. The trans-Saharan trade therefore greatly expanded. The Berbers had always engaged in some trade with the darker peoples to their south. In particular, they wanted to get gold, which was abundant in West Africa and could be eventually sold to the people beyond the desert in the Mediterranean areas, people who placed a much greater value on gold than the West African peoples did. The gold could also be sold to Arabs and eventually to European peoples. But so far the trade had been rather sporadic. With the introduction of the camel that trade now greatly expanded.

One of the principal sources of gold during the medieval period was the ancient empire of Ghana. Ghana is not to be confused with the modern country called Ghana. Ancient Ghana was much further to the north and west of modern Ghana, encompassing Southern Mauritania, parts of Senegal, and Southern Mali. The modern country of Ghana assumed the name of Ghana when it became independent in 1957 as a tribute to the power and importance of the ancient kingdom of Ghana. The main inhabitants of Ghana were a people called the Soninke, who were traditional enemies of the Berbers, though they also traded with them. In the distant past these people living in the savannah grassland, south of the Sahara, were highly successful fishermen, hunters, and farmers, growing crops like millet and sorghum. Their success was largely due to their expertise at ironwork which enabled them to develop better farming tools and techniques. The Soninke are part of the much larger Mande group, a very prominent African-language group whose branches extend as far as the forest (Ajayi and Crowder, 132). Their society was originally organized into villages, but certain village chieftains eventually came together, perhaps in the face of ever-increasing pressure from the Berbers, to form a loose kind of kingdom which eventually became the Empire of Ghana.

Ghana and its Soninke people were very strategically placed to take a leading role in the trade in gold and salt. They were midway between the large-scale producers of the gold to the east and south in the area known as Bambuk and the Berbers who wanted to exchange their salt for the gold. Ghana eventually became very wealthy and prosperous. As the trade in gold and salt expanded, particularly with the introduction of the camel, North African Arabs became involved in it and subsequently came to play a leading role also. Some might even say that they came to dominate the trade since they had more access to what could be regarded as capital and were more directly in touch with the demand for gold in South East Asia and Europe. Travel was easier, and these Arab merchants now traveled extensively in the area. As they traveled, they tried to take Islam with them and introduce it to the native African peoples with varying degrees of success.

It is to these Arab travelers and merchants that we owe some of the most compelling accounts of the great Empire of Ghana, the first of the great medieval West African or Sudanic empires. Ghana is first mentioned towards the end of the eighth century by the Arab Al-Fazari, although his account is not very detailed. He refers to Ghana as "the land of gold," a nomenclature later used by other Arab writers also, and he suggested that Ghana's fame as a center for the gold trade extended to various places in the Asian Middle East. The most detailed account of Ghana, however, is to be found in the writings of Al-Bakri, writing in the eleventh century. Al-Bakri writes of a great king whose conduct is praiseworthy, who is loved and respected by his people and is a great administrator and lover of justice. He describes the capital of Kumbi Saleh as consisting of two great towns. The reason for this was that one of the towns was set aside almost exclusively for Muslim: the traders, merchants, and scribes who were in Kumbi Saleh in large numbers. The Muslim town had about a dozen mosques. This would suggest that although the religion of the people of Ghana at this time was traditional African religion, the rulers practiced religious tolerance and welcomed Muslims, many of whom were used by the rulers as scribes and other functionaries because of their literacy. The king's own town was about ten kilometers from the Muslim sector, and the palace itself was surrounded by conical huts, and the whole surrounded by a fence. The king conducted ceremonies with tremendous pomp and grandeur in his palace. In the king's court were sons of vassal chiefs, who were there almost as hostages, to prevent their fathers from rebelling. The wealth of the people of Ghana derived from the trade in gold, salt, and other commodities. The king's own wealth derived from the taxes imposed on these commodities. No tax was imposed on the sale of gold as such, but the king nevertheless derived great wealth from it by taking the gold nuggets for himself and allowing the people to keep only the gold dust (Shillington, 100; Ajayi and Crowder, 135). There was no regular standing army, but, because of the king's relations with vassal kings and chiefs, he was able to raise an army of about two hundred thousand at short notice. Even in the king's court there are mosques for Muslim ambassadors; the king's interpreters are Muslims as are his treasurer and most of his ministers. From the writings of Al-Bakri and other Arab writers we therefore get a picture of a very powerful and wealthy Ghanaian king presiding over a very efficient administration, engaging quite successfully in trade with his neighbors and various other nations, his people living in well-constructed and imposing structures, practicing religious tolerance, and maintaining law, order, and justice.

The Empire of Ghana reached its zenith in the middle of the eleventh century. There is some debate about the real reasons for the decline of the Empire of Ghana. Ajayi and Crowder, echoing the writer Ibn Khaldun, assert that Ghana was overrun by the Almoravids in 1076, as a result of which the empire was converted to Islam (Ajayi and Crowder, 139). For Shillington the matter is not that clear, and the conversion to Islam might have been a voluntary and peaceful one. Certainly, the conversion did not take place suddenly and in one blow, as a jihadic conquest would have occasioned. Nevertheless, it seems true that the power and influence of Ghana declined largely as the result of military and religious pressure, exerted over time, by the Almoravids who were intent on extending their religion as far as possible. The decline was intensified by the changing dynamics of the gold trade which Ghana had dominated. The opening of the Bure Goldfields to the south of Ghana in the eleventh century meant that that area, rather than Bambuk, became the main producer of gold and new trading routes were opened over which the Empire of Ghana had little control, and the importance of some other peoples began to rise.

The Empire of Mali

The decline of the Empire of Ghana caused certain peoples, like the Sosso and the Malinke, who were related to the Soninke of Ghana but were subject peoples of the empire, to take advantage of the situation and begin to assert their independence. Of these, the Sosso were the most aggressive. During the twelfth century they took over large portions of Ghana and extended their authority over neighboring peoples, some of whom had, like themselves, been subject to Ghana. Under their powerful leader, Sumunguru, they were able to establish an independent state and to bring large sections of the Malinke and the Soninke under their control. The Sosso were a brutal, oppressive, and tyrannical people who were able to extend their authority by conquest, murder, and massacres, and they extorted tributes from their subject peoples. Inevitably, some of the subjects of the Sosso began to resist this tyranny, and the Empire of Mali took its rise from this resistance.

The leader of the Malinke resistance against the Sosso was a chieftain called Sundiata (or Sunjata) who was able to organize an alliance of Malinke chieftains against Sumunguru. Sundiata, who features prominently in the Mali oral tradition, particularly in the Sundiata Epic, is generally regarded as the founder of the Mali Empire. The Mali Empire was much more extensive than the Ghana Empire, most of which it included. It extended southwards and eastwards from Ghana. Where Ghana lay largely in the Sahel, the scrubland area bordering the Sahara, the Empire of Mali pushed much further southwards as far as the fringes of the forest and included the savannah grasslands. Ibn Khaldun writes about a great king of Malinke, called Mari-Djata, who was able to mobilize the Malinke and unite them into a single powerful force. Mari-Djata is almost certainly the same as Sundiata of the oral tradition. Before the emergence of Sundiata there had been chieftains or kings among the Malinke, some of whom had begun to be converted to Islam, but it was Sundiata who was able to mobilize them into a powerful force and into the state called Mali. Having united the Malinke, he led them against the Sosso under Sumunguru, defeated them at the battle of Kirina in 1235, and killed their leader. Sundiata's exploits are recorded in the masterly epic that bears his name and in other forms of the oral tradition, where he is regarded not just as a hero, but even as a magician pitting his wits against another powerful magician, Sumunguru, and finally overcoming him. With the defeat of Sumunguru and the Sosso Mali became the superpower in the area and Sundiata vastly extended its influence and its territories. He built up what could only be called an empire. Mali included most of what was Ghana and all the Soninke peoples. It extended from the fringes of the forest and the southern savannah grasslands where Bure, the main goldfields, and Niani, the capital, were located, eastwards and northwards across the savannah to include much of the Niger valley, and cities like Timbuktu at the bend of the Niger River. The expansion of Mali northwards, eastwards, and westwards meant that it was now in complete control of all the major trade routes, including the gold trade routes, and was therefore in a position to dominate the gold trade.

At the time of the establishment of the Mali hegemony by Sundiata most of the Malian peoples adhered to their traditional religion, although conversion to Islam was already beginning and proceeding gradually. Sundiata himself was a traditionalist. As the leader, he was the one who was most in tune with the spirits of the ancestors and therefore deserving of great reverence and respect. His subjects approached him on their knees. His great wealth, derived from the empire's success in the gold trade, also enhanced the king's majesty and awe. Sundiata was also a great administrator. Under his rule were a number of vassal kings or chiefs in the outlying areas who were allowed to administer their territories as long as they paid tribute to the king and were loyal to him. The king himself employed literate Muslims as scribes and financial officers. Sundiata maintained a large and powerful standing army and the commanders were also important officials, thus enabling the king to exert control over the army.

Sundiata's immediate successors were not as effective as the legendary king, although some of them continued to expand the empire. By now most of the kings and rulers had been converted to Islam and some of them even made the pilgrimage to Mecca. However, there were rivalries and tremendous mismanagement and incompetence, culminating in the usurpation of the throne towards the end of the thirteenth century by Sakura, a freed slave. The fact that Sakura was a freed slave is of tremendous significance.

It tells us something about the nature of slavery in Africa and points to some of the differences between African slavery and the later trans-Atlantic slavery. The slave in Africa could eventually regain his freedom and some slaves were used in the king's administration and could rise to very high office. In Sakura, we know of at least one slave who became emperor. Sakura was actually a great king. He expanded the empire and greatly increased trade. He even made the pilgrimage to Mecca and actually died on the way back from the pilgrimage. On his death the throne passed to the descendants of Sundiata once more, and eventually Mansa Musa, a grandson of Sundiata's brother, became emperor in 1312.

For many, Mansa Musa was Mali's greatest emperor. By the time of his accession the country, or the ruling class at least, had been completely converted to Islam. Indeed, while Mansa is the Malian expression for king, Musa is the Islamic equivalent of Moses. Mansa Musa was arguably the greatest emperor the Mali Empire ever had. Sundiata is revered as the founder of the empire, but it was Mansa Musa who, apart from extending its boundaries, greatly consolidated its reputation and influence. Taking great advantage of Mali's position in the gold trade, he greatly extended Mali's wealth and his own personal fortune. Mali controlled all the internal trade routes over which gold was carried. Some of the Arab writers credit Mansa Musa with the conquest of important centers like Gao and Timbuktu, though others suggest that Mali may have acquired these cities before Mansa Musa came to the throne. However, there is no doubt that it was he who built these cities' reputations, particularly that of Timbuktu, with its great university and a center, not just of Islamic learning, but of learning in general. Students and scholars from all over Western Africa, the Mahgreb, and South West Asia went there to study subjects like mathematics, astronomy, accounting, medicine, philosophy, and so on, as the research of scholars like Henry Louis Gates has shown. The textbooks used by these students and their scholarly teachers are still preserved and can be examined. Respected as a man of high intellect himself, Mansa Musa attracted and invited scholars from far and wide. He was very well known outside Mali and he wanted his country to be well known also. He attracted not only scholars, but other travelers like geographers and historians. Even after his death in 1337, these travelers and scholars continued to flock to Mali, including the famous Ibn Battuta to whom we owe much of our knowledge of the situation in Mali at the time.

As already indicated, Islam was already firmly established in Mali by the time of Mansa Musa's accession. Even if the majority of the population still adhered to the basics of their traditional religion, the upper classes, the leadership, and the royalty were firmly Muslim. Mansa Musa decided to make the pilgrimage to Mecca in 1324–25, and the details of that pilgrimage have become famous. He took a large entourage with him, including 100 camels loaded with gold. This was a magnificent display of the wealth and power of Mali for all to see. Mansa Musa was also very generous with his gifts of gold at all the various places he stopped on the way to and from Mecca. These places included Egypt where the sultan was highly impressed by Mansa Musa's power, wealth, and intellect. It is reported that Mans Musa's generosity with his gifts of gold caused the value of gold in Egypt to be devalued for another 12 years. On the way back from Mecca Mansa Musa ordered that a mosque should be built at every spot where he stopped on Friday, the Muslim holy day. This accounts for the tremendous number of mosques in the empire. He also took back a famous architect with him who not only built new mosques, but redesigned old ones like the famous mosque at Gao. This also accounts for the architectural splendor of most of the mosques in Mali, like the great mosque at Djenné, one of the world's architectural wonders.

After Mansa Musa's death, the power of Mali started to decline, largely because of dynastic struggles. The reigns of the succeeding mansas were brief and troubled, although some of them did their best to maintain the empire's reputation in the outside world. For instance, Europe became so interested in Mali that the country began to feature in European maps of the fourteenth century. One such map shows the Malian emperor seated on his throne, holding a nugget of gold. Mansa Musa was succeeded by his son, Magha, who reigned for only four years before he was succeeded by Mansa Musa's brother, Mansa Sulayman. Sulayman was actually a very effective ruler who continued to ensure Mali's prosperity, but he could not fend off the dynastic struggles. On Sulayman's own death his son's succession was questioned and civil war broke out. There then ensued a period of short reigns, murders, assassinations, coups, plots, and counter-plots during which the power and influence of Mali inevitably declined. Other neighboring states also inevitably took advantage of the decline of Mali to assert their independence or their own dominance.

Songhay

The people who took the most advantage of the decline of the Mali Empire were the people of Songhay who not only asserted their own independence but went on to take over large sections of the Mali Empire and form their own empire, the last of the great West African medieval empires, towards the end of the fifteenth century and the early sixteenth century. At its height the Songhay empire covered an area of half a million square miles. It was based on the Niger River, eastwards and southwards from Mali.

The Songhay state had been formed in the ninth century on the Middle Niger by Sorko fishermen and hunters who welded their boating and hunting skills into a military weapon they used to dominate local farmers. The town of Gao on the Niger bend had been founded by Berber and other merchants and the people of Songhay traded with them and provided them with food items in exchange for salt and other products. Contact with these Berber Muslims resulted in the leaders of Songhay becoming Muslim themselves and Gao became their capital. Not long after, however, Gao and large sections of Songhay became part of the great Mali empire. As already indicated, Songhay took advantage of the decline of Mali to assert its independence. The kings of Songhay at this time were called sunnis (or sonnis), the name of the dynasty, and it was their first sunni leader, Sunni Sulayman, who built up a remarkable army consisting of horsemen and war canoes and started expanding Songhay territory up the Niger River. However, it was their first great leader, Sunni Ali, who established the empire, an empire that was to become even greater than Mali.

Sunni Ali reigned from 1468 to 1492, and his entire reign consisted of an endless and even brutal campaign to expand the Songhay Empire. He saw the importance of the cities of Timbuktu and Djenné as centers of the gold trade that he had to bring under his control if he was to dominate that trade; he also saw the importance of the fertile Niger plain as a food-producing enclave crucial to the economy of the entire region. He therefore set out on a campaign of military conquest. Under his leadership Songhay conquered Timbuktu in 1468. The city had actually been taken from Mail by Berbers in 1438, and Sunni Ali now drove out the Berber governor who fled taking some of the scholars with him. Sunni Ali also took Djenné in 1473. Sunni Ali was also a brilliant administrator who appointed officials loyal to him as governors of cities and gave them responsibility for ensuring good governance and collecting taxes. Largely because of his conquest of Timbuktu and the flight of the Muslim scholars, Sunni Ali was actually hated by Muslims who felt he was not Muslim at all. It is certainly true that he showed great disdain for the Muslim scholars and authorities in the areas he captured, and that the University of Timbuktu, from which a number of scholars fled, suffered greatly under him. The Arab and other historians and chroniclers represent him as oppressive, arrogant, and ruthless. The Songhay oral tradition, on the other hand, presents him as the great hero who founded the Songhay empire (Shillington, 116).

Sunni Ali died in 1492 and he was succeeded for a very brief period by his son Abu Bakr. Sunni Ali had never been really liked by the other leaders because he was not Muslim and there was little love for his son whose allegiance to the Muslim faith was also very dubious. Various groups, including military leaders, were disaffected and rose up in rebellion. The chief of these was one of Sunni Ali's generals, Askia Muhammad. It is believed that Askia Muhammad tried unsuccessfully to persuade Abu Bakr to pledge allegiance to Islam. The chaos culminated in a battle in 1493 in which Askia Muhammad was victorious and he became the emperor. One of the reasons he later gave for taking over the empire from Abu Bakr was that Abu Bakr was not a Muslim and he had got the blessing of Muslim authorities to take over non-Muslim states. This also illustrates the importance of Islam in the development of the West African empires.

Askia Muhammad was another great emperor of Songhay. He ruled until he too was deposed in 1528, and he should be credited with the great expansion of the Songhay Empire. He introduced very strong political organization and by the time of his deposition in 1528 the Songhay Empire was greater than any other in West Africa before or since. He was a shrewd king who realized the power of Islam and even made use of Islam to reinforce his authority, even though he permitted religious freedom and did not try to impose it on those of the ordinary people who still adhered to the basics of their traditional religion. To show his respect for the Muslim faith, he made the pilgrimage to Mecca and, unlike his predecessor who had sacked Timbuktu, he restored that city to its previous position as a bastion of learning. He also vastly increased trade and therefore the wealth of the empire. However, he was deposed by his own son in 1528. Songhay did not really "decline" as the other West African empires had done. It continued to preside over the gold trade and in spite of drought and disease and dynastic struggles the economy continued to flourish during most of the sixteenth century. The Moroccans decided to invade because they wanted to control the gold trade, and so Songhay was overrun by a Moroccan army in 1591.

Great Zimbabwe

The ancient state of Great Zimbabwe in Southern Africa flourished between the thirteenth and the fifteenth centuries. The area is very fertile and suitable for the raising of cattle and the production of crops like wheat. It could therefore serve as the breadbasket for a much larger area, as it did once even in the twentieth century. The ancient state of Zimbabwe therefore started as a great farming center, famous for the rearing of animals and the production of crops, not to mention interesting wildlife such as elephants, useful for their tusks. Ownership of cattle determined the extent of one's wealth and therefore led to the rise of classes and the difference between rich and poor. The main inhabitants were the Shona, which even today is one of the most important ethnic groups in modern Zimbabwe. The king's wealth depended on the tax imposed on the trade passing through the capital from the interior to the coast, and on the tribute in gold, ivory, and foodstuffs paid by subsidiary chieftains.

Great Zimbabwe is famous for its massive stone structures, consisting of huge towers and massive circular enclosures. These structures are all the more fascinating because no mortar was used in their construction, and they nevertheless stood for hundreds of years. They were almost certainly built between 1200 and 1450. Although the building of stone enclosures to protect cattle and the homes and properties of the wealthy was not unknown in Southern Africa, here in Great Zimbabwe they appear at their most elaborate. Some of these elaborate structures are built on hills and some in valleys. Some of the walls are ten meters high and some of the towers are even higher. The art of erecting these structures had been perfected by 1400, a tremendous testimony to the skill of the Zimbabwe craftsmen and stonemasons. The purpose of these structures is not particularly clear. Since the enclosures encircled the homes of kings and rulers, they may have been constructed for defensive purposes, to keep enemies at bay. They may simply have been constructed to show off the wealth and power of the ruling classes. The greatest enclosure surrounded the residence of the king, but there were other enclosures round the homes of major government officials. The towers were probably intended as storehouses for surplus grain.

Great Zimbabwe was abandoned round about 1450, and the area is now mostly in ruins. Over-grazing, over-cultivation of the land and consequent decline in agricultural production, and the fall in the demand for gold have all been given as reasons for the decline of Great Zimbabwe and the abandonment of the area. It certainly became much less important as a center of trade than it had been. Still, the architectural achievements of this southern civilization were considerable.

This survey has shown the nature of the situation in Africa before the massive movement of the Portuguese and other Europeans to Africa began in the fifteenth century. Far from being a barbaric entity with no civilization and organization, Africa had many organized states, empires and kingdoms, with political, social, and economic structures that worked and were meant to ensure law and order. In most cases they also ensured justice and prosperity. This is not to say that pre-colonial African society was perfect or ideal. Like all human organizations, there were some brutal and chaotic societies, and there were several examples of incompetence and deterioration. These also happen in modern societies, because all societies are human. For the most part, however, African societies and systems were not very different from those elsewhere or from those that exist even in the modern world. African ingenuity, innovation, and capacity for mastering systems and mechanisms designed to solve problems and ensure progress are also displayed. In a sense, the intervention of the Europeans disrupted and set back the onward movement that had been going on in Africa for thousands of years.

References and suggestions for further reading

Abun-Nasr, J. M. 1987. *A History of the Maghrib in the Islamic Period*. Cambridge: Cambridge University Press.
Ajayi, J. F. A. and Crowder, M. 1971. *History of West Africa*. Vol. I. Harlow: Longman.
Austen, R. (ed.). 1999. *In Search of Sundiata: The Mande Epic as History, Literature and Performance*. Bloomington, IN: Indiana University Press.
Azevedo, M. (ed.). 2005. *Africana Studies: A Survey of Africa and the African Diaspora*. Durham, NC: Carolina Academic Press.

Brett, M. and Fentress, E. 1996. *The Berbers*. Oxford: Blackwell.

Connah, G. 2001. *African Civilizations: Precolonial Cities and States in Tropical Africa*. 2nd ed. New York: Cambridge University Press.

Davidson, B. 1995. *Africa in History*. New York: Touchstone Books.

Ehret, C. 2002. *The Civilizations of Africa: A History to 1800*. Oxford: James Currey.

Fage, J. D. 1995. *A History of Africa*. 3rd ed. London: Routledge.

Falola, T. (ed.). 2000. *African History Before 1885*. Durham, NC: Carolina Academic Press.

Garlake, P. 1973. *Great Zimbabwe Described and Explained*. London: Thames & Hudson.

Henze, P. 1999. *Lepers of Time: A History of Ethiopia*. London: Hurst.

Hunt Davis Jr., R. 2005. "Africa and the Genesis of Humankind." Pp. 55–70 in M. Azevedo (ed.), *Africana Studies*. Durham, NC: Carolina Academic Press.

Laremont, R. and Kalouche, F. (eds.). 2002. *Africans and Other Civilizations: Conquest and Counter-Conquest*. Trenton, NJ: Africa World Press.

Lassen, M. 1994. *The Oromo of Ethiopia: A History, 1570–1860*. Trenton, NJ: Red Sea Press.

Levtzion, M. 1973. *Ancient Ghana and Mali*. London: Methuen.

Mazrui, A. 1986. *The Africans: A Triple Heritage*. London: BBC Publications.

Newman, J. L. 1995. *The Peopling of Africa: A Geographic Interpretation*. New Haven, CT: Yale University Press.

Phillipson, D. W. 2012. *Foundations of an African Civilization: Aksum and the Northern Horn, 1000 BC–AD 1300*. Oxford: James Currey.

Shillington, K. 2019. *History of Africa*. 4th ed. London: Red Globe Press.

Stringer, C. 2016. *The Origin of Our Species*. London: Penguin.

Toynbee, A. 1950. *War and Civilization*. New York: Oxford University Press.

Trevor-Roper, H. 1965. *The Rise of Christian Europe*. New York: Harcourt, Brace & World.

Wildung, D. (ed.). 1997. *Sudan: Ancient Kingdoms of the Nile*. New York: Flamarion.

Wilkinson, T. 2016. *The Rise and Fall of Ancient Egypt*. London: Bloomsbury.

2 Slavery

Although in this chapter we shall be discussing slavery in Africa in general, we shall place emphasis mostly on the trans-Atlantic slavery associated with the European intervention in Africa and its impact on the continent in general. The trans-Atlantic slavery was the most devastating phenomenon that sub-Saharan Africa ever suffered. It will not be an exaggeration to say that it was the African equivalent of the Holocaust, a brutal activity that resulted in the premature death of millions of Africans and changed the direction in which the continent was moving. The nature and impact on the continent of this phenomenon cannot possibly be underestimated or downplayed as some modern scholarship and discussion have attempted to do. For instance, some scholars have come up with ridiculously low estimates of the number of Africans who were forcibly abducted and shipped to the Americas, thus suggesting that the impact of the slave trade on Africa could not have been all that devastating. Others have emphasized the fact that slavery was in existence and widespread in Africa before the coming of the Europeans and have pointed to the participation in slavery of groups other than the Europeans, such as the Arabs. This chapter will certainly discuss the nature of slavery within Africa and the role played by the Arabs in slavery in Africa and apportion appropriate responsibility, but there is no doubt that the trans-Atlantic slavery was much more elaborate, much more organized and systematic, and much more brutal than any form of slavery that had been seen in Africa before.

The slave trade was the ultimate result of a new European interest in Africa in the early fifteenth century. Of course, contact between Europe and North Africa goes way back, if only because both European and North African states bordered the Mediterranean. The Romans fought a significant war with Carthage, now identified with modern Tunisia, in which the great general Hannibal crossed the Mediterranean, went over to Europe, crossed the Alps with his elephants, approached Rome from the north and almost brought about its total destruction. The Almoravids, too, had conquered significant parts of Spain, and there was religious interaction between these two areas because of the establishment of both Christianity and Islam. There was economic interaction too, as Berbers and Arabs from North Africa traded with Southern European nations. This was particularly so with the gold trade which was dominated by the Arabs who served as the middle men between the Sahelian dwellers who brought the gold from the south and the Europeans who wanted it and valued it highly. We also know of at least one Portuguese map in which the great Malian Emperor Mansa Musa is represented seated on his throne holding a nugget of gold. So the Portuguese knew of Mansa Musa. However, before the early years of the fifteenth century there had been little or no contact between Europe and sub-Saharan Africa. All this would now change.

DOI: 10.4324/9781003111733-3

In the later Middle Ages there were certain trends that would change the view of Europeans towards both the Mediterranean and the Atlantic. Hitherto, the Mediterranean had been the world's most important waterway. Gradually, however, this focus would change to the Atlantic. There were certain nations located on the Atlantic, which were small in area but quite enterprising, like Portugal, England, and Holland. These were poised to take advantage of this change in focus. The entire west coast of Africa was on the Atlantic and this fact put that area within the sights of the Europeans, especially Portugal. There were other, much more important reasons for this new European interest in and contact with Africa. The most important of these was the gold trade which had been going on for centuries. Hitherto, this trade had been dominated by the Arabs who, because of religious and other reasons, had not been the favorites of the Portuguese. The Portuguese now wanted direct access to the gold mines and gold-producing areas of Western Africa. Portugal, at this time, was not particularly well-off, and dominance of the gold trade would bring both great wealth and economic importance. The Portuguese were also interested in discovering a sea route to India. India was fairly well known among Europeans because of both its ancient and exotic culture and as the home of spices which were highly prized and highly desired in the West to pep up the rather bland European diet. So far, however, these spices could be acquired only by making hazardous voyages overland passing through some very dangerous countries. This greatly affected the price of the spices apart from the threat to the lives of the merchants. A sea route to India would not only greatly reduce the cost of the spices, but would open up a vast Asian area with tremendous possibilities.

The Europeans were also anxious to make the acquaintance of a legendary monarch of Ethiopia they had heard of. According to them, he was called Prester John. There is no evidence of the existence of a king of Ethiopia by that name, but Ethiopia, then known by most Europeans as Abyssinia, had long been a Christian country, and an alliance with its monarch would greatly help the Europeans to contain the Arabs and loosen their hold not only on the North African gold trade, but also on the East African trade which the Arabs now dominated also. The Europeans also wanted the assistance of this king to expel the Muslim Moors out of the conquered parts of the Iberian Peninsula. Such an alliance therefore had strategic and economic advantages. Finally, the new interest in the Atlantic and in the west coast of Africa was an aspect of the new spirit of adventure characteristic of the Renaissance which was now at its height in Europe. Renaissance humanism involved not only the expansion of man's inner horizons, but of the outer ones as well. There was a drive to explore and find out more about the world, and the many voyages of discovery made during this period were a part of that drive.

And so the Portuguese started their exploration of the west coast of Africa. They captured Ceuta, on the North African coast, in what is now Morocco, appropriately on the border between the Mediterranean Sea and the Atlantic, and they appointed the young Prince Henry as its governor. Henry was consumed with the new spirit of adventure and exploration and recognized its importance, although he never became an explorer himself. However, he played a leading role in the establishment of a school for navigators at Sagres, and thus earned the name of "Prince Henry the Navigator." As the fifteenth century progressed the Portuguese proceeded to capture and occupy a number of islands off the West African coast and set up stations on the coast. They took Madeira in 1419 and the Azores in 1434. They occupied the Arguin Islands in 1444 and colonized the Cape Verde Islands in 1460. In 1462 Pedro da Cintra arrived in Sierra Leone, giving the country that name. One story goes that he heard the rumbling of thunder and thought it was the roaring of lions in the mountains, so he gave the area the name Sierra Leone or "Lion Mountain." Another suggests that the name derives from the appearance of one of the hills overlooking the bay, a hill which closely resembles a crouching lion. Before leaving the area he carved his name and the date on a rock just outside the harbor. These can be seen even at the present day. The Portuguese also laid claim to the Island of Goree off the coast of Senegal and built a fort and trading station at Elmina in present-day Ghana. In so far as the attempt to discover a sea route to India was concerned, Bartolomeu Dias succeeded in reaching the southern tip of the continent in 1487 but was frightened by storms from proceeding further. Ten years later in 1497 Vasco da Gama not only rounded the Cape of Good Hope (which Dias had called the Cape of Storms) but also succeeded in reaching India.

At the start of their association with Africa the Portuguese were only interested in what Alpha Bah calls legitimate trade (Bah, 72). Primarily, they wanted African gold, and they brought copper, brass, and European cloth which they traded for the gold. This trade went on quite peacefully and prosperously for a while. Recent research has shown, however, that the Portuguese were not above engaging in a secondary traffic in slaves. They got the slaves from the Kingdom of Benin and sold them to the Akan people of modern Ghana (Shillington, 174). There were some very rich gold mines in Ghana, particularly in Ashanti land, and extra labor was needed to work the mines, so the Ashantis got the extra labor from the Portuguese, and this trade started only when the Portuguese arrived. As we have seen, the Portuguese built forts and trading stations on the islands off the African coast and on the African coast. Some of these Portuguese merchants and traders actually settled in the islands and the coastal regions of Africa. They established plantations for growing sugar, modelling these plantations on similar ones that had been established on Mediterranean islands and in Southern Spain and Portugal during the fourteenth and early fifteenth centuries. These Southern European sugar plantations made use of unpaid "workers" from North Africa and from the Slavs of Russia, hence the word "slave" which derives from the word "Slav." In their plantations in Africa, therefore, the Portuguese were accustomed to a system that made use of largely unpaid labor on plantations. All the evidence suggests, however, that this system was relatively benign and could certainly not be compared to what eventually came to exist on the American plantations. These Portuguese settlers, who were called "lancados," became quite Africanized. They adopted African customs and intermarried with the Africans thus producing a hybrid group of people called Afro-Portuguese. They became extremely useful as middlemen between the local population and the visiting Portuguese and other merchants.

Generally speaking, the relationship between the Portuguese and the local Africans up to this point was comparatively cordial. It was based largely on the legitimate trade in gold. Soon, however, this trade was to be replaced by the much more sordid trade in human cargo. The main reason for this was the "discovery" of the "New" World by Christopher Columbus in 1492. It is interesting to note that Columbus's motive in setting out on his epic journey was not to find America; like many of the other navigators, his intention was to discover a sea route to India. Unlike the other navigators, however, he decided to go westwards because it had by then been confirmed that the world was round; so, if one could get to India by going eastwards, one could surely also get to it by going westwards. He was also imbued by the spirit of adventure characteristic of the Renaissance. It is also worth noting that there is evidence that the Scandinavians had actually got to North America well before Columbus arrived in the Caribbean.

Columbus actually stumbled on the Caribbean islands and America by accident. Indeed, it is quite possible that he thought he had got to parts of India, which is why he gave the area the name "West Indies."

The practical result of Columbus's activities was that European nations, such as Spain, Portugal, England, France, and Holland, now took possession of large tracts of America and the Caribbean islands, and established plantations to grow crops like sugar, cotton, and tobacco. The first to establish plantations were the Portuguese and the Spaniards, and the plantations were modeled on those the Portuguese had been accustomed to in Africa. At first, they used local natives as unpaid labor, but the local populations were quite unsuitable for this kind of work. Moreover, they easily succumbed to the new diseases the European conquerors had brought with them, diseases to which they had no immunity. Whole local nations were wiped out completely, particularly on the Caribbean islands. The Portuguese, of course, had had experience of the plantation system in Africa. They had used Africans efficiently on those plantations and knew that Africans were tough, resilient, and adaptable. They therefore developed the idea of going to Africa to get labor to work on their American and Caribbean plantations. This was the origin of the trans–Atlantic slave trade.

Oriental slavery

Slavery did not start with the trans–Atlantic slave trade. In fact, it has a very long history worldwide. The Romans, whom some people hold to be one of the most "civilized" peoples in history, were notorious for owning slaves. The Egyptians had slaves and so had the Greeks. Slaves are mentioned several times in both the Old and New Testaments. A statement by Saint Paul says that in Christ there is no bond or free and it is clear that there were slaves among the Israelites. Slavery as an institution was therefore well known and common in the ancient world. Slavery had also existed on the continent of Africa before the institution of the trans–Atlantic slave trade. We have already seen that the Portuguese actually got slaves from the Kingdom of Benin and the Ashantis also needed and acquired slaves to work their gold mines. Then there was the trans–Saharan slave trade carried on mostly by the Arabs between North Africa and Asia and between North Africa and parts of Europe. After the establishment of Islam in the seventh century CE the Arabs moved to North Africa and conducted jihads or holy wars with the intention of converting as many Berbers and other Africans as possible to Islam, and they would do this by force. Captives in battle were often taken into slavery and sold to Arab merchants for further sale to people in South Western Asia or even Southern Europe. There is evidence that the Berbers, who had been converted to Islam, also participated in the trade. Since Islamic law forbade the enslavement of other Muslims, the Muslim merchants had to look for their slaves elsewhere and they found them in the captive or conquered "infidels" of the Sahel or the Western Sudan. The traffic in slaves thus became a feature of the general trans–Saharan trade. It was only one aspect of the "oriental" slave trade. It was called oriental because it was largely practiced by the Arabs and the slaves were sent eastwards to the Arabian peninsula and other parts of South Western Asia. The other aspect of the oriental slavery was conducted in North Eastern Africa along the borders of the Red Sea, the Horn of Africa, and Eastern Africa. This was also dominated by the Arabs and perpetrated through trade along the east coast and jihads. The slaves were then sold to Arabia and other parts of Asia. There is evidence that some Africans in this area also participated.

So the Arabs had been active in the slave-trading business long before the arrival of the Portuguese in Africa. And yet there are significant differences between the oriental slavery and the new trans-Atlantic slavery. Some may say that slavery is slavery is slavery, and one cannot make distinctions between forms of slavery. In a sense, this is true, as is aptly demonstrated by a scholar such as Henry Louis Gates in his videos about Africa. One must condemn slavery wherever it occurs and whatever form it takes. Yet the scale of the trans-Atlantic slavery was monstrous, and it is necessary to make some distinctions. Oriental slavery was not done primarily for commercial reasons. The profit motive, though significant, was not paramount. It can almost be said that the Oriental slavery was a by-product of the jihads and the Arab interest in extending the influence of Islam. The slaves were largely conquered in war and taken as prisoners of war. They were not captured in raids solely designed to procure slaves. The oriental slavery was not plantation slavery. The captured slaves were not taken to the Arab world to work on plantations. Where the economy of the South of the United States, to which many of the slaves were taken, was dependent on slavery, the economic system of the Arab world was not based on slavery. The slaves were largely used for domestic purposes though some of them might have worked on farms.

The Arabs who captured slaves and took them to the Arab world were largely interested in women and children, though men were sometimes taken and made into eunuchs to supervise the harems of their slave masters. To be put in charge of harems, even though they had been castrated, suggests that the male slaves enjoyed some measure of trust. This was quite different from the trans-Atlantic situation were slaves were regarded with tremendous distrust. Some of them were wrongly suspected of poisoning or wanting to poison their masters and were even executed in consequence. The women who were abducted to the Arab world became concubines, but the Arab slave masters quite often married their female slaves and integrated them into the society. They did not sell them, and they certainly did not sell the offspring they had with them. Once again, this was quite different from the trans-Atlantic situation. In the Americas, particularly in North America, slave masters never married their female slaves. They might see them as being sexually desirable and might even have children with them; but they never married them. We know, for instance, that Thomas Jefferson, widely regarded as one of the greatest American presidents, had several children by a female slave whom he never married. Their descendants are only now discovering their white cousins. In the trans-Atlantic situation white slave masters quite often regarded their female slaves as breeders with whom they could beget more slaves that would then be sold into further slavery. They quite often sold their offspring with their female slaves, as is depicted in Alex Haley's realistic novel based on slavery, *Roots*.

Furthermore, racism did not play a part in the oriental slavery. One of the main reasons why European slave owners and captors had no compunction about capturing Africans and selling them as commodities was the belief that Africans were somehow sub-human and little better than horses or cattle. That was why they branded their slaves before loading them on to the ships or after they had been sold. Even in later, apparently more enlightened, days, it was calculated that a black person was worth only two-thirds of a white human being. The Arabs never regarded their African slaves as being sub-human. If they did, they would not have married them and integrated them into their society. Finally, there is the question of the total number of slaves involved. As is the case with the trans-Atlantic slave trade, numbers vary depending on the sources of information. However, it has been generally estimated that no more than five million Africans were taken from Africa by the Arabs, and the number of people of African descent living in the Arab world at the present time as a result of slavery is no more than two million. This is considerably less than the situation in the Americas.

Slavery within Africa

Let us now take a look at the nature of slavery within Africa itself before the trans-Atlantic slavery. There is no doubt that slavery was common in Africa before the beginning of the trans-Atlantic slave trade. We know that there were slaves in the Empire of Ghana and even in the later Empires of Mali and Songhay. The slaves were often captured in war, but many of them were used by the monarchs in their administration either because they were literate or were good at record-keeping. They became thoroughly integrated into the society. Some of them eventually came to occupy very high positions in their masters' administrations. This was because the monarchs trusted them completely since, as outsiders originally, they could not belong to rival ruling families and therefore posed no threat to the throne. Because of their influence and importance, slaves often intervened in succession crises. We know of at least one case where an individual who was originally a slave actually came to be emperor. This was Sakura who usurped the throne of Mali during the chaos and dynastic struggles that followed the death of Sundiata. And he was a great ruler indeed. It is clear that as the power of these medieval empires grew and as they converted to Islam, they regarded the non-Muslim states with contempt, referred to them as infidels, and had no qualms in conducting raids into their territories, with the excuse that they were conducting jihads, though some of these raids might have been deliberately intended to get slaves to sell to the Arabs.

In this matter of slavery in Africa a lot depends on the definition of the word "slave." A good number of the people who were referred to as slaves were actually domestic servants, working in the homes of their masters and not on farms or mines. Bah gives the very interesting account of a slave woman among the Fulani who was really a nanny and was responsible for the upbringing of her master's children and even grandchildren. She became so thoroughly integrated into the family that she regarded the children as her own children and grandchildren and they regarded her as their mother and grandmother (Bah, 76). Her position in the family and the attitudes of all concerned were hardly the same as those in North America when the slave trade was at its height. In certain parts of Africa there was a caste system, and those belonging to the lowest caste were sometimes referred to as slaves. Referring to them as slaves was certainly reprehensible, but there was a still a great difference between the situation of these people and the slaves in the Americas and the West Indies. For instance, among the Igbos of Eastern Nigeria there was a group of people called "Osus." They were sometimes referred to as slaves, but they were really outcasts because they were supposed to have been dedicated to the gods. They could not cut their hair or live with other people. They could only marry among themselves, and when they died they were buried, not where other people were buried, but in the so-called "Evil Forest." Chinua Achebe in his seminal novel *Things Fall Apart* gives a graphic presentation of the situation of these people.

In certain parts of Africa, a slave was someone given to a priest to work for that priest, or even perform sexual favors, in expiation for a crime that had been committed by that person's family. Once more, this was certainly reprehensible and unjust, but the situation was very different from that of the slave in the Americas.

All the evidence suggests that the situation of the "slave" in Africa was generally much better than that of the slave in the Americas and the West Indies. The "slave" who was a domestic servant quite often played a very important role in the master's household and could regain his or her liberty. Many slaves were used by the rulers in their administration, played leading roles in the state and could also regain their liberty. Slaves were seldom deliberately captured as a result of raids deliberately intended for that purpose. They were mostly prisoners of war who had been captured in battle. Slaves were often criminals or prisoners who were forced for a certain length of time to atone or pay for their crimes by working without pay. Also, unfortunate people who had fallen on hard times often offered their services voluntarily as slaves to work without pay in return for food and shelter. As we have seen, slaves were often domestic servants and were later integrated into the family for whom they worked. Some of the females married their masters or some other prominent members of society. Only in one case, the case of the Ashantis, do we definitely know of slaves who were deliberately recruited to work in the mines; and this happened after the beginning of the trans-Atlantic slave trade. The slaves were usually bought from Portuguese middlemen.

The trans–Atlantic slave trade

Let us now turn our attention to the trans-Atlantic slave trade itself, concentrating largely on its impact on Africa. It was caused by the "discovery" of the Americas, the need for heavy labor on the plantations, and the unsuitability of the native tribes for that kind of labor. The slaves were generally captured in the interior of Africa by the locals and then brought to the coast to be sold to the European slavers. At this stage, the Europeans never dared to penetrate into the interior because they were afraid of what they might find in there, the interior of the continent being, as yet, unexplored. Furthermore, the nature of the terrain inhibited penetration of the continent at this stage. As we have seen, there were rapids and cataracts very close to the spots where the rivers entered the ocean, and these would have to be traversed before penetration into the interior. Even at this stage, slaves were quite often prisoners of war who had been captured in battle and were sold to the slavers by their enemies. As states were formed or expanded, local wars inevitably ensued and the conquering states sold their captives. For instance, the expanding state of Benin sold captives to the Portuguese from as far back as the fifteenth century. In the sixteenth century, the Mane in what is now Sierra Leone occupied the highlands of that country and sold the conquered local peoples into slavery. In the early eighteenth century the Fulbe people in the Futa Jalon of what is now Guinea fought a holy war against neighboring tribes and sold the captives into slavery (Shillington, 180). There is evidence that the European slavers actually encouraged this ethnic rivalry among the peoples of West Africa, in particular, because it would result in their having many more slaves. But slaves were also captured through raids intended for the purpose and this was now done by local African peoples. The European slavers thus had African collaborators who did the dirty work for them. Some of the rulers were actively involved in slavery. The kings of Dahomey were notorious for organizing raids and selling even their own people into slavery. So, to a lesser extent, were the rulers of Benin and parts of the Cameroon. At times they used specially appointed officials for the purpose. They and the officials became rich and powerful as a result. We do know of some African individuals who made slave raiding a career and amassed fortunes in consequence. In a sense this was surprising since the slaves were sold for little more than what would now be considered trifles, such as cheap cloth, metal hardware, and beads. But they were also sold for guns, and this introduced a new level of violence into African society. The possession of guns increased the hold of tyrannical rulers over their subjects and promoted more inter-ethnic strife. The researches of scholars like Professor Akosua Perbi have revealed the extent of the Indigenous African participation in the slave trade.

The progress of the trade: the middle passage

The captured slaves were transported to the coast and sold. They were housed in deplorable conditions in the fortresses that had been built at places like Elmina castle in Ghana, Bunce Island in Sierra Leone, the Island of Goree off the coast of Senegal, and Quida in what used to be Dahomey and is now Benin. It is still possible to visit these fortresses and see the quarters in which the slaves were kept. The slaves came from various countries from Mauretania, Senegal, and the Gambia in the north to Angola in the south. Bah has identified six main sources of supply of the slaves who were taken to North America, Brazil, and the West Indies. The first was the Senegambia area populated by four main ethnic groups: the Mandingo, the Fula, the Wollof, and the Jola. The slaves had been kidnapped or were debtors, criminals, destitutes, or war captives. Kunta Kinte in Alex Haley's *Roots* is supposed to have come from this area. The second area was that around the modern Sierra Leone, extending from the Sherbro River to the Ivory Coast. It included tribes like the Bassa, Kru, Mende, Gola, Temne, Kissi, and Kono. The third slave-producing area was the Gold Coast, now Ghana, and it included ethnic groups like the Akan and the Fanti. The devastating internal turmoil which characterized this area and which eventually led to the establishment of the Ashanti confederation, made it a fertile source of slaves. Two fortresses in this area, Elmina Castle and Cape Coast Castle, were among the most famous slave fortresses. The fourth area was the Dahomey area, known as the slave coast, and dominated by the Ewe, the Yoruba, and the Bini. It was also dominated by the notorious kings of Dahomey, now Benin, and it provided the largest number of slaves every year. It was described as the greatest slave-trading place on the Guinea coast, providing more slaves than all the other areas put together (Bah, 80). Fifth on the list was Benin in Nigeria and the Niger Delta. This was an area inhabited by ethnic groups such as the Igbo, the Ibibio, the Edo, and the Ijaw. Finally, the sixth major slave-providing area was South Western Africa: Cameroon, Congo, Angola, Gabon, and the Democratic Republic of the Congo.

One might well ask what the role of the Church was in all this, particularly the Roman Catholic Church which was dominant at the start of the trade and during most of it. The Roman Catholic Church had also been instrumental in the explorations and "discoveries" that led to the establishment of the plantations in the West. There is a report that after the "discovery" of 1492, the Pope felt it incumbent on himself to prevent the rivalry developing between two major Catholic nations about the possession of various territories in South America. He therefore took his pen and drew a line from north to south, declaring that all new countries to the left of that line would belong to Spain, and all to the right would belong to Portugal. Hence it is that while most of South America belonged to Spain and is still Spanish speaking, only one country, Brazil, belonged to Portugal and is Portuguese speaking. But Brazil is by far the largest country on the continent. It is not generally known that about 40 percent of all the slaves transported across the Atlantic actually went to the plantations in Brazil. The Church was instrumental in all this and could have done a lot towards alleviating the condition of the slaves. However, the Church turned a blind eye to the activities of the slavers. In fact, it can be said that the Church gave its blessing to the slavers' activities provided that the slaves were baptized and converted to Christianity either before being loaded on to the ships or just after they were sold. One of the slave ships was apparently called "Jesus of Lubeck." The Church was therefore complicit in the slave trade, and some churches actually benefited from the profits of that trade.

The process whereby the slaves were transported across the Atlantic to the Americas is generally called "the middle passage." The slaves were chained, kept mostly naked, left to wallow in their own filth, and allowed hardly any exercise. Inevitably, diseases broke out among them, and those who were seriously ill were thrown alive overboard and left to the mercies of the sharks. A sick slave was of no use to the slavers; he was, in fact, a great liability. Some of the slaves actually committed suicide by jumping overboard themselves because they preferred that kind of death to being owned by white slave masters who they feared might even eat them. Again numbers vary, but it is generally estimated that about half of those slaves who were loaded on to the ships died during the middle passage. However, some slaves managed to stage riots and rebellions. In 1730, the ninety-six slaves on board the *Little George*, who were being taken from West Africa to the Americas, overwhelmed their captors, forced the crew to take refuge in the ship's cabinet, and turned the ship back. They then sailed up the Sierra Leone River, and jumped overboard to dry land in Sierra Leone, thus regaining their freedom. In 1839 some slaves who were being taken from Mendeland in Sierra Leone to North America on a ship called the *Amistad* rebelled against their captors. Led by a young man called Joseph Cinque, they overwhelmed them, and took control of the ship. They eventually arrived in the United States, where the company that had owned the ship and the slaves still claimed possession and took the case to court. The slaves' case was taken by a former president, John Quincy Adams. Adams won the case and the slaves were repatriated to Sierra Leone. A famous movie, directed by Steven Spielberg, was made out of the slaves' experiences.

There is tremendous controversy among scholars and researchers about the total number of Africans who were abducted from the continent and transported to the New World. In a sense, this was inevitable, since some of the researchers had a hidden agenda to minimize or downplay the extent of the trade and its impact on Africa. It was therefore in the interest of these people to assert that the numbers were much lower than previously supposed. However, the problem is further complicated by the difficulty of getting accurate figures from such a distant time. Philip Curtin, in a work entitled *The Atlantic Slave Trade: A Census*, put the estimate of the number of slaves taken from Africa at 11.5 million. Of these, he estimated that 9.5 million reached the Americas. This sparked the controversy, because Curtin's figures were considerably lower than those previously accepted or those that other scholars had put forth. For instance, Edward Dunbar and R. R. Kuczynski had estimated that at least 15 million slaves actually reached the Americas, which would suggest that many more actually left Africa. Oliver Martin had estimated that at least 20 million left Africa. On the other hand, some highly respected scholars like W. E. B. DuBois, J. D. Fage, and Basil Davidson put the number abducted from Africa at 50 million (Bah, 77). Another notable scholar, J. E. Inikori, challenged Curtin's figures, and called into question his data, his motives, and his methodology. Curtin's calculations were partly based on the annual rates of increase of the black populations in the British colonies. Working backwards, therefore, he had estimated what the original black populations must have been, and this is obviously unreliable. Also, Curtin had based his calculations on tax records, which are also unreliable because tax transactions are usually under-reported. Curtin had excluded Jamaica from his calculations, although everyone knew that Jamaica, like other parts of the West Indies, was a major destination for the slaves. Other scholars, while not casting aspersion on Curtin's motives, still expressed reservations about the accuracy of his calculations. The problem was that many of the slave merchants and slave owners did not keep accurate records of the slaves they owned or the slaves that left the African continent. Then there was the tremendous issue of those who died during the voyage, calculated by some scholars as being almost half. This is why it will be impossible to get accurate figures. The only real judgment one can make is that Curtin's figures are probably much too conservative, while DuBois', Fage's, and Davidson's are slightly exaggerated. The figure lies in between, probably leaning more towards 50 million than 12 million.

In what ways was this new trans-Atlantic slavery different from the kind of slavery that had gone before: the oriental slavery and internal African slavery? We have already seen some of the differences; let us highlight the main ones. The first major difference lay in the sheer scale of the trans-Atlantic slavery. It was a highly organized and intentional phenomenon involving several European nations and designed solely for the purpose of abducting black people for sale as unpaid laborers. It was not the incidental or collateral by-product of a jihad or ethnic struggle. The slaves were not merely prisoners of war who had been captured in war. The raids were made deliberately at the request of Europeans who had traveled long distances over the ocean for this sole purpose of acquiring slaves. Secondly, the enterprise was purely economic and commercial. The economies of the slave-receiving areas, such as the Southern United States, the West Indies, and Brazil, were entirely dependent on slave labor. One certainly cannot say that the economies of the parts of Asia to which the slaves were taken by the Arabs were dependent on slavery. Nor were the areas within Africa where slaves were used.

Thirdly, the profit motive was paramount with the trans-Atlantic slavery. The European slavers arranged for the slaves to be captured because slave-trading was a highly profitable activity. A lot of Europeans grew rich from the trade and its consequences. A famous concept that evolved from the trade was the so-called "unholy triangle." This referred to the process whereby capital from Europe went with the slave merchants to Africa. This was the first side of the triangle. The capital was then used to purchase slaves who were then transported across the Atlantic to the Americas, the second side of the triangle. The profits were then sent back to Europe, thus constituting the third side of the triangle, before the whole process started all over again. It was the Europeans and their colonists in the Americas and the West Indies who made enormous profits from the process. We know from Jane Austen's novel *Mansfield Park,* for instance, that the fortune of the patriarch Sir Thomas Bertram was almost entirely dependent on his plantation, in the West Indies, on which slaves were used.

The trans-Atlantic slavery involved the most abominable racism. Africans were abducted and used on plantations almost as animals or beasts of burden because it was thought that they were not quite human. They were little better than animals and could also be regarded as chattels, things that one could own or possess. Before they were forced to leave their continent, or after they arrived in the New World, they were branded as horses or cattle would be. They were chained like animals and they were often whipped to make them work harder, just as horses would be whipped to make them go faster. Racism involves detestation of and brutality towards other races simply because they were thought to be different or inferior. At this time in world history, the later Renaissance, racism was at its height in Europe as can be seen in attitudes towards Jews and Moors even in the plays of Shakespeare. The white man in Europe felt absolutely superior. But, more than that, he felt that the black man was the embodiment of "the other," a conglomeration of all the evils the white man hated, little better than a beast. The references to the Moor Othello in Shakespeare's play of that name, references such as "old black ram," "the beast," and a "jennet," prove the point. Later when slavery had been established as an institution in the United States, we see the brutality with which slaves were treated. Some were actually burnt alive, showing that for their masters the slaves' lives had no value whatever, except for a monetary value, like cattle and horses. Finally, as we have seen, the trans-Atlantic slave trade involved the most unspeakable cruelty and brutality. Even if one excluded the treatment of the slaves in the New World, what other adjectives than cruel and brutal could there be to describe a treatment that involved chaining humans, keeping them in the same place throughout a journey that lasted for more than three months, and leaving them wallowing in their own filth and suffering from horrible diseases?

Consequences of the slave trade

What were the consequences of the trans-Atlantic slave trade? The first was demographic. Africa's population stagnated for three hundred years while the populations of other continents increased. Up till recently, Africa was a continent where the inhabitants hardly practiced birth control, and so the rate of population growth is normally quite steep. Even with the practice of birth control in some parts of contemporary Africa, the population has topped the one billion mark and is expected to top three billion by the end of the century. Had the slave trade not occurred, Africa's population would have grown steeply during the sixteenth, seventeenth, and eighteenth centuries. The stagnation of the population was bound to have devastating effects on the continent's development.

   The second consequence was, as might be expected, economic. The forcible removal of between 12 and 50 million people from the continent was bound to have devastating consequences on economic development. Moreover, the people who were removed were those who were at the height of their productive capacity, the ones who formed the productive labor force. The slavers were not interested in old people or in the very young. They were interested in those who could immediately be put to work on the plantations, or who could be used in a very few years, and whose labor could be used for a long period of time. These were the ones who could be profitably sold. They were the people who were at the height, not just of their physical powers, but also of their intellectual powers. Their removal was bound to affect all areas of development. Walter Rodney is surely right in suggesting in his book *How Europe Under-developed Africa* that the slave trade was largely responsible for Africa's comparatively slow rate of development in modern times. Of course, he blames not only the slave trade, but imperialism as well. The slave trade affected commerce and the patterns of trade that had been established over the centuries. The slave raids were bound to affect the trade routes over which trade had been carried for centuries. The removal of the most productive part of the labor force was bound to affect not just commerce, but agriculture as well, and agricultural development is a very important part of economic development. People would be reluctant to go to work on farms if they had no guarantee that a slave raid would not pounce on them to take them to a land they did not know and separate them permanently from their relations and the environment to which they had been accustomed. The slave trade was also bound to affect the enhancement of culture, since it was those who could make the most solid contribution to cultural development, those who were involved in the singing and the dancing and the arts and crafts, the most productive part of the labor force, in other words, who were abducted.

The slave trade also had tremendous social consequences for Africa. The forceful abduction of able-bodied men and women from their native environment meant that many homes lost fathers, mothers, and children. The loss of fathers was particularly significant, because in the African environment fathers were generally regarded as heads of households, having particular responsibilities to discharge. Consequently, not only did many homes lose their heads of household, the women had to step up to the plate and assume the responsibilities their men had discharged. This imposed an additional burden on women and significantly affected the household dynamics. It also inevitably affected the larger dynamics of the village, the town, and the clan. Related to this was the psychological impact of the loss of loved ones on those left behind. It is easy to imagine what this must have been like, but the television series *Roots* gave a very compelling presentation of the impact on Kunta Kinte and on his family of his abduction and separation from the environment he had always known. One can only imagine the impact of the forceful seizure and the horrible voyage across a vast ocean on the minds of people who slowly became aware that they would never see their loved ones again and they were destined for lands and experiences they had never known before. Of course, all this did not occur to the abductors because, as far as they were concerned, the slaves were hardly human and were not subject to the feelings and attitudes that normal human beings experienced.

Another consequence of the slave trade was the enhancement of the ethnic rivalries that had existed on the continent. Many of the slaves who were transported were actually captured in war. The slavers therefore came to realize that the more wars there were on the African continent the more slaves they were likely to have and they actually played a significant role in fomenting and encouraging these ethnic rivalries. African rulers also realized that there was a viable and lucrative market for their enemies captured in battle and this did not reduce their appetite for war. The guns which the slavers gave in exchange for the slaves also introduced a new and terrible dimension into warfare in Africa.

The slave trade also gave the European powers a toehold in Africa. It gave them experience in dealing and negotiating with Africans and it increased and heightened their contempt for the African. All this helped to pave the way for the imperial conquest and the imperial process that was to follow hard on the heels of the abolition of the trade when it occurred. It is also generally agreed that the slave trade stifled the innovation, inventiveness, and ingenuity that had been apparent on the continent up to this point. As we have seen, the trade was bound to affect cultural and intellectual development. At the start of the slave trade crafts and arts like pottery, basketry, glassmaking, masonry, weaving, and the manufacture of silver, gold, and iron goods were flourishing. Many of the craftsmen and women were transported to places like the United States, as can be seen today in the American islands off the shores of Georgia and South Carolina where these crafts now flourish among the Gullah people, the descendants of the Gullahs who came from Sierra Leone. Finally, a major consequence of the slave trade is the plight of millions of people of African descent in the African diaspora, particularly in the United States. Not only did the slaves have to endure the most unspeakable cruelty during the period of slavery itself, their descendants have been subjected to all forms of discrimination which have not been totally eradicated by the civil rights laws. This has included poverty, inadequate housing and inferior education opportunities, and higher levels of incarceration. And the list goes on.

Economically the continent itself did not benefit from the slave trade. A few rulers, like the kings of Dahomey and the Ashantis, might have made some profit, and some of their henchmen might have enriched themselves through the trade, but these were very few and far between. Most of the middlemen and collaborators got little more than foreign cloth and other trifles, worth far less than the compatriots they exported.

Decline and abolition of the slave trade

There were several reasons for the decline of the slave trade. First, there were religious, humanitarian, and philosophical reasons. These, of course, were all linked. It is significant that the drive towards abolition was strongest in Britain. This was largely because Britain was by this time the most important slave-trading nation. Britain brought more slaves from Africa than any other nation, and more than half of all the slaves transported from West Africa to the Americas were carried in British ships (Shillington, 256). It is therefore not surprising that the hue and cry against the trade was most pronounced in Britain. The eighteenth century saw the rise in Britain of the Quakers and of Methodism, founded by John Wesley. John Wesley had great influence both in Britain and the United States, where he actually lived for some time. The Quaker leaders actually moved from Britain to the United States, where they went on to affect the development of American history quite considerably. These new Christian sects, unlike the more established ones like Roman Catholicism and the Church of England, could not turn a blind eye to the cruelty and barbarism of slavery, which they saw as denying the inherent dignity of every human being and opposed to the basic tenets of the Christian religion. We thus see the link between the religious, the philosophical, and the humanitarian. The Quakers were the first Christian group to condemn slavery and the Methodist John Wesley became a champion of the anti-slavery movement, vehemently calling for the Christianization of the slaves and their eventual emancipation.

The humanitarian impulse was further strengthened by the publication at about this time of some memoirs by black people who had gone through the slave experience themselves. The two most famous of these were by Olaudah Equiano, otherwise known as Gustavus Vassa, and Ottabah Cugoano. Born about 1745 in Igboland in Eastern Nigeria, Equiano was captured when he was about 11 years old and put on a ship bound for the West Indies. He was not actually sold in the West Indies but was taken to Virginia in the USA where he was purchased by a British naval captain and taken to England. He then spent the next few years as a slave on British navy ships, but was eventually able to purchase his freedom in 1766. Cugoano was born in Ghana in 1757. He was captured and taken to the West Indies in 1770, but after a year as a slave in Grenada he was bought by an Englishman and taken to England in 1772, where he regained his freedom and converted to Christianity. He learnt to read and was able to mingle in high society. He eventually became a great friend of Equiano's and the two of them collaborated on various ventures to put an end to the slave trade. Their memoirs are among the most famous slave narratives extant. Equiano, for instance, gives a very eloquent account of his life in his native Eastern Nigeria and of his abduction and transportation to America. Both men had therefore been slaves, but had managed to make their way to England and gain their freedom. They eventually became highly educated and were thus able to write their fascinating memoirs, in which they exposed the evils of slavery. Equiano's book was and is still very popular. Both men became champions of the anti-slavery movement, and their books served to arouse the consciousness of the British people and give momentum to the movement for abolition.

A number of events soon happened which revealed that a number of leaders of opinion in Britain had been inspired by the new trend and the courage and rectitude of the Methodists and the Quakers. Lord Mansfield, a leading judge, in a famous court ruling of 1772, declared that the master of a slave called James Somerset, who had fled to Britain from the West Indies, could not take him back by force to those islands. Somerset thus became free. His case had been championed by a leading philanthropist called Granville Sharp. Sharp now collaborated with William Wilberforce, a member of the British House of Commons, and the issue of slavery was raised in the British Parliament. Sharp eventually became Chairman of the newly formed Abolition Committee. Other famous philanthropists who championed the movement for abolition included Lord Macaulay and the Clarkson brothers, Thomas and William.

Meantime, in North America, events were happening which would reinforce the case for the abolition of slavery. The war of independence had been fought between 1776 and 1783. It is interesting to note that many slaves in America fought on the side of the British, largely because they were opposed to their slave-owning masters, who included Jefferson and Washington. The British promised these slaves not only their freedom at the end of the war, but also substantial allocations of land. This in itself was recognition that the slaves would have to be freed. Unfortunately for the slaves, the British lost the war and could not live up to their original promise. They therefore offered the slaves who had fought on their side land in Nova Scotia, in present-day Canada, which the British still owned. However, the slaves, most of whom had been accustomed to the climate of the Deep South, found Nova Scotia much too cold and very inhospitable. They therefore asked to be repatriated back to Africa, and the British granted them their wish. Thus began the very important "back to Africa" campaign, which turned out to be a significant aspect of the movement towards abolition. The slaves were taken to Sierra Leone where a settlement was formed. It was supervised by the British via a company formed with the support of the Clarkson brothers. Indeed, one of the brothers, Thomas Clarkson, became the first governor of the settlement, and therefore, in a sense, the first governor of Sierra Leone, whose capital has since that time been called "Freetown." Incidentally, when my alma mater, the Prince of Wales School, was established in Freetown, Sierra Leone, in 1925, the four "houses" into which the school was divided were named after four of the philanthropists that played such a leading role in the abolition movement: Granville, Wilberforce, Macaulay, and Mansfield.

There were also political reasons for the abolition momentum. The slaves in both North America and the West Indies were beginning to be rebellious, and it was becoming obvious that it would be difficult to keep on holding, as captives, slaves who were increasingly demanding their freedom. Of course, as Shillington shows, slaves had always resisted their captivity right from the very beginning. There had been revolts and attempts to escape. In seventeenth-century Brazil, for instance, runaway slaves established an independent republic known as "Palmares" which lasted for one hundred years before it was eventually overthrown by the Portuguese. Now, however, the slave resistance grew in intensity. In the United States there was the unsuccessful revolt led by Gabriel Prosser in Virginia in 1800. The most famous of the slave revolts, however, was that in

Haiti in 1791. The island was owned by the French who had established plantations on it producing sugar cane, cotton, cocoa, and coffee. By 1791 there were 400,000 slaves in Haiti. It was by far the most prosperous of all the French possessions, but the condition of the slaves was absolutely miserable. Of course, the French Revolution had happened in 1789, and the slaves on the island were themselves imbued with the revolutionary spirit. The black slaves wanted to be completely free, and a slave priest called Boukman called on his fellow slaves during a church service to rise up against their masters and ask for compensation for the work they performed (Bah, 84). They also asked for better conditions of work. A bloody revolution followed in which two thousand whites were killed. The French government, which was itself a revolutionary government that had rebelled against authoritarianism and oppression, decided to give freedom to all the slaves, but it was quite obvious that this was merely a ploy to buy time and also to stave off the threats from the British and the Spaniards who were also interested in possessing such a rich island. The French still wished to retain control of the island and keep the slaves in servitude. The rebellion thus continued and became a war of liberation that lasted for 12 years. The French had imprisoned Boukman soon after the start of the revolt, but a very charismatic new military leader now emerged called Toussaint L'Ouverture. Under his leadership the slaves went on to achieve victory after victory, not just against the French, but against British and Spanish forces who wished to take over the island. Napoleon, the French emperor at the time, engineered a ruse that led to the removal of L'Ouverture, but the spirit of resistance had been kindled and the rebellion went on. The slaves eventually won a tremendous victory against the French army, the greatest army in the world at the time, and the revolt ended in the proclamation of the first black republic in the world, the Republic of Haiti. It would be impossible to overestimate the significance of the Haitian rebellion in world history, especially in the history of liberation struggles, and the endeavor to liberate all who are enslaved or oppressed. This was the successful revolt of black slaves against their captors, in the process of which the slaves had won some significant battles against some of the best armies in the world. It showed not only what blacks could achieve, but what oppressed peoples can achieve, and the revolt became an iconic event in the history of liberation struggles and of colonized and oppressed peoples all over the world. Toussaint L'Ouverture himself remains a black hero.

Some would claim that the major reason for the decline of the slave trade was economic. The brilliant Trinidadian scholar and future prime minister Eric Williams rejected the view held by many Western historians that the reasons for abolition were mainly philanthropic, religious, and humanitarian. These historians, he suggested, had put forward these reasons in order to mask the involvement of Western nations in the slave trade. Two extremely important factors at work here, he argued, were the over-production of sugar cane and the consequent slump in the price of sugar, and the increase in the cost of slaves. The French, in particular, had been too successful in the production of sugar cane in the plantations in their colonies. The price of sugar thus fell and the international market was flooded with cheap sugar. At the same time, African middlemen and collaborators were asking more for the slaves they sold to the West. The unholy triangle or trade was therefore bringing less financial returns for Western businessmen and investors who still had to spend more on the slaves they bought from West Africa. They therefore cut down on the number of slaves bought or went out of business altogether.

We must bear in mind the period in which all these events were happening. It was towards the end of the eighteenth century, when the industrial revolution was gaining steam. The invention of things like the spinning jenny and the steam engine was about to bring about an economic revolution such as the world had never seen. In some places there was a gradual shift from an agrarian culture based on plantations and farming to a commercial and industrial culture based on manufacturing. Of course, agriculture would not be allowed to suffer extensively because every nation needed a creditable food supply. However, some capital and other resources had to be diverted from agriculture to manufacturing. Investors found out that it was much more profitable to invest in factories than in slaves and plantations. Some even felt that it was better to keep the Africans working on farms in Africa that produced the raw materials needed by the new factories in cities like Liverpool and Manchester in Britain. Work in factories was emphasized, and for this kind of work slaves were quite unsuitable. The industrial revolution therefore led to a gradual decline in the need for slaves and in the drive to get them from Africa. The economic reason was therefore perhaps the most important, but all of these factors played a part, and we cannot attribute the decline of the slave trade to just one factor.

Of course, these things tend to happen gradually, not all at once. The slave trade would continue for some time, but the trend was towards abolition. In 1807 laws were actually enacted by the British Parliament and by President Jefferson in the United States, formally abolishing the slave trade. The British law included the stipulation that any British ship that encountered a slave ship on the high seas was empowered to attack and board the ship, free the slaves, and take them to the haven that had been established for freed slaves in Freetown, Sierra Leone. This was the beginning of the end of the trans-Atlantic slave trade. Of course, it would go on, underground as it were, for some more years, well into the 1830s. It was not until 1834 that slavery was finally abolished in British colonies, and in the French colonies it lasted until 1848. Within America itself slavery continued until President Lincoln's emancipation proclamation in the 1860s.

References and suggestions for further reading

Bah, A. 2005. "Legitimate Trade, Diplomacy, and the Slave Trade." Pp. 71–90 in M. Azevedo (ed.) *Africana Studies*. Durham, NC: Carolina Academic Press.

Curtin, P. 1969. *The Atlantic Slave Trade: A Census*. Madison, WI: University of Wisconsin Press.

Davidson, B. 1961. *The Atlantic Slave Trade*. Boston: Atlantic-Little Brown.

Fage, J. D. 1995. *A History of Africa*. 3rd edition. London: Routledge.

Inikori, J. E. 1976. "Measuring the Atlantic Slave Trade: An Assessment of Curtin and Anstey." *Journal of African History* XVII (2): 197–223.

Law, R. 1991. *The Slave Coast of West Africa, 1550–1750: The Impact of the Atlantic Slave Trade on an African Society*. Oxford: Clarendon Press.

Lovejoy, P. 1983. *Transformation in Slavery*. Cambridge: Cambridge University Press.

Miers, S. and Igor K. (eds.). 1977. *Slavery in Africa*. Madison, WI: University of Wisconsin Press.

Miers, S. and R. Roberts (eds.). 1988. *The End of Slavery in Africa*. Madison, WI: University of Wisconsin Press.

Patterson, O. 1967. *The Sociology of Slavery*. Rutherford, NJ: Fairleigh Dickinson University Press.

Perbi, A. 2004. *A History of Indigenous Slavery in Ghana from the 15th to the 19th Century*. Legon-Ghana: Sub-Saharan Publishers.

Reynolds, E. 1986. *Stand the Storm: A History of the Atlantic Slave Trade*. New York: Allison & Busby.

Rodney, W. 1972. *How Europe Underdeveloped Africa*. Dar-es-Salaam: Dar-es-Salaam University Press.

Williams, E. 1944. *Capitalism and Slavery*. New York: Praeger Books.

3 Imperialism in Africa

Imperialism can be defined as the annexation and occupation of an alien country and the subjection of its people. In this sense imperialism had been a feature of world history for ages. Still, the kind of imperialism that happened from the Renaissance onwards was unique and has had a much more profound impact on the world than anything that went before. This kind of imperialism was massive; it involved the occupation and subjugation of entire continents like North America, South America, Africa, and most of Asia. It was almost exclusively done by people from the continent of Europe who must have felt that they were superior to the peoples they found on these continents; that these peoples were, in most cases, sub-human; and that they had a perfect and almost God-given right to take over the countries, subjugate the people, and exploit the resources.

In the case of Africa, European conquest actually took place within a comparatively short period of time, even though contact between Europe and Africa had been going on, as we have seen, since the fifteenth century. It actually occurred during the nineteenth century. A look at the extent of the European holdings in Africa prior to the mid-nineteenth century will reveal that they were comparatively sparse. The Portuguese, the first European nation to make contact with Africa in the early fifteenth century, had set up trading stations along the coast in places like Angola and on some islands off the coast such as the Azores and Madeira, had engaged in legitimate trade in gold, and had established plantations along the coast without venturing to penetrate inland. Later, they built forts along the coast when legitimate trade was replaced by the slave trade. With the rounding of the Cape of Good Hope and the mastery of the new sea route to India in 1497, the Portuguese interest in the East African coast and the East African trade was aroused and they now built trading posts in Mozambique. The Portuguese also settled colonists in these trading stations, some of whom intermarried with the local population and became settlers. However, it was a company that supervised these stations and settlements, not the Portuguese government.

The French had been active in the north. They had invaded Algeria in 1830, occupied the cities of Algiers and Oran, and put an end to Ottoman rule in that area. The French also had a foot-hold in the West Central area of Africa, in the area now known as Gabon, in which they had a few trading posts. The British were in Sierra Leone where a haven for freed slaves had been established towards the end of the eighteenth century under the supervision of a company and some philanthropists. As in other cases, the settlement was largely along the western coastal areas. In 1808, The British declared the whole area a crown colony, thus bringing it under the influence of the government and making it a British possession, but they still had not yet penetrated the interior. The

DOI: 10.4324/9781003111733-4

British were also influential in Egypt where they had forced the evacuation of the French who had temporarily occupied Egypt under Napoleon. After the departure of the French, however, Egypt was ruled by a dynamic leader with Ottoman connections named Mohammed Ali, whose successors continued the rule of the dynasty until late in the nineteenth century.

The British were also in South Africa. The Dutch had actually preceded them from as far back as the seventeenth century, when they established a small permanent settlement on the Southern shores of Table Bay, because they realized that the Southern Cape of Africa was strategic in order to protect their interest in India and the activities of the East India Company, established after the mastery of the sea route to India. The settlement continued to prosper, but in 1795 the British seized the colony from the Dutch because they realized its strategic importance in protecting the route to India and British interests in India. By this time, India was a flourishing part of the British Empire. The British gave the colony back to the Dutch in 1803, but they retook it in 1806, partly because they realized its importance during the Napoleonic wars, and this time they retained control. This forced the Dutch settlers to move further inwards which brought them into conflict with local peoples like the Zulus.

Generally speaking, then, European possessions in Africa in the early nineteenth century were few and far between. They consisted mostly of stations, towns, and forts along the coast, thus suggesting that during the first three or four centuries of European contact with Africa the Europeans had preferred to consolidate their positions along the coast without laying claim to the interior of the continent. However, by the end of the nineteenth century the entire continent, with the exception of Ethiopia and Liberia, had fallen under the control of the European powers and imperialism was at its height. So, what happened?

The first factor in bringing about the occupation of Africa by Europe was the great exploration of the interior of Africa which started at about the same time as the decline of the slave trade towards the end of the eighteenth century and was intensified during the nineteenth. Some might wonder why there was this new drive to explore the continent. Why was the erstwhile fear of the interior of the continent now replaced by intense curiosity about what it contained? There are those who would argue that the great exploration of Africa was due to the desire for more knowledge about this mysterious continent. Others would say that the Europeans went in to convert the Africans to Christianity and win them away from barbarous practices like slavery, which was still going on in some places, particularly along the eastern coast. In other words, the drive behind the exploration of the continent was scientific, educational, religious, and humanitarian. No doubt, these reasons were important and will be discussed. But it now seems incontestable that the new enthusiasm for the exploration of the continent was largely due to economic, commercial, and ultimately political motives. With the decline of the slave trade and the rise of the industrial revolution the patterns of trade were changing and the new factories of Europe needed cheap sources of raw materials. It was just possible that these could be found in Africa. It is quite significant that many of the explorers into the interior of Africa used the famous river courses like the Senegal, the Niger, the Congo, the Nile, and the Zambezi. These were seen as the arteries of Africa, the new trade routes along which commerce could proceed. It is now quite clear that many of the explorers and the groups that sponsored them were merely disguising their real commercial and political motives behind the veneer of altruism, humanitarianism, science, and religion. Once they got into the interior, many of them were much more interested in making treaties with the local potentates that would give economic and political advantages to various European nations.

The activities of the Association for Promoting the Discovery of the Interior Parts of Africa were typical. Simply known as the African Association, it was formed in England in 1788 by a group of wealthy Englishmen with the intention of sending an expedition to the famous city of Timbuktu which even then had an almost mythical grip on the imaginations of Europeans. The members of the association were supposedly interested in Timbuktu's reputation as a medieval center of learning, and they wanted to explore the Niger River to its source. However, it was also clear that their interest had been partly aroused by the reports of the abundance of gold that was to be got from this area. Moreover, the constitution of the association stipulated that any information derived from the exploratory journeys should be kept secret. This was in direct contradiction to the practice in Europe from the Renaissance onwards of disseminating new information (Shillington, 328). Obviously, the association felt that keeping the information secret would be to the commercial advantage of Britain.

Reasons for Europe's colonization of Africa

Let us now review the reasons and the factors which explain the colonization of most of Africa by European powers in the nineteenth century. Although there is controversy among scholars about the relative importance of these factors, it seems that the economic reason, as we have seen, was the most important. With the decline of the slave trade and the rise of the industrial revolution in Europe, there was a need for raw materials to fuel the factories of Europe, particularly in England in places like Liverpool, Manchester, and Birmingham. The products needed included rubber, cotton, coffee, ivory, palm oil, peanut oil, animal skins, and metals like copper and iron. Of course, diamonds and gold were also welcome. Europeans believed that Africa was a vast source of all these products, and the explorers vouched that Africa had all of them in abundance. Furthermore, these newly revealed countries could become markets for the goods produced by the factories. The slave trade had taught Europeans that Africans could be encouraged to develop an appetite for the goods produced in Europe. Any country that had extensive possessions in Africa would automatically have a free market. The surplus profits and capital generated by the success of industrialization could also be invested in Africa in things like stores and mines.

There were, of course, numerous non-economic factors. We do not have to choose between the economic reasons and the others because they all played a part. There were religious reasons for the European drive to expand into Africa. There was a tremendous outburst of evangelicalism in Europe during the nineteenth century, as we can see from some of the novels of the period like Dickens's *David Copperfield* and Charlotte Brontë's *Jane Eyre*. Some of the writers, like Dickens, might make fun of the evangelical drive, but it was real, nonetheless. The Church at home was coming under attack largely because of new theories like that of evolution and the rise of certain academic disciplines. Darwin's theory of evolution, for instance, suggested that the human being evolved over hundreds of thousands of years from other primates, whereas the Bible and the Church asserted that man was created in a moment at the end of the six days of the creative process. Evolution therefore challenged the traditional teaching of the Church and there were vigorous and memorable debates on these issues at universities, such as Oxford in England. The Church was also challenged by the rise of geology as an academic discipline. Where the Church had traditionally taught that the earth was created in six days, geology posited that the process took millions of years as is attested by the different ages of various layers of rocks. The Church was therefore under tremendous pressure at home, and there was a need to find new converts elsewhere to compensate for the loss of interest and the growth of skepticism at home.

Some Europeans were motivated by altruistic considerations. There were some, of course, who merely concealed their real economic and political motives under the veneer of altruism, but others were genuine. They saw the conquest and occupation of Africa as the only viable way of putting an end to the curse of slavery and other barbaric practices. Some genuinely good Europeans, like David Livingstone, were horrified by the fact that slavery was still going on in Africa even though it had been formally abolished by the British and other powers. They experienced slavery at first hand. Livingstone, for instance, must have come into contact with the brutal slavery that was still going on in Eastern and Central Africa. After all, Livingstone was exploring Eastern and Central Africa at about the same time as the notorious slave trader Tippu Tip was amassing a massive army to raid villages and take slaves in the same area. For these Europeans, then, conquest and occupation would rescue Africans from their fellow African predators and put an end to the slave trade.

Europe had also made great scientific and technological advances during the nineteenth century. Mark Twain visiting London in the 1890s declared that the progress that Europe had made in knowledge during the nineteenth century was greater than in the rest of the ages put together. Discoveries were being made and theories put forward in all the disciplines. In 1851 Queen Victoria's husband, Prince Albert, staged the Great Exhibition in Hyde Park. It was intended to showcase the great advances Britain and Europe had made in science and technology. There was a desire to acquire more and more knowledge in all fields: anthropology, geography, languages; and Africa seemed fertile virgin territory where even more knowledge could be gained.

Because of the great scientific and technological advances that had been made, Europe in general was extremely self-confident and had a sense of world superiority. We must once more stress the significance of the fact that imperialist conquest and occupation were done by Europeans, and this stemmed partly from the sense of world superiority that Europeans had at the time. They felt they had the right not only to go to other continents and traverse them from end to end, but to occupy them and subjugate their peoples. Some might have felt that they had the right to export their culture and lifestyle and impose them on other people, because theirs was superior. Associated with this sense of superiority was a kind of racism. Africans were generally considered to be sub-human by many of these imperialists. They were the embodiment of "the other," all those qualities and attitudes that were considered to be repugnant. Stanley in his writings refers to Africans as "savages" who could only respond to force, and Cecil Rhodes held more or less the same views. In his groundbreaking book about the mind-boggling brutality practiced by the agents of King Leopold II in the Congo, *King Leopold's Ghost*, Hochschild presents a graphic vignette of an African being hung upside down and cooked to death over a slow fire, like a pig (Hochschild, 234). To some of these imperialists the African was sub-human, like an animal, right at the bottom of Darwin's evolutionary scale, and was not therefore entitled to the same decencies and considerations that other people were.

The sense of cultural and scientific superiority was evident, not just in Britain, but in Germany, which was the rising European power in the later years of the nineteenth century. Germany won the Franco-Prussian war against France, another major European power, in 1870–71, inflicting a humiliating defeat on the latter, and taking over some of her territory like Alsace-Lorraine. Apart from the sense of technological superiority, Germany emerged from the Franco-Prussian war as the most powerful nation in continental Europe. It therefore felt it needed colonies to justify its military superiority. It also needed overseas markets for the products of German industry. France, on the other hand, had been humiliated. It had lost the Franco-Prussian war, and it had also lost territory to Germany. It had also lost much of its national pride and sense of power. It therefore hoped to compensate for its losses and regenerate France by acquiring as much territory as possible in Africa and in Asia.

There was much the same attitude in Britain, of course. Britain was feeling superbly self-confident, with the greatest navy in the world and tremendous industrial and economic success. It was the leading industrial nation in the world, and for most of the nineteenth century its empire was expanding. Up to about the middle of the nineteenth century Britain had encouraged a "free trade" policy, a kind of "laissez faire" that allowed each European country to trade wherever it wanted in Africa. This meant, of course, that this kind of trade would be dominated by Britain because she had more resources and a better infrastructure than the others. Britain also had the tremendous advantage of being the world's greatest financial power, with its capital, London, being the world's financial center, and the British pound being the currency of world trade. The pound held the same position and importance that the dollar does today. British financiers and industrialists could invest their capital in Africa and find markets there for the products of their factories. However, in the second half of the nineteenth century Britain was beginning to face competition from Germany, the United States, and, to a certain extent, even from France. After the Civil War ended, the United States was beginning to get its act together and was also becoming a rising industrial power. Increased competition drove Britain from "free trade" to a certain amount of "protectionism" and its competitors realized that they also needed colonies in order to operate on a more equal footing (Shillington, 334). All this posed a threat to Britain's importance and success, and she also needed a new sphere of activities. And so the British also saw the great advantages of having colonies. Colonies would provide a cheap source of raw materials and a ready market for the products of Britain's factories, and Britain and her colonies would constitute a powerful trading area.

There was also the technological gap between Europe and Africa, which had been exacerbated by the slave trade. Europe had excellent steamships that could not only transport settlers and soldiers to Africa, but could also bombard African territories. Europe also had superior weaponry. Although Africans had become familiar with guns since these had been sold or given to them in exchange for captured slaves during the days of slavery, Europe had made great advances in gun technology and in this area the Africans could not compete. For instance, Europeans had the repeater rifle and the Maxim gun, which was a machine gun. The Africans had no weapons like these and that made all the difference. There was also the traditional weakness of individual African states, and rivalries within states as well as between states. Ethnic rivalries were particularly evident, and the Europeans did their best to exploit these. There were occasions when some African tribes thought the agreements they were making with the Europeans involved only protection from their ethnic enemies, only to discover later that they had actually ceded their territories to the European nation concerned.

Finally, there were strategic reasons. The British, for instance, had to have a hold on Egypt, particularly after the opening of the Suez Canal in 1869. It was crucial for the canal to remain open and provide access for Europeans to South West Asia and India. The same was true of South Africa. The Cape had to be protected to ensure the free passage of ships to India and the Far East.

The exploration of Africa

From 1788 onwards numerous European explorers traversed the continent of Africa. Mungo Park was one of the first to be sponsored by the African Association which lasted until 1815. His description of the nature of his journey actually laid bare the real purpose of the African Association: "rendering the geography of Africa more familiar to my countrymen, and opening to their ambition and industry new sources of wealth, and new channels of commerce" (Park, 2). Park made two journeys to Africa. The first was in 1795 to the areas around the rivers Gambia and Niger. He was captured and imprisoned by Africans during his journey, but he escaped and made his way back to Britain. Like many of these explorers, he gave highly sensationalized accounts of his journey on his return to Europe in 1797. He knew that his fellow Europeans had an insatiable appetite for the exotic and the barbaric in so far as Africa was concerned and he presented the Africans as barbarous and untrustworthy and generally inferior to Europeans. However, his account served to awaken the enthusiasm of other adventurers and of the British government which now sponsored his second journey to Africa. He left England in 1805 with the ostensible intention of exploring the Niger River and following it to the sea. However, in the course of his exploration of the river he was attacked by African warriors. In an attempt to escape he jumped into the river and was drowned.

In 1827 the Frenchman René Caillié, who disguised himself as an Egyptian, became the first European to visit the city of Timbuktu. Caillié also visited Senegal and Sierra Leone and crossed the desert to reach Morocco. Other explorers pressed on with what had been Mungo Park's task of solving the mystery of the mouth of the great Niger River. The mystery was eventually solved by the two Lander brothers who in 1830 followed the Niger to its mouth and demonstrated that what had previously been known as the "Oil Rivers" was actually the Niger Delta. The achievement of the Lander brothers clearly demonstrated the real motives of the sponsors of African exploration, for it delighted the merchants and traders who now realized that there was a major navigable waterway into the heart of West Africa with all the commercial possibilities that this entailed.

Missionaries were also interested in going to Africa to spread the gospel. Some of them also wanted to acquire knowledge of African languages and African traditional customs. They therefore joined the cohort of explorers of Africa and traveled extensively. For instance, two German missionaries, John Kraft and John Rebman, were the first Europeans to get to Mount Kilimanjaro in East Africa, Africa's highest mountain. Largely because the missionaries were able to acquire a fund of information that would later be extremely useful to the imperialist occupiers, it might be argued that they paved the way for imperialism. It must be noted, however, that the missionaries were generally opposed to imperialist annexation of the countries they visited because that would stand in the way of converting the local Africans to Christianity. So were some of the merchants who knew that their success as traders depended on the goodwill of the African people. However, the very presence of the missionaries and merchants gave the political occupiers a pretext for annexation because they could claim that they needed to protect their nationals.

Some of the explorers had their own entourage, others found it more effective to simply join existing trading caravans. Some even disguised themselves. Richard Burton was one explorer who delighted in disguise and in passing for anyone other than a European. He was helped by the fact that he was fluent in Arabic, which enabled him to pass as an Arab, something that was extremely useful in areas with large Arab populations. Using that disguise, he visited the city of Harar in a remote part of Eastern Ethiopia. Harar was then a Muslim city forbidden to Europeans and adherents of other religions. Burton was obsessed with "discovering" the source of the Nile, which was of great interest at this time to Europeans as possibly the world's greatest river and the source of Egypt's fertility. In 1858 he made an expedition to Africa to do just that, accompanied by another adventurer, John Speke. His destination was the Great Lakes region of Africa. Traveling through Somalia and Ethiopia, they managed to reach Lake Tanganyika. Both men fell seriously ill during the voyage. Burton was so ill that he could not continue, and Speke went on alone. He became the first European to see the great African lake Lake Nyanza, which he renamed Lake Victoria, after the British Queen. It was also clear to him that the lake was the source of the Nile River. In 1860 Speke returned to the area with another explorer named James Grant. He was able to confirm that Lake Nyanza was indeed the source of the Nile River and that the river flowed from the northern shores of the lake. As far as Europeans were concerned, this was a great "discovery" indeed. Grant and Speke had demonstrated that the great Nile River was navigable for most of its length. Although Burton had been forced by illness to abandon the trip on which he and Speke had embarked, he was able to soldier on and get to places like Dahomey and the coast of Cameroon. In 1864 Samuel Baker reached Lake Albert, and other British explorers followed to the area. All this was extremely important for Britain in particular, because it gave that country added interest in West Africa, but also all along the four-thousand-mile length of the Nile River, right into the heart of the continent.

One of the most remarkable of the explorers of Africa was the Scotsman David Livingstone. He was quite different from the others because his motives were genuine and were untainted by any hidden commercial or economic considerations. He was a genuine Christian missionary who was interested in converting the Africans to Christianity, but also in curing their diseases and caring for their welfare. A medical doctor by profession, he was genuinely disgusted by the slave trade which was still going on in certain parts of Africa and one of the reasons why he advocated the conversion of the Africans to Christianity was that it would eventually put an end to slavery. As Bah puts it, unlike people like Mungo Park, Livingstone was genuinely sensitive to the suffering of the African people and had great respect for African traditions (Bah, 110). It was not therefore surprising that the African people he met loved him. Livingstone was sent out to Africa as a missionary by the London Missionary Society in 1844 when he was only 27. At the time, missionaries were expected to stay in the chosen country for a while, but to return home eventually. Livingstone stayed in Africa until his death there in 1873. The London Missionary Society, alarmed by his long absence, asked another explorer, Henry Morton Stanley, to look out for him on one of his own trips. Stanley succeeded in finding David Livingstone in the heart of Africa and greeted him with the now famous words, "Dr. Livingstone, I presume." Livingstone pursued his missionary activities in Africa, but he also traveled extensively in the heart of the continent. He traversed

Southern and Central Africa three times, from 1851 to his death in 1873. He traveled from the Zambezi River to Luanda on the west coast, and it was on this journey that, according to Shillington, he was astounded by the ravages of the slave trade which was still going on (Shillington, 330). Turning back, he traveled right across the continent from the west coast to the east coast. Later he led an expedition to Lake Malawi and he spent the rest of his life exploring the lake and the river systems of South Central Africa.

Livingstone died in 1873 on Lake Bangweulu in what is now Zambia. He had done tremendous work in Central and Southern Africa, and the Africans he had served with such devotion loved him so much that they decided to embalm his body in preparation for taking him back to Scotland. The process of the embalming is itself another index of African ingenuity and knowledge of some complex scientific principles. It was supervised by Livingstone's friend and companion called Chuma. The embalming over, Livingstone was taken in a caravan of 60 men, led by Chuma, to the coastal town of Bagamoyo, from where the corpse was transported to Britain. It took Chuma and his men ten months to complete the journey. Incidentally, though Chuma had accompanied Livingstone in almost all of his journeys and made the "discoveries" with him, he is never given any credit for these "discoveries" and is seldom mentioned.

Northern Africa was extensively explored by two Germans, Heinrich Barth and Gustav Nachtigal. Here, once more, the commercial and economic motive was paramount. Barth was actually sponsored by a group of British merchants, and he succeeded in negotiating trading concessions with some of the leaders for all British merchants. For instance, he got the sultan of Sokoto to grant a franchise guaranteeing security for all British merchants and their property while passing through the sultan's dominions.

In the heart of Africa lies the great Congo River, one of the largest in the world. The volume of water it pours into the ocean is second only to that of the Amazon. It is with the exploration of that river and its basin that we shall now be concerned. It will become clear that the explorers of this area were really intent on establishing the bastions of imperialism. The most famous names in this regard are Henry Morton Stanley, Count Pierre de Brazza, and King Leopold II of the Belgians.

Exploration and annexation: Stanley, De Brazza, and King Leopold II

The activities of Henry Morton Stanley, Count Pierre de Brazza, and King Leopold II of the Belgians ably exemplify the relationship between exploration and political annexation, leading to rivalry among the European powers. Stanley is also a prime example of an explorer with sinister ulterior motives while pretending that he was driven by altruistic and humanitarian concerns. A Welshman by birth, of obscure parentage and very little education, his real name was John Rowlands, and he eventually found his way to the United States where he first worked as an assistant to a trader named Henry Stanley and changed his name to Henry Morton Stanley. He had numerous adventures, and his tremendous flair for writing about the battles and other events he had been in led to his becoming a journalist. Eventually, he was commissioned by the *New York Herald*, in collaboration with the London Missionary Society, to go to Africa and find David Livingstone who was traveling in the heart of Africa and had not been heard of for a long time. Thus it was that Stanley made his first visit to Africa in 1871. He found Livingstone on the shore of Lake Tanganyika and they traveled together around the shores of the lake. He tried to persuade Livingstone to return home with him, but the latter refused, since he was bent on continuing his work with the Africans and his search for the source of the Nile.

On his return from this first trip to Africa, Stanley published an account of his travels called *How I Found Livingstone*, which gave a most sensational and misleading account of Africa and the Africans, whom he totally despised. However, *How I Found Livingstone* was enormously popular and Stanley acquired the reputation and fame of a kind of rock star. In 1874 both the *New York Herald* and the British paper the *Daily Telegraph* asked Stanley to return to Africa and complete Livingstone's work of exploring the great central African lakes. During the three years duration of the trip, Stanley mapped out Lakes Victoria and Tanganyika. This trip also confirmed Stanley's reputation for using unspeakable violence towards his porters as well as the local Africans who had welcomed him cordially. The peoples in the areas he traveled in eventually came to realize that he was bent on conquest and not just on the acquisition of knowledge, and they felt their security threatened by his activities. They therefore started to resist, and he responded ruthlessly. He continued to explore the area around the Congo River before finally returning home in 1877. He had crossed the continent from east to west, from Zanzibar in the east to the mouth of the Congo in the west. On his return, he published an account of his trip called *Through the Dark Continent*, which was also an instant success.

Stanley now tried, but failed, to secure the interest of the British government in supporting a return journey to Africa, the purpose of which was to establish British and European hegemony over the heart of Africa. He also failed to interest the Americans in the project; they preferred him to go to the North Pole instead. However, Stanley's journeys and writings had served to arouse the interest of King Leopold II of the Belgians. Leopold was a very energetic and ambitious man, but he was king of a very small and rather insignificant country that had made very little contribution to European affairs and was hardly known outside its own borders. Leopold therefore had delusions of grandeur, seeing himself as master of a vast and prosperous empire with millions of subjects. He had read *Through the Dark Continent*, and Stanley seemed to be the answer to his prayers. Ownership of a large chunk of the heart of Africa would give a boost not only to his own personal position, but also to his country as an important European player. At first he cloaked his aspirations under the veneer of altruism and humanitarianism. In 1876 he formed the International African Association, and he summoned a conference to discuss the exploration and civilization of the continent. He therefore attracted sympathetic support from most Europeans, many of whom saw his efforts as an attempt to put an end to barbaric practices such as slavery.

In 1879 Stanley returned to central Africa, but this time as King Leopold II's representative with a mandate to establish stations in the Congo, ostensibly for the purpose of studying the Upper Congo. Clearly, these stations were centers, not of study, but of exploitation. For the next five years, Stanley worked tirelessly for the king, setting up stations and negotiating treaties with local African potentates who had no understanding of the documents on which they placed their marks. Some of the treaties handed over the territories of the Africans to Belgian control; some of them stipulated that the Africans should produce and turn in certain quantities of commodities such as rubber and ivory to the king's representatives, failing which penalties would be exacted. Stanley also had a mandate from the king to construct a road linking Boma with Malebo Pool. He also established ports on the Congo River. Clearly, this was colonialist annexation and occupation. The European occupation of Africa had begun and Stanley had proved a most deceptive conman. Stanley's capacity for violence was mind-boggling. Even at this stage, when Belgian ownership of the Congo had not yet been formalized, he had no qualms about murdering the native peoples and looting their ivory. He, in fact, established the foundations of what came to be called the Congo Free State.

Stanley worked for the Belgian king; another famous explorer worked for the French in the same area of Africa. He was Count Pierre de Brazza who was Italian by birth. De Brazza had explored the area now known as Gabon, and he returned to Africa in 1880. Like Stanley, he negotiated treaties with local kings, some of whom unwittingly ceded their territories to him and the French. He also established ports on the Congo River thus demonstrating that he was on a mission of conquest and occupation on behalf of the French. For instance, he established a port named Brazzaville after himself, on the north bank of the river. The next year, Stanley came to the same spot, claimed the south bank for King Leopold II and named it Leopoldville. Leopoldville became the capital of the Congo Free State until independence in 1960 when its name was changed to Kinshasa. Brazzaville is still Brazzaville and the country De Brazza established was once called Congo Brazzaville, but is now called the Congo Republic. In establishing French rule, De Brazza used as much force as Stanley, including forced labor in constructing roads.

Cecil Rhodes and Southern Africa

Apart from Eastern and Central Africa interesting things were happening in other parts of the continent. This brings us to the activities of Cecil Rhodes, perhaps the most notorious imperialist of them all. He was the one who enabled the British to gain control of almost the whole of Southern Africa. He was an extremely astute businessman who ruthlessly exploited the mineral resources of Southern Africa and thus made for himself an enormous fortune which he used to expand British ownership of the southern part of the continent. He was a passionate believer in the destiny of the British Empire which he thought should be made to embrace as much of the world as possible. However, as far as he was concerned, this "British" community of civilized peoples was not meant to include members of the black race who, in his opinion, were no better than savages incapable of being nurtured. Indeed, he can be said to have laid the foundations of the apartheid system in South Africa.

Born in England in 1853, Cecil Rhodes originally tried to enter University College, Oxford, but he was rejected in 1873, the same year in which a young African graduate of Fourah Bay College, Sierra Leone, named Christian Frederick Cole, was accepted by the same college; Cole went on to gain an honors degree four years later and then went to the Inns of Court to train as a barrister. He became the first black barrister to practice in England. It is ironic that Rhodes, who would later rant about the backwardness of the African, was originally rejected by Oxford University, while a black African who was a descendant of liberated slaves was accepted. Although Rhodes later returned to England to enroll at Oriel College, Oxford, he did not receive his degree until 1881 because he had to keep going back to South Africa to supervise his business. Diamonds had been discovered in South Africa, so Rhodes and his brother turned their attention from agriculture, in which they had failed, to mining, and though his brother was soon disillusioned and gave up, Rhodes, a man of tremendous determination, pressed on and became enormously successful. In 1880 he formed the DeBeers Mining Company together with another young man called C. D. Rudd. The company soon became the world's most famous and successful diamond mining company, and still is. Rhodes decided to use his enormous fortune to help Britain gain ascendancy over the whole continent, "from Cape to Cairo." He entered the parliament of the Cape Colony in 1881, and played a leading role in the establishment by Britain of a protectorate over Bechuanaland (now Botswana), and became prime minister in 1890. However, he was removed as prime minister in 1896 because of the failure of a raid called the Jameson Raid, which he organized in 1895 into the Transvaal which, together with the Orange Free State, were more or less independent Dutch enclaves.

Even while he was prime minister, Rhodes had used his wealth to gain mining concessions in what are now Zambia and Zimbabwe, and had encouraged the British government to establish protectorates over the people. Rhodes had heard of the rich gold mines in the area and he was determined to secure them for both himself and the British. In 1889 he received a charter from the British government to form the British South Africa Company which was given the right to rule, police, and make new treaties over a vast area of Southern Africa including what are now Zambia and Zimbabwe. His aim was to establish British sovereignty. At first he tried to outwit the king of the Ndebele people, King Lobengula. He gave the king the impression that he was allowing only a few prospectors into his country, whereas, in reality, the king was ceding his country to Rhodes's agents. The relations between the king and Rhodes is a typical example of the immoral and deceptive practices that most of the imperialists used to gain territory. This was Rhodes the conman at his worst. Shillington reports that the document that the king signed was deliberately mistranslated by the Reverend Helm, the resident British missionary (Shillington, 356). When Lobengula discovered how he had been tricked, he resisted vigorously and war inevitably broke out between both the Ndebele and the Shona on the one hand, and Rhodes and the British on the other. Of course, the British, with their superior weaponry, won. In 1890 a group sent out by Rhodes to stake mining claims in Mashonaland, discovered that the mines there would be less productive than they had anticipated. In desperation they destroyed ancient historical sites including Great Zimbabwe. Rhodes and his vandals thus destroyed irreplaceable markers of civilization and world development. However, as far as his colonists were concerned, his ventures were so successful that the two territories were eventually named Northern and Southern Rhodesia after him.

Although Rhodes was removed as prime minister of the Cape Colony in 1896, he continued to meddle in the affairs of the Transvaal and the Orange Free State. This time, the British government that had removed Rhodes as prime minister because of the uproar in Britain against the Jameson Raid, now saw things as Rhodes saw them. The British distrusted Kruger, the leader of the Transvaal, because they thought he was bent on an alliance with Germany, one of Britain's strongest competitors. Moreover, they did not wish that Germany should have access to the enormous gold resources of the Transvaal. Rhodes had also suggested to the Boers that Transvaal, the Orange Free State, and the Cape Colony should form a federation. His aim, of course, was that the federation would be dominated by the British. The Boers rejected the idea and war ensued, the Second Boer War between the Boers and the British, lasting from 1899 to 1902. This time the Boers were defeated, and this led ultimately to the formation of the country of South Africa.

Although Rhodes's enormous wealth derived from the exploitation of the resources of the African people, he had tremendous contempt for them and did everything in his power to marginalize them. As prime minister of the Cape Colony he passed acts directed at eroding the position of the blacks. The Glen Grey Act pushed black people from their lands to make way for industrial development. Other acts disenfranchised the black population, with Rhodes arguing that the black man was like a child and should be denied the vote. One of his most egregious acts was the creation in his will of a foundation called the Rhodes Scholarship which made provision for brilliant white graduates from nations of what became the British Commonwealth (including South Africa, Canada, Australia, and New Zealand, as well as the United States) to study further at Oxford University for two years. The privilege was not to be extended to blacks, not even blacks in South Africa. It was not until recently that African Americans became eligible for the scholarship, and black South Africans were not made eligible until Nelson Mandela became president of South Africa. 2020 saw the rise of a movement at Oriel College to remove Rhodes's statue from the university because of his racist attitudes and imperialistic activities, and the board of the college voted in favor of removing the statue.

Events in North and West Africa

The opening of the Suez Canal in 1869, giving Europe easy access to the East African coast, India, and the East, and the need to protect it, meant that the canal became the pivotal point in British colonial policy. British interest therefore shifted to Cairo and continued all along the Nile River right up to the Great Lakes. The British were now interested in the entire Nile valley, and huge sections of East Africa, right up to Central Africa. Of course, the Egyptians were restive and in 1882 there was a tremendous battle at El Kebir between the British and the Egyptian army, in which the British were successful, and this meant that they had controlling interest all along the Nile. However, this also meant that there was the possibility of conflict with the Belgians who were dominant in the Congo Free State.

The French were also active. They were bent on disrupting the British near-monopoly of trade in Africa, and in 1879 they embarked on the construction of a railway to connect Dakar in their colony Senegal with the Upper Niger valley. This would give them a huge market in West Africa. They already had Algeria, and in 1882 they occupied Tunisia and declared protectorates over Porto Novo and Pointe Noire on the West Coast of Africa. This move thus gave France control over a whole swathe of territory in West Africa and threatened British control of important trade routes. De Brazza's activities had also given France a foothold not only in the Gabon area of West Africa, but along the Congo in the heart of Africa. Stanley's activities had secured large tracts of the Congo basin for King Leopold II of Belgium which threatened to bring him into conflict with the Portuguese in Angola. The Portuguese also claimed rights slightly further north, near the mouth of the Congo. To make matters worse, the British supported the claims of the Portuguese in Angola and near the mouth of the Congo. Thus, there were now at least four European powers clashing for supremacy in the heart of Africa: Britain, Portugal, France, and Belgium. Right into the middle of this impending chaos came another major player, Germany.

Germany's role and the Berlin Conference

Germany was now ruled by the so-called "Iron Chancellor," Bismarck, who had led the country to victory in the Franco-Prussian war. Bismarck embodied the German sense of superiority and consequent yearning for colonies. With the British, the French, the Belgians, and the Portuguese striving with each other for the possession of African territories, he concluded he needed to move fast if Germany was to get anything at all. In

1884, therefore, he got Germany to acquire Togoland, Cameroon, and South West Africa by merely proclaiming them protectorates over which Germany had control. To consolidate German gains and prevent European countries from going to war over African possessions, Bismarck summoned a conference at Berlin, subsequently known as the Berlin Conference, which lasted from 1884 to 1885, to discuss the partitioning of Africa.

The Berlin Conference was one of the most momentous events in world history and it would affect the subsequent development of the continent profoundly. Fourteen European countries were represented, but there was no African present. The conference was an incontestable demonstration of Europe's towering arrogance and sense of world superiority. It also showed their superb contempt for the African and their belief that he did not matter, that Africans were hardly human beings. Europeans could take their pens and the map of Africa and simply partition the continent among themselves by drawing arbitrary lines, with complete disregard for which African nation lived where. Anyone looking at the map of Africa today will see that many of the boundaries are simply straight lines. In some cases, rivers, lakes, and mountains were used as boundaries. Hardly any of the men attending this conference had been to Africa, and they operated from total ignorance of the African situation. The continent was divided up into about 55 different countries and all but two of them allocated to various Europeans as their possessions or part of their spheres of influence. Only Liberia and Ethiopia escaped, Liberia because it was protected by the United States which had played an important role in its establishment. The artificial partitioning of Africa at the Berlin Conference would have tremendous consequences for the continent and its peoples.

Consequences of the Berlin Conference

The first major consequence was that the Congo was given, not to the country Belgium, but to King Leopold II as his personal property. So an entire country, which was almost the size of the whole of Western Europe, was handed over to an individual as his personal property. Furthermore, this individual had never set foot in Africa. Leopold, taking full advantage of his new possession, proceeded to exploit the Congo, which he now called the Congo Free State, with unspeakable brutality. Leopold's rule and exploitation of the Congo is about the most horrible illustration of the horrors of imperialism. He was particularly interested in rubber and ivory. Rubber was then in great demand for the factories of Europe, and the Congo was one of the most important sources of supply. Leopold got his agents to set quotas that each village or community should turn in by certain dates. When they did not, whole villages were, at times, exterminated. Individuals were brutally killed, and village elders were forced to send the amputated hands of individuals to show that they had been punished for not meeting their quotas. Indeed, the amputation of hands became a favorite form of punishment by Leopold's agents in the Congo. The extent of the brutality was simply mind-boggling, even by the usual imperialist standards. Not even small children were exempt from the vicious punishment and slaughter. Adam Hochschild in *King Leopold's Ghost* recounts several of these instances of mindless cruelty, including the report of one Lefranc. On tracing the howls to their source, Lefranc found

> some thirty urchins, of whom several were seven or eight years old, lined up and waiting Their turn, watching, terrified, their companions being flogged. Most of the

urchins in a paroxysm of grief … kicked so frightfully that the soldiers ordered to hold them by the hands and feet had to lift them off the ground … 25 times the whip slashed down on each of the children.

(Hochschild, 120)

The children were being punished for laughing in the presence of a white man, and the instrument used was a *chicotte*, made of sun-dried hippopotamus hide, cut into a long sharp-edged cork-screw strip, and applied to the bare buttocks. Twenty-five strokes could mean unconsciousness and a hundred or more, which was not uncommon, were often fatal.

Hochschild is of the opinion that some of Leopold's agents and their activities provided prototypes for Joseph Conrad's presentation of the Congo imperialist experience in the famous novella *Heart of Darkness*. One of the prototypes was Leon Rom who displayed a row of severed African heads around his garden, something that occurs in *Heart of Darkness*. Another was Guillaume Van Kerckhoven who told a traveler that he had paid his African soldiers five brass rods for every human head they brought him. He had done this in order to stimulate their prowess in the face of the enemy (Hochschild, comments on photographs after 120). We not only have written reports of the brutality in the Congo, some of them secondhand, but there are also photographs. One of the most heart-rending is of a man looking at the severed hand and foot of his five-year-old daughter. There are also graphic ones of adults without hands and of men being severely beaten with the *chicotte*. Millions of Africans lost their lives through the actions of Leopold's agents. This was nothing but genocide, as bad as the Holocaust. In the end, thanks to the reports of some missionaries and colonial administrators like Sir Roger Casement, even the conscience of Europe was aroused and revolted by the incredible brutality. The result of the outcry was that in 1908 the Congo was taken away from Leopold and handed over to the Belgian government.

Another consequence of the artificial partitioning of Africa by the European powers was the fracturing of national identities leading to political and military upheaval. Because of European ignorance of ethnic configurations, whole nations which had been kept intact, and should have remained intact, were now inadvertently split up and found themselves the subjects or in the spheres of influence of different European nations. Thus one whole proud nation might find its members split up and allocated to three different African countries belonging to the French, the British, and the Italians. The Somali people suffered most because of this. Some found themselves in Italian Eritrea, some in Italian Somaliland, some in French Somaliland, some in British Somaliland, and some even in British Kenya. The opposite of this was equally devastating: nations that were separate, and should have been kept separate, found themselves hounded together into one country or into the sphere of influence of one European nation. Nigeria was an example of this: the Yorubas, the Igbos, and the Hausas, each of them a great nation with millions of people, were forced together to form the country of Nigeria. This would later give rise to one of the most daunting problems in Africa, civil wars and wars among nations, as a nation that had been splintered tried to come together again and regain its old identity, or a nation that had been forced into some kind of union with others tried to break away and regain its former identity. The first process is called irredentism and the second secession. The Somalis present a typical example of irredentism as they try to regain national identity and wholeness. This has been the cause of numerous wars and upheavals in the Horn of Africa which continue to the present day and ensure that Somalia is one of the most unstable countries in Africa. Nigeria is a typical example of the second process. In 1967 the Igbos attempted to break away from the Nigerian federation, thus causing a bloody civil war known as the Biafran War that lasted until 1970.

A further result of the Berlin Conference was that Germany was recognized as an imperial power and was even able to acquire a fourth colony, Tanganyika. The agreement reached at Berlin among the European countries had stipulated that if a European country could demonstrate actual occupation of an African country, it was entitled to that country. This enabled Bismarck to proclaim a protectorate over Tanganyika because of effective occupation, since a German agent named Carl Peters had made treaties with local African leaders.

As far as the Europeans were concerned, perhaps the most important consequence of the Berlin Conference was that, in the aftermath of the conference, there was hardly any conflict among these powers who had been competing for supremacy within Africa and were almost on the point of coming to blows when the conference was held. In this regard, Bismarck's ruse was a great success. There were two exceptions, two occasions when Europeans powers came close to exchanging blows. One was the so-called Fashoda incident, which happened in 1898 along the Nile River. A small French expeditionary force under the command of Jean-Baptiste Marchand faced off against a much bigger Anglo-Egyptian force led by the famous Sir Herbert Kitchener, which was building a road up the Nile. Kitchener ordered Marchand and his men to retreat, and the latter were forced to do so because, outnumbered as they were, they could never have had a chance in an actual confrontation. It was a small incident involving no fighting, but it had tremendous consequences. It meant that the British were left unchallenged and Britain was the only European country with influence all along the Nile from Egypt to the Great Lakes. Having gained control of Egypt and the Nile, the British still had to defend them, and from now on they were involved in a complicated set of diplomatic maneuvers involving the Portuguese, the French, and King Leopold II of Belgium who took delight in playing one major European nation against another. In the end the Nile was secured for Britain. The French had to be content with moving westwards into unproductive near-desert areas. Indeed, in 1899 they renounced all claims to the Nile valley.

The second incident was between the Portuguese and the British. With the Portuguese in Angola and the British influential among the Shona and the Indebele in Southern Rhodesia, there was always the possibility of a clash. This almost happened when the Portuguese explorer Serpa Pinto annexed the Macololo people in 1898. The British saw this as an intrusion into their sphere of influence and issued an ultimatum to the Portuguese, who gave in. In the end both countries agreed to a treaty that ratified the boundaries of Mozambique, Nyasaland, and Southern Rhodesia. The incident was a humiliating defeat for Portugal whose government was forced to resign. Britain's ascendancy as the world's greatest colonial power was confirmed. By the end of the century Britain had colonies on all the continents and her empire comprised about a quarter of the world's population.

The Italians and Ethiopia

The Italians attempted to colonize Ethiopia but failed miserably. Ethiopia became the only indigenous African nation not to be colonized by a European power. This was largely due to the humiliating defeat it imposed on massive Italian forces at the battle of Adowa (or Adwa) in 1896 under its Emperor Menelik II. The battle of Adowa has become an iconic event in African and even world history, and its significance cannot be overestimated. It suggested that a well-trained European army could be defeated by Africans on African soil; it represented what African competence, ingenuity, and efficiency could achieve; and it was a major landmark in the determination to remain free and the resistance to oppression and tyranny. The Italian army was defeated largely because of the brilliant military strategy of the Ethiopian leader Menelik II in drawing out the Italians from their secure position in the mountains, but also because of the incompetence of the Italian commanders who chose an unpropitious moment to advance and attack. The defeat of the Italians also showed that the almost total occupation of Africa by the European powers was not achieved without strenuous resistance from many African peoples. This resistance had started before the Berlin Conference and the scramble, and it continued well after. It was not until the start of World War I in 1914 that the Europeans could be said to be in total control.

Resistance to imperialist occupation

At the start of the period of European intrusion there was little resistance, largely because the African peoples were not quite sure of what was happening. At that time, the Europeans preferred to negotiate and use guile rather than military force. They often presented themselves as friends of the African people who would help to protect them against their enemies and who were interested in trade and bringing a new God to them. The local people welcomed the Europeans as allies against enemy tribes, not realizing that in most cases they were condemning themselves to subservience. Once the Africans realized what was happening, however, there was strong resistance. States in the interior, or that extended from the coast into the interior, were larger and better organized and more prepared to resist the imperialists than coastal states. These states included the Shona and Ndebele, the Zulus, the Ashantis and others. We shall now look at a few examples of resistance, starting with West Africa.

After the Berlin Conference, the French and the British advanced across West Africa. Generally speaking, the French acquired large but arid and unproductive states, while the British got places like Sierra Leone, the Gambia, the then Gold Coast and Nigeria, which were rich in mineral and agricultural resources. Both the French and the British sought to bolster their positions, but they were met by fierce resistance from some quarters.

Samori Toure's resistance against the French

The Madinka emperor Samori Toure, whose empire had been part of ancient Mali, has become almost as legendary as some of the emperors of ancient Mali, whose glories his people hoped to emulate. Shillington refers to Samori Toure as "France's single most formidable military opponent in Western Africa" (Shillington, 338). The accolade is well deserved. Samori Toure had an army of 30,000 men, including an elite cavalry corps; he also had some modern weaponry bought from the British in Sierra Leone. The French found this army almost invincible. They were therefore forced to sign a treaty with Samori Toure in 1887, but it was clear that they were doing this only to buy time and that they were bent on establishing total control and ensuring the total defeat of the Madinkas. Eventually, the French invaded in 1891, largely because they realized that

Samori's position had been weakened by internal struggles. Samori, aware of his weakened position, resorted to guerrilla tactics and a scorched earth policy, thus depriving the French of much-needed supplies. But there were new forces to be dealt with further to the east, such as the British and the Ashantis. Though he won some spectacular victories, he was forced to surrender to the French in 1898 and was exiled to Gabon where he died. He remains, however, one of West Africa's great traditional heroes.

The Ashantis

The Ashantis offered stubborn resistance to the British. A proud and enterprising people in what is now central Ghana, they were very active in the gold trade and subsequently in the trade in palm oil which was much needed by the factories of the West. For a while they traded amicably with the British, but tensions arose when they realized that the British, like themselves, wanted to dominate the gold and palm oil trade. The British invaded Ashantiland in 1874 in an effort to assert their authority, defeated the Ashantis, and burnt their capital, Kumasi. This was before partition and the British did not yet wish to formally occupy Ashantiland. After partition, however, the British saw the entire area as belonging to their sphere of influence, and they had to show that they were the ones who controlled the entire Gold Coast. The British therefore invaded again in 1895, occupied the Ashanti kingdom and proclaimed a protectorate over almost all of the Gold Coast. However, in 1900 the Ashanti army which had survived intact, rose up in rebellion against the British and real war ensued. The Ashantis won some very significant victories and came very close to defeating the British, but in the end superior British military armaments prevailed. The whole of the Gold Coast was declared a colony of Britain and the Asantehene (the Ashanti monarch) was exiled to the Seychelles.

Namibia and resistance to the Germans

The Herero and Nama peoples of South West Africa, or what is now Namibia, offered some of the fiercest resistance to the imperialists, in this case the Germans. Namibia is also a glaring example of imperialist consolidation of power by exploiting the conflicts among African peoples. This part of Southern Africa, from the Namib Desert to the west to Bechuanaland and the Okavango River to the east, had long been inhabited by two major ethnic groups: the Nama to the south and the Herero to the north. Unfortunately, these two peoples were traditional enemies, an enmity largely arising from the need to control the trade with the British in cattle, ivory, and ostrich feathers. In 1884 the Germans, using as a pretext the need to protect their traders and missionaries, declared the whole area a German protectorate. After the Berlin Conference Germany decided to consolidate its hold by playing the old game of "divide and conquer." It made a treaty with the Herero which involved protecting them against their traditional enemies the Nama and attacked the Nama. Although the latter fought bravely in the war that followed, they were finally defeated. The Germans then turned their attention to the Herero, taking advantage of succession struggles to establish their authority. They took vast tracts of land from the Herero and allocated them to German settlers; they imposed taxes and forced labor. The Herero rose up in rebellion, but their rebellion was brutally crushed and their leaders executed. The Germans were in control, but the Herero and the Nama were not to be so easily written off. In the early twentieth century the Germans continued to introduce white settlers into the area, taking huge tracts of land from the natives. The new settlers also forcefully took away the people's cattle to stock their new ranches. The Herero were the first to rebel and their rebellion was fierce. They killed over 100 German settlers and reoccupied the land that had been taken away from them. They would probably have won the struggle had their natural enemies the Nama supported them, but that did not happen until it was too late. The German commander put out a proclamation that all the Herero must leave the territory and that any Herero found inside German territory, armed or unarmed, would be shot. This amounted to nothing less than ethnic cleansing, the complete removal of the Herero from their native and ancestral lands. By 1905 only 16,000 Herero, out of a previous population of 80,000 were left, but only 2000 refugees reached Bechuanaland (Shillington, 378). This was one of the most notorious events in the history of imperialism. The Nama also rose in rebellion, waging a vigorous and largely successful guerrilla operation. It was not until 1907 that the rebellion was finally put down, thanks, once again, to superior German weaponry. Once the war was over the Germans brutally punished the surviving Herero and Nama. They seized all their cattle and deposed their chiefs. Both groups were reduced to total impotence and were forced to occupy menial jobs in the homes and farms of their German masters.

The Maji Maji rebellion in East Africa

It should be clear that the two major forces working against Africans in their rebellion against the imperialists were ancient ethnic animosities and superior European weaponry, particularly European possession of the machine gun. The question is often asked, why Africans, who had been so ingenious in the past in finding solutions to obstacles and in the use of what can be called African science, could not find a suitable answer to European aggressiveness and European weaponry. The Maji Maji rebellion in what is now Southern Tanzania provides a good example of an attempt to do just that. The people in this part of what was then Tanganyika believed in the power of a magic fluid or magic water called "maji maji" that could turn bullets into water. This would be a formidable antidote to the machine gun. The belief in maji maji brought the people of Southern Tanganyika together in a demonstration of rare unity against the Germans. The revolt spread and the people scored major successes. This led to greater belief in the power of the magic water and more successes by the people. The Germans were completely stupefied by the extent of the rebellion's success and the fact that it was all due to a magic fluid. Eventually, however, the rebellion was put down and the Germans characteristically punished the people brutally by destroying villages and laying waste huge tracts of land. Famine followed, and more than 50,000 more people died in consequence (Shillington, 379).

It can be seen, then, that although imperialism formally started with the Berlin Conference and the partition of Africa in 1884–85, many African peoples continued to put up fierce resistance for a long while after that. The process of putting an end to this resistance and establishing the authority of the imperialist powers went under the ironic title of "pacification." The use of the term "pacification" to describe the process was the most egregious misuse of a term ever recorded. In effect it involved the most brutal suppression of all resistance in order to bring about the total subjugation of the African people involved. It was not until the start of World War I in 1914 that the resistance can be said to have been completely eliminated. Germany lost the war and all its African colonies in consequence. They all became trust territories of the League of Nations and were given to other nations to administer on behalf of the League of Nations. Thus, the Cameroon went jointly to France and Britain, South West Africa went to South Africa, Tanganyika went to Britain, Togo to France, and Burundi and Rwanda went to Belgium.

The administration of colonial territories

Generally speaking, the colonizing powers imposed taxes in order, as they claimed, to raise funds to pay wages and finance the reforms they were introducing. They also introduced forced labor and established an army and a police force, both consisting of local men, but with the colonizing power providing the officers. By and large, these were the commonalities among the systems of the various colonial powers. However, there were also differences. It has been generally held that one of the major differences between the French and British systems of administering their colonies was that the French practiced the policy of assimilation while the British used the system of indirect rule.

The French had always held an exalted view of their culture which some of them felt to be superior to any other culture in the world. Originally, therefore, they sought to assimilate all the members of their empire into French culture. This would involve putting them through a thoroughly French system of education during which they would imbibe French values and attitudes, irrespective of their skin color. This meant that those in Africa would regard themselves and be regarded as black French men and women. They would have full French citizenship, with the right of full representation in the French parliament, and they would be subject to and protected by French laws. Some might see this intention of the French as being very laudable. After all, they were saying that everyone in the French empire was equal in all respects and had the same opportunities open to him or her, irrespective of race or place of origin. This would be a considerable movement away from the basic tenets that launched both the slave trade and imperialism itself. It is also one of the major aims of most civilized societies. There were, however, a few obstacles to the achievement of total assimilation. In the first place, it meant admitting that the cultures of the African peoples were inferior to French culture, and, even worse, should be completely forgotten. Some would say that this implied a kind of unjustifiable arrogance. It even undermined the supposed belief in equality and was opposed to all notions of diversity and the strength that could derive from such diversity. Was it possible to devise an educational system that would create black Frenchmen and women out of Africans, and was such a system even desirable? It now seems to us quite laughable that young African children attending school in some of the French colonies were expected to recite every morning that their ancestors were "Gauls."

The second major obstacle to the success of the assimilation policy was the numbers involved. In the early twentieth century the people in the French Empire numbered tens of millions. How were all these to be assimilated? In practice, therefore, the French abandoned the plan of assimilation for all, and only a few select and highly educated people were actually assimilated. The rest were regarded as "sujets" or subjects of the empire. Some of the assimilated ones actually held important positions in France. For instance, Leopold Sedar Senghor, who became the first president of an independent Senegal, and Houphuet Boigny, the first president of an independent Côte d'Ivoire, were not only members of the French Assembly, but also ministers in the French government. Senghor was a member of the French Academy and was also one of a committee entrusted with the task of ensuring the purity of the French language.

There were also unenviable consequences even for those who became assimilated. Some of these people, having been put through a French system of education in their home countries in Africa, were then sent to France for the continuation of the system. There it dawned on them that they had been completely alienated from their roots in the African tradition. Hence arose the concept of alienation. These people also discovered that although they were supposed to have the same legal and political rights as French men and women born in France, they were not totally accepted as being French. They were therefore in a kind of cultural limbo and were going through an identity crisis. They therefore embraced the literary and philosophical concept of "negritude," which meant an embracing of black-ness and "African-ness" as these people tried to get back to their roots.

Having realized that French legal and political rights could not be extended to all the subjects of their empire, the French started placing emphasis on local government and appointed local chiefs to collect taxes, recruit forced labor and generally keep the people in line. For the most part, these chiefs were not local traditional rulers accepted and respected by the people, as were those that were used by the British in their adminis-tration. They therefore did not have the kind of mystique that traditional rulers would normally have. The French also dispensed with customary law, largely because these appointed chiefs lacked both the mystique and the knowledge to administer it.

The British, on the other hand, largely used the policy of "indirect rule." This meant making use of and ruling through the local administrative systems that they encountered. Although they had largely subdued the people and were in charge, they preferred to keep the local kings and chiefs in place and use them in their administration to collect taxes, execute the laws, and maintain order. The system is largely associated with Lord Lugard, who was governor of Nigeria. In his book *The Dual Mandate in British Tropical Africa* (1922) Lord Lugard explained how he had worked out the system as he tried to find a way to administer the Sokoto Emirates of Northern Nigeria. The system was so successful that Lugard recommended it be used throughout British Africa, and his advice was largely accepted. The system was inexpensive and effective. The people, who might not have listened to an alien official, knew that they had to respect and obey their king or chief. In fact, the British came to believe so strongly in the new system that they went on to appoint so-called "warrant chiefs" in the so-called "stateless societies" where there were traditionally no kings or chiefs, such as among the Igbos in Eastern Nigeria. This gave rise to some dissatisfaction. The system also involved keeping in place large parts of the traditional system, especially the laws of succession. Unlike the French who regularly imposed appointed chiefs on the people, the normal laws of succession were observed by the British who accepted the chiefs and kings that those laws produced. This also meant that customary law was largely retained and observed and there was little inclination among British administrators to obliterate local custom, local traditions, and local beliefs. This was quite different from French attitudes. It must be noted, however, that a few French colonies practiced a form of indirect rule called "association." The indigenous authorities were allowed to exercise power while the French authorities remained aloof, intervening only when power was abused.

The Portuguese method of colonial administration was like that of the French. They believed that a small number of their subjects, the elite, could be exposed to Portuguese values and Portuguese culture. They were called *civilisados* or *assimilados*, and were exempt from the taxes imposed on the less fortunate mass of Portuguese subjects. They could also not be recruited for forced labor. However, unlike the French, they were never given the political and legal rights that the French *assimiles* enjoyed.

The Belgians practiced what can only be referred to as direct rule from Belgium. There was no question of assimilation or of indirect rule. King Leopold II and his successors in the Belgian government did not believe that the African was capable of exercising power. He used Belgian agents and representatives appointed by himself to subdue and rule the people of the Congo with the utmost brutality. A form of direct rule was used in Southern Rhodesia and South Africa, because those countries were occupied by British and Dutch settlers who were generally given free rein to run their own affairs in these semi-autonomous states.

The impact of imperialism

Imperialism in Africa lasted only for about 80 years, from the 1880s until the 1960s, yet its impact was profound. The entire continent was transformed in ways that could not have been imagined. The transformation was economic, political, social, educational, and even religious. The economic impact was probably the most profound. The fact that African economies were now directed by alien European powers meant that patterns of production and trade that had been developing over hundreds and even thousands of years were radically altered. Since a major reason for the European expansion into Africa was to procure cheap raw materials, the colonial powers encouraged their new subjects to concentrate on the so-called "cash crops," the crops that were needed for the factories of Europe: rubber, palm oil, cotton, coffee, tea, ground nuts, cacao. This meant that, in some cases, attention was diverted from the subsistence crops, such as rice and millet, with all kinds of consequences for food production in later years. Emphasis was also placed on mining and minerals such as copper, iron, gold, and diamonds, which led to changes in the patterns of migration as some young men were forced to or voluntarily moved to work in the mines. Africans were therefore brought into the "money economy," because the farmers who produced these commodity crops were paid for their produce, but they did not derive much benefit from it because they used the money to purchase goods from Europe which, at times, were of no use to them. Also, although many people became farmers because the European colonialists wanted as much produce as possible, the Africans were not really large-scale farmers. For all practical purposes, they were like peasant farmers. They did not have plantations as was the case with the British settlers in places like South Africa, Southern Rhodesia, or even in Kenya. There the settlers had taken away huge tracts of African land; this option was not available to individual African farmers. Still, these small African farmers performed yeoman service in the production of these commodity or cash crops and certain areas became famous areas of production. Senegal and the Gambia were assiduous in the production of groundnuts; Nigeria and Sierra Leone were prolific producers of palm oil; the Gold Coast (now Ghana) excelled every other country in the production of cacao. In fact, its economy became almost entirely dependent on it. This suggests one disadvantage of over-specialization in the production of cash crops. A country that concentrated on the production of one or two cash crops to such an extent that the entire economy depended on it was likely to suffer if demand or the price of the crop declined. This actually happened to the Gold Coast after it became independent Ghana when the price of cacao fell drastically. The colonial powers should have realized that over-specialization was inadvisable and should have encouraged diversifying the economy. They did not because they were interested in their own profits and not the future welfare of their colonial territories.

Of course, these African countries, having exported their raw materials rather cheaply to Europe, were then encouraged to purchase the manufactured products from the colonizing country. Thus Nigeria, having exported palm oil and palm-kernel oil to be used in the factories of Britain, purchased margarine, soap, and cosmetics made out of these products; Ghana, having exported cacao to Britain, purchased the cocoa drink and chocolates made out of cacao; and Senegal and the Gambia, having exported groundnuts to France, purchased peanut butter made out of groundnuts in the factories of France. The colonial countries could not teach their colonies how to make these products because they would have lost huge markets and the diversification of the economies of their colonies was not to their advantage.

Imperialism also had political consequences. Tried and tested systems that had worked were replaced by the rule of an alien power represented by just one man, the governor, whose word was law. Some scholars argue that the dictatorial behavior of some modern African leaders derives, not from traditional models, but from the observation of the powers and activity of colonial governors. As Azevedo points out, political expression against the colonial regime was strictly forbidden and prior to 1945 the colonized people did not participate in the decision- making process.

Social consequences

The social impact of imperialism was just as important as the political, and the most important of the social consequences was the impact on the condition of African women. The European imperialists came to Africa with their own peculiar view of how women should behave and what women should be permitted to do. On the other hand, women in traditional Africa had played extremely important roles. For instance, they were mostly responsible for agricultural production. The imperialists, however, believed that women should be subordinate to men and the most important tasks in the community should be done by men. Therefore, only men should be entrusted with the production of the all-important cash or commodity crops intended for export. Men were therefore brought into the cash economy whereas the women were confined to growing the "minor" subsistence crops. This also affected the distribution of land. Men now had greater access to the best land, because that was needed for the growing of the cash crops. In fact, women in most African societies were deprived of the right to ownership of land, a situation which continued in most countries until after independence.

The imperialists emphasized the building of cities and ports as new centers of administration and outlets for the goods from the interior. The growth of cities in turn attracted a number of people, including young men and women, to these new centers where wealth and influence were supposed to be concentrated. In most circumstances, however, the expectations were groundless, and this led to social evils like crime and prostitution. Azevedo states, "The lure of the city—education, health, jobs, and good living—was often an illusion which contributed to poverty, despair, slums and ghettos, prostitution and crime. During this social transformation, individualism began to replace African communalistic traditions ..." (Azevedo, 119).

Religious and cultural consequences

The most important cultural consequence of imperialism was the introduction of Christianity to areas in tropical Africa that had adhered to traditional religions. Missionary activity had actually preceded imperialism, but it was reinforced by imperialism. As we have seen, the political administrators went into African territory partly because they felt they had to protect their missionaries operating there. The missionaries had a mission to expand Christianity, and this they did quite effectively. Unfortunately, this occasionally involved introducing contempt for traditional beliefs and traditional customs. Most missionaries tried to convince the African peoples that their previous ways were pagan or barbaric and must be abandoned. Converts were given "Christian" names or had to adopt Christian names before they could be accepted into the church or the school established by the church, and they were taught to believe that most things associated with traditional religion or culture, like the masquerades, were evil.

Some positive effects of imperialism

It must be acknowledged that the impact of imperialism was not entirely negative. It is to Western imperialism that Africa largely owes the exposure to Western education, which opened the door for some Africans to certain beneficial careers. This does not mean that African societies did not have their own educational systems and structures before imperialism; it means that Western imperialism offered new perspectives and skills that were highly beneficial and necessary for Africa's interaction with the rest of the world. Some African societies, like Ethiopia, were literate before imperialism, but it was not until the interaction with the West that literacy was achieved in some others. However, the introduction of Western-type education had its disadvantages. As we have seen, it sometimes led, particularly in the French colonies, to the alienation of some Africans from their roots in the African tradition. The psychological and social consequences of this were sometimes devastating. It must also be stressed that the European imperialist powers did not spend as much money on African education as they ought to have done. It was not until after World War II that some colonial governments started taking an interest in African education. Higher education was almost entirely neglected and most Africans who wanted exposure to it had to travel to the colonizing countries for further studies. Although Fourah Bay College in Sierra Leone was established in 1827, it was not until after World War II that universities were established in Ghana, Nigeria, and parts of East Africa.

Another positive effect of imperialism was the construction of a viable infrastructure: ports and harbors; railways; roads; and communications systems, such as telegraph and postal services. Of course, in the construction of these the imperialists were largely motivated by self-interest; the railways and roads were necessary to bring the valuable cash produce from the interior to the coastal ports and harbors in order to be exported to Europe. The roads and the railways also enabled the European administrators to move about the country and therefore be in a position to establish their authority. Telegraph and postal systems were necessary in order to communicate with the authorities back home. Moreover, the construction of the infrastructure was partly paid for with the taxes imposed on Africans. However, the infrastructure made a positive contribution to the development of colonial territories, and it is significant that some independent African governments failed to sustain and maintain them, with adverse economic consequences.

The introduction to Western-type health services was another positive result of imperialism. The construction of hospitals and the use of Western medicines and drugs were highly beneficial. The European doctors and nurses, especially those who were missionaries, were highly trained and dedicated and one must admit that they did a world of good. Drugs were cheap and readily available and in many cases they were free. Of course, there was the downside. These services were only available to a tiny section of the African population. In many places there was no hospital or doctor within a radius of one hundred miles. However, there were the African medicine men and women and these were often extremely effective. One of the faults of the imperialist medical system was that not much was done to study the impact of these traditional healers and to integrate them into the medical system, as is now going on.

The debate about the ultimate effect of imperialism will continue. Some will suggest that the advantages outweigh the disadvantages; others will assert that on balance it had a positive impact especially when one considers what happened to African countries after independence when most things seemed to be in decline. Some will say that the forceful occupation of other people's countries is incontestably wrong, in any case, and one must not even consider whether there were advantages. The real nature of the situation was that imperialism was not meant to benefit Africans, and one must not therefore be surprised if it had some very deleterious effects. It was meant to benefit Western Europe and that it did tremendously. In the process there were some positive effects for Africans, but there were also some terrible consequences as well.

References and suggestions for further reading

Arendt, H. 1968. *Imperialism.* New York: Harcourt.

Azevedo, M. 2005. "European Exploration and Conquest of Africa." Pp. 109–122 in M. Azevedo (ed.). *Africana Studies.* Durham, NC: Carolina Academic Press.

Davidson, B. 1987. *Modern Africa.* London: Longmans.

Fieldhouse, D. K. 1965. *The Colonial Empires: A Comparative Survey from the Eighteenth Century.* New York: Delta.

Hobson, J. 1902. *Imperialism: A Study.* London: George Allen and Unwin.

Hochschild, A. 1999. *King Leopold's Ghost.* New York: Mariner Books.

Langer, W. 1935. "A Critique of Imperialism." *Foreign Affairs,* Vol. XIV, October: 102–115.

Liebowitz, D., and C. Pearson. 2005. *Stanley's Mad Journey through the Congo.* New York: W. W. Norton.

Pakenham, T. 1991. *The Scramble for Africa, 1876–1912.* New York: Random House.

Park, M. 1983 [1799]. *Travels into the Interior of Africa.* London: Eland Press.

Porter, A. 1994. *European Imperialism.* London: Macmillan.

Robinson, R. E. and J. A. Gallagher. 1961. *Britain and the Partition of Africa.* London: Macmillan.

Rodney, W. 1972. *How Europe Underdeveloped Africa.* Washington, DC: Howard University Press.

Rotberg, R. 1973. *Africa and its Explorers: Motives, Methods, and Impact.* Cambridge, MA: Harvard University Press.

Rotberg, R, and M. F. Shore. 1988. *The Founder Cecil Rhodes and the Pursuit of Power.* New York: Oxford University Press.

Shillington, K. 2019. *History of Africa.* London: Red Globe Press.

Tamarkin, M. 1996. *Cecil Rhodes and the Cape Afrikaners: The Imperial Colossus and the Colonial Parish Pump.* London: Cass.

Wright, H. 1961. *The New Imperialism: Analysis of Late Nineteenth Century Expansion.* Boston: D. C. Heath and Company.

Zewde, B. 1991. *A History of Modern Ethiopia, 1855–1974.* Oxford: James Currey.

4   African nationalism and the drive towards independence

The first point to stress is that the drive towards autonomy, self-rule, and independence on the part of African countries was part of a global movement which had been going on long before the rise of African nationalism and which, in a sense, can be said to have given momentum to African nationalism. It also included the American civil rights movement and can therefore be said to be a movement dedicated to the liberation of all peoples of African descent from subjugation and oppression and to giving them the means whereby they could take charge and either govern themselves and others or participate fully in government. It included the belief that Africans and people of African descent had been treated badly by the West and if liberated and given the chance could do very well by themselves. It is quite significant that the civil rights movement reached its culmination in the 1960s, at about the same time as most African countries were achieving independence. It can be argued that both the civil rights movement and African nationalism were spawned by the Pan-African movement or were, at least, closely related to it.

The Pan–African movement

The Pan-African movement goes way back to the last quarter of the eighteenth century in America and is related to the war of independence and the subjugation characteristic of slavery. It started as a drive by freed slaves of African descent to return to the homeland Africa and establish an independent country where they could govern themselves and be free of oppression and subjugation and to which all peoples of African descent could belong. At this time, it was called the "back to Africa" campaign. Two principles thus fueled the pan-African movement at its inception: freedom and black self-determination. The back to Africa campaign was associated with two African countries: Sierra Leone and Liberia, both in West Africa. Those slaves who fought on the side of the British during the American War of Independence were given their freedom after the war and were eventually transported to Sierra Leone because they preferred to go back to Africa rather than the inhospitable Nova Scotia. Since the British had lost the war, these liberated slaves could not stay on in the United States. By that time, the British had designated Sierra Leone as a haven for liberated slaves. These liberated slaves were joined by rebellious black soldiers from the West Indies called "maroons," some poor black people belonging to the lowest and most deprived classes from London, and black people who were being taken into slavery but were liberated on the high seas by the British and taken to Sierra Leone. As for Liberia, it was founded in 1847 by the American Colonization Society as a place in Africa to which liberated slaves who wanted to go back to Africa could be sent.

DOI: 10.4324/9781003111733-5

The activities of several individuals and institutions at this time demonstrated the tremendous enthusiasm there was in the United States for a return to Africa and participation in a country in Africa run by free Africans. Paul Cuffe had been the first to organize a serious attempt to get liberated slaves of African descent to return to Africa and his efforts met with tremendous enthusiasm, but he died unfortunately in 1817 before he could achieve his objectives. Robert Campbell and Martin Delaney actually travelled to Africa in 1859 and acquired land from an African chief on which returnees would be settled, but the incipient Civil War put a halt to their activities. In 1858 Henry Highland Garnet founded the African Civilization Society whose aim was to "strike a death blow to American slavery" and "to establish a grand center of Negro nationality." He too was unable to realize his objectives largely because of great opposition from those, like Frederick Douglas, who preferred the freed slave to become an equal part of American society.

Activists and intellectuals of the "Back to Africa," Pan-African, and nationalist movements

The concept of a "return to Africa" was promoted not only by free blacks from the United States, but also from the Caribbean and South America. A leading exponent of the concept was Edward Wilmot Blyden who later emerged as one of the leading African intellectuals of his day. Born in 1832 in St. Thomas in the Virgin Islands, he was a missionary associated with the West Indian Church Association. Although he was the son of free parents, he was refused admission to an American university in 1850 and so he went instead to Liberia which was independent and ruled by black people. He became editor of a local paper called the *Liberian Herald* and used this and other means to spread his views about the glories of the African past, especially the achievements of the ancient African kingdoms and empires. He obviously took tremendous pride in Africa. However, as a missionary, he believed that Africa could be saved by being exposed to Western Christian values, and he was a passionate advocate of introducing these enlightened Western values to Africa. For this reason he has often been accused, like Garnet, of being paternalistic and "Eurocentric." However he demonstrated what could only be called African nationalism and pan-Africanism: his belief that the Republic of Liberia could serve as a model for a free African state, governed by blacks, spreading along the whole length of West Africa. His writings show that he was a towering intellectual, and his efforts resulted in a number of like-minded blacks from the United States and the Caribbean returning to Africa.

Edward Blyden was a missionary and, in a sense, his career illustrates the role played by the African church in the Pan-African movement. The African church was appropriately concerned about the sufferings of the lowest classes of blacks in the United States and it was precisely this class of blacks who were the most anxious to return to Africa where they felt their lot would be easier than it was in the West. The activities of Bishop Henry Turner also forcefully illustrate this trend. Henry Turner was a bishop in the African Methodist Episcopal Church, a denomination that eventually took strong roots in Africa. Like some of the other Pan-Africanists, he became well acquainted with Africa through his many trips there, and he was a very forceful advocate for black emigration to Africa. He was convinced that the poorer classes of blacks would have a better life there and in this he was supported by many others including leading blacks. He really believed that African Americans who returned to Africa could help to build a strong, powerful, and independent nation that all black people could be proud of. In reality, he was able to transport only a few blacks to Africa, but his vision was, nevertheless, very popular. Turner's work was continued by Chief Alfred Charles Sam in the early twentieth century. Chief Sam was born in the then Gold Coast, present-day Ghana, and he actually formed a company, the Akim Trading Company, which would sponsor the resettlement of blacks from the United States in the Gold Coast. He travelled extensively in the United States, selling shares in the company to poor blacks. Some might now regard his views and activities as laughable, but his action in forming a resettlement company was essentially no different from that of the British, Portuguese, or Dutch who formed companies to sponsor the settlement of their nationals in Africa. A major difference, however, was that he was sponsoring the resettlement of people whose ancestors had been forcibly removed from the continent. His activities were not ultimately successful because, although he was able to take some black emigrants back to Africa, they were disillusioned by what they encountered, and the British authorities were not very cooperative.

In the vision of Henry Turner and Chief Sam, a slightly new nuance in the Pan-African outlook could be detected. There is still emphasis on the idea of a return to Africa, but there is also the beginning of a greater emphasis on the building of a strong and free African country that all black peoples could be proud of. This was largely due to the nature of the times and some ground-breaking events that had happened. The American Civil War had ended, a war that had been fought over the issue of the emancipation of black slaves, but there was still the ongoing question of the extent to which the emancipated blacks could actually be free. The emphasis was therefore on freedom and liberation. On the other side of the Atlantic the European powers had selfishly partitioned and occupied almost the entire continent. Imperialism was at its height, and reports were beginning to seep through about the brutalities perpetrated on the subjected Africans by the occupying powers. In trying to accomplish their aims, people like Turner and Chief Sam had interacted with many Africans and had learned at firsthand about the atrocities committed by the European imperialists and the suffering of the Africans. Therefore, there was an intensification of the Pan-Africanist drive with a view to securing the liberation of the African continent, followed by the formation of a strong African nation that would be powerful enough to prevent further occupation. The Pan-Africanist drive thus absorbed the drive towards self-determination.

Another thing of moment that happened towards the end of the nineteenth century was the emergence of Karl Marx and the publication of his *Communist Manifesto*. The result was the rise of Marxism which stressed that the bourgeoisie owned the commanding heights of the economy while the proletariat, those at the lowest end of the social ladder who did the actual work, suffered. Marxism was therefore anti-capitalist, but it also equated capitalism with imperialism. Imperialism involved the ownership of the commanding heights of an alien people's economy by a European imperialist power who exploited not only the economy but also the labor of the subjected people. At this time, therefore, many people who were anti-imperialist also gravitated towards Marxism. However, while Marx stressed the relationship between capitalism and class, they stressed the relationship between capitalism and race. It was mainly black people, they claimed, whose labor and economic potential were exploited, in Africa and elsewhere, by a white bourgeoisie. It is not surprising, therefore, that some of the Pan-Africanists, who were strongly anti-imperialist by this time, were drawn towards Marxism.

Two Pan-Africanists who emerge out of this kind of context were, perhaps, the most famous of them all: Marcus Garvey and W. E. B. Du Bois. Marcus Garvey was born in

Jamaica in the West Indies in 1888. His grandfather had been a slave, but his parents were free. However, they were extremely poor and could not even afford to give their son a decent education. However, what Garvey lacked in so far as a formal education was concerned, he more than made up for in his tremendous energy and drive, organizational ability, breadth of vision, eloquence, ingenuity, and entrepreneurship. He became one of the leading black people the world over during the first half of the twentieth century. His first job was as a trade unionist, and he became involved in a strike which went wrong and so he was forced to become a journalist. It was while working as a journalist that he became aware of the inequities of the system. He had also visited places like Costa Rica and London and these visits had reinforced his impression. As a result, he formed the Universal Negro Improvement Association and the African Communities League. Both bodies were dedicated towards the amelioration of the condition of black peoples all over the world, but Garvey's ultimate aim was the transplantation of all black people in the African diaspora to form one vast African nation that would be free and independent, certainly independent of the European imperialists. He did not find much support for his ideas in Jamaica, so he relocated to the United States, after an invitation by Booker T. Washington. There he found the support he wanted, although he also made some enemies, particularly among African American intellectuals who resented his lack of education, saw him as an impetuous megalomaniac, and found his objectives ridiculous, extreme and unworkable. They also saw him as being similar to the Ku Klux Klan since he was also preaching a doctrine of racial separation. However, Garvey inspired a great mass movement which some have called "Garveyism." He was charismatic, but also an exhibitionist and a flamboyant showman. He enjoyed staging great parades through the streets of New York, with himself attired as a military commander or emperor in full regalia. In fact, he proclaimed himself "Provisional President of Africa," the Africa that would be formed as a result of the transplantation of most black people in the diaspora and the liberation of the entire continent from the clutches of the imperialists. But Garvey did not just dream; he also demonstrated some of the ways in which this Africa would achieve success. He formed vast companies, such as shipping companies and others, in which ordinary people had shares, partly to finance the resettlement campaign, but also to show what the black man was capable of if given the opportunity; and for a while the companies were hugely successful. Supporters were awed by the fact of a black man owning shipping companies. He had chapters and sections of his movement in every corner of the African world and at one time the membership was said to be in excess of six million (Williams, 178). Marcus Garvey genuinely believed that the African motherland could be wrested from the hands of alien exploiters and that an African nation with an African government that would compel the respect of the whole world could be established there. Obviously, the imperialist European powers did not like this, nor did the American government, so they engineered Garvey's downfall by accusing him of fraud. He was arrested, tried, and sentenced to a term of imprisonment. Most scholars now agree that the arrest and imprisonment were political. On his release he went back to his native Jamaica, but he was not too happy there, so he relocated to London where he died. His remains were subsequently moved back to Jamaica where he now enjoys the status of a hero. There is no doubt, however, that his movement was a very powerful forerunner of the drive towards African nationalism.

W. E. B. Du Bois, the other great advocate of Pan–Africanism, could not have been more different from Marcus Garvey. Where Garvey received little formal education and was largely self-taught, Du Bois was one of the most highly educated African Americans ever. Born in 1863, he attended universities in both the USA and Germany and was the first African American to receive a doctorate from Harvard University. His doctorate was in sociology. Where Garvey might leave the impression of being uninformed and simplistic in his approach to important issues, the learned Du Bois showed in his prolific writings, including his classic *Souls of Black Folk*, that he was aware of the complexities and had mastered them, and he was able to make informed suggestions about matters such as race and equality to bodies such as the League of Nations. Where Garvey was the impetuous, exhibitionist orator, Du Bois was the restrained, calm, rational professor giving courses at Atlanta University. They shared some common beliefs. They were both Pan-Africanists who believed that both Africans and African Americans should be united in a common purpose: bringing about the total emancipation of peoples of color on both sides of the Atlantic. But, unlike Garvey, Du Bois was lukewarm about the total physical transplantation of African Americans from the United States to Africa. He strove throughout his life to achieve equality for African Americans through integration, not through total separation and transplantation, as Garvey would. Like Garvey, Du Bois accepted the concept of "Africa for the Africans" and the total liberation of African countries from European occupiers, but he rejected the idea that this liberated Africa should be then ruled by African Americans, as was definitely implied in Garvey's styling himself "Provisional President of Africa." Driven by his concern for the plight of people of color all over the world, Du Bois founded the National Association for the Advancement of Colored Peoples, or NAACP, in 1909. It is still a powerful organization today. Indeed, one major reason why Garvey and Du Bois could never bring themselves to collaborate is because they saw their organizations as rivals. Du Bois once referred to Garvey, whom he probably despised, as "the most dangerous enemy of the Negro race in America and the world."

Unlike Garvey who never set foot in Africa. Du Bois visited Africa several times and eventually relocated to Africa and died in the newly independent Ghana in 1958. He was one of those Pan-Africanists who saw the connection between capitalism and racism, inclining more and more to socialism and becoming increasingly disillusioned with conditions in the West. The fact that Du Bois actually died in Africa illustrates the nature of the relationship that came to exist between the leaders of Pan-Africanist thought in the United States and African Pan-Africanists and emerging leaders of African nationalism. Pan-Africanists in the United States had been interacting with their counterparts in the Caribbean and Africa even before the end of the nineteenth century, and this had given rise to a number of Pan-African conferences like the Chicago Congress on Africa in 1895, the Atlanta Congress on Africa in 1895, the Pan-African conference in London in 1900, and the First Universal Race Congress in London in 1911. Du Bois himself organized Pan-African congresses in 1919, 1921, 1823, and 1927; and Marcus Garvey's Universal Negro Improvement Association organized Pan-Africanist conventions in the United States between 1920 and 1925. It was obvious that leaders on both sides of the Atlantic who believed that Africa should be liberated from the clutches of European imperialists were coming together and planning.

Largely inspired by the activities and views of Garvey and Du Bois, some Pan-Africanists and advocates of the liberation of black people from the colonial yoke who lived in the Caribbean or were Africans living in Britain also came together. In 1917, people of African descent from the Caribbean and West Africa formed the Union for Students of African Descent. In 1918 came the African Progress Union, and in the 1920s the very powerful West African Students Union was formed (Williams, 179). The movement gained steam in the 1930s. Famous names like George Padmore and C. L. R. James from the Caribbean joined the ranks and became very active. Both, like Du Bois, leaned towards socialism. Padmore formed the International African Friends of Abyssinia and the African Service Bureau. Quite significantly, some very important emerging African nationalists joined them in their efforts: Jomo Kenyatta who later became the first prime minister and president of Kenya and led Kenya to independence and I. T. A. Wallace-Johnson, a redoubtable African nationalist from Sierra Leone. Both of these figures were living in London at the time and Jomo Kenyatta was the publisher of a Magazine called *The Negro World*.

Pan-Africanists were also active in the French territories, especially after World War I. France was a leading imperialist nation that had appropriated more African land than any other. The peace conference at the end of World War I was held at Versailles with no African voice present, although Africans and people of African descent had fought in the war. This set up France to appear as the veritable symbol of European indifference to real African welfare, and several Pan-African organizations arose in France. These included the Ligue Universelle pour la Défense de la Race Noire, founded by Marc Houenou of Dahomey, and the Comité de la Défense de la Race Nègre, founded by Lamine Senghor from Senegal. Apart from their interest in the liberation of Africa, these organizations were also concerned about the plight of black people in the diaspora and were attracted to the ideas of Marcus Garvey.

All this culminated in the staging of perhaps the most important Pan-African Congress of them all, the fifth held in Manchester, England, in 1945, at the end of World War II. One of the reasons for its importance was that a prominent participant was Kwame Nkrumah, an emerging African nationalist who would lead his country, the then Gold Coast, to independence as the new Ghana, the first sub-Saharan African country to achieve its independence. Nkrumah would also become the leading advocate, in fact the embodiment, of the concept of Pan-Africanism and African unity on the African continent. Nkrumah had organized the congress jointly with George Padmore, and it was attended by almost all the noted Pan-Africanists and several representatives from African countries. According to Michael Williams, more native-born Africans attended this congress than all the others before it (Williams, 181). The participants realized that, with the end of World War II, the world would never be the same again and it was time to press on with the liberation of African countries from the imperialistic yoke. The most important concern of the congress was the formulation of a strategy for bringing this about. The Pan-Africanist movement was thus firmly wedded to African nationalism and this congress gave great impetus to the drive for African independence.

Forces fueling the drive towards independence

Let us now look at the forces that fueled the drive towards the independence of African countries. We have seen the role played by the fifth Pan-African Congress of 1945. Mention must also be made of the misguided Italian invasion of Ethiopia in 1935. Italy had always had its eyes on Ethiopia. Its invasion of that country in 1896, during the heyday of colonialism, resulted in a most humiliating defeat at the battle of Adowa. Ethiopia thus became an iconic symbol in the struggles for African liberation, independence, and autonomy. However, the Italians did not give up, and they tried again in 1935 under the dictator Benito Mussolini. They did this partly as a revenge for their humiliating defeat in 1896 and partly to satisfy Mussolini's own grand ambitions. During the four years during which the Italians occupied Addis Ababa they perpetrated tremendous violence including the use of poison gas. However, they were never able to occupy the entire country. An attempt was made in 1937 to assassinate the Italian Viceroy Rodolpho Graziani, and the Italians responded by killing about 6000 Ethiopians in three days in Addis Ababa. A total of 30,000 Ethiopians were massacred in revenge (Shillington, 410). All this while, Europe turned a blind eye to the invasion and its aftermath probably because Europe was preoccupied with its own existential problems such as the rise of Nazism and Fascism and the Spanish Civil War. However, Africans, and others in the African diaspora, saw this indifference to the invasion of an iconic symbol as one more demonstration of the fact that the West could not be trusted, and that Europeans in particular were people of bad faith who wished to perpetrate Western hegemony over Africa and other places. The growing antagonism towards European powers thus gained force. It was not until Italy declared war on Britain in 1940, occupied British Somaliland, and invaded Egypt, which Britain controlled, that the British took action. They decided to expel the Italians from Ethiopia, but in order to do so they brought together a coalition that involved African troops from several African countries. It was the African soldiers that bore the brunt of the fighting and played the major role in the liberation of Ethiopia. This was a source of great pride and a demonstration of what Africans could do to liberate themselves.

A major force, however, was World War II itself. The war and its consequences played a tremendous role in fueling African nationalism and the drive towards independence. Numerous young Africans from the French and British colonies actually fought in the war on the side of the Allies. The French and British had used two very effective methods to persuade or encourage these young men to fight with them. They promised them extremely good jobs and the possibility of further training in the West if the Allies won the war. I personally know of at least two men (one an uncle) who got such promises. One was later trained in communications and eventually headed the country's communications network; the other was trained in water technology and eventually headed the country's water supply system. The European colonialists also represented the war as a great fight for freedom. If the Allies lost the war, they argued, almost the entire world would come under the ferocious tyranny of Germany and the Nazis. Every colony was therefore asked to make its own contribution to the war effort. Of course the British, especially, continued to receive from Africa supplies of fibers, metals, and other raw materials needed to produce war equipment. The colonies in Africa were extremely proud of the role they played in the war. Long after the war ended, some of them continued to commemorate the notable skirmishes their soldiers had been involved in. African soldiers were particularly useful in the struggle in the Far East, in places such as Burma, against the Japanese, because they knew about the forest and were therefore good in jungle warfare. However, it occurred to these soldiers, both during and after the war, that although they had been supposed to be fighting for freedom, they themselves were not free in their own countries. This helped to fuel the drive for freedom within African countries. The same thing was happening in the USA in so far as the African Americans were concerned. Thousands of African Americans fought in the war and it occurred to them that, in spite of Lincoln's Emancipation Declaration and relevant amendments to the constitution, they were not really free in the United States. They were hardly able to exercise the franchise or get access to normal education or normal housing. They were not even "free" within the military. One must remember that the "Tuskegee Airmen," an air-force squadron consisting of blacks only, were separated from the rest of the military even though they were brave, accomplished, and efficient. It was not until 1948, with an executive order issued by President Truman, that the American military became fully integrated. The experiences of these military personnel in the war, then, helped to fuel both the civil rights movement in the United States and African nationalism in Africa and give further demonstration that the movement was global.

The war also exposed Europe's vulnerabilities. These African soldiers had fought both with and against Europeans. They had confirmed that European countries could be defeated and the white man successfully resisted. After all, France, a major colonial power, had been occupied during the war, as were some other European countries. Ultimately, Germany itself, another colonial power, had been defeated. Some of these African soldiers had fought in Europe and had observed poverty among Europeans. They had also seen that many Europeans were uneducated. Their respect for Europe was sadly diminished. Far from finding common ground, the European countries had been engaged in a fight almost to the death with one another, a fight which almost brought down Western civilization. At least, this was how the Africans saw it. Britain had fought heroically, resisting the German attempt to invade in the Battle of Britain in 1940, and fighting almost singlehandedly until the Americans entered the war after the Japanese attack on Pearl Harbor in December 1941, but she was now exhausted. A lot of manpower and other resources had been devoted to the war effort and large sections of the country were almost in ruins. Rationing was still going on and, in spite of the allied victory, the country was not in the same towering position she was in at the start of the war.

With the end of the war, the United States was propelled into prominence. The Allies would almost certainly not have won the war without American intervention, and it was now quite obvious that the United States had the greatest military in the world and was now poised to be the most powerful nation. However, the United States was generally against colonialism. Indeed, five or so years earlier when the British prime minister and war leader Winston Churchill was trying to persuade President Roosevelt and the United States to join the war, the two men had a summit during which they drew up what has come to be known as the Atlantic Charter. The Charter strongly endorsed the view that all peoples had the right to self-determination and stipulated that one of the conditions for America's joining the war was that at its end Britain would give independence to her colonial territories. It has never been quite clear whether Churchill intended to stick to the agreement, but the attitude of the United States towards colonialism was quite clear, and the rest of the world knew this.

The end of World War II also propelled the Soviet Union into prominence as a world power. The Soviet Union had made a significant contribution to the defeat of Germany and it now brought about the division of Europe into two distinct blocks: Western Europe allied to the United States and committed to democracy, and the Eastern or Soviet bloc dominated by the Soviet Union and committed to Marxist communism. Although operating from an opposite ideological stance, the Soviet Union, like the United States, was antagonistic to imperialism. Since it embraced Marxist principles it was antagonistic to capitalism and believed that capitalism and imperialism went hand in hand. Indeed, imperialism was an extension of the capitalist ethos. The Soviet Union thus actively supported emerging independence and liberation movements in many parts of Africa: in Guinea, Mozambique, and Angola. Several of the leaders of these movements were pro-Marxist. Indeed, at the fifth Pan-African Congress in Manchester in 1945 some of the resolutions had a distinctly Marxist slant, and some of the prominent participants, figures who would play an important part in the independence movements and even governments of soon-to-be independent countries, were expressing Marxist sentiments. The Soviet Union and communism became forces to be reckoned with and their support greatly energized the emerging African leaders.

A major factor was that the burgeoning nationalism in Africa gave rise to a new and powerful group of leaders determined to lead their countries to independence. Between the two world wars there had been a certain level of political agitation in African countries. However, it was much more muted than what happened now. This was largely due to the nature of the political leaders. The leaders at the time were members of the elite who had nothing to do with the masses and were not therefore in a position to mobilize the masses. Nor did they really want to. The new breed of leaders was completely different. Some of them, like the charismatic Kwame Nkrumah, had been educated, not by missionaries or in the prestigious European universities, but in the United States where they had been exposed to the agitation for equality. Some of them, like Julius Nyerere and Hastings Banda, had had their education in Scotland at universities which, though prestigious, were infused with the great Scottish interest in the welfare of Africans that was not always present in England. Some, like Jomo Kenyatta of Kenya, had been involved in the Pan-African movement whose vision for Africa they shared and they were also associated with people like Wallace Johnson who had formed the West African Youth League. Some, like Tom Mboya of Kenya and Sekou Toure of Guinea, were actually trade unionists interested in ameliorating the condition of workers and alleviating some of the disadvantageous effects of capitalism. They had all arisen from the masses and could be called "men of the people." And they were successful because they had the vison and the organizational ability to mobilize the masses. Apart from Kwame Nkrumah himself, they included Nnamdi Azikwe and Obafemi Awolowo of Nigeria, Sekou Toure of Guinea, Jomo Kenyatta and Tom Mboya of Kenya, Julius Nyerere of Tanganyika, Kenneth Kaunda of Northern Rhodesia, and Hastings Banda of Nyasaland (now Malawi).

The rise of the Labour Party in Britain was another event that had a marked impact on the liberation of British colonial peoples in general and Britain's African colonies in particular. At the end of World War II, Winston Churchill, the victorious British prime minister, called a general election thinking that, given the recent victory over the Germans, he and his Conservative Party were bound to win. Contrary to expectations, however, the Conservative Party was signally defeated by the Labour Party which won with a majority of nearly two hundred seats. It was an overwhelming victory and it was the first time that Britain's Labour Party had won an absolute majority. However, the Labour Party was generally against colonialism, and the forces outside Britain as well as within it, which had been moving for the liberation of the colonies, gathered steam. The first consequence of this was the independence of India in 1947. India had been the jewel in the British crown, possibly the most important country in the British Empire. Its agitation for independence had been led by the visionary and saintly Mahatma Gandhi whose doctrine of non-violent resistance became a model for the liberation struggles on both sides of the Atlantic. When India became independent in 1947 under its new prime minister, Jawalarhal Nehru, it gave a tremendous boost to the drive for independence in African countries. If India could do it, the African leaders thought, so too could they. African nationalism was really afoot.

Finally, the establishment of the United Nations in 1945 was another important factor. The League of Nations had been singularly ineffective in preventing another world war, and so at the end of World War II a new organization was founded that was much better organized and more determined and intentional in its aims than the League had been. The United Nations was definitely anti-colonialist. Powerful anti-colonialist nations like the United States and the Soviet Union had permanent seats on the Security Council. Soon resolutions were being passed calling for the liberation of colonial territories, and the European colonial countries soon realized that the United Nations meant business.

The move towards independence

Given the agitation for the liberation of colonized peoples that followed the end of World War II, the transition to independence for African countries went relatively smoothly, with a few exceptions. Taking their cue from Mahatma Gandhi, most of the protests and demonstrations were generally non-violent, with the people resorting to civil disobedience instead. Force, when it was used, came from the other end, the imperialist end. The two major colonialist powers, Britain and France, had decided, with effect from the late forties, to give some measure of participation, or the semblance of participation in the decision-making process, to the indigenous people. Local councils were elected or appointed, the franchise was extended to include certain groups, and there was now indigenous representation on the legislative councils. In some cases, as in the Gold Coast, Africans were actually in the majority on the legislative council (Shillington, 420), but in other cases, as in Sierra Leone, the African representation was scanty. In all cases, however, most of the Africans were either nominated or were traditional rulers. The colonialists were still the wielders of power. It is doubtful whether the colonialists were thinking, at this stage, of actual independence, and, in the case of Britain, the changes that were introduced would probably not have been made, were not the Labour Party in power. However that may be, the agitation and mobilization for self-government and independence gathered steam and new parties and movements were formed, such as the United Gold Coast Convention, through which Kwame Nkrumah came to prominence. In French West Africa and French Equatorial Africa, reforms were similarly made. Both entities could together now send ten delegates to the French National Assembly, but the representation was still scanty, amounting to only 2.5 percent of the total seats in the Assembly. It was quite clear that the African representatives were not being treated as equals, and this led to some dissatisfaction. The African delegates now formed their own political party, the Rassemblement Democratique Africaine (RDA) under the leadership of Felix Houphouet-Boigny, who later became the first president of Côte d'Ivoire. Tensions within the RDA led Leopold Sedar Senghor, the first president of Senegal, to break away in 1948 and form his own party, the Bloc Democratique Senegalaise (BDS).

It will be seen that the responses by various colonialist governments to the rising demand for liberation and independence varied. The British, though generally accepting the principle of self-determination under the Labour Party, was rather reluctant to grant independence when the liberation movement really gathered steam. The great Winston Churchill, whose Conservative government succeeded the Labour Party's in 1951, is reported to have said that he did not become prime minister in order to preside over the dissolution of Her Majesty's empire. Eventually, however, the British were forced to recognize that the tide could not be stemmed and a pattern gradually emerged whereby the British would regard the leaders of the independence movements as agitators. They would even imprison some of them for a while, but would have to free them and make them leaders of government business or chief ministers or prime ministers. The French, similarly, had not really thought of granting complete independence to their dependent territories. However, unlike the British who had initially merely desired to continue a form of indirect rule, the French had still harbored a vision of all their colonies joining them in a grand French community of civilized peoples. However, faced with certain pressures they were forced to make concessions and agree to major reforms in 1956 when the African territories became fully self-governing entities with fully elected assemblies. However, they were not yet fully independent, and the French still controlled foreign and military affairs and economic planning. This was change indeed, and further change was on the way. Both the British and the French would come to realize that continuing to run empires was a very expensive business in a changing post-war world. Moreover, it was probably better to hand over power to fairly moderate independence movements, like Nigeria's Northern People's Party or Sierra Leone's People's Party, that would support the West, than wait and have to hand over anyway to much more radical movements that would probably support the Soviet Union.

The case of the Mahgreb countries of North Africa

The first African countries to gain their independence were not sub-Saharan countries, as one might have expected, but North African countries in the so-called Mahgreb. With the exception of Algeria which is a special case, all these countries had certain things in common which probably explain why it was easier for them to gain their independence. Most of them were parts of the Ottoman Empire and when that empire declined, Turkish-style leaders were left behind who were called beys and were sometimes used as puppet kings by the European powers. All these countries were declared protectorates, not colonies strictly speaking, and so, when the movement for freedom got going, it was easier for them to lay claim to it. The imperialist countries imposed themselves on these countries as "supervisors of the finances" when the economies started going wrong and it was easy to move from being a "supervisor" to being a "protector." Finally, when independence was granted, the controlling imperialist power imposed a puppet king who was soon removed in a (sometimes) military revolt, whose effects are still being felt today. These countries include Egypt, Tunisia, Libya, Morocco, and the Sudan. Let us look at each in turn.

After Alexander the Great's conquest of Egypt in 332 BCE, the country was ruled by various foreign powers including the Ottomans. Some of these rulers, like Mohamad Ali who actually came from Albania, were de facto kings. The British had always had their eyes on Egypt both because of the need to protect the Suez Canal and their desire to construct a Cape to Cairo railway. As for the French, they were joint financiers of the canal. So in 1882 an Anglo-French fleet seized military control of Egypt. This was ratified and legalized in 1914 when a protectorate was declared. Strictly speaking, therefore, Egypt was not a colony, but it was under the control of the British and the French. Egypt was granted independence in 1922, but for all practical purposes remained a protectorate with a puppet king in charge. In 1952, the then puppet king, Farouk, was overthrown by the military under General Naguib and Colonel Nasser. Libya had also been part of the Ottoman Empire. The Italians seized it in 1931. The Italians lost World War II and the territory, of course, and the country was divided into a British zone and French zone. The British and the French were therefore "protectors" of the protectorate Libya. The British zone consisted of Cyrenaica and Tripolitania and they recognized

Idriss al-Sanussi as the Emir of Cyrenaica, another puppet figure. In 1949 the United Nations, which was generally responsible for countries controlled by the defeated powers, established the independence of Libya with Idris al-Sanussi as King. However, in 1966 Idris was overthrown and killed in a coup led by Colonel Muamar al-Guaddafi. Tunisia also came within the ambit of the Ottoman Empire and was ruled by a bey when the French invaded in 1882. Before this (in 1869) the bey had been forced to submit to an Anglo-French-Italian supervision of the country's finances. In 1956 the French recognized the country's right to independence and this was granted with the bey as king. The bey was deposed in 1957 and Habib Bourguiba was elected president. Morocco was not actually part of the Ottoman Empire although the Turks were influential there. It was ruled by a sultan. In the twentieth century the French took upon themselves the right to supervise the country's finances and in 1912 they declared the country a French protectorate, but the sultan was still in office, a puppet king, so to speak. Following agitation which was led by the sultan himself, the French decided to depose the sultan. It was a grave mistake because the nationalists raised an army and restored the sultan to power. The French were forced to recognize the independence of Morocco in 1956. Probably because the sultan was himself the focus of nationalist opposition to the French, the monarchy has survived to this day. As for Sudan, after the 1898 defeat of the Mahdi who had inflicted a humiliating defeat on British forces under General Gordon in 1885, Sudan was jointly administered by Britain and Egypt. It was called the Anglo-Egyptian Sudan. Eventually, Egypt wanted Sudan to be united with it, but the British were opposed to this. So Sudan got its own constitution and independence in 1956.

Sub-Saharan countries and independence

The first sub-Saharan country to achieve its independence was Ghana (the then Gold Coast) under its charismatic leader in 1957. Both Nkrumah and Ghana have therefore become iconic in the story of the drive by African countries for independence. As we have seen, Nkrumah was very active in the Pan-African movement. He was the joint organizer of the highly influential congress of 1945 and he was inspired by people like Marcus Garvey and W. E. B. Du Bois. He was also very much in touch with all the other leaders like George Padmore, Jomo Kenyatta, C. L. R. James, and I. T. A. Wallace Johnson. He had been educated at American universities, and on his return to Ghana joined the teaching profession. When the United Gold Coast Convention was formed in 1947, he was invited to be its secretary. This was Nkrumah's chance. It provided an opportunity to set about the task of realizing the aims of the Pan-African movement. Indeed, Nkrumah would become the most ardent proponent of Pan-Africanism and African unity within the African continent. When, in 1948, some ex-servicemen demonstrated peacefully in Accra against the high cost of living, police opened fire on them, and the British government who now saw Nkrumah as an agitator suspected that he was behind the demonstration. They arrested him and sent him and some of the other leaders of his party to prison for several months (Shillington, 421). When, as a consequence of the demonstration, the British government was forced to change the 1946 constitution, Nkrumah recognized the power of the demonstration and the power of mass action. On his release, therefore, he formed his own party, the famous Convention People's Party (CPP). The difference between the CPP and the others that had preceded was that it was truly a party that mobilized the masses. Nkrumah would never have succeeded if he had not had the support of the masses, including market women and laborers. But his appeal was a threat to the British government who re-arrested him and imprisoned him once more. However, when an election was held in 1951 in which universal adult suffrage was used, Nkrumah contested as a candidate though he was in prison, and his party won a resounding victory. The British government was forced to release him and name him "Leader of Government Business." He was the one who led Ghana to independence as prime minister in 1957.

Other African countries learnt some very valuable lessons from Ghana's and Nkrumah's experience. One of the most important was singlemindedness in pursuit of the goal of independence. Nothing short of independence would do. Nkrumah, who was fond of using biblical language, once paraphrased a saying from the Bible and declared, "Seek ye first the political kingdom and all other things will be added unto you." Another lesson was the importance of getting the undiluted support of the masses. Mass political movements with the goal of independence sprang up over most of Africa, particularly in the British colonies, in places like Tanganyika, Uganda, Nyasaland, Northern and Southern Rhodesia, and, of course, Nigeria. In some cases, unfortunately, some of these mass parties did not embrace the entire country because of ancient ethnic rivalries. A mass party at times became identified with one ethnic group. This was the case with Nigeria and partly accounts for the fact that Nigeria gained its independence after Ghana. The Nigerian leaders, people like Nnamdi Azikwe, Obafemi Awolowo, and the Sardauna of Sokoto, were brilliant and, in a sense, their parties were well organized. But each party drew its mass support from one particular region or ethnic group. Thus Obafemi Awolowo's Action Group was largely the party of the Yorubas from the west; Nnamdi Azikwe's National Council of Nigeria and the Cameroon (NCNC) largely drew its support from the Igbos in the east; and the Sardauna of Sokoto's Northern People's Party (NPP) was largely supported by the Hausas and the north. It proved difficult for these leaders to become united for a common purpose and to work out a system that would bring the whole of Nigeria into freedom under one leader. In other words, the task of creating a whole independent nation out of these various entities, each with its own independent traditions, proved difficult. In a sense, the problem had been created by the imperialists who should never have forced all these entities into one country. In the end, a federal system was designed, with each region retaining some autonomy under a premier, and with a federal national government under a prime minister, with limited powers. There was still the issue of who would lead the federal government. Eventually, a northerner, Alhaji Abubakar Tafawa Balewa, became prime minister of the whole country since his party, the Northern People's Party, had the largest number of seats in the federal assembly and the northern people were the largest in population. An alliance was worked out between the Northern People's Party and Azikwe's NCNC whereby Azikwe eventually became a ceremonial president of the Republic of Nigeria, while Tafewa Balewa was prime minister. Obafemi Awolowo's Action Group and the west were left out in the cold and had to be content with being the opposition. All this was to give rise to tremendous problems later. The march to independence was afoot though. Nigeria gained its independence in 1960, and Tanganyika, and Uganda followed. Sierra Leone got its independence in 1961.

Independence and the French territories

The agitation for independence and freedom was not as strident in the French territories as it was in the British ones. This was largely due to the French administrative policy of assimilation whereby the leaders of the people, through their education and training, had become very much associated with France and were not imbued with the spirit of rebellion and the need for detachment that prevailed in the Anglophone countries. Some of them were members of the French Assembly and at least one was a member of the French cabinet. Although in the forties and early fifties the French still had the vision of a vast French community of civilized peoples, the Francophone countries could not be isolated from the vigorous drive for African liberation. As we have seen, some French-speaking Africans in France had been associated with the Pan-African movement (Williams, 179). There was also dissatisfaction among Francophone leaders in the French Assembly who suspected that they were not considered the equals of the other members of the Assembly and therefore not really regarded as being French. They had begun to think of their countries as self-governing and autonomous entities. The problem was that the leaders of the Francophone countries could not agree among themselves about the nature of the future relationship among them, which would then enable them to negotiate with France in order to determine the nature of the future relationship with France. All this came to a head when General De Gaulle took over the leadership of France in 1958. Unlike former French leaders, he was not committed to the idea of one grand French entity of civilized nations. He had been quite sympathetic to African countries in the French Empire largely because many of them had sent troops to help France fight in the war against Germany. At a Free French conference held in Brazzaville in 1944 he had promised a new deal for Francophone countries (Shillington, 416). He now became quite frustrated over the bickering among the Francophone leaders, and he took the world by surprise when he decided to give Francophone countries an ultimatum. A referendum would be held in each country, and there would be one choice on the ballot: either (a) independence and autonomy, but with continuing links with France and membership of a French community (rather like the British Commonwealth); or (b) a total and utter break with France. Each individual would vote "*Oui*" or "*Non*" to choice (a). A "*Non*" vote would mean a complete break with France. All but one of the Francophone countries voted in favor of independence but with continuing links with France. That country was Guinea, whose leader Sekou Toure had come under the influence of the Soviets and was a Marxist. In revenge, the French left Guinea taking everything they could carry, including the country's telephones. Guinea was left completely destitute. It had to begin almost all over again and it had no choice but to intensify its Marxist orientation and turn to the Soviet Union. In some ways, the other countries benefited from the continuing link with France. Their currency the CFA was still tied to the French franc, which ensured financial stability and gave some protection against the economic malaise which soon started plaguing the Anglophone countries. Also, the fact that France reserved the right of military intervention either in cases of external attack or internal commotion meant that for a while there was greater political stability. To this day, there is a greater relationship between France and her former colonies in Africa than between Britain and hers.

The settler territories

The struggle for independence was most acrimonious in the so-called settler territories. These were the countries where the imperialist occupiers had encouraged millions of their own people to settle and make a home. These countries included Algeria, Kenya, Southern Rhodesia, and South Africa. The pleasant and equable climate in these areas made European settlers especially welcome. They found environments which were, in some cases, much better than the ones they had left behind in Europe, especially those millions who had not done very well for themselves in Europe. French men and women flocked to Algeria and British flocked to the pleasant highlands of Kenya and to Southern Rhodesia and South Africa. The Boers had started going to South Africa from the seventeenth century and they claimed that they had a better right to the land in certain parts of the country because they got there before indigenous people like the Zulus. West and Equatorial Africa were spared this European invasion because of the heat and a little insect, the mosquito, which put off European settlers even after the discovery of quinine. In the new country the settlers had a much more comfortable life than they could have dreamt of in their home countries. Land was taken away from the Africans and given to them to enable them to become prosperous farmers, and some of them found their fortunes in the mines. Generally, they became the ruling class and looked down on the native Africans who in many cases became their servants or were segregated and forced to live in the worst areas in the most appalling conditions. However, with the rising tide of universal adult suffrage and independence, there was the real possibility that these black people or people of color would now become the rulers and masters of the country and many of the settlers might have to leave. The settlers would not have it, and so they resisted as strongly as they could.

The resistance by the native Algerians to French imperialism began in 1954. It was led by a well-organized movement called the Front Liberation Nationale, or FLN. Soon there were bloody incidents in which many were killed. The French, who at this time had not the least intention of granting independence or leaving Algeria, responded by sending thousands of French troops to put down the revolution. By 1958 there were about half a million French troops in Algeria (Shillington, 426). But the revolution could not be crushed. The turning point came in that same year when De Gaulle assumed power in France. He decided to go with the prevailing wind and give independence to Algeria, but the French in Algeria resisted. Many of them had been born there and that was their only home. They could also not tolerate the idea of native Algerians being in charge of government and wanted to remain a part of France. The war now took a different turn with French Algerians fighting French soldiers and it became very bloody indeed. At one stage an attempt was made by the French Algerians to assassinate President De Gaulle. It failed, and in the end the liberation movement and De Gaulle won. Algeria became independent in 1962 with the FLN leader, Ben Bella, as president.

The situation was almost as bloody in Kenya. The settlers there had taken the best land from the native Africans and were largely farmers, rearers of cattle and sheep, and growers of tea and coffee. They were extremely prosperous and had no intention of leaving. They were also the ruling class, the enablers of the administration. The resistance was led by the redoubtable Jomo Kenyatta, a leading figure in the Pan-African movement who had been the publisher of *Negro World* during his days in London. Kenyatta formed a movement called the Mau Mau movement, which was a secret society whose members took an oath to resist the British and reclaim their country by whatever means was necessary. They took to the forest, resorted to guerilla warfare, and became a much-dreaded force. A large number of the British were killed, and the administration responded by killing thousands of Kenyans whom they accused of either being Mau Mau themselves or supporters of the Mau Mau. They imprisoned thousands more, some of whom they tortured in an effort to get them to confess that they had taken the oath. The British Conservative government in London was, at first, opposed to the liberation struggle and wished to preserve the status quo. I can recall one of the leading newspapers denouncing Kenyatta when he was put on trial and suggesting that he was preaching "a calculated hymn of hate." Kenyatta was imprisoned and the carnage went on. It became fashionable to kill Africans on the slightest suspicion that they were supporters of the Mau Mau. In the end, the British government realized that Kenya, too, would have to be freed. Kenyatta was released from prison, and when the party which he formed, the Kenya African National Union (KANU), won elections, he became prime minister and ultimately the first president of Kenya.

The situation in Southern Rhodesia was complicated by racism and segregation as it was in South Africa. Southern Rhodesia, which had been supervised by a company set up by Cecil Rhodes, was largely ruled by white settlers who, though numerous, formed a very small percentage of the population. The Shona and the Ndebele were the major African ethnic groups. The white settlers were extremely prosperous, had the best land which they had taken away from Africans, and treated the Africans like dirt. Southern Rhodesia, though part of the British Empire, was hardly regarded as a colony; it was completely autonomous. To strengthen their political and economic domination, the Rhodesian settlers proposed to the British government that a federation be formed that would encompass Southern Rhodesia, Northern Rhodesia, and Nyasaland. However, the Africans in Nyasaland and Northern Rhodesia protested strongly against the proposed federation. The problem was that, while Southern Rhodesia was almost directly British, Nyasaland and Northern Rhodesia were only protectorates, and joining the federation would diminish their legal status. Also, there were fewer settlers in these countries than in Southern Rhodesia and the Africans therefore did not wish to come under the predominantly white domination that existed in Southern Rhodesia. However, in spite of the growing protest and unrest in Nyasaland and Northern Rhodesia, the British pushed the federation through in 1953. This gave rise to more protests and the rise of the real liberation movement. The leaders of the liberation movement at this time were very weak, however, and their movements were banned. New leaders now came to the fore in the persons of Kenneth Kaunda in Northern Rhodesia and Hastings Banda in Nyasaland. Kenneth Kaunda formed a mass party, the United National Independence party (UNIP), and Hastings Banda, who had studied medicine at Edinburgh and was practicing in Scotland, returned to Nyasaland to lead the liberation movement, called the Malawi Congress Party. Eventually the British had to cave in and Kenneth Kaunda became another freedom fighter whom the British first imprisoned, but later released to eventually become a head of government. Nyasaland and Northern Rhodesia became independent in 1964. Northern Rhodesia changed its name to Zambia and Nyasaland to Malawi.

The situation continued to be very dire, however, in Southern Rhodesia where the settlers were determined to cling to power. However, they attracted the world's antagonism and even the British government itself, under the Labour prime minister Harold Wilson, turned against them, determined to grant majority rule to the Africans. Sanctions were imposed by various bodies and countries, but the settlers were adamant. Their leader, Ian Smith, even made a unilateral declaration of independence (UDI) in 1965, severing the ties with Britain, and thereby incurring more sanctions. The liberation movement in Southern Rhodesia was called the Zimbabwe African National Union (ZANU), and it escalated its resistance to the Smith regime, resulting in skirmishes and some bloodshed. However, the resistance movement was comparatively weak. It had a rival, the Zimbabwe African People's Union (ZAPU), and the rivalry made things worse.

Eventually, ZANU got a new leader, Robert Mugabe, who was not only able to mobilize his supporters and wage a more effective guerilla campaign against the Smith regime, but was also able to get heavy support from outside bodies such as Marxist liberation movements from Mozambique and Angola, and this made all the difference. The Smith regime was forced to cave in and an agreement was reached in London in 1979 which stipulated the holding of free elections followed by the eventual independence of the country. The elections were held in 1980 and Robert Mugabe's ZANU won a resounding victory. Southern Rhodesia became independent as Zimbabwe in 1980 with Robert Mugabe as its first prime minister and eventual president.

Although South Africa had been granted independence by the British as far back as 1910, it was not really until 1994, when Nelson Mandela became its first black president, that it could really be said to have achieved independence. Most blacks were denied the vote before this, and the country was ruled by a white minority, although blacks outnumbered whites by five to one. It was a completely autonomous, self-governing country, whose prime minister regularly attended meetings of the prime ministers of the white independent Commonwealth countries. There were racist regimes in one or two other parts of Africa, such as Southern Rhodesia, but the difference between these and South Africa was that racism and racial segregation were institutionalized. It was part of the country's legal structure, and it was called apartheid. One might even say that this system of discrimination was enshrined in the constitution of 1910 which allocated only 7 percent of the land to blacks while most of the remaining land was reserved for the whites. In 1948, the system of apartheid really got going when the racist, Boer-dominated National Party won the elections and its leader, Dr. Malan, became prime minister. People were designated by law as whites, non-whites, blacks, and coloreds; blacks were banned from appearing in certain areas; pass laws were passed requiring blacks to produce passes when so required; sexual relations between people of different race were banned. It was a most egregious and hateful situation. Later, the so-called Bantustans were established in which Africans would live separately from the whites. The Bantustans were horrible and few Africans were in favor of them. Inevitably, the situation gave rise to serious resistance. The main resistance movement in South Africa, the African National Congress (ANC), was actually founded as far back as 1912. The leaders at the time were much less vocal than later leaders would become, largely because they believed that the government would be persuaded to see reason. This hope proved futile. In 1943 the youth wing of the ANC decided on a more aggressive approach. The leaders were Nelson Mandela and Oliver Tambo. In the meantime other resistance movements emerged, like the Pan-Africanist Congress which organized a demonstration in a town called Sharpeville to protest against the pass law. The government responded by ruthlessly opening fire on innocent demonstrators and 70 people were killed. The incident has since been called the Sharpeville massacre. In 1963 the main leaders of the ANC, including Nelson Mandela, were arrested and Mandela was sentenced to life imprisonment. Oliver Tambo took over the leadership of the ANC and went into exile. In the end, South Africa incurred the hatred of the world. Various countries imposed crippling sanctions. This would hit where it hurt most, because at this time South Africa was incontestably the economic powerhouse of Africa. Even the United States, which at one time was sympathetic to the South African government, was forced to impose sanctions, and the divestment movement gained strength. This involved companies in the United States that had investments in South Africa, "divesting," that is, withdrawing their investments. The world also responded by giving awards of various kinds to leaders of the protest movement, like Chief Albert Luthuli and Archbishop Desmond Tutu who were both awarded the Nobel Prize for Peace. The South African resistance which had gone underground also received military and financial help from a number of sources, including countries like Mozambique and Angola. Eventually, the sanctions and the effective guerilla effort took their toll and South Africa was forced to the negotiating table. Nelson Mandela was released in 1990, and after four years of negotiations, an agreement was reached which made provision for universal adult suffrage and the holding of free and fair elections. In the elections that followed Nelson Mandela and his ANC won handily and Mandela became the first black president of a really independent South Africa.

The Belgian Congo

The Belgians Congo's drive towards independence illustrates the continuing duplicity and capacity for exploitation characteristic of the Belgian administration of the Congo, even though the country had been taken away from King Leopold II, and the Belgian government was now in charge. The Belgians still wanted to retain the rich resources of one of the largest countries in the world and they therefore had no intention to allow it to become independent. Indeed, according to scholars like Shillington (439), they deliberately kept the Congolese people isolated from the trends sweeping throughout Africa by refusing to expand educational facilities. No attention was paid to higher education. Indeed, it is thought that at the time of actual independence there were no more than four African graduates in the Congo. The Belgians governed the Congo directly and, unlike the other colonial powers, they took no steps, however minimal, to prepare the people for a possible participation in government. There was no legislative council on which Africans were represented and no African-run newspapers. There were no Africans in the senior positions of the civil service. The most educated Africans were low cadre teachers, clerks, and shopkeepers.

However, the continental tide could not be stemmed and the few people with some education started making political demands and holding rallies. At the same time, political parties began to emerge. Unfortunately, the political parties reflected the ethnic tensions and rivalries characteristic of this vast country. This would prove the bane of the Congo for the foreseeable future. Kasavubu formed the Bakongo Cultural alliance (ABAKO), drawing support from the Bakongo people; Moise Tshombe formed the CONAKAT, drawing support mainly from the people of Katanga; and Patrice Lumumba formed the Movement Nationale Congolais, drawing support mainly from his own home area. These three leaders regarded each other with jealousy and even hatred, and could never come together with a common purpose. A pivotal event at this time was Lumumba's participation in an All African People's conference in Ghana in 1958. Ghana had just received its independence from Britain in 1957 and its charismatic leader, Kwame Nkrukmah, was a beacon of inspiration to other Africans. Lumumba returned determined to hasten the move towards total independence and when his party held rallies that deteriorated into riots he was thrown in prison on charges of incitement to violence. The Belgian government, realizing that something had to be done to prevent anarchy, summoned the leading Congolese politicians to a conference in Belgium in January 1960. Quite astonishingly, instead of mapping out a plan for the move towards independence, the Belgian government offered the Africans independence immediately. This was in itself a recipe for disaster seeing that there had been no preparation for independence and the leading politicians were most inexperienced. Furthermore, there were ethnic tensions to be resolved. Some scholars believe that the Belgian government panicked because it did not want an Algeria-type revolution on its hands. Others, like Ludo de Witte, suggest that the Belgian government's action was a deliberate and calculated move to prevent the politicians from adopting a more radical agenda, like leaning towards the Soviet Union. Granting independence in 1960 would mean that Belgium would still be influential in so far as the exploitation of the Congo's rich resources was concerned. They could manipulate and control Lumumba and the others and ensure that the Congo government did not fall into the wrong hands. This latter view has been backed by historical research.

The Congo gained its independence on June 30, 1960. At the independence ceremony the Belgian king made an arrogant and completely misguided speech, hailing King Leopold II as a visionary hero and genius, and referring to Belgium's civilizing mission in the Congo. It seemed as though this was almost calculated to invoke the wrath of genuine Congolese nationalists, and Patrice Lumumba, who had become prime minister with Kasavubu as president, roundly condemned the speech as well as Belgium's brutality during the days of occupation. This annoyed the Belgian king and some Western observers, and from that day on they were determined to get rid of Patrice Lumumba. The problem was complicated by the fact that Lumumba was a Marxist with leanings towards the Soviet Union. His orientation was solidified when the Belgians, in revenge for his condemnatory speech, left the country taking almost everything with them, as the French had done in Guinea. Lumumba had no choice but to be more responsive to Soviet advances. The Belgians and the USA now decided to use the ancient ethnic rivalry among the Congolese tribes to get their revenge and get rid of Lumumba. They encouraged and endorsed Tshombe's decision to declare Katanga independent and make that enclave secede from the Congo. The country was thrown into chaos and there was virtual civil war. Lumumba appealed to the United Nations for help in protecting the territorial integrity of his country, but that body was dominated by the USA and Western powers like Britain who hated Lumumba and wanted him gone, so the UN did nothing. The problem was that the Cold War was going on, and the West was not prepared to allow a vast and potentially rich country in the heart of Africa like the Congo to fall within the Soviet ambit. Eventually, the CIA, with support from hostile Congolese like Moise Tshombe and Kasavubu, engineered the assassination of Patrice Lumumba. The result was that the Congo was plunged into even further chaos which continues to this day.

The Portuguese territories and independence

The Portuguese territories in Africa were among the last to gain their independence. This was because the Portuguese were resolute in their determination not to even consider independence. Moreover, Portugal, at the time, was ruled by a fascist dictator, General Salazar, whose word in Portugal was law. The result was that vigorous and powerful liberation movements sprang up in all the Portuguese territories, determined to win independence by force, if necessary. Moreover, all these movements were strongly supported by the Soviet Union and were Marxist in orientation. In Guinea Bissau and Cape Verde, Amilcar Cabral formed the Partido Africano da Independência da Guiné e Cabo Verde (PAIGC); in oil-rich Angola Agostino Neto founded the Movimento Popular de Libertação de Angola (MPLA); and in Mozambique Eduardo Mondlane founded the Frente de Libertação de Moçambique (FRELIMO). When Mondlane was assassinated in 1969, Samura Machel assumed the leadership of FRELIMO. Since these movements were supported by the Soviet Union they were powerfully armed and were therefore able to wage strenuous guerilla war against the Portuguese. It was not until Salazar's removal from office in 1974 that independence became a reality. All the three countries gained their independence in 1975.

References and suggestions for further reading

Beinart, W. 2001. *Twentieth Century South Africa*. 2nd edition. Oxford: Oxford University Press.

Birmingham, D. 1995. *The Decolonization of Africa*. Athens, OH: Ohio University Press.

Birmingham, D. 1998. *Kwame Nkrumah: The Father of African Nationalism*. Athens, OH: Ohio University Press.

Davidson, B. 1978. *Let Freedom Come: Africa in Modern History*. Boston: Little, Brown.

De Witte, L. 2001. *The Assassination of Lumumba*. Trans. A. Wright and R. Fenby. London: Verso.

Digre, B. 1990. *Imperialism's New Clothes: The Repartition of Tropical Africa, 1914–1919*. New York: Peter Lang.

Esedebe, O. 1982. *Pan-Africanism: The Idea and Movement*. Washington, DC: Howard University Press.

Freund, B. *The Making of Contemporary Africa: The Development of African Society since 1800*. Bloomington, IN: Indiana University Press.

Geis, I. 1972. *The Pan-African Movement: A History of Pan-Africanism in America, Europe and Africa*. New York: Africana.

Hargraves, J. 1988. *Decolonization in Africa*. London: Longman.

Kanza, T. 1972. *Conflict in the Congo: The Rise and Fall of Lumumba*. London: Penguin.

Malopba, W. O. 1993. *Mau Mau and Kenya*. Bloomington, IN: Indiana University Press.

Manning, P. 1998. *Francophone Sub-Saharan Africa, 1880–1995*. 2nd edition. Cambridge: Cambridge University Press.

Martin, T. 1982. *The Pan-African Connection: From Slavery to Garvey and beyond*. Cambridge, MA: Schenkman.

Mazrui, A. and M. Tidy. 1984. *Nationalism and New States in Africa: From about 1935 to the Present*. London: Heinemann.

Nelson, S. 1994. *Colonialism in the Congo Basin, 1880–1940*. Athens, OH: Ohio University Press.

Nkrumah, K. 1963. *Africa Must Unite*. New York: International.

Ofuatey-Kodgoe, W. (ed.). 1987. *Pan-Africanism: New Directions in Strategy*. New York: New York University Press.

Padmore, George. 1971. *Pan-Africanism and Communism*. Garden City, NY: Doubleday.

Rodney, Walter. 1967. *How Europe Underdeveloped Africa*. Dar-es-Salaam: Oxford University Press.

Ross, R, Mager, A. K. and Nasson, B. 2011. *The Cambridge History of South Africa. Vol. 2: 1885–1994*. Cambridge: Cambridge University Press.

Sampson, A. 1999. *Mandela: The Authorised Biography*. London: HarperCollins.

Williams, M. 2005. "The Pan-African Movement." Pp. 173–186 in M. Azevedo (ed.), *Africana Studies*. Durham, NC: Carolina Academic Press.

5 African politics

This chapter will examine the nature of governance and the political structures that existed in Africa up to the achievement of independence by African countries and the structures that have been in existence since then. It will be concerned with the arrangements that were made and the systems that existed for the governance of states and countries.

Political organization up to imperialism

Let us remind ourselves about the formation of settlements and, subsequently, states. Settlements arose when man moved from the hunter-gatherer stage to that of purposive agriculture, since agriculture required settled communities. Once settlements arose there was the need to regulate relations among the members, hence laws and rudimentary forms of governance also developed. At this stage the structures that were used in Africa were lineage and kinship. In other words, members related to each other regulated relations among themselves and ensured the maintenance of order and discipline. The kin or lineage group could be as big as a clan, embracing the entire village or town, as long as all the members could trace their ancestry in some way to a common ancestor. Centralized bureaucracies were rare. This was the situation until about 2500 years ago in sub-Saharan Africa. Of course, countries to the north, like Egypt, had evolved centralized bureaucratic state systems long before this.

The emergence of centralized states and kingdoms paralleled economic development. Surpluses resulted in trade, not only within communities, but also among neighboring and even long-distance communities. There was therefore a need to control not only trade, but also the trade routes. To do this, more centralized organization was needed, and so states emerged. As the states gradually developed, certain lineages, and the leaders of those lineages, gained superiority either because of their wealth or their numbers, and so kings, ruling families, and kingdoms emerged. But these centralized states still retained kinship-based social organization, and there was a kinship-based superstructure. One had to belong to a certain lineage or certain lineages to qualify for the kingship. Indeed, we do know that even after colonization there were certain states that had no kings and were not centralized. The Igbos of Eastern Nigeria are an excellent example of this. In one of the most famous episodes of Chinua Achebe's *Things Fall Apart* the newly arrived white missionaries ask the people in the Umuofia community for their king, and the people reply that they have no king; they only have priests and elders. They still retained kinship and lineage as the main method of ensuring justice, progress, and stability. These were the so-called "stateless societies."

DOI: 10.4324/9781003111733-6

The first states in Africa were in Egypt and in Kush. Later there was Axum, which is roughly equivalent to the modern Ethiopia. This was the situation right up to the first millennium BCE. Afterwards, Carthage, equivalent to the modern Tunisia, arose around the first millennium BCE. It was a very powerful state on the Mediterranean whose people were called Phoenicians and were experts at shipbuilding. It is particularly notable for fighting a memorable war with Rome in which its famous general, Hannibal, almost brought Rome to its knees by crossing the Alps with his elephants and approaching Rome from the north. Then came the kingdoms along the Senegal River like Tekur established about 2000 years ago, round about the start of the first millennium CE. Later arose the great West African empires already mentioned: Ghana, Mali, and Songhay. There were others like Kanem (modern Chad), Bornu in Northern Nigeria, and Mossi. Some of these were emirates ruled by emirs.

All these states were all centralized states whose rulers, including the emirs, were supreme. We do know that, in the case of Egypt, the pharaoh was revered as a god. His word was law even though he ruled with the help of ministers or advisers. Rulers like Sundiata were absolute monarchs, so political activity consisted in jockeying among the ministers, advisers, and others in similar positions for the attention or favor of the king. Although the monarch was absolute, he nevertheless had to listen to the advice of his ministers or the governors of his provinces. In some cases these constituted a council that would discuss issues before the king took a final decision. In a few cases, also, there were secret mechanisms for removing the king should he become too cruel. We do know of quite a few kings, like Askiya Muhammad of Songhay, who were deposed. In these centralized states there was no opposition, formal or informal, though there was discussion until something like a consensus was arrived at. In the stateless societies, decision-making was based on discussion among elders or members of councils until consensus was reached. As one Cameroonian proverb puts it, "we talk until we are one." In some of the stateless societies decision-making took the form of summoning all the males in a community to meetings. The issues would then be discussed and decisions taken by consensus. Achebe's novel *Things Fall Apart* illustrates this perfectly in a scene where the Igbo community of Umuofia summons a meeting of the males to decide whether or not to go to war with a rival clan. It is interesting to note that this was precisely how Greek communities in Athens, which is supposed to be the home of democracy, took decisions. In all these states there was no opposition and there was no concept of taking decisions by majority vote. This was the situation right up to the start of imperialism in the later nineteenth century. It can be seen that the Europeans came to a situation where there were structures that worked. In a sense, the imperialists destroyed some of the structures that they found.

Political organization under imperialism

Let us now look at governance and political organization in Africa under imperialism. As we have seen, the colonial powers never intended to grant self-government or independence to their colonies, so there was never any real preparation for those aspects of governance. Apart from the armed resistance to imperialist occupation which went on with various levels of intensity throughout the period of colonial occupation, there was never any real sign of what we have come to regard as political activity during the early phase of colonial rule. As we have seen, the British mainly used the system of indirect rule, which meant making use of traditional rulers in local government. This generally happened in the centralized states where there were already viable central systems of government. The British used these systems because the task of administration was made much easier by using the traditional chiefs and rulers. The traditional rulers were used to collect taxes, recruit labor, communicate the wishes of the colonial government to the people, and generally help in maintaining order. In the stateless societies where there were no traditional rulers, the British even went to the extent of appointing so-called "warrant chiefs." Since these did not have the mystique of traditional rulers, they did not always have the total support or respect of the people, but they still did what the British expected of them. The use of the traditional rulers in some levels of government meant that customary law and traditional culture were left intact, more or less, since the chiefs who presided over them were knowledgeable. Still, there was no doubt that the British were in charge and the traditional rulers were little more than their agents.

The French still clung to their ideal of assimilating all their colonial subjects into one vast French cultural entity with the full rights of French citizenship and representation in the French National Assembly. In practice, this inevitably proved impossible and only a small fraction could be "assimilated." The vast majority of French subjects had to be governed as subjects on the spot. The French broke up each of their colonies into smaller units. At the head of each country was a French governor and various French officials were in charge of smaller units. The French, like the British, also used local "chiefs" in the lower levels of local government, but unlike the British system, these chiefs were appointed by the French; they were not traditional chiefs and therefore lacked traditional mystique. They were little better than minor black French officials who carried out the orders of the French government and could be dismissed at will. The appointment of chiefs who were not traditional and therefore not steeped in customary law and culture inevitably led to the erosion of these aspects of traditional society in the French colonies.

In the British territories there was a governor at the head, representing the British government and responsible for carrying out the colonial policies of the British government, in so far as that territory was concerned. Senior British officials were in charge of the various departments such as Education, Health, Finance, Agriculture, and Works. They were later called "directors" and they formed what came to be called the executive council with the governor at its head. They actually formulated and executed policies. When legislative councils came into being, these officials also constituted the majority of the legislative council that was responsible for passing laws for the territory. Later, a handful of indigenous people were added to the legislative council, but these were generally appointed by the governor and were mostly traditional chiefs. The system was designed to ensure that the British were in charge, and a similar system existed in the French territories.

Real political activity in most African colonial states started in the period between the two world wars and was largely coterminous with the gradually rising tide of agitation against colonial rule and the emergence of African nationalism associated with other movements like the Pan-African movement. By the start of World War I pacification had largely come to an end and, although there was continuing armed resistance in various parts of the continent, Africans were beginning to come to terms with the reality of colonialism. But, with the failure of the armed resistance, they were also beginning to consider how eventually to overthrow it. There was growing agitation and workers were beginning to form unions and stage strikes. Africans were also beginning to form self-help associations and protesting against local injustices (Shillington, 403). With the introduction of Western-style education, largely by the missionaries, there was a growing cadre of educated clergymen, teachers, clerks, traders, and interpreters who were becoming increasingly conscious of the implications of imperialism: the injustices and evils that were being perpetrated, the arrogant dominance of the European imperialists, and their own exclusion from participation in the governance of their own countries. These constituted a growing conscious elite that was also becoming aware of the aims and aspirations of the Pan-African movement. In the French territories the concept of "negritude" was gaining strength. This was a movement in both French Africa and the French African diaspora that was dedicated to establishing the autonomy and the value of black people. It was mainly cultural and philosophical, but it also had political objectives as well, and one of its leaders was Leopold Senghor, one of the "assimilated" individuals who would later represent Senegal in the French National Assembly and would eventually become Senegal's first president.

It was precisely this growing elite that formed the bulk of the membership of the political movements that emerged between the two world wars. They were the focus of organized opposition to colonial authority and could therefore be said to be engaged in political activity. Their ranks were reinforced by professionals, and they were led by these professionals, people like lawyers and doctors, who were themselves largely missionary educated or Western educated. Even though some of these movements included universal adult suffrage among their long-term objectives, they were not, at this stage, calling for independence, nor were they by any means mass parties. They were mostly interested in the amelioration of the condition of people like themselves. These movements included the Tanganyika African Association (TAA), established in 1929, and the National Congress of British West Africa, NCBWA, founded in 1919 by John Casely-Hayford, a Cambridge-educated Gold Coast barrister. The NCBWA was a West African, not just a Gold Coast movement. It called for equal employment and promotion opportunities for both Africans and Europeans in the civil service at a time when the senior positions in the civil service were held only by British people, even though some of the Africans in the service were more qualified. It also called for higher educational opportunities for Africans and a clearer separation of the judiciary from the colonial administration (Nyang'oro, 165). Apart from promoting heightened awareness of the issues, these intra-war movements did not achieve much because their methods, membership, and goals were limited, and their leaders did not really have much contact with the masses. After Casely-Hayford's death the NCBWA fell apart.

Really intensive and intentional political activity in Africa emerged during and after World War II with the rise of a new breed of African leaders, like Kwame Nkrumah, Obafemi Awolowo, Nnamdi Azikwe, Jomo Kenyatta, Tom Mboya, Sekou Toure, and Kenneth Kaunda. Some of these new leaders, like Nkrumah and Kenyatta, had been very active in the Pan-African movement; some had been educated, not by missionaries or in prestigious British universities, but in the United States; some like Mboya and Toure were leaders of the trade-union movement. They had all arisen from the masses and had the ability to mobilize and organize the masses. Their parties were therefore mass political parties, and they were calling for outright independence. Indeed, some of the older breed of leaders despised the new breed. For instance, J. B. Danquah of the then Gold Coast was quite hostile to Nkrumah and his Convention People's Party, and H. C. Bankole Bright of Sierra Leone's National Council despised Milton Margai's Sierra Leone People's Party. They looked on the new leaders as upstarts. However, it is these new leaders who would lead their countries to independence.

Shortly after the war the British government began to introduce consultative forms of government and allow some local people to be elected to the legislative councils. But the franchise was still limited and the few Africans so elected were members of the elite. The British still continued to be in charge. However, with the rising tide of nationalism and the clamor for independence, the British were forced to extend the franchise and hold elections that brought Africans into the majority, with the new leaders eclipsing the old breed of leaders and becoming chief ministers and ultimately prime ministers of soon-to-be independent countries. The French, at this stage, were determined to keep their colonies as members of a vast French civilization or state. However, even they were forced to introduce reforms when the increasingly disgruntled African delegates to the French National Assembly formed a political party in 1946 called the Rassemblement Democratique Africain (RDA), led by Felix Houphouet-Boigny. In 1956 they introduced further reforms which established self-government and fully elected councils for most of their territories (Shillington, 424). The drive towards independence was under way. As we have seen the process was concluded by General De Gaulle.

The political legacy of imperialism

All African countries achieved independence under a constitution largely written by the colonial power but with both parties acceding. It was a constitution that was supposed to enable the country to achieve full development and take its rightful place in the modern world. The colonial powers simply assumed that the political system that would best do this was one rather like that operating in their own countries: liberal democracy involving political pluralism. Not much thought was given to whether the system would work in an entirely different environment with people of a different culture, different worldview, different history, and having different attitudes. It was simply assumed that this was the best system. There was even evidence that the system was not working as it was supposed to do in certain parts of the Western world. After all, France itself had just been through a period of political paralysis and military humiliation, partly due to the multiplicity of political parties that led to the emergence of General De Gaulle as a kind of dictator. Nevertheless, the system was still thought to be best for the emerging African nations and little thought was given to alternatives. The cynical might say that the relevant colonial power devised a system that would enable it to retain a hold on the African country, continue its manipulation of the economy in its favor, and ensure that the country continued its ideological leanings towards the West. This was almost certainly part of the calculation.

In the former British territories, the constitution always provided for universal adult suffrage, free elections, the formation of as many political parties as were desired, and political competition. After the elections, the party that won the majority of seats in the parliament formed the government with its leader as executive prime minister. Members of the majority party chosen by the prime minister became ministers of government and formed the cabinet with the prime minister at its head. The leader of the party with the next highest number of votes, usually the party that lost the election, would become leader of the opposition. Decisions would be taken and laws passed by majority vote in parliament, which meant that the will of the party in power always prevailed. The Queen was, in theory, still the ceremonial head of state, and she was represented in the country by a governor-general normally chosen on the recommendation of the government of the country concerned. This was the system known as the Westminster model because it was practically the system that obtained in Britain. The system devised for the former French colonies was also almost the same as that in effect in France. Political parties were free to operate and each nominated a candidate for the presidency. The candidate who won became president and executive head of government with the right to choose ministers belonging to his own party. Usually he was supported by a party that had the majority in parliament. There may or may not be a prime minister, but the president was head of government and head of state. All the former French territories, with the exception of Guinea, belonged to the French community just as the former British colonies belonged to the British Commonwealth with the Queen as its head. However, the relationship among the members of the Commonwealth was much looser than that between France and her former colonies. France still retained certain rights and privileges that exist up to this day.

Let us also look at some of the institutions inherited from the colonial situation at independence. The first was the rule of law. Whatever one might say about the imperialists and their oppression of the African people, one has to admit that as far as relations among individuals were concerned the rule of law prevailed, and this was handed over to the African governments at independence. The rule of law is certainly one of the bastions of democracy. Ordinary citizens must have the assurance that if for some reason they fall foul of the government, they can have a fair and unbiased hearing in the court system. In other words, the constitution and the laws must protect the citizens and their rights. This was certainly the case at independence. I can remember an episode in Sierra Leone shortly before independence when a local politician actually took the British governor to court, and the case was fairly heard. In other words, the judiciary was independent and there was a clear distinction between the executive and the judiciary, a distinction that is necessary for democracy. The police force was also independent and there was little of the corruption that became typical later. The press was also active and operated freely. Indeed, the press had been very active during the drive to independence and in the days leading to independence as it supported the concept of self-determination and cast its fortunes with one political party or the other. There was also a fairly efficient and honest civil service. Once it became clear that the colonial territories had to be granted self-determination, some of the imperialist powers, like the British, did their best to prepare the local people to shoulder the responsibilities. This was particularly true of the civil service. The British began to select qualified local people and place them in positions where they would get the training necessary for the positions they would hold in the civil service of an independent country, positions like permanent secretaries and officials in the foreign service. This ensured integrity and efficiency in the civil service at the dawn of independence. The military was also disciplined and independent of politics. In British West Africa at that time it was called the West African Frontier Force, and there were battalions in each British West African territory. In other words, at the time of independence quite a few of the institutions necessary for the effective working of democracy were in place.

There were downsides to this system inherited from the Western powers. In the first place almost everything, including matters of tremendous national interest, was decided by majority vote, where the majority could, at times, be quite wrong. This was in direct contrast to the traditional African system where it had been customary to take decisions by consensus, decisions that everyone would then adhere to, precisely because it represented the will of the people as a whole and not just one segment of the people. In the traditional system, as we have seen, there could, at the start, be quite a variety of opinions or ideas as to what steps should be taken, but as a result of thorough discussion and even argument, a solution was arrived at that everyone or almost everyone could support. The system of government and opposition inherited from the West at independence meant that in most cases the opposition felt it had to say or suggest the opposite of what the government was suggesting and oppose the government's proposals, even if these were reasonable. The opposition was therefore at risk of adopting strange or unreasonable ideas and opposing some that might be quite reasonable. Of course, this happens even today in some Western democracies where all the members of the opposition feel they must oppose everything the government says and does, and they do it as though they have been programmed to do so, and with hardly a dissenting voice. All this must have sounded strange to many Africans.

The concepts of political pluralism and political competition might sound attractive and civilized on the surface. However, political competition means that the "winner takes all." This results, at times, in very significant parts of the population being excluded from the business of government for considerable periods and from meaningful participation in the decision-making that would affect their lives for years to come. They could always hope, as is the case in the Western world, that they would be the winners in the next election, but in most of Africa this seldom happened, and the results were disastrous.

With regard to the issue of political pluralism and the formation of political parties, it is very important to remember that in Africa, both before and after independence, political parties tended to be associated with ethnic groups, and people's primary loyalties were to their ethnic group or tribe rather than to the nation. If an ethnic group that was in the majority formed a political party, it meant that that party and that group would be in the majority in parliament and form the government for the foreseeable future and the other groups would be in opposition and be excluded from government. This was a recipe for disaster. The idea of the majority party forming the government also meant that some of the most able and qualified people in the country were excluded from participation in government because they belonged to the opposition and not to the governing majority party. This was catastrophic in some areas where there was a shortage of qualified people.

There were other challenges to the smooth operation in Africa of the inherited democratic system. Up to the time of the institution of a measure of self-government, what the new leaders and their people had experienced as far as governance was concerned was essentially an authoritarian system. The colonial governor was completely in charge even though he had an executive council that executed policies. He was the one who was solely answerable to the colonial government in Europe. There was no representative or consultative government. If one goes further back to the traditional African past and the days before imperialism, one finds that, with the exception of the stateless societies, most of Africa was governed by authoritarian emperors or kings, even though these potentates might have had councils and advisers. Some of them might have been benign; others were ruthless. In other words, the models that the new leaders had, in both the imperialist and the pre-imperialist eras, leaned more towards authoritarian rule than democratic or representative or consultative forms of governance. The new leaders had witnessed the governor's authoritarian rule. They had experienced attempts by the governor and his advisers to crush resistance by military force if necessary. They had experienced at first hand the ambience of the governor with all its majesty, panoply, and splendor. They had also heard of a similar ambience surrounding the African traditional rulers. It is not surprising that they also yearned to behave like governors or like traditional kings. In other words, there was inevitably a tension, in the new states, between authoritarian leanings and the new democratic templates that the new constitutions introduced.

Another challenge relates to the abilities of the people who were now called upon to be leaders, such as ministers of government, and therefore to execute the demands of the new democratic constitution. The level of education that many of them had received was not particularly high. This was partly the result of European colonial education policy. As we have seen it was not the policy of the colonial powers to educate their colonial subjects to the point where they could run the government themselves or man the higher levels of the civil service. The colonial educational system was designed to produce a small "elite" that would man the lower levels of the civil service. It produced clerks, clergymen, small business owners, some teachers, and traders. These were precisely the cadre of people who provided leadership for the new mass parties that led their countries to independence. It was this lower cadre of leaders who now formed governments in many parts of Africa and were the ministers and ambassadors to foreign countries. Most of them had no experience of administration, let alone of government. Yet they were expected to navigate their way through complex issues of national development and foreign transactions.

Rise of discontent after independence

At the dawn of independence there was tremendous optimism about Africa's future. In almost every country there was the expectation that the leaders would be true to their word and deliver the fruits of independence. After all, Nkrumah had declared, "seek ye first the political kingdom and all other things will be added unto you." The political kingdom had been achieved, and now the people expected that the government would deliver on promises of higher education and health facilities, adequate electricity and water supply, adequate infrastructure, adequate housing, full employment, and so on. In order to achieve all these, huge financial resources and qualified manpower, including knowledgeable planning teams, were needed. Both were in short supply. The financial returns that some countries expected from their natural resources did not always materialize because of all kinds of factors, many of which were beyond the control of the government. Manpower was available but had to be trained, sometimes at enormous cost. There was a lot of good will towards Africa at independence, and aid was coming from some countries and international agencies. However, the aid money sometimes went towards the wrong projects or into the wrong pockets. The result was that most of the independent African countries were slow in achieving their aspirations, and dissent, frustration, and disappointment set in among the general population. Various protest groups, like those organized by students, teachers, and workers, began to emerge. Governments felt their positions threatened and realized that unless something was done, they would lose their hold on power. They would certainly be voted out of office at the next election, and they did not want that. The solution they found to the impasse was the one–party system.

The one–party system and its justification

By the end of the 1960s and throughout the 1970s the one-party system was the dominant political structure in most of Africa. This meant that the democratic template inherited from the colonial powers had been completely abandoned. The only two countries where it can be said quite categorically that the system never existed were Botswana and The Gambia. African leaders gave some very interesting reasons for the move away from political pluralism to the one-party system. Firstly, they claimed that the idea of a "loyal opposition" was unknown in Africa and alien to the African temperament. In referring to the "loyal opposition" they were mocking the concept which operated in the British Parliament where the opposition was sometimes referred to as "Her Majesty's loyal opposition." The term implied that although the opposition was expected to criticize the government, it did so peacefully and with the utmost propriety; it never resorted to violence and it certainly did not seek to subvert the government. In fact, it was "loyal" not only to the Queen, who was head of state, but to all the country's institutions. And it was a formal and recognized opposition with its leader holding a position recognized and sanctioned by the state. This concept seemed ridiculous to many Africans. Countries in traditional Africa had never had a formal opposition. The people opposed to the king or state had been regarded as rebels who had tried to subvert the state. There had been differences of opinion, but these had been generally resolved in open discussion until a consensus was achieved. Besides, the African leaders argued, a formal opposition could always be used by hostile foreigners to undermine the state and its leadership. Furthermore, having an opposition was a tremendous waste of human resources in a situation where there was a shortage of qualified manpower and where all the resources of the country needed to be harnessed for the purpose of development. The qualified people in the opposition party or parties should be collaborating with the government in promoting development.

Secondly, African leaders claimed that the multi-party system was an obstacle to the all-important task of creating national unity. Most of these countries consisted of several ethnic groups or tribes, and individuals demonstrated greater loyalty to their tribe than to the state that had been established at independence. Some of these ethnic groups were, in fact, nations with populations running to several millions. African leaders were very conscious of recent events such as Katangas's attempt to break away from the Democratic Republic of the Congo and Biafra's to break away from the Nigerian Federation. These two groups were regarded by some as "nations" whose members owed greater loyalty to the Katanga or Igbo tribe or area rather than to the Congo or Nigeria. There was a need to fuse all these tribes or nations into a viable state. This was essential for development. It did not escape the attention of leaders that most of the areas threatening to secede or break away contained the most valuable resources of their countries. In a situation where political parties were identified with ethnic groups, it would be easy for a disgruntled tribal political party to engineer the secession of its particular ethnic group, and this would be disastrous. The creation of national unity was a top priority, and a multi-party system would hinder that process through the activities of parties that might collaborate with hostile foreigners and undermine the state or encourage secession and thus jeopardize development and the state's territorial integrity.

African leaders also argued that multi-party elections were wasteful of much needed financial resources and were also likely be violent and thus pose a threat to the nation's security. It is true that African election candidates spent a lot of money to overcome their opponents and secure election. Most of the money was spent, not in advertising or traveling around the constituency, but in hiring groups of armed supporters, who were thugs in reality. The moment an individual declared his candidacy in the pre-one-party environment, his first act was usually to employ a large body of thugs whose task it was to intimidate opponents and their supporters by any means necessary. Election campaigns mostly consisted, not of rallies, but of various sets of thugs fighting each other. In many cases this resulted in several deaths. The thugs had not only to be paid for their services but fed as well throughout the election campaign.

Of course, there were other reasons that African leaders could not, and did not, mention. Most of these leaders were not wealthy by any standards when they were elected to parliament and became ministers of government. Some had been clerks, low-level teachers, traders, small business owners, and so on. On becoming ministers their new salaries were phenomenal, several times greater than what they previously earned. Besides, some of them were able to make much more than their salaries through graft and corruption. Their lifestyle was now incomparably better. Some of them had been able to build mansions and owned several cars in addition to the official flag-bearing car, usually a Mercedes Benz, with an official chauffeur. They were highly respected, and they were able to give lavish parties and send their children to expensive schools, at times overseas. And, of course, the laws that regulated the lives of ordinary citizens did not always apply to them.

These new ministers also presided over the elaborate system of patronage or "clientelism" as it was called. In return for political support, they performed all kinds of favors for their relatives, friends, and members of their constituencies. They were the ones to go through if one wanted access to the corridors of power. They were the ones whose help one had to enlist if one wanted a scholarship for one's child, if one was aspiring to become a member of a corporation board, like the electricity commission, or the water board, or the income tax commission. They could be helpful if one needed a business license or if one wanted the monopoly for importing certain commodities, and they could also intercede with the police or even the judiciary if one got involved in illegal activities. They therefore automatically became extremely important people in the community. All this would be lost if their party lost a multi-party election.

Some of these leaders, like Agostino Neto of Angola, Sekou Toure of Guinea, and Samora Machel of Mozambique, were Marxist in orientation anyway, and the one-party system had always been a necessary corollary to Marxism. They therefore had an automatic argument for moving towards the one-party system. Finally, as already indicated, the growing frustration in many African countries led to agitation by groups like trade unions, student organizations, and teachers' organizations. All of these were now hostile to the governments concerned, as were some religious groups. If these groups threw their support behind an opposing party in a multi-party election, the government would almost certainly lose the election, and this, as far as the new leaders were concerned, would be disastrous. Thus it was that, from the late 1960s, most African countries moved towards the establishment of one-party systems and centralized state control.

Transition to the one-party system

What process did they use in order to achieve this? They gave the appearance of going according to the constitution. In most cases, the government held a referendum asking the people to say whether a one-party system should be instituted. In every case the people apparently voted in favor of a one-party system, but it was quite clear that the referendum had been rigged. The percentage of people who apparently voted in favor was always in excess of 90 percent. Emboldened by the referendum result, the government would then change the constitution to allow for the existence of only one party. If the country was not already a republic, the constitution was also changed to establish a republic, with a president as head of state. This was done in order to further weaken the influence of the former colonial power, particularly in the former British territories. The government sensed that there would be antagonism in Britain to the institution of a one-party system. There was also the complication that, at this time, the judicial systems of all the former British territories were still linked to that of Britain, in the sense that the British House of Lords was still the highest court of appeal for the former British territories, as it was in Britain. It was therefore possible for the citizens of a country that had declared a one-party system to appeal to the House of Lords which might uphold the appeal and block the one-party system. To avoid this, these African countries severed the links between their judicial systems and that of Britain, establishing a supreme court as the highest court of appeal in their countries. The African governments also passed laws banning all other parties apart from the single established party, usually the party which was in power and formed the government. Those individuals who retained their membership of banned parties or declared their adherence to such parties were thrown into prison. Some were even murdered. Although few opposition politicians were actually forced to join the single party, it was made quite clear to them that they would have to live in the political wilderness, have no access to the corridors of power, and be excluded from the system of patronage if they did not. In other words, they would be reduced to being nonentities. In a few cases, some of the leaders of the rival parties were quietly absorbed into the dominant single party and offered compensatory ministries or other high-level jobs. This happened in Sierra Leone, for instance, where the All People's Congress became the single party and absorbed the leader of the SLPP opposition, Salia Jusu Sheriff, offering him the Ministry of Education. By the end of the 1970s the transition to the one-party system was complete.

Nature and effects of the one-party system

Let us now look at the nature and effects of the one-party system. At election, only the single party could put up candidates. In many countries, there was only one candidate per constituency, the single-party candidate. There was also only one candidate for the presidency, and that candidate, usually the sitting president himself, unwaveringly received almost 100 percent of the vote. In some countries, like Sierra Leone, two or more candidates per constituency were allowed to stand, but they all belonged to the same single party. In other words, the voters were given some kind of choice, but the choice was based, not on ideology, policies, or principles, but on the personalities and characters of the candidates. Even so, the candidate the government wanted to win usually did so, as the votes were rigged anyway. Here is a hilarious example of how the rigging usually worked. Three candidates in one of the constituencies in Sierra Leone were competing for the seat. However, the government had a preference for one of the candidates and was determined to secure his election. At the time, to ensure that voters voted for the candidate of their choice even if they were illiterate and could not read names, the photographs of the candidates were displayed on the ballot boxes, and the voters simply put their ballot into the box of their preferred candidate. In this case the ballot boxes were in the process of being transferred to the central counting station for the counting of the votes. However, the government had given instructions to the soldiers accompanying the boxes to remove most of the ballots from the boxes of two candidates and place them into the ballot box of the third, the preferred candidate of the government, to ensure that he would win the election. The preferred candidate was bald, and the soldiers' instruction was that they should place almost all the votes into the bald candidate's box. Unfortunately, one of the other two candidates was also bald, and the soldiers opened the boxes and placed most of the ballots into the box of the other bald candidate; he was therefore the one who won the election. He was himself the most surprised person when it was announced that he had won the election. This incident also illustrates the fact that under the one-party system elections were a farce.

A major consequence of the one-party system was that it led to the consolidation of the position and power of the president. There being no possibility of another candidate being put up by a rival party to threaten his re-election, the president was sure of re-election almost indefinitely. Some of them even became presidents for life. There were no checks and balances on his actions. His position was secure as long as his party wanted him, and no one from his party ever rose to challenge him because no one wanted to incur his displeasure, since they were all hoping for positions in the government or other positions such as ambassadors or directors or board members of important corporations. The president had the absolute right to choose ministers, heads of departments, heads of universities, the head of the police, and the head of the military, the justices of the supreme court and so on. Some felt they had the power of life and death over their citizens, for they could contrive, and in some cases actually did contrive, the false accusation, arrest, trial, and conviction of those who opposed them. Presidents in Africa came to feel that they were above the law or could dictate the laws. Thus, the one-party system encouraged the rise of dictatorships in many African countries.

The one-party system meant that patronage was concentrated in the hands of the single party. One had to be a member of the party or connected to a prominent member in order to get a good job or a scholarship for oneself or one's children, or licenses to operate certain businesses. This inevitably meant the marginalization of individuals or groups that could not support the party. In most cases, these individuals were among the best in the country. The party extended its influence to every sphere of activity and every sector of society: the civil service, the universities, the student organizations, and the media. This meant the politicization of the police force, the military, and the judiciary. It also meant a total lack of accountability at all levels. If one was a member of the party one could avoid being charged for crimes or misdemeanors; or one could easily get a judgment in one's favor. The lack of accountability started at the top, the presidency, and permeated downwards. But perhaps the most unfortunate effect of the one-party system was that a whole generation of young people grew up without knowing that there could be dissent, or that there could be two sides to a question. They grew up, in other words, without knowing about the power, nature, and effect of debate. They became accustomed to a situation where everyone literally toed the party line.

The one party-system inevitably led to the enhancement of the power and condition of the military. The absence of free and fair elections, the decline of the economy, and the curtailment of freedom in general that were characteristic of most one-party states, meant that there was tremendous frustration and anger among the citizens, and the governments therefore felt it necessary to keep the populace in check. In order to do this, they needed the support of the army, so they went out of their way to ensure that the army was satisfied and well provided for. While the majority of the people were starving and deprived, the army had all the food it wanted at low cost. While the vast majority of the people lived in inadequate housing, the army had reasonable quarters. The army also received their pay on time while almost every other sector of the population had to wait for their pay for weeks, in some cases. The leaders of the army were feted by the government and in areas where there was an abundance of precious stones and other minerals, as in Sierra Leone, leaders of the army were permitted to own their own mining plots and engage in illicit mining. Some African countries spent as much as 42 percent of their budget on the military. In spite of this pampering, the military had little to do. There were hardly any foreign armies to fight, so the main task of the army was to maintain order domestically. However, African leaders would soon come to regret their pampering of the military.

The military's rise to power in Africa: military coups

It is now common knowledge that from the mid-1960s Africa was ravaged by military coups. The first coup in sub-Saharan Africa was in Togo in 1963. One of the most notable coups in Africa happened in Ghana in February 1966 with the overthrow of Kwame Nkrumah. Nkrumah had been an icon of the African liberation movement. He was the first leader in sub-Saharan Africa to wage a successful struggle for independence against a major colonial power and he led his country to freedom. Other African leaders lionized and looked up to him. The rest of the world had its eyes on Ghana to see what an African country would make of independence. Nkrumah had been a champion of the Pan-African movement and was the most outspoken advocate in Africa of the concept of African unity. Indeed, he and two other leaders, President Tubman of Liberia and Emperor Haile Selassie of Ethiopia, were mostly responsible for the establishment of the Organization of African Unity in 1963. His removal from office in a coup while he was on a foreign visit was therefore earth-shattering. However, the great promise that Nkrumah and his party held out had not materialized. The economy had declined considerably, due largely to a fall in the price of cacao, Ghana's major export, a decline over which Ghana had little control and which was partly engineered by Western powers who had become disillusioned with Nkrumah and his leftist ideas. But Nkrumah had also established a one-party system within which he himself had developed into an authoritarian dictator. His word was law and his opponents were sometimes brutally treated. One of his names was "Osagyefo," which means he was regarded as being almost god-like. Though he had been a leader with tremendous vision, and he had done some great things for Ghana, his overthrow was not surprising. Another notable coup was that in Nigeria in January 1966. In fact, in 1966 alone there were no less than four coups in Africa. After these coups others followed in Africa with astonishing rapidity, and some are even occurring in the present day. What were the causes of these coups?

The most obvious cause was that the military coup was the only means of removing a leader and a government that had become extremely unpopular because they were corrupt, incompetent, and brutal. With the abandonment of free and fair elections, these leaders could not be removed by the ballot box. There was therefore no accountability and the governments became even more corrupt and brutal. Only the military had the power and the means to remove them. In some cases, the military had become so important that the government itself realized it was a threat to be regarded with some suspicion. The military leader would then stage a coup as a pre-emptive strike to prevent the government from removing him. This was almost certainly the reason for Idi Amin's successful coup against Milton Obote of Uganda in 1971. As we have seen, the military in most countries was pampered by the government; in fact, it was the force that maintained order in the country and kept the government in power. It was, de facto, the most powerful institution in the country, so it must have occurred to the military leaders that they might as well take over the government as well.

Table 5.1 Number and type of military coups in African countries, 1960–2012.

Year	Successful	Failed / Attempt
1960	1 (DRC)	1 (Ethiopia)
1961		1 (Somalia)
1662		1 (Senegal)
1963	3 (Togo, Congo, Benin)	1 (DRC)
1964		4 (Ghana, Tanzania, Gabon, DRC)
1965	5 (Benin, Algeria, DRC, Benin, Benin)	1 (Burundi)
1966	8 (CAR, Nigeria, Uganda, Ghana, Burkina Faso, Burundi, Nigeria, Burundi)	2 (Togo, Sudan)
1967	3 (Togo, Sierra Leone, Benin)	1 (Ghana)
1968	3 (Sierra Leone, Congo, Mali)	
1969	4 (Libya, Sudan, Somalia, Benin)	
1970		3 (Congo, Togo, Guinea)
1971	1 (Uganda)	4 (Sierra Leone, Uganda, Sudan, Chad)
1972	3 (Ghana, Madagascar, Benin)	2 (Congo, Benin)
1973	2 (Swaziland, Rwanda)	1 (Côte d'Ivoire)
1974	3 (Burkina Faso, Niger, Ethiopia)	5 (Uganda, Uganda, Angola, CAR, Madagascar)
1975	2 (Chad, Nigeria)	3 (Benin, Sudan, Mozambique)
1976	1 (Burundi)	6 (CAR, Nigeria, Niger, Uganda, Mali, Sudan)
1977	1 (Seychelles)	6 (Benin, Sudan, Congo, Chad, Angola, Uganda)
1978	3 (Comoros, Ghana, Mauritania)	3 (Mali, Somalia, Sudan)
1979	3 (Ghana, Equatorial Guinea, CAR)	2 (Chad, Ghana)
1980	5 (Mauritania, Liberia, Uganda, Guinea Bissau, Burkina Faso)	1 (Zambia)
1981	2 (CAR, Ghana)	4 (Mauritania, Equatorial Guinea, Liberia, Gambia)
1982	1 (Burkina Faso)	5 (Mauritania, CAR, Zimbabwe, Kenya, Ghana)
1983	2 (Burkina Faso, Nigeria)	5 (Equatorial Guinea, Liberia, Ghana, Cameroon, Niger)
1984	2 (Guinea, Mauritania)	2 (Ghana, Cameroon)
1985	3 (Sudan, Uganda, Nigeria)	3 (Liberia, Guinea, Liberia)
1986	1 (Lesotho)	1 (Equatorial Guinea)
1987	2 (Burundi, Burkina Faso)	2 (Sierra Leone, Comoros)
1988		1 (Uganda)
1989	2 (Sudan, Comoros)	1 (Ethiopia)
1990	1 (Chad)	2 (Nigeria, Zambia)
1991	2 (Mali, Lesotho)	4 (Djibouti, Togo, Chad, Togo)

(Continued)

Table 5.1 (Cont.)

Year	Successful	Failed/Attempt
1992	2 (Sierra Leone, Algeria)	3 (Burundi, Benin, Comoros)
1993	1 (Nigeria)	2 (Guinea Bissau, Burundi)
1994	1 (Gambia)	2 (Burundi, Liberia)
1995		3 (Sao Tome & Principe, Comoros, Sierra Leone)
1996	3 (Sierra Leone, Niger, Burundi)	3 (Guinea, CAR, Sierra Leone)
1997	1 (Sierra Leone)	1 (Zambia)
1998		1 (Guinea Bissau)
1999	3 (Niger, Comoros, Côte d'Ivoire)	
2000		3 (Comoros, Sierra Leone, Côte d'Ivoire)
2001	1 (DRC)	5 (Côte d'Ivoire, Burundi, CAR, Burundi, Comoros)
2002	1 (Côte d'Ivoire)	
2003	3 (CAR, São Tomé & Príncipe, Guinea-Bissau)	1 (Mauritania)
2004		4 (DRC, Chad, DRC, Equatorial Guinea)
2005	1 (Mauritania)	
2006	1 (Chad)	2 (Madagascar, Côte d'Ivoire)
2008	2 (Mauritania, Guinea)	
2009		1 (Madagascar)
2010	1 (Niger)	2 (Guinea-Bissau, Madagascar)
2011		3 (DRC, Niger, Guinea-Bissau)
2012	2 (Mali, Guinea-Bissau)	

Source: Barka and Ncube. 2012. Political Fragility in Africa: Are Military Coups d'Etat a Never-Ending Phenomenon?

This suggests that the motives of most of the military leaders who staged coups were far from being altruistic. There were, of course, solid reasons to justify the removal of the leaders who had coups staged against them. In almost every case, the government was incompetent and corrupt, and the economy was in free fall. Something had to be done, but this was not the reason for the coups d'état. Military leaders staged coups mostly to protect themselves or to realize their own political or economic ambitions. And so the coups happened with astonishing regularity. Between 1952 (when the first African coup was staged in Egypt by Colonel Abdel Nasser and General Neguib against King Farouk) and 1984 there were 70 successful coups in Africa (Gordon, 79). At any one time during the 1980s, 65 percent of Africa's peoples and well over half of its states were under military administration (Decalo, 547–548). Some countries had several coups. Sierra Leone had about five, Liberia had at least three, and Nigeria had many more than that. Indeed, for more than a generation, both Ghana and Nigeria had only one brief period of civilian rule sandwiched between much longer periods of military dictatorship. At first, the people welcomed the coups because they were sick of corrupt and incompetent governments. Most of them were also living in extreme poverty and privation and were desperate for a change. They therefore saw the military as deliverers and their intervention as a godsend. This was certainly the case in places like Sierra Leone, Ghana, Nigeria, Zaire (the Democratic Republic of the Congo), Ethiopia, and Liberia. However, they would soon be disillusioned.

Military intervention solved absolutely nothing. In fact, in some cases it made matters much worse. The economy continued to deteriorate under the military who were just as, if not more, corrupt than the civilians, largely because there was even less accountability. General Mobutu of the Democratic Republic of the Congo, for instance, treated that country as his personal property and became enormously rich in consequence. The political situation did not improve either. These military regimes were absolute autocratic regimes that made no pretense about ruling with the people's consent and will. The autocratic civilian regimes had at least gone through the motions of getting the consent of totally submissive legislatures; the military regimes ruled by decree. The first act of military leaders after taking power was usually to suspend the constitution and abolish the legislature. They gave orders and the people obeyed because the military were pointing their guns at them. In most cases, the orders were misguided and not properly thought out. To an even less extent than the civilian leaders, the military who took over had no experience of administration, or of the complexities of economic or international matters. Indeed, the level of ignorance among the members of the military who formed governments was monumental and most of them refused to listen to whatever advice they received. They were arrogant wielders of the power of the gun. Since the leaders of the military under civilian administrations had largely been in collusion with the governments, the members of the military who took over belonged, at times, to the lower levels of the army hierarchy. Given the qualifications that were required for entry into the army in Africa in those days, some of them inevitably had very little education. For instance, the coup in Liberia in 1980 was led by Master Sergeant Doe, who was barely literate. That in Sierra Leone in 1992 was led by Captain Valentine Strasser. Idi Amin, who took over in Uganda in 1971, was barely literate also.

Government brutality in Africa was also even worse under the military regimes. One of the first acts of some of the new military governments was to execute their predecessors. In Liberia, for instance, Master Sergeant Doe executed all the members of the previous government of President Tolbert without due process. Some reports state that the ministers were stripped down to their underpants, made to play soccer on the beach with a coconut for a soccer ball, and then tied to stakes before being shot to death. When Captain Jerry Rawlings took over in Ghana in 1979, he also executed three former leaders of military governments: Lieutenant General Afrifa, General Acheampong, and Lieutenant General Akuffo. Civilians were also executed by military governments on trumped-up charges, without due process.

There are those who are prepared to argue that not all the military or dictatorial rulers in Africa were worthless. Some of them genuinely had the interest of the country at heart, saw that the country needed to move in a new direction, and were determined to do everything in their power to effect this. Rawlings, for instance, who took over twice in Ghana, instilled a much-needed discipline on his country and was largely responsible for the turn in Ghana's economic fortunes which has continued to this day. General Murtala Muhammed who took over from General Gowon in Nigeria in 1975 was highly respected within and outside Nigeria and was credited with restoring a moral compass to a nation that had been plagued by corruption and brutality and introducing some much-needed reforms. Some people even talk of "benevolent dictatorships," referring to those leaders who, though ruling autocratically and dispensing with the forms of democracy, imposed discipline and order, improved the country's economic fortunes, and were genuinely concerned with the welfare of the ordinary man or woman. Such leaders, however, were very few and far between.

Civil wars

Africa has been ravaged, not only by military coups, but also by civil wars. Countries where civil wars have occurred include Nigeria, Sierra Leone, Liberia, Côte d'Ivoire, Sudan, South Sudan, Angola, the Democratic Republic of the Congo, Mozambique, Somalia, the Central African Republic, Chad, and Djibouti. This list is by no means exhaustive. Some of these wars, like those in Somalia and the Central African Republic, are still going on. Indeed, it can be said that the Democratic Republic of the Congo has been plagued by a civil war ever since independence in 1960. What are the causes of these civil wars?

Some of the civil wars were caused by ethnic or tribal tensions, which are themselves part of the colonial legacy. We have seen how, at the Berlin Conference, the European powers partitioned Africa without regard for the boundaries between tribes and nations. Nations that had long been separate were hounded together into one state, and whole nations were divided up among several countries. This was the case in Nigeria where the Hausas, the Yorubas, the Igbos, and other tribes were put together into the country that became Nigeria. Both before and after independence there was a struggle for dominance among the ethnic groups. At independence federal power largely fell into the hands of the northern Hausas, the largest ethnic group. This was bound to embitter other groups, even though the country was divided into states with each ethnic group being dominant in its own state. The Hausas in the north became bitterly antagonistic towards the Igbos in the east after the first Nigerian coup in 1966, because the coup had largely been led by Igbos and the man who became head of state in the new military regime was an Igbo. The Hausas suspected the Igbos of being behind the coup in which the Hausa prime minister of the federation, Sir Abu Bakarr Tafawa Balewa, and the premier of the north, the formidable and influential emir of Sokoto, had both been killed. The result was disturbances in which Igbos living in the north were massacred. The Igbo east then seceded from the federation, thus precipitating the brutal Nigerian civil war, otherwise known as the Biafran War, in which millions lost their lives.

Ethnic tensions were also behind the civil war in Rwanda which also involved one of the worst genocides in Africa, although in this case the ethnic differences were exacerbated by issues of class. The major difference between the Hutu and the Tutsi was not so much of ethnicity as of class. From time immemorial the Tutsis regarded themselves as superior to the majority Hutu. Indeed the word Hutu originally meant "peasant," while Tutsi was associated with wealth and status (Shillington, 444). The Belgian colonialists, who were administering the country on behalf of the United Nations, reinforced this division by encouraging the belief in Tutsi superiority and giving preference to the Tutsi in all matters including educational opportunities and government positions. By independence, however, it was clear that power had to be given to the majority Hutu who had their own political party. Several Tutsis fled into exile and they and their descendants invaded the country under Paul Kagame in 1993. When it became clear that the Hutu president was prepared to negotiate with them, more militant Hutus, who had formed a secret society vowing to eliminate all Tutsis, assassinated him by shooting down his plane, and thus began what has become known as the Rwanda genocide.

Civil wars in the Horn of Africa have been caused by the Somalis, who were divided up and found themselves in about four countries after the Berlin Conference, trying to regain their nationhood. To do so, those in Eritrea had to rise up against the government of that country, and those in Ethiopia had to do the same.

The abuse and monopolization of political power was certainly a major cause of the civil wars in Africa. The fact that the military dictators had absolute power, as did leaders in one-party states, meant that there was a lack of freedom and accountability and the people had no means of redress. Where there were elections, as in Uganda, Sierra Leone, and Liberia, they were fraudulent and rigged, and the people had no real choice. So the same authoritarian leaders remained in power. Some were removed by military coups. In some cases, however, the grip of the authoritarian regime was so strong that there had to be a resort to civil war. Quite often, the civil war was started by exiles, with the support of some outside forces. The exiles were in a position to advocate for outside support and to raise the funds and the armaments necessary for a successful military venture. The civil war in Sierra Leone, for instance, was launched by exiles in Liberia, some of whom had been trained in Gaddafi's Libya, and they were largely supported by Charles Taylor, who had just come into power through a similar civil war in Liberia. The civil war in Rwanda was similarly started by exiles, and the war in Uganda that resulted in the ousting of General Idi Amin was the result of a collaboration between exiles and President Nyerere of Tanzania who masterminded the invasion.

Quite often, the civil war was not motivated by an altruistic desire to rid the country of a ruthless and corrupt regime and give back freedom to the people; it was caused by a blatant desire for power and, more importantly, by the need to control and exploit the country's valuable mineral resources. In Sierra Leone, for instance, it soon became clear that the main issue in the war was who would control the nation's diamond-mining industry. Foday Sankoh, the rebel leader, might have started out with idealistic ideas about getting rid of the corrupt Momoh administration, but he soon became caught up in a scramble for possession of the nation's rich diamond fields. He and his movement were supported by Charles Taylor, the then Liberian leader who had been promised his own share of the diamond booty. In the Nigerian civil war, oil was an extremely important factor, although there were other major causes. Nigeria was then, and still is, one of the world's most important producers of oil, from which a substantial percentage of the country's revenue derives. But the oil deposits were largely in the east, which was dominated by the Igbos, and so the east could never be allowed to secede and walk away with a substantial proportion of the nation's revenue. The control of oil resources also played an important role in the civil war in the Sudan. The government was dominated by people from the north, with leanings to the Middle East and the Arabs, but the oil resources lay largely in the south. However, the people in the south felt they were being poorly treated although the country's main source of revenue came from their area. Of course, the strife between the north and the south had been going in one form or the other ever since independence in the 1950s, but it was largely enhanced by the discovery of oil. In the end the south succeeded in their bid to secede because, as part of the treaty that ended the war, they were allowed to secede and form their own state of South Sudan in 2011.

Religion is often a cause of civil war. The conflict could be between Christians and Muslims, or between rival sects of the same religion, like Islam. Religion certainly played a major role in the conflict in the Sudan. The north, which dominated the government, was predominantly Muslim with ties to the Middle East and the Arabs, while the south was predominantly Christian and black. The Dafur catastrophe resulted when the government, in response to disturbances, sent Muslim "Arab" militias, backed by government air power, to attack Dafur. These militias were known as the "Janjaweed." The activities of the "Janjaweed," which some people saw as amounting to ethnic cleansing or genocide, resulted in the displacement of about 100,000 people who mainly fled to neighboring Chad. Most of the civil conflicts in North Africa had religion at their base. The brutal civil war in Algeria, which started in 1991, was caused by the refusal of some sectors of the country, including the political elite, to accept the success of a Muslim fundamentalist party, the FIS, in the elections held that year. A similar situation currently exists in Egypt.

Of course, greed on the part of leaders and the general decline in the economic situation have been major causes of civil wars. This was the case in Sierra Leone and Liberia, where the political elite exploited the country's resources for their own benefit while the rest of the population languished in poverty and privation; it was certainly the case in the Democratic Republic of the Congo where President Mobutu treated the country as his own mere property and practically seized the revenues from the exploitation of the country's resources. In some countries, the resulting youth unemployment led to large numbers of young people becoming radicalized and joining rebel groups. Sometimes they went out of the country to join these groups or to explore the radical ideas that were being spawned. Numbers of unemployed high school and college graduates from Sierra Leone, for instance, found their way to Libya where they came under the influence of supporters of President Gaddafi who had published his *Green Book*.

Finally, differences in ideology played a part in fomenting civil wars. This was particularly true of countries where the leaders, even before independence, had leanings towards Marxism or communism. In Angola, for instance, Agostino Neto, who became the first president after independence, had always been a Marxist. At independence he tried to steer the country in a Marxist direction, but he was opposed, and had always been opposed, by others like Jonas Savimbi who adhered to more liberal economic and political doctrines and were supported by the United States and South Africa. The result was civil conflict.

It must be noted that these civil conflicts led to great humanitarian problems as hundreds of thousands of refugees were displaced and had to flee from their homes to other countries, thus placing a tremendous strain on the host country's infrastructure and economic base. Thousands fled from the civil war in Liberia to neighboring Sierra Leone. Similar numbers fled from Sierra Leone to Guinea and the Gambia. About 100,000 fled from Dafur to neighboring Chad. The problem of displaced persons is one of the major problems still facing the continent of Africa.

End of authoritarian rule

An end did come to this bleak period of authoritarian rule in Africa. With the beginning of the 1990s it became obvious that most of Africa was no longer prepared to tolerate military rule or authoritarianism. The main catalyst precipitating change was the collapse of the economy of most African countries. There was massive unemployment, massive inflation, massive decline in the value of currencies, and massive decline in exports. All this was largely due to the incompetence of governments, and it was therefore easy for new protest groups to emerge. This time the protest groups would not be silenced. With economies in decline, many African governments were forced to apply to bodies like the International Monetary Fund and the World Bank for assistance, largely in the form of loans. These bodies demanded political reform as a condition for their assistance. They argued that it was incompetence, caused largely or nurtured by the nature of the political system, that was responsible for the malaise. Lending money without a reform of the system would be taking a great risk. Most of the African countries had no choice but to accept this condition. Another important factor was the fall of the Berlin Wall in 1989 and the subsequent fall of communism in all the Eastern European Marxist states. These countries had been bastions of one-party authoritarian rule. The Soviet Union itself, the chief bastion of authoritarianism, collapsed and its constituent members moved away from totalitarianism. Authoritarianism and one-party rule were breaking down all over the world, and Africa was not left behind. Even states that had not come under military rule, like Zambia and Malawi, were forced to accept political reform. Great external pressure was thus brought to bear on African countries, and, with the new decade of the 1990s, there was a rapid move towards democratization in almost all of Africa. Comparatively free elections based once more on the multi-party system were soon held in Ghana, Sierra Leone, Angola, Zambia, Malawi, and so on, and in some cases, leaders who had been popular at one time and had even led their countries to independence, like Kenneth Kaunda of Zambia, were swept out of office by the ballot box. In some cases a military leader simply converted himself into a civilian and contested the elections. It did not really matter, since he had to contest the elections in a new democratic system and face challengers. This was the case with Jerry Rawlings of Ghana who had been a long-time military ruler of his country. He won the elections and served for two terms as president, before giving up completely because the constitution prevented him from standing again.

Democratization did not proceed without hiccups, though. In Nigeria, the first presidential election since 1983 was held in June 1993 and won by Moshood Abiola. However, the sitting military president, Ibrahim Babangida, nullified the election result, claiming fraud. There followed a long period of political jockeying in which some dictatorial presidents resigned, some were ousted by military force, and others died by natural causes. Abiola never became president. However, the situation was eventually resolved, and Nigeria returned to democratic rule in 1998. By the end of the decade, the century, and the millennium, almost all of Africa was democratized. The exceptions were largely the North African countries where dictators like Gaddafi in Libya, Ben Ali in Tunisia, and Mubarak in Egypt remained in power until the "Arab Spring," before being overthrown. But even the "Arab Spring" did not solve the problem, as can be seen in the continuing turmoil in Libya and Egypt.

A survey of the nature of African politics in the post-colonial era cannot be complete without noting the attempt of some African countries to implement a Marxist or socialist model of government that the leaders believed would enhance development in Africa. Some of the African leaders, like Sekou Toure of Guinea, Samora Machel of Mozambique, and Agostino Neto of Angola, had embraced the Marxist ideology before independence anyway. They had seen colonialism as a feature of capitalism and believed that to be anti-colonialist meant being anti-capitalist. Their anti-colonial movements had received great help from the Soviet Union. The countries that attempted to implement a Marxist approach included Guinea, Mozambique, Angola, Algeria, Mali, and Tanzania. Like European Marxists, the Marxists in Africa believed in the class struggle between the proletariat and the bourgeoisie who they felt were in charge of African governments; they also believed in the abolition of private ownership, particularly of the means of production, and in centralized state control, especially of the country's economic institutions (Serapaio, 194). These countries and their leaders are sometimes referred to as Afro–Marxists, because they claimed to be slightly modifying the traditional Marxist Approach. Some scholars believe that, in effect, they only paid lip service to socialism (Shillington, 479). Some of the basic tenets of socialism, such as the redistribution of income or the enactment of social policies to improve the condition of the workers and ordinary people, remained un-attempted and unrealized. In any case, it is debatable whether one can talk of the struggle between the proletariat and the bourgeoisie with regard to Africa, unless by "bourgeoisie" one means the governing elite. In most African countries, there were just the two divisions: the governing elite and the rest of society who were the ordinary people.

Julius Nyerere, president of Tanzania, was very different from the other African socialists because he attempted arduously to practice some of the principles of socialism and to give his brand of socialism a truly African character. He described his brand of socialism in detail in what has come to be known as the Arusha Declaration of 1967. The main plank of his agenda was the idea of "villagisation" or "Ujama." This involved bringing the people together in large villages, essentially collectives. Nyerere believed that large-scale farming, rather than small subsistence farms, was the key to success in agricultural production, but the large farms should be owned, not by capitalist individuals, but by the people, working collectively. This was the "African" component of the program: the idea of communal ownership and communal work. The large villages would have better access to government-provided facilities such as education, health, utilities, and so on, and there would still be central government control.

In practice, all attempts at implementing a socialist or Marxist agenda in African countries failed. Even Nyerere's failed for various reasons, the main one being the frustration of farmers much more accustomed to subsistence and small-scale farming of their individual land than to communal work on land that was communally owned. Nyerere, however, was honest enough to admit failure and change direction toward the end of his presidency. This is one of the reasons why he became probably the most respected and admired of African leaders.

With the exception of most of the Mahgreb countries, the trend towards democratization has continued in Africa. Most countries practice some form of democracy, though the situation is far from being perfect. In Kenya, for instance, election results were challenged, there were allegations of rigging, and there were suggestions that the governing party wanted to stay in power by all means. There was a similar situation in Zimbabwe. In Côte d'Ivoire the contested election results led to a civil war situation. All this has led some commentators to suggest that Africa is backsliding from the hopeful position of the early 1990s. The real issue is that there are problems with the form of democracy now being practiced in most African countries. Generally, African countries merely went back to the form of democracy that had failed in the past. This is largely the form of democracy being practiced by Western countries, but there are problems even in the Western countries as is quite evident in the case of the United States of America where many commentators are complaining that their democratic institutions are in peril. Far from devising a form of democracy that would be suitable to African conditions and African attitudes, the framers of the new African constitutions merely went back to the Western model: political pluralism and competition and the winner takes all. Some of the new African constitutions, like that of Nigeria, mainly follow the American model; at one time in Nigeria the two political parties were called the Republican Party and the Democratic Party, as in the USA. Some constitutions, like that of Sierra Leone, look like the French model. The new constitutions fail to take into account the fact that a major problem was the exclusion of large segments of society from the decision-making process for long periods of time, even indefinitely, by the winner takes all concept. This is particularly striking in areas where political parties are still identified with ethnic groupings. African countries still have to work on a political structure that, while being democratic in the sense that everyone votes freely and those who want to stand for election are free to do so, makes it possible for the inclusion of all segments of the population in the decision making-process at the highest possible level. The emphasis must be on inclusion rather than exclusion. Some countries have been moving in this direction. It is unthinkable that African countries will slide back to the chaos that preceded the 1990s. The signs are therefore very hopeful. Democracy is not an easy system to operate, but it is more than likely that African countries will continue to muddle through to an eventually ideal situation.

References and suggestions for further reading

Babu, A. M. 1981. *African Socialism or Socialist Africa?* London: Zed Books.

Ball, N. 1981. "The Military in Politics: Who Benefits and How?" *World Development* 6: 569–582.

Barkan, J. (ed.). 1994. *Beyond Capitalism vs. Socialism in Kenya and Tanzania.* Boulder, CO: Lynne Rienner.

Bratton, M. 1888. "Second Elections in Africa." Pp. 18–33 In L. Diamond and M. F. Plattner (eds.). *Democratization in Africa.* Baltimore, MD: Johns Hopkins University Press.

Bratton, M. and N. van de Walle. 1999. "Towards Governance in Africa: Popular Demands and State Responses." Pp. 27–55 In G. Hyden and M.l Bratton (eds.). *Governance and Politics in Africa.* Boulder, CO: Lynne Rienner.

Chazam, N. et al. 1988. *Politics and Society in Contemporary Africa.* Boulder, CO: Westview Press.

Clark, J. 1997. "The Challenge of Political Reform in Sub-Saharan Africa." Pp. 23–39 in J. F. Clark and D. Gardiner (eds.). *Political Reform in Francophone Africa.* Boulder, CO: Westview Press.

Cooper, F. 2002. *Africa since 1940: The Past and Present.* Cambridge: Cambridge University Press.

Cowan, M. and I. Laasko. (eds). 2002. *Multi-Party Elections in Africa.* Oxford: James Currey.

Cox, T. 1976. *Civil–Military Relations in Sierra Leone: A Case Study of African Soldiers in Politics.* Cambridge, MA: Harvard University Press.

Crockett, R. 2010. *Sudan, Darfur and the Failure of an African State.* New Haven, CT: Yale University Press.

Decalo, S. 1976. *Coups and Army Rule in Africa: Studies in Military Style.* New Haven, CT: Yale University Press.

Doro, M. 1995. "The Democratization Process in Africa." *Choice* (October): 245–257.

Gordon, D. L. 2007. "African Politics." Pp. 57–107 in A. A. Gordon and D. L. Gordon (eds.), *Understanding Contemporary Africa.* Boulder, CO: Lynne Rienner.

Hirsch, J.L. 2000. *Sierra Leone Diamonds and the Struggle for Democracy.* Boulder, CO: Lynne Rienner.

Hodder-Williams, R. 1984. *An Introduction to the Politics of Tropical Africa.* London: George Allen & Unwin.

Hoffman, D. 2012. *The War Machines: Young Men and Violence in Sierra Leone and Liberia.* Durham, NC: Duke University Press.

Legum C. and G. Mmari (eds.). 2002. *Mwalimu: The Influence of Nyerere.* Oxford: James Currey.

Mamdani, M. 1996. *Citizen and Subject: Contemporary Africa and the Legacy of Late Colonialism.* Oxford: James Currey.

Martinez, L. 1999. *The Algerian Civil War. 1990–1998.* London: Hurst.

Nugent, P. 2012. *Africa since Independence: A Contemporary History.* Basingstoke: Palgrave Macmillan.

Nyang'oro, J. E. 2005. "Africa's Road to Independence (1945–1960)." Pp. 163–172 in M. Azevedo (ed.), *Africana Studies: A Survey of Africa and the African Diaspora.* Durham, NC: Carolina Academic Press.

Osaghae, E. E. 1998. *Crippled Giant: Nigeria since Independence.* London: Hurst.

Poggo, S. S. 2009. *The First Sudanese Civil War: Africans, Arabs and Israelis in the Southern Sudan, 1951–1972.* Basingstoke: Palgrave Macmillan.

Prunier, G. 2005. *The Rwanda Crisis: History of Genocide, 1959–1994.* Kampala: Fontana.

Serapaio, L. B. 2005. "The Contemporary African World." Pp. 189–206 in M. Azevedo (ed.). *Africana Studies: A Survey of Africa and the African Diaspora.* Durham, NC: Carolina Academic Press.

Shillington, K. 2019. *History of Africa* (4th ed.). London: Red Globe Press.

Tvedten, I. 1997. *Angola: Struggle for Peace and Reconstruction.* Boulder, CO: Westview Press.

Tangri, R. 1985. *Politics in Sub-Saharan Africa.* London: James Currey and Heinemann Educational Books.

Vandewalle, D. (ed.) 2011. *Libya since 1969: Gaddafi's Revolution Revisited.* Basingstoke: Palgrave Macmillan.

van der Veen, R. 2004. *What Went Wrong with Africa: A Contemporary History.* Amsterdam: KIT Publishers.

Young, C. 1994. *The African Colonial State in Comparative Perspective.* New Haven, CT: Yale University Press.

6   African social systems

This chapter will be concerned with the social relations existing among Africans. It will consider the nature of these relations in the traditional past and also how these relations and procedures have been carried over into the present or how they influence Africans in the present. Three major issues that are extremely important to African life will be examined: lineage, family, and marriage. Let us start by noting some caveats. It is very easy to generalize about African life and believe that a particular practice or procedure exists everywhere in Africa. It is also easy to believe that certain attitudes and beliefs in the past, or in traditional rural areas, also characterize the present or are to be found in modern urban areas. Not all Africans practice polygamy, although it was a feature of the African past and is still common in several parts of Africa. In the past most African marriages were arranged, and though this is still done in some parts of Africa today, numerous modern young Africans meet at school, at work, or at university, engage in courtship, and decide to get married, without waiting for their families to decide who their partners will be. Africa is a vast continent, and, although there are commonalities which we will stress, there are also differences in behavior, attitudes, and practices. Also, because of globalization, strides in education, travel, and advances in communication, age-old practices are being modified or even abandoned altogether. We have to be sensitive to these issues in order to get a reasonable picture of the nature of social relations in Africa.

The family

As we look at these features of African social relations we will discover that many of these are quite different from practices and beliefs in Western society. In no area is this more obvious than in the concept of the family. When one mentions the family in Western society, people automatically think of what has become known as the "nuclear" family: the father, mother, and the children. When one talks of the family in African society, one usually means the "extended" family. That certainly includes the nuclear family, but it goes way beyond this to include grandmothers, grandfathers, aunts, uncles, cousins, nephews, nieces, great-aunts, and great-uncles, and so on. Every individual member of this extended family knows that they have responsibilities towards the others. The concept of the extended family has proved amazingly effective in areas where there might be poverty, privation, or even oppression. The old who are no longer able to work, or who might not have children to provide for them, know they can depend on the other members of the extended family to ensure that they do not starve or want for anything. Grandmothers or great-aunts who have lost their husbands know that they can

DOI: 10.4324/9781003111733-7

stay with their children and grandchildren without being considered a burden. That is the expected thing. They will be properly looked after and respected. They will not be put into old people's homes, because there are no old people's homes. These homes have never been considered necessary. In fact, the issue of homelessness hardly exists in most African societies because normally everyone can find a home within the extended family system. There is an old Krio proverb in Sierra Leone which, roughly translated, says, "no matter how cramped the house is, the chicken will still find space to lay its egg." In other words, there will always be space in the house for a relative who needs a home. If the relatives do not make provision for this kind of person the entire extended family will be disgraced. The members should have realized that they have a responsibility towards the more unfortunate members of the group. In most of these environments there is no social security because the economy cannot sustain it. However, the members of the extended family are expected to provide their own social security. Members of the extended family can visit each other without warning or invitation and stay for as long as they want. I can remember a colleague in Sierra Leone asking to borrow money because several of his extended family from the provinces had just descended on him without warning. He was expected to house and feed them for as long as they chose to stay. He realized he had a responsibility towards these members of the family which he had to discharge on pain of disgrace. In Western society, even if these members would be welcome, they would have had to call and give notice of the visit, or they would have had to be invited. The system is quite different.

The extended family provides an excellent ready-made support group. The members know they can depend on each other in times of stress or any kind of trouble. I can remember my father telling me about an aunt of his who never had children herself but always determinedly stood by and championed any member of the family who was in trouble or had problems of any kind. Children who lose their parents know they can count on aunts or uncles to take them into their homes and provide for them, to the extent of seeing them through school or even university. And those aunts and uncles do it as part of their responsibilities, not as a favor. A parent who lives in the provinces could send his son to a member of the extended family living in the city for the purpose of going to school or finding a job. In this kind of system the old are not only provided for, they are highly respected, because they are the senior members of the family and the repositories of wisdom. One of the most arresting scenes in Ali Mazrui's documentary series *The Africans: A Triple Heritage* is that in which a learned professor and government consultant in Nigeria visits his grandfather in the village, genuflects to him, and listens to his words of wisdom.

In traditional Africa the family is the unit that has responsibility for ensuring that children are properly brought up, trained and educated in the ways of decency and propriety. By family here one means the larger extended family, not just the parents of the children. Hillary Clinton once said it takes a village to raise a child. She was referring to the fact that in many parts of the world it takes a much larger unit than the nuclear family to raise a child. This is certainly true of traditional Africa. Aunts, uncles, grandparents, and others can play as important a role in this as the parents. In some societies, as we shall see, the uncle might play a much more important role in mentoring the child than the actual biological father. The uncle, in these matrilineal societies, is more like a father than an uncle. An aunt who sees a child doing wrong can discipline the child, and the child's mother, far from being angry with the aunt, will be grateful to her.

In traditional Africa, the smaller family unit, that is the parents and the children, is often an economic unit designed and organized to produce a livelihood. This means that the children also help to produce the means whereby the family survives. This has often been given, in fact, as a justification for polygamy, because the more wives a man has, the more children he is likely to have to help work on the farm. Productivity will therefore be greater. Even in some urban areas today some mothers expect their daughters to help them sell goods in the market. This might sound ominous to people in the West who believe, with great justification, that children should be in school and should not work before they reach a certain age. With expanding education and greater opportunities for both boys and girls, the practice is being gradually discontinued. However, it must be noted that in traditional Africa, particularly the Africa of the past, working on the farm or helping to look after animals was part of the informal educational system. If a boy is to become a successful farmer or herder of animals, he must learn by observation the means of achieving this. Being part of the production unit gave children useful training for the future.

Marriage

Marriage in Africa is almost universal. In traditional Africa all men and women are expected to marry and have children. There are hardly any bachelors. This is why most marriages are arranged. The young man's parents would not wait until he shows an interest in marriage. As soon as he gets to a certain age they start looking around for a suitable wife for him. Of course this happened mostly in traditional Africa; in modern urban Africa young men and women are allowed more flexibility. However, arranged marriages still persist. I once went to a Muslim wedding where the gentleman who gave the introductory remarks at the mosque told the assembled guests that the father of the bridegroom had gone to their family and said that he was interested in their daughter as a wife for his son. This might have been a formal way of putting it, but it still suggests that it is acceptable in some quarters for the father to take the initiative in arranging for a wife for his son, and the concept of arranged marriages is not altogether dead.

Why is there such an insistence on marriage in Africa? Marriage is necessary in order to produce children who will serve as an insurance policy for the future. In societies where there were no welfare schemes or state provision for the old, one had to ensure that one had children who would look after one in old age. This still obtains in many parts of Africa. The importance of marrying and having children is also related to a concept that still exists in many parts of traditional Africa. This is the notion of immortality. In most African religions, immortality largely consists in being remembered. One is immortal as long as one has descendants who will remember one. The more children one has, therefore, the more likely it is that there will be descendants who will continue to remember one for a long time. It is therefore absolutely necessary to marry and have children in order to ensure immortality. In traditional Africa, childlessness is regarded almost as a curse. Children are supposed to be a gift from God and should therefore be welcomed. This is why birth control is hardly practiced in traditional Africa. It is almost tantamount to going against the will of God or the gods. It is extremely important for Western advocates of birth control in Africa to remember this. Of course, there is need for population control in Africa because the economy of certain countries and the inherent poverty of the African soil will not support huge populations, but this has to be done in ways that show sensitivity to the religious, cultural, and social assumptions of the

African peoples. The story is told of a rather interesting poster in a West African capital advertising the need for birth control. On one side of the poster was a handsome young man in a three-piece suit and his equally beautiful young wife. They were flanked by their two good-looking children, a boy and a girl, very well dressed and obviously healthy and very well fed. The four of them were smiling radiantly. On the other side of the poster was a scruffy looking man dressed almost in rags and flanked by his equally emaciated and ragged wife. Behind them were about nine equally ragged children. The lesson that the poster obviously wished to inculcate was that life is much better in a very small family. A line of passersby had formed, admiring the details on the poster. However, they were admiring, not the handsome couple and their beautiful children, but the ragged couple and their nine children. One passerby was heard to say, "This man is so blessed; he has so many children." The poster had achieved the opposite of its intention because the framers had not taken into account the people's social, cultural, and religious beliefs.

One marries also to have children because children are a sign of wealth in certain parts of traditional Africa. When the narrator in Chinua Achebe's *Things Fall Apart*, a novel set in the last decade of the nineteenth century, gives an account of Okonkwo's wealth, he mentions, not only his barns of yams, but also his wives and his numerous children. The concept of children as a sign of wealth can also be found in certain parts of modern Africa. I can remember taking my car to a garage and overhearing the mechanics complaining about how the bourgeois elite want to take away their (the mechanics' and the poorer people's) children away from them, through birth control, without realizing that children were their own wealth. The elite may have their money and their property, but they (the poorer people) had their children, and that was their own wealth.

It is important to note that marriage in Africa, especially in traditional Africa, is not merely a personal matter between the two people. Marriage is the bringing together of two families: the family of the bride and the family of the bridegroom. This is one of the reasons why it has to be approached with a tremendous amount of caution. This is also one of the ways in which marriage in Africa is different from marriage in the West. In the Western world a young man can go down on his knee, propose marriage to a young woman, and be accepted, without consulting or even informing either his own family or the family of the young woman. If the couple want to, they can get married without any further consultation or even without the approval of their respective families. This is unheard of in Africa. The marriage would involve the bringing together of two families for the foreseeable future. This is one of the reasons why marriages are arranged. Each family knows about the other beforehand and is sure that both are compatible. If the families do not know about each other beforehand, they do a lot of what is called "tracing," in order to find out as much as possible about the other family. They try to find out whether the other family has a record of hereditary or stigmatized diseases, insanity, or crime. It would be problematic to be associated with such a family for life. If the "tracing" produces the desired results the marriage can proceed. The fact that two families are involved helps to give stability to the marriage. There are more experiences to derive sustenance from, if the couple so desires, and more people to give counsel, if needed.

African engagement and marriage rituals are very elaborate. In some traditional societies the engagement ceremony, during which the bridegroom's family comes to ask the bride's family for the hand of the bride and which is sometimes called the "asking," is just as elaborate as the wedding ceremony itself. This can be seen, for instance, in the novels of Achebe which are set in traditional Igbo society, *Things Fall Apart* and *Arrow of God*. Probably, these ceremonies have to be elaborate because they involve the whole community, not just the families of the bride and bridegroom. They must reflect the values and customs of the entire community. As is commonly known, the concept of community is extremely important in Africa. The community, in many traditional African societies, is even more important than the individual. And so for these very important rituals the whole community is involved.

Let us look at the engagement procedures or ceremony in a particular society, in this case, the Creoles of the Western Area in Sierra Leone. The choice of the Creoles is important because they have often been thought to be too "Westernized" or "Anglicized," yet some of their marriage and funeral rituals contain very African elements. I am myself a Creole. The engagement ceremony starts with a delegation from the bridegroom's family setting out on a "mission" for the home of the bride and her family. The mission is to ask for the hand of the bride as a wife for "their son." It is noteworthy that the bridegroom-to-be plays no role in the ceremony. It is a delegation consisting of his relatives that goes to the family of the bride to do the "asking." The delegation usually consists of middle-aged and old people, people with experience in these matters, in other words. Both sexes are represented, but the delegation chooses a spokesperson who is usually a male. Relatives and friends would gather in the home of the bride's parents and the bride's family would also choose a male spokesperson. Both spokesmen are expected to be extremely smart and articulate because they would soon be involved in complicated reasoning and bargaining. A "watchman" is usually posted by the bride's family to alert them when he "sights" the delegation from the bridegroom's family approaching, and there would be shouts of "they are coming" swirling all around. The members of the bride's family then scramble to shut all the doors and the windows and then sit down quietly waiting. On arrival, the leader of the other delegation knocks three times on the main door. The spokesman for the bride's family responds with a tone of tremendous anger and irritation, demanding to know who has come to disturb his peace at this time of night when he and his family have gone to bed. He suspects, he says, that they must be thieves who have come for his property. Then follows a period of wrangling and argument in which the bride's family's spokesman continues to repeat his suspicions and the leader of the other delegation tries to reassure him that they have come to see his family with very good intentions. The spokesman for the bride's family then pretends to relent, opens the door and lets the delegation in.

After the opening pleasantries, the leader of the delegation then stands up and launches into an interesting narrative. He was passing by this house once, he says, when he noticed an extremely beautiful rose, more beautiful than any other rose he had seen. He decided that he must have that beautiful rose, and he has come to ask the owner of the house to give him that rose so that he could give it to his son. It is noteworthy that the leader of the delegation uses imagery and metaphors. He does not refer to the bride-to-be directly, although everyone present knows that that is who he is talking about. All this contributes to the elaborateness and beauty of the occasion. The spokesman for the bride's family once more pretends to be mightily annoyed. He had been persuaded to let the delegation in, he says, because they assured him they had come with good intentions. But now the leader was asking for his most beautiful rose. He has the good mind to ask them to get out of his house again. The wrangling now continues as the leader of the delegation tries to persuade the bride's family that their intentions are good. The spokesman for the bride's family then pretends once more to relent, and he asks the leader of the delegation about the arrangements that have been made to take care of this most beautiful rose. If he should give his rose to them, would they take the utmost care of it? Would they ensure that it is regularly watered and nourished? Would they protect it from "jealous eyes"? Would they make sure that thieves do not come in the night to steal it? The leader of the delegation promises that they would do all this and more. The spokesman of the bride's family pretends to relent once more and asks the women of the family to bring the "rose."

Now comes an interesting segment of the ceremony during which anything up to six young women, who are not the bride-to-be, are brought out in turn by the women of the family. The leader of the delegation has to assure the family that although each of them is very beautiful, they are not the rose he saw. Eventually the real bride to be is brought out, very radiantly dressed, and the leader of the delegation cries out rapturously that this is indeed the rose, and he does so to tremendous cheering and applause. Then follows the segment where the leader of the delegation hands over to the spokesman for the bride's family an amount of money and some other objects that the delegation has brought. The spokesman and senior members of the family withdraw to examine the gift. They then return to say that they are satisfied and there is general rejoicing and dancing to a song which informs everyone that the bride's mother has said "yes." At times the dancing spills over into the street. The visiting delegation then returns to the home of the bridegroom to announce that the parents of the bride have agreed to give their daughter in marriage to the delegation's "son."

We can see that this is a very elaborate ceremony in which neither the bride nor the groom plays any part at all. The bride only appears for a short time, and the groom never appears. He sends a delegation from his family to represent him. This is probably a hangover from the days when the marriages were actually arranged and neither bride nor groom had any part in the negotiations. Both spokesmen have to be extremely intelligent, forceful, and erudite to engage in the kind of wrangling that goes on and to entertain the audience, because the ceremony is expected to provide entertainment, and the audience expects to hang on every word that the spokesmen say. It is significant that Creoles in the diaspora still use this ceremony as they try to retain their cultural identity.

In many African societies the family of the bridegroom gives a certain amount of money or some property to the family of the bride at the time of the engagement. This is what is usually referred to as "bridewealth" in the West. It is almost certainly a misnomer because it involves much more than a purely economic arrangement, as the term "bridewealth" would imply. The practice has led some Western commentators to propagate the view that African husbands "purchase" their wives who then become their mere property. This is a wrong-headed view. As Azevedo suggests, "the bride is not his property in any case, but his dependent and partner to whom he is responsible for providing the material and social support to raise and feed a family" (Azevedo, 375). The form and amount of the gift can vary greatly from society to society and from period to period. It can be as small as a mere token or as large as amounts of property; in some cases it consists of several heads of cattle. It can also vary according to the status and position of the bridegroom. In some contemporary African societies, for instance, a bridegroom who is a doctor, lawyer, or university professor would be expected to give much more than a clerk, even where the women are of the same status. This suggests that the practice is not purely economic and we are not talking about purely economic value.

There are several reasons for the existence of the practice, a practice which exists even in contemporary Africa where bridegrooms who are doctors, lawyers, and university professors would be offended at the suggestion that they have bought their wives. In the first place, the transfer of property or large amounts of money is quite often a form of insurance. It is an insurance against separation or divorce or an eagerness by the woman to go back to her parents' house should things not work out as she had anticipated. In many societies, the gift has to be returned to the man's family if the woman goes back to her parents or if separation of any kind occurs. In most cases it would be virtually impossible for the woman's family to raise the amount of money necessary since this might happen several years after the marriage and the money might have been spent. In some cases, the "gift" might even have been used by the younger males of the woman's family to help them find wives for themselves. Some might think it unfair for the younger males in the family to use part of the gift or all of it to find their own wives, but there it is. The provision of that amount of money or property plays a role in ensuring continuing good relations between husband and wife. In almost all societies, the transfer of property suggests the value the bride's family places on her, and therefore the esteem in which the new bridegroom should hold her. And this value is not just economic; it is pre-eminently social. The gift is an indication by the bridegroom that he is prepared to hold the bride in as high esteem as her family held her. This is not very different from the situation in the West where a bridegroom-to-be would give an expensive engage-ment ring to the fiancée. And as is the case in some parts of Africa, the value of the ring depends on the status of both man and woman. The ring is an indication of esteem and value and a token of love.

Among the Creoles of Sierra Leone whom we have already mentioned, the amount of money given to the bride's family during the engagement ceremony is to enable her to get her bridal equipment, which includes the bridal dress and, sometimes, the dresses of the bridesmaids. But traditionally, she also uses part of the money to equip herself to move into her new home. It is this money that she uses to buy crockery and cutlery, to make curtains, chair covers, and bedclothes for her new home. This is why traditionally the gift is referred to as the "trousseau" money. It thus has a practical importance. Aze-vedo also mentions the fact that in some traditional African societies, especially pastoral societies, the bridal gift to the family of the bride is an indication by the husband that he intends to claim paternity over all the children produced by the marriage. This is because in pastoral societies where the people are almost continually on the move, it is quite possible that a child might not be the husband's biologically. In spite of this, he intends to claim paternity because he needs all the hands he can muster in herding his animals, and he wants no ambiguity in deciding to whom his herds should belong in the event of his own demise. Azevedo claims that what is "purchased" "in a marriage contract involving a large amount of bridewealth is the right to paternity over all the children born of the woman" (375). Claiming paternity over a child one suspects might not be one's own is not strange in Africa.

Polygamy in African society

A very important aspect of African marriage is the practice known as polygamy (or polygyny). This is the situation where one man has more than one wife, and it is quite common even in contemporary Africa. It was a very common practice in traditional African society where it was, in fact, the norm. The practice was even further enabled by Islam which allows a man to have up to four wives as long as he is in a position to take care of them all and treat them all fairly. Of course, Christianity adheres to the one man one wife concept, but it is significant that polygamy was sanctioned by the Old Testament, which is a bastion of belief for many Christians. Figures like Abraham, Jacob, and David had more than one wife. Polygamy is, in fact, not unique to traditional African society. It is also important to remember that it is not just traditional men who favor polygamy. Numbers of African women are in favor of it, probably because it is the only system they have known as far as relations between husbands and wives are concerned. I once heard a highly educated African woman academic say that the fact that her husband might practice polygamy does not diminish her as a woman. There was once a radio report of some modern African women saying that they do not mind their husbands practicing polygamy because it gives them their own space and more opportunity to follow their own pursuits. In teaching Mariama Ba's *Une Si Longue Lettre* to a class of African students not so long ago, I thought I would stimulate discussion by emphasizing the downside of polygamy as illustrated in the text. The male students in the class, all of them modern young men, made their views strongly known. They not only supported polygamy, but some of them said they intended to be polygamists because it was the tradition.

The supporters of polygamy in Africa are prepared to give several reasons to support their views, and some of these may have been the reasons why the practice started and flourished in Africa in the distant past. Polygamy ensures sexual and other provisions for all adults in the society, especially for women. In societies where there was frequent warfare there must have been more women than men. To insist on the one man one wife concept would mean to exclude some women from sexual activity, especially in communities where adultery was taboo. It also ensured that every woman had the possibility of having children of her own in a society where children were very important. Polygamy also made economic sense because it meant that every woman had someone to provide her with those items she herself could not, and it ensured a bigger labor force. A man with more than one wife was likely to have more children and therefore more hands to work on the farm.

In many traditional African societies, it was taboo for a nursing mother to have sexual relations. One must remember that, in these societies, all mothers breastfed their children, since modern food for babies, like formulas, did not exist. And many mothers did not wean their children until they were about two years old. In the meantime, sexual provision had to be made for the husband, in a society that frowned on adultery and prostitution. Polygamy was the answer. Polygamy also ensured more children, and having several children was a good insurance policy for the future. It ensured that there was someone to look after one in old age; it also ensured "immortality."

Of course, there are downsides to the practice of polygamy. It could result in tremendous jealousy among the wives and among the children by the various wives. This is illustrated in various novels by African writers, particularly novels by Buchi Emecheta, Flora Nwapa, and Mariama Ba. But we also have experience of it in actual life. I can remember a male student, who was not doing well in the class, blaming his poor performance on his father's second wife whose children had not been able to go to university. The second wife, he claimed, had secretly cut off a strand of his hair while he was sleeping and taken it to the medicine man to ensure that he would become stupid and not get his degree. The entire story sounds quite fantastic, but the evidence of jealousy in a polygamous household is there. The system requires great inter-personal skills to be effective. A lot depends on the personal skills of the husband. He must be fair in his treatment of all his wives and refrain from demonstrating any favoritism. All traditional societies expect polygamous husbands to be fair in social, economic, and sexual arrangements. In this connection, the position of the "senior wife" is important. The senior wife is usually the first wife and she holds a special position, as far as traditional society is concerned. One of her most important roles is to help the husband maintain order and discipline. She is the "leader" of the wives, so to speak.

Generally speaking, all the evidence suggests that polygamy works reasonably well in the traditional setting. However, it does not do so well in the modern and urban setting where economic and other pressures might undermine the position of the husband and prevent him from demonstrating the fairness expected of him. This might lead to a breakdown of order and discipline in the household.

Polyandry, the practice of one woman marrying several husbands, is rare in traditional Africa and hardly exists in modern Africa. Eugenia Shanklin mentions one instance among the matrilineal Lele people in the Democratic Republic of the Congo. A woman could become the "village" wife, married to members of a particular age set group. These groups are formed every 15 years or so, and young men are initiated into them. The group would build a house for its "wife," a woman who might have been captured in war. If the woman bears girls, these could be claimed as "village wives" (Shanklin, 273). It is quite obvious that this system makes it possible for several men to have access to the sexual favors of the same woman. It does not give the woman influence over the men as the polygamous system does.

LGBT issues

A lot of Africans feel that homosexuality is virtually unknown in Africa and that it is largely a Western phenomenon. This is, of course, a false assumption. Homosexuality exists everywhere since it is biologically and psychologically and not environmentally determined. We know that King Mwanga II, a nineteenth-century king of Buganda, was homosexual. Among the Langi people, effeminate men were "married" to other men and treated as women. Open homosexuality is more prevalent in some areas than in others, probably because of some deliberate human efforts to suppress it or because some social or societal arrangements have the unintended effect of containing it. This is almost certainly the case in Africa. The emphasis on manliness in traditional Africa and the need for males to be ready to go into battle almost at a moment's notice against enemy tribes or clans must have led to the discouragement of any unmanly or "feminine" tendencies. There are even reports of ritualistic procedures in some societies designed to "purge" or sublimate "unnatural" tendencies before they take root. However, apart from homophobia, the most important factor working against homosexuality in Africa is the universal insistence on marriage and having children. People who might have been disinclined to find lifelong partners in the opposite sex find themselves obligated to do so because of relentless societal and familial pressure and because, once they get to a certain age, partners are found for them in any case.

Homosexuality in most African countries largely goes on underground, although LGBT groups are springing up in a few countries. Generally speaking, most Africans and most African countries are vehemently opposed to homosexuality and some very draconian laws have been passed against it in countries like Uganda, Nigeria, and Zambia. In the Sudan convicted homosexuals were liable to the death penalty until the law was changed in 2020, but it still exists in parts of Somalia. Recently, there were reports of the very harsh treatment of gay men in Nigeria, Sierra Leone, and Egypt, and there are often reports of people being rounded up and imprisoned. A few countries, however, are beginning to demonstrate that LGBT rights are a very important component of human rights. South Africa is a shining example of this. There the rights of gay people are enshrined in the constitution. Ghana is another country that has adopted a very "civilized" attitude towards gay people. However, gay rights constitute one aspect of human rights where Africa has to make progress.

Lineage and ancestry

In modern Western society, family membership and ancestry are traced through the family lines of both parents. One can trace one's relationship to all the members on the side of both the parents of one's father as well as one's relationship to all the members on the side of the parents of one's mother. This is what is referred to as the bilateral or bilineal method of tracing relationships or ancestry. In traditional Africa one traces relationships and ancestry either through the mother's line or the father's line. Tracing relationships through the father's line is referred to as the "patrilineal" method and societies that do this are called "patrilineal." Tracing relationships through the mother's line is the "matrilineal" method and societies doing so are "matrilineal." These methods are extremely important when it comes to matters of inheritance or even succession. In patrilineal societies one inherits property through one's father's line, or a father could give his property to his children. In a matrilineal society a father does not necessarily give his property to his children; rather, he gives it to his sister's children. Or, to put it another way, one can inherit property from one's mother's brother. In a patrilineal society, the people that an individual will recognize as his real cousins and as real kin are his father's brother's children, both sons and daughters, and these are referred to, not as "cousins," but as "brother" and "sister." In a matrilineal society, it is the children of the mother's brother and sister that are real kin. The system becomes incredibly complicated, as the writings of scholars like K. A. Busia have shown. All this suggests that in considering family relations in traditional Africa we must, as it were, be prepared to redefine certain terms. Take the terms "brother" and "sister," for instance. In some traditional African societies, particularly the patrilineal societies, there are no words, in the language, for "cousin." Your father's brother's children, both males and females, are regarded as your "brothers" and "sisters." The ties among these relations are much stronger than among "cousins" in the Western world and as strong as among siblings in the Western world. The same applies to the terms "son" and "daughter." One's brother's children are one's sons and daughters, particularly if their own biological father has died or if one has assumed responsibility for their welfare. In a sense, one is their "father." This is why Babamukuru, in Tsitsi Dangarembga's novel *Nervous Conditions*, refers to himself as the "father" of his brother's daughter, Tambu: "'Now. What is the matter, Mai? There is no need to bring up all that. Tambudzai is my brother's daughter, I am her father. I have the right to discipline her. It is my duty'" (Dangarembga, *Nervous Conditions*, 172).

The majority of African traditional societies are patrilineal, but there are several that are matrilineal. Patrilineal societies in Africa include the Tiv and Yoruba of Nigeria; the Gikuyu of Kenya; the Swazi of Swaziland (now renamed Eswatini); the Malinke of Senegal, Mali, Guinea Bissau and Côte d'Ivoire; the Zulu of South Africa; and the Gala of Ethiopia (Azevedo, 373).

In a patrilineal society there are various levels of relationships. First, there is what one might call the immediate family consisting of the father, wife or wives, and the children.

But there is also the lineage, a more extensive group of related members. It consists of all those in a local area who can claim to be descended from a common male ancestor. The lineage can serve as an administrative group, especially in the so-called stateless societies, because it can take decisions on matters that affect all its members. Finally there is the clan, which can also serve as a powerful administrative group, and which can consist of several lineages. However, they are lineages that are somehow related to each other, and all the people in the society recognize that they are kin, even if they cannot trace the exact nature of the relationship. At times, the whole village is the clan, as we can see from Achebe's novels, such as *Things Fall Apart*, where the village of Umuofia is, in fact, a clan. This gives vibrancy to the notion that it takes a village to raise the child, because the whole village can be a clan of related members and related lineages all of whom recognize a familial relationship and responsibility to each other.

In matrilineal societies people trace their family membership through the mother's line and through female kin to a common ancestress. It is not quite clear how or why this practice started. It is quite possibly due to the notion that a child can be absolutely sure about who the mother is, but not always the father, something that becomes quite important in matters of inheritance and succession. In any case, the matrilineal system emphasizes the importance of the "female principle" in African affairs. Examples of matrilineal societies include the Yao of Malawi, Mozambique, and Tanzania; the Bemba of Zambia; the Wollof of Senegal; and the Baule of Côte d'Ivoire. In some matrilineal societies the wife continues to live with her parents and the husband joins her. More often, however, men seek to live near their sisters or near their kinsmen that could be traced through their mother. In the matrilineal system the mother's brother is extremely important. It is the mother's brother, not the father, who disciplines the children and is responsible for some decisions. We can see this, for instance, in Ama Atas Aidoo's play *Anowa*, which is set in an area of Ghana that is matrilineal. It is the woman's brother, not the father, who belongs to the same kin group as her children. In matrilineal societies the bond between brother and sister is sometimes stronger than that between husband and wife. It is noteworthy, though, that although the female principle is emphasized in matrilineal societies and relationships are traced through the mother's line, it is still the men who wield authority. For instance, it is the mother's brother who disciplines the children.

In traditional African societies there are many taboos. Adultery and incest are usually taboo and divorce is frowned upon. However, in some societies a man is allowed to marry the wives of his deceased brother. In some cases he does not actually marry her, but he has children with her in the name of his deceased brother. This practice continues even into modern times. Once more, the main object is to ensure provision for the wife or wives of the deceased brother. At times it is to ensure that whatever property the dead man had remains in the family.

The social arrangements in traditional African society were highly beneficial and ensured social stability. They also gave individuals a sense of belonging. Kinships and extended family systems ensured that the old, the unfortunate and the underprivileged were cared for and the individual could count on a bastion of support from his kin in times of trouble and difficulty. Marriages were largely stable because many more people than the husband and wife were interested in ensuring their success. Divorce, adultery, and prostitution were rare. Of course there were wars, civil and international, as there have always been in all societies, but there was not the kind of gratuitous violence one often has in modern Western societies. There were hardly instances of children killing parents and vice versa, or of family members butchering each other, or of psychotic people going on killing sprees, or of people killing babies and young children, or of mass murderers. The social system ensured that the conditions producing such states of mind either did not exist, or, if they did, they would have been taken care of before they produced such states of mind. Madness did exist in traditional African societies, but it was rare. Because the entire village or clan felt itself responsible for keeping an eye on the young and educating them about the proper values.

However, these social patterns and attitudes were bound to be affected by modern or contemporary forces and trends like the expansion of Christianity, urbanization, the exposure to Western education and culture, and globalization, which is really the expansion into other societies of Western capitalist attitudes and values through travel, trade, and the media. Attitudes to marriage probably took the hardest hit. As young people go through high school or university education and become exposed to Western ideas and the Western media, they choose their partners because they fall in love. Marriages among such Africans are no longer arranged. The families on both sides still play a part, but couples are beginning to accept their own responsibility for making the marriage succeed. One result is that divorce has become such more common. Most Africans still make use of the traditional rituals, although some of them have been modified. The bridewealth concept has certainly been modified. An educated young man is no longer likely to give cattle to the family of his bride; he is much more likely to give a sum of money instead. With regard to polygamy, the Christian Church officially condemns it. Polygamy occurs less and less among educated and middle-class Africans. Such people tend to live in urban areas where economic and other pressures make it impossible to sustain the polygamous ideal anyway. Some African men, while adhering to the idea of monogamy, still have affairs outside of marriage and therefore are polygamous in a sense. They are therefore adhering to the traditional concept of one man having more than one woman, but without the responsibilities and duties that actual polygamy would entail. This means that adultery is much more common and even accepted in the contemporary urban setting than in the traditional.

Urbanization has had a marked impact on traditional African social arrangements. In the cities people tend to be far away from their lineage and their kinsmen in the traditional area, and some of them might therefore not feel the same sense of obligation they are expected to. Life in the city is also expensive and stressful and this might affect the ability of some to discharge their obligations within the lineage, kinship, or extended family systems. Nevertheless, the kinship and extended family systems are still holding their own even in the urban areas. People still send their children to relations in the city for upbringing or with the expectation that they might help them find jobs and make progress. Meetings of family groups are held in the cities, and at times of celebration or misfortune the entire lineage in the city might come together. It is also well known that, no matter how prosperous Africans become in the city, many of them still make annual pilgrimages to their native villages and build huge mansions there. Of course, there are temptations in the city and, being far away from the constraints and sanctions of traditional life, some young people succumb to these temptations and drift into a life of crime or prostitution. These are rife in the city. The youngsters might succumb to these out of sheer necessity because they cannot always count on the support of a traditional system that would sustain them until they could stand on their own feet, or out of attraction to the illusory glamor of the scene. Youngsters might also succumb to drug abuse which is becoming rife in African cities. This has been fostered by globalization, but also by the numerous civil wars that have plagued the African continent. It is well known that commanders in Africa gave drugs to their soldiers, some of them no more than boys, in order to bolster their courage in battle. The youngsters become addicted as a result, and most of them find their way into the cities when the war is over.

Some aspects of the African social system are being inevitably modified by contemporary forces. However, many of them still stand, thus showing the resilience of African life and the relevance of these systems.

References and suggestions for further reading

Achebe, C. 1959. *Things Fall Apart*. New York: Anchor Books.

Ajayi, J. F. A., and T. Falola. (eds.). 2000. *Tradition and Change in Africa: The Essays of J. E. Ade Ajayi*. Trenton, NJ: Africa World Press.

Ayisi, E. O. 1988. *An Introduction to the Study of African Culture*. London: Heinemann.

Azevedo, M. 2005. "The African Family." Pp. 371–382 in M. Azevedo (ed.), *Africana Studies*. Durham, NC: Carolina Academic Press.

Azevedo, M., and G. Prater (eds.). 1982. *Africa and its People*. Dubuque, IA: Kendall/Hun.

Colson, E. 1974. "Plateau Tonga." Pp. 36–95 in D. M. Schneider and K. Gough (eds.). *Matrilineal Kinship*. Berkeley, CA: University of California Press.

Dangaremgba, T. 1988. *Nervous Conditions*. Seattle, WA: Seal Press.

Douglas, M. 1969. "Is Matriliny Doomed in Africa?" Pp. 121–135 in M. Douglas and P. M. Kaberry (eds.). *Man in Africa*. London: Tavistock.

Ekong, J. M. 1992. *Bridewealth, Women and Reproduction in Sub-Saharan Africa: A Theoretical Overview*. Bonn: Holos.

Fortes, M. 1950. "Kinship and Marriage among the Ashanti." Pp. 252–284 in A. R. Radcliffe-Brown and D. Forde (eds.), *African Systems of Kinship and Marriage*. Oxford: Oxford University Press (for International African Institute).

Fox, R. 1967. *Kinship and Marriage*. Harmondsworth: Penguin.

Kuper, A. 1982. *Wives for Cattle: Bridewealth and Marriage in Southern Africa*. London: Routledge & Kegan Paul.

Lesthaeghe, Ron. 1989. *Reproduction and Social Organization in Sub-Saharan Africa*. Berkeley, CA: University of California Press.

Mwamwenda, T. S., and L. A. Monwoe. 1997. "Status of Bridewealth in an African Culture." *Journal of African Social Psychology* 137: 269–272.

Oppong, C. 1981. *Middle Class African Marriage*. London: George Allen & Unwin.

Parkin, D., and D. Nyamwaya (eds.). 1989. *Transformations of African Marriage*. Manchester: Manchester University Press.

Radcliffe-Brown, A. R. and D. Forde (eds.). 1950. *African Systems of Kinship and Marriage*. Oxford: Oxford University Press (for International African Institute).

Shanklin, E. 2007. "Family and Kinship." Pp. 265–292 in A. Gordon and D. Gordon (eds.), *Understanding Contemporary Africa*. Boulder, CO: Lynne Rienner.

Wiesner, T. S., C. Bradley, and P. L.Kilbride (eds.). 1997. *African Families and the Crisis of Social Change*. Westport, CT: Bergin & Garvey.

7   Africa's environmental problems

The problems facing the African environment are enormous. They include deforestation, soil erosion and land degradation, desertification, droughts and floods, inadequate or contaminated water resources, the deposition of toxic waste, and threat to wildlife. The list is by no means exhaustive. Having been ignored in the distant and more recent past, attention is now being paid to them because it is now realized that there is a definite connection between the environment and human development, which includes national prosperity or failure, and starvation or a well-fed healthy people. It is small wonder that the protection of the African environment is currently one of the United Nations' sustainable development goals. Some of these problems are obviously caused by Mother Nature but it is also obvious that many are man-made and could be solved or alleviated by human intervention. This chapter will look at the interaction between Africans and their environment both in the past and in the present, and will examine some of the issues listed above.

Lest the above list suggests that Africans do not care about their environment, it must be stressed right at the outset that in the traditional setting, Africans are much more intimately connected with their environment than people in the West. The connection is not just economic, but also social and spiritual. In traditional Africa there is the belief, as we shall see in the chapter on religion, that there is a force permeating the whole of nature, holding together the whole of nature, and influencing everything in nature. There is thus an interconnectedness among spirits and other supernatural beings, humans, the rest of biological nature, and even inanimate objects. Spirits and other supernatural forces are supposed to live in streams, trees, mountains and other forms of nature, and these forms of nature are therefore regarded as sacred and must not be desecrated. The earth itself, which produces food to nurture human beings, is regarded as sacred and in many African religions there is a god or goddess of the earth who is one of the most powerful deities. During the act of circumcision in many African communities, the blood of the male trickles on to the earth and binds the initiate not only with the earth but with the living dead, so to speak. The urge to protect the earth in order that it may produce enough to nurture human beings can be seen, for instance, in the traditional Igbo belief, enunciated by Chinua Achebe in his novel *Things Fall Apart*, that people who die of certain diseases should not be buried in the earth. This might sound harsh, but it probably originated in the people's desire to protect the earth and keep it pure so that it may produce abundantly.

It is also important to stress that there is an intimate relationship between the environment and development. African nations, who are very much concerned with development, are beginning to realize this. The recent problems in the Sahel, where drought

DOI: 10.4324/9781003111733-8

and the encroaching Sahara Desert caused hunger, starvation, movements of population, and setbacks to the economies of several countries, brought this starkly to our attention, if only because we were forced to look at photographs in the media of emaciated, skeletal, and dying adults, children, and animals. Degraded land will affect agricultural production and therefore availability of food for the population, leading to the need to import food, with all kinds of consequences for the economy and the health of the people in general. Water supply contaminated by toxic waste or by the by-products of indiscriminate mining will lead, not only to lessened agricultural production, but also to a deterioration of the people's health with all kinds of consequences for the economy. Governments do engage in revenue-generating activities that will, nevertheless, have disastrous effects on the environment and on the economy itself eventually. Of course, some African governments will argue that in order to promote development they need to generate revenue and therefore have to strengthen industries like the timber or logging industry, with consequent disastrous impact on the environment. One must concede that these governments do have a point. The problem is how to promote development, that is provide the resources to promote such development, and at the same time protect the environment for our children who would need that environment for their own development. This is what scholars and experts have referred to as sustainable development. Development which destroys the environment cannot be called sustainable because that environment will no longer be able to provide the means for continuing such development.

Although the relationship between the African environment and African development is a fairly recent preoccupation, concern over the African environment is not itself new. As far back as 1935 E. P. Stebbing published an article in which he warned the then colonial governments, such as Britain and France, about the expanding Sahara Desert and the dangers to the Sahel. The Sahel is the semi-arid region bordering the Sahara and it is part of several West African countries like Burkina Faso, Niger, Nigeria, and Chad. Stebbing recognized that the growing infertility of the area meant that it would soon be desert-like, and that the Sahara was encroaching. Stebbing made suggestions about the measures that needed to be taken, but the colonial governments at the time did not pay attention. They were much more interested in the exploitation of the region for their own benefit than in the protection of the environment for Africans of the future. Indeed, some of the activities of the colonialists were harmful to the environment, but they benefitted from them and were therefore unlikely to stop them. For instance, the emphasis on cash crops or commodities like cacao, tea, coffee, and cotton to fuel the factories of Europe meant devoting huge tracts of land for the cultivation of such commodities; that meant cutting down the trees in such areas and leaving less and less arable land for the cultivation of subsistence crops. Ordinary farmers consequently had to engage in more shifting cultivation to provide arable land for their purposes. If the measures suggested by Stebbing in 1935 had been adopted, the tragedy that occurred in the Sahel from the 1970s might have been avoided.

The environmental problems in Africa captured the world's attention in the 1970s with the events in the Sahel when it became apparent that large sections of the population of West Africa were on the verge of starvation because of dwindling rainfall and reduced soil fertility for crop cultivation (Nyang'oro, 237). It was also recognized that the situation in Africa had global ramifications and demanded a global effort to produce solutions. From then on, several international conferences on the environment were held, all of them showcasing Africa's problems. In 1972 the United Nations Conference on the Human Environment was held in Stockholm. This conference highlighted global concern for the world environment in general, but also for the African environment in particular. It led to the establishment of the United Nations Environmental Programme (UNEP), and it is significant that the headquarters were located in Nairobi, the capital of Kenya. In 1992 the United Nations Conference on the Environment and Development (UNCED) was held in Rio de Janeiro. This conference, which was also called the "Earth Summit," drew up a program of action called "Agenda 21." Agenda 21 focused on the balance between creating and protecting a healthy environment and promoting the development of the world's economies (Nyang'oro, 235). Next came the World Summit on Sustainable Development held in Johannesburg in 2002. As the name implies, this conference focused on sustainable development, stressing the need to promote development and end poverty while protecting the environment at the same time. The conference drew up the "Johannesburg Plan" that came to be known as the "Millennium Development Goals" (MDGs), and all the participants committed themselves to implementing it. It is significant that one of these important conferences was held in Africa and the headquarters of the agency that resulted from another was located in Africa. This emphasized Africa's and the world's determination to promote development in Africa while protecting the environment at the same time.

Some of Africa's environmental problems have been caused by geological factors and by the continent's geographic location. Africa is a very old continent, much older than North America or Europe. The soil is of ancient origin and its nutrient capacity has been diminishing for a much longer period than in other continents. This leaching from the soil of the continent's nutrients over a very long period of time is a very important factor (see Lewis and Berry). It has resulted in the African soil being much less fertile than that of other continents, with significant consequences for agricultural production and for the continent's ability to sustain huge populations. Africa's geographic location has also had interesting environmental consequences. As we have seen, most of the continent (about 75 percent) lies within the Tropics of Cancer and Capricorn. This means that temperatures are generally extremely high and most of the continent has a tropical climate. The high temperatures mean that matter decomposes very easily and quickly in the soil, unlike the situation in more temperate latitudes. The high temperatures generally lead to heavy rainfall, but this occurs in most cases during one period of the year, unlike the situation in temperate latitudes where rainfall occurs throughout the year and is fairly evenly distributed. In many areas of Africa there are only two seasons: the dry season and the rainy season. The combination of high temperatures and heavy rainfall in most areas means that matter easily decomposes and is easily leached into the seas. Nutrients therefore stay in the African soil for shorter periods than in other continents. This is a further contribution to the infertility of the African soil. Let us now look at some specific problems of the African environment.

Deforestation

Deforestation is the cutting down of trees for various purposes. It might be to provide more space for the cultivation of crops, to provide firewood for cooking, to provide timber, to provide land for grazing, to provide space for the construction of houses as urban populations expand, or to conduct mining operations if minerals have been discovered in the area. Whatever the purpose, it can have a very adverse impact on the environment and can lead to some other major environmental issues such as soil erosion and desertification. Deforestation affects the nature of the landscape. Some areas where the trees have been cut look like an eyesore. This is particularly true of a country like Sierra Leone where trees have been cut down on some beautiful hillsides to make room for the construction of some ugly shacks. The resulting landscape looks like a slum.

Africa is particularly attractive to those who for one reason or the other wish to cut down trees. Africa has one of the world's densest rainforests; it is located in the basin of the Congo River, in the Democratic Republic of the Congo, and in Cameroon which, according to Nyang'oro, has the world's second largest contiguous tract of rainforest after the Amazon Basin (Nyang'oro, 243). The rainforests are extremely important to the world's ecological system, but they are to be found in very few parts of the world. Nyang'oro states that a UNEP study (1990) revealed that just three countries—Brazil, the Democratic Republic of the Congo, and Indonesia—have most of the world's tropical forests. Africa has 17 percent of the world's forests and the DRC has over 20 percent of Africa's forests (Nyang'oro, 240). This is because of the very heavy annual rainfall these regions have. Nyang'oro goes on to mention that there are two forest types: the closed tropical rainforest, with a tight canopy of evergreen trees, and the open tropical forest, with a non-continuous canopy. Because of the temperature and heavy rainfall, both are present in Africa. The forest in the DRC is a closed tropical forest, but there are open tropical forests in many other countries like Sierra Leone, Ghana, Cameroon, and Kenya. Africa therefore has a huge proportion of the world's forests, but these are being seriously depleted and their depletion is bound to affect the world's ecological system. The depletion is worse in some countries than in others. For instance, it is worse in Cameroon and Côte d'Ivoire than it is in the DRC; nevertheless, according to Nyang'oro, closed forests in Africa are expected to disappear within 25 years unless necessary steps are taken to avoid the catastrophe (Nyang'oro, 240, quoting World Bank Report, 2000, 42). There has thus been a lot of deforestation in Africa. In a sense, it has been going on for a long time, but it accelerated dramatically after World War II.

Let us now look at the reasons for deforestation in Africa. The first is the need to provide space for crop cultivation both for subsistence and for the production of the so-called cash or commodity crops, such as cacao and coffee, for export to the Western world. The cultivation of the cash crops, in particular, requires extensive removal of trees. The situation is made worse by the inherent poverty of the African soil. Much more land is required and many more trees have to be removed because one can plant on a particular piece of land for only a limited number of years before the land appears to be exhausted. This means that after a certain number of years that piece of land, where the nutrients are almost exhausted, has to be left to lie fallow while the trees and shrubbery in another area are burnt down to provide more cultivable land. However, because of rising populations and the need to provide more crops, the farmer might return to the original piece of land before he is supposed to and before the land has recovered its nutrients. The land therefore produces less and less and eventually becomes completely exhausted and useless for farming. This is the process which is known as "shifting cultivation" because the farmer moves from one piece of land to the other. It has been calculated that shifting cultivation accounts for 70 percent of deforestation. It has to be noted that the trees that were growing in the area before it was burnt down for crop cultivation may not have grown back before the farmer plants there again. Once forests are cleared for agriculture there is no guarantee that the trees will grow back. Shifting cultivation, therefore, is a very important agent of deforestation (Nyang'oro,

242). But perhaps the ultimate responsible factor here is the inherent poverty of the African soil which compels farmers to shift from one piece of land to the other.

Another important cause of deforestation is poverty, both of individuals and of countries as a whole. Most Africans' source of energy is fuel wood or charcoal. This is because most Africans are too poor to afford alternative sources of energy like electricity and gas. It may also be that a particular country is too poor to be able to produce electricity for all the people all of the time. It is also well known that even where the government is able to provide electricity it may not be available all the time because of inefficiency or corruption. For instance, Nigeria, Africa's most populous country and one of the world's most important producers of oil which is important in the production of electricity, has numerous power outages and the electricity-producing corporation NEPA is famous as the butt of many jokes and ribald songs. Ninety percent of Africans use fuel wood or firewood for cooking, and wood and brush supply 52 percent of all energy sources. To provide the firewood, trees are cut down and the bundles of firewood transported to cities and other areas in trucks. At times the wood is further burnt down to produce charcoal which is used by all even at the present day because of the unreliability of the electricity supply. With rising populations the demand for fuel grows even further and the woodland becomes even more vulnerable. It has been calculated that every year Africa loses woodland areas the size of the Netherlands. One very tragic case is that of the island country of Madagascar, or the Malagasy Republic, which has lost 80 percent of its forests. The situation is tragic because Madagascar was home to some of the most exotic flora and fauna in the whole world. Some of these species of animals and plants are only to be found in Madagascar. The speculation is that they were brought to the island, and only to that island, by current drifts from the Indian Ocean. All these species are now endangered because of the loss of habitat. This will inevitably have an impact on Madagascar's tourism industry, but the deforestation itself will lead to land degradation and climate change.

Commercial logging

Commercial logging is a major cause of deforestation in Africa. Commercial logging is the cutting down of trees to provide timber for the construction of buildings, the manufacture of furniture, and so on. It is very crucial to the economy of several African countries such as Ghana, Sierra Leone, Cameroon, and Gabon. These countries realized that the export of timber which they had in abundance could provide much-needed revenue and foreign exchange and therefore give a boost to their ailing economies. The so-called structural adjustment policies, that some of these countries, like Ghana, were forced to adopt, greatly accelerated the export of timber. These policies were stipulated by financial bodies like the World Bank and the International Monetary Fund to whom some African countries applied for loans. A condition stipulated by these financial institutions for granting the loans was that the African countries should cut down on imports and increase exports in order to generate the foreign exchange and revenue that were needed to pay back the loans and give a general boost to the economy. Some of the countries that accepted the policies saw the export of timber as an automatic source of revenue and foreign exchange. For instance, timber exports from Ghana increased between 1983 and 1989 from 16 million dollars to 99 million dollars (Nyang'oro, 243). In 2010 Ghana earned 137.9 million euros from timber exports compared to 128.2 million in 2009. Some might argue that a country has the right to export whatever it needs to in order to revive its economy, and the economy of a country like Ghana was in dire need of rejuvenation. The problem is that the intensified cutting down of trees leads to deforestation, especially if it is not properly planned and directed, and deforestation can lead to dire consequences. The problem of commercial logging is probably worst in Cameroon. About 75 percent of that country's forests have been logged or allocated for logging concessions. Less than 20 percent has not been logged and only 6 percent is protected as parks or reserves. All this is particularly unfortunate as Cameroon's forests are the most biodiverse (Nyang'oro, 243, quoting World Resources Institute).

Conflicts

Strange as it might sound, civil wars can lead to deforestation. The fact is that civil conflicts can cause enormous displacement of people who then become refugees in a neighboring country. Guinea, for instance, had to take in hundreds of thousands of refugees from Sierra Leone and Liberia during the conflicts in those countries and both Sierra Leone and Liberia took in thousands from each other during their own civil conflicts. These refugees do not just go into the houses of friends in the host country. Enormous camps have to be built for them as well as improvised individual shacks. In order to do this, vast tracts of land have to be cleared and this leads to deforestation. Moreover, these refugees have nothing but firewood to use as a source of energy.

Effects of deforestation

Soil erosion and land degradation

Deforestation has several devastating consequences. One of them is land degradation which will then have dire consequences for food production and agriculture in general. Trees provide cover, and their roots hold the soil in place. When there are no trees the soil is loosened and is easily vulnerable to heavy rainfall and floods. The heavy downfall of rain carries away large amounts of loose soil, a process known as soil erosion. Huge amounts of nutrients might also be leached. The problem is further exacerbated by the fact that in many areas of Africa the rainfall occurs and is concentrated in certain months of the year. It is thus very heavy and likely to erode large amounts of loosened soil. The land thus becomes degraded and not as productive as it otherwise would have been. It is interesting that shifting cultivation which is practiced in order to increase food production might lead to deforestation and soil erosion which might, in fact, affect the production of food. But the erosion of the soil can have even more dire consequences. The erosion causes the soil to lose its firmness and strength and buildings put on it are at tremendous risk from floods and heavy rainfall. This happened very recently in Sierra Leone. The trees on a once beautiful hillside near the capital, Freetown, were removed to make way for shacks and larger ugly-looking buildings. These improvised buildings had a magnificent view of the Atlantic Ocean, but they were on a very weak foundation since the once-firm soil was now considerably loosened. Eventually a heavy downpour occurred causing a tremendous flood which swept away hundreds of houses leading to the loss of over one thousand lives.

Forest dwellers' lifestyle

Nyang'oro insists that deforestation can affect the lifestyle of people who live in or depend on the forest. According to him, rural dwellers, who account for 75 percent of the African population, depend on the forest for a number of products such as fuelwood, fruit, nuts, dyes, and medicines. In Ghana, for instance, two million people depend on the forest for their livelihood. Another 75 percent depend on food got from the forest to supplement their diet (Nyang'oro, 244). Deforestation can therefore lead to malnutrition. Indeed, deforestation can affect almost every aspect of the lives of these rural dwellers.

Desertification

Deforestation can also lead to desertification, which is the conversion of once arable land into arid, desert-like wasteland. It can be caused by drought, but also by the degradation of the land through soil erosion and the leaching of nutrients. It can also be caused when crops are over-cultivated, or rangelands overgrazed. All these factors have been held responsible for the situation in the Sahel, where land that was once productive and suitable for cultivation has become arid, with terrible consequences. It has been calculated that since World War II about 650,000 square kilometers of land once suitable for agriculture has been lost to the Sahara Desert. The continent as a whole is losing about 36,000 square kilometers of land to the desert every year (Nyang'oro, 246). The problem is particularly serious in Niger, Mali, Burkina Faso, Mauretania, Northern Nigeria, Northern Ghana, Senegal, Gambia, Chad, Sudan, and Egypt (Nyang'oro, 247). Desertification is, in fact, one of Africa's major environmental problems. Of course, desertification can also be caused by sustained drought. This is almost certainly one of the major causes of the desertification in the Sahel where there was considerable diminution in levels of rainfall for several years.

Climate change

Deforestation can also lead to climate change, which is one of the factors threatening the very survival of the planet itself. Trees take in carbon dioxide through their leaves and release oxygen into the atmosphere. It is, of course, quite beneficial for the atmosphere to have more oxygen and less carbon dioxide because the presence of carbon dioxide in the atmosphere is one of the forces causing global warming. Fewer trees means less oxygen and more carbon dioxide in the atmosphere. This is one of the reasons why Africa's environmental problems are of global concern. Deforestation in Africa can lead to global warming which is a global concern.

Loss of wildlife

The cutting down of forests means that the wildlife inhabiting the forest area loses its cover. Africa is famous for its wildlife, much of which lives in the grassland areas and attracts tourists from all over the world. However, a lot of the wildlife, such as leopards and deer, lives in the forest areas and when this is diminished, so is the animal cover and some of the smaller animals that the bigger ones depend on. Inevitably, the numbers of these animals decrease. Quite a few of the animals in Africa are already on the endangered species list. Some, like those in Madagascar, are well on the way to becoming extinct. Their loss hampers nature's way of maintaining a balance.

The nature of the African soil

We have already seen that soil erosion and desertification, which are related to deforestation, are in and of themselves major environmental problems in Africa. So is the nature of the African soil itself. Because the African soil is very old, it is not as infused with nutrients as some of the other continents and is therefore less fertile. It is also more subject to soil erosion. The African soil therefore has diminished carrying capacity; that is, the ability to sustain human activity. It is assumed in some quarters that, because of the enormous size of the continent, Africa can support many more people than it currently has. This is not true, because the infertility of the soil makes the continent incapable of sustaining much more human activity. This becomes extremely important for issues like population control. Africa is not under-populated as some assume, because the available soil cannot sustain an enormous population. Moreover, half of the potentially arable soil has a lot of laterite which is unsuitable for sustained agricultural activity. Of the land that is arable, only 7 percent has rich alluvial soils (Nyang'oro, 247, quoting Revell, Lewis and Berry). Indeed the reason why huge areas are unsettled is because they cannot support sustained settlement.

Drought and floods

We have already seen some of the impact of both. Desertification is partly caused by drought. This is almost certainly the case in the Sahel. Since 1968, rainfall in the Western Sahel has been below the historical mean. One of the consequences is that Lake Chad, once one of Africa's largest lakes, has shrunk considerably. It is estimated that 60 percent of Africa is subject to drought. While some areas experience extreme drought conditions, others have devastating floods with dire consequences for agricultural production. One such case is Mozambique. That country had been doing extremely well since independence in 1975. It had been doing so well that it applied for membership and was accepted as a member of the British Commonwealth of Nations in 1995 although it had not been a British colony. But then came the devastating floods of March 2000, caused by very heavy rainfall and the bursting of the Limpopo River. The flooding was a severe economic setback. In March of 2019 monstrous flooding following Cyclone Idai left hundreds dead and more than 100,000 displaced. Because of its position on the African coast facing the Indian Ocean, Mozambique is particularly susceptible to floods.

The oil industry

Many African countries have discovered oil, but the exploitation of this resource has had a devastating impact on the environment in some cases. In most cases the oil is inland and not offshore, and in order to get at it oil companies have to drill deep into the earth. As a result, huge mountains of matter are removed from the center of the earth and piled on the surface. These mountains of matter are not only a tremendous eyesore, but they also affect the quality of the soil and cause land degradation. The extracted matter can seep into the water system and since some of it is poisonous it causes great health problems for the inhabitants. The oil is usually exploited by foreign companies that have no interest in the preservation of the African environment. They are interested only in profit. It is interesting that many of the oil-producing areas in Africa which should be among the most developed and beautiful, if only because they are producers of wealth, are among the worst-looking and the most neglected. The impact of the oil industry on the environment has led to protests from the people. The most famous case was that in Nigeria toward the end of the last century. Nigeria is, of course, one of the world's leading oil-producers. The oil comes mostly from the east. A famous activist and writer,

Ken Saro-Wiwa, led the protest against the industry's destruction of the environment in that area. To silence him and his movement and allow the oil companies to proceed with their activities un-hindered, the Nigerian government of the day arrested Ken Saro-Wiwa and eight others in 1995 on trumped-up charges of treason and sedition. They were put on trial, convicted, and hanged. Generally speaking, the oil industry in Africa causes ecological disturbance, pollution, explosions, and the infusion of dangerous fluids into the soil.

Toxic waste

Many Western nations now make use of nuclear energy. This is good, since it means less dependence on fossil fuels which contribute toward global warming. However, the creation of nuclear energy results in by-products and waste that can be toxic or even radioactive. Obviously, this presents enormous health hazards. Consequently, some people in the Western world do not want the by-products and waste from nuclear energy buried in areas near where they live. They therefore arrange with the leaders and other individuals in some poor African nations to dump their toxic waste there in return for the payment of huge sums of money. The poor countries need the money, for development some would claim, and the Western nations have places to dump their toxic waste and thus preserve the health of their people. It is common knowledge that in most cases the money paid to leaders for the depositing of toxic waste finds its way into the pockets of individuals and never contributes to development. Other kinds of toxic waste apart from nuclear waste products were regularly deposited in Africa. A UNEP report on Somalia of April 22, 2016 states that from the early 1980s, and continuing into the civil war, the hazardous waste dumped along Somalia's coast includes radioactive uranium waste; lead; cadmium; mercury; industrial, hospital, chemical waste products; and other toxic waste. In 2009, it was reported that tons of toxic waste collected from municipal dumps in Britain were being illegally sent to Africa in breach of Britain's laws stipulating that defunct television sets, computers, and other gadgets should be disposed of safely. At times individuals in these African countries discover that toxic waste has been dumped on their property without their knowledge and consent. In 1981, for instance, some Italian businessmen and Nigerian officials agreed to dump five shiploads of hazardous materials in 8000 drums in a Nigerian citizen's backyard without his knowledge. There was the famous incident in the village of Koko in Nigeria in 1988 in which Italian companies Ecomar and Jelly Wax arranged to pay a local farmer $100 per month to store thousands of barrels of hazardous waste materials. The amount varies, according to the reports one reads, between 2000 and 18000 barrels. It was later discovered that some of the barrels were unsealed and leaking, with serious health effects on the people. This arrangement that sometimes occurs between African governments and other individuals on the one hand, and some Western people on the other, to dump toxic waste on the continent, is one of the most egregious features of the relationship between African and Western countries.

These activities led to the Bamako Convention of 1991 in which 12 African countries decided to take action to prevent Africa from becoming a dumping ground for toxic waste. It came into effect in 1998. However, the Bamako Convention did not put an end to the practice which continues in many forms up to the present. In 2006 there was the infamous *Probo Koala* scandal in Côte d'Ivoire. In 2009 there was the report about toxic waste from British municipal dumps being sent to Africa. Concerns about the continuation of this activity were expressed in 2011, 2016, and 2018 by various organizations including UNEP. This was the main reason why a second convention of the interested parties was held in Abidjan in January 2018 to review the progress that had been made since the first convention of 1991 and make plans for the future.

Inadequate water resources

In examining Africa's environmental problems, we must take a look at Africa's water resources. In this connection we are considering, not just the availability of water for purposes of agriculture and food production, but for other purposes like, drinking, cooking, and general household use. As far as agriculture is concerned, some areas are lucky to have adequate rainfall; others are not and must depend on irrigation to a certain extent. Some areas are lucky to be watered by river systems. In many areas it is the unavailability of water for general purposes that is most striking. The water supply is inadequate, not just because of the lack of rainfall, but because of the pollution of the available sources of water, like rivers and streams, by seepage of debris and human waste. The water that some Africans depend on for cooking, drinking, and other household purposes would be described in other parts of the world as simply filthy. This is no fault of the people. They do not have access to the kind of resources that would lead to clean, filtered, or treated water. And of course, this would have serious consequences for their health. It must be noted that even where rainfall is heavy, there is often a shortage of clean water and the people have to depend on water from streams and rivers. This is because proper arrangements have not been made for storing water. Sierra Leone, for instance, has annual rainfall of about 150 inches, and yet, during certain months of the year, there is a serious shortage of water. This is because there aren't proper arrangements for storing the water in suitable reservoirs, and most of the water runs to waste into the ocean. More attention has to be paid to providing proper water storage and proper water treatment. It should also be possible for arrangements to be made for water sharing among neighboring countries.

Africa's environmental problems are obviously enormous, and they threaten development. What is to be done? In the first place, something must be done to slow down deforestation which is really at the heart of most of the problems. This calls for good management of Africa's forests. One must admit that countries have the right to engage in logging in order to provide revenue for development, but this has to be properly regulated. Attention must be paid to the replacement of trees that have been cut down, for whatever purposes, and serious consideration must be given to the number of trees to be replanted. In this connection, mention must be made of the heroic efforts of the late Professor Wangari Maathai who launched the Green Belt Movement in Kenya that was concerned with replanting trees. For her efforts she became the first African woman to win the Nobel Prize for Peace, which she did in 2004. More movements like hers are needed in Africa. The cutting down of trees for fuel and energy is very problematic because it is a question of poverty. The solution here would be both national and global, because deforestation in any one part of the world would have consequences for others, and the measures that are needed would probably be beyond the capacities of just one country. If we are going to say to people that they must stop using firewood for fuel and must use gas or electricity, then we must make it possible for them to afford the gas or electricity. This would therefore mean getting the people out of poverty and it would involve economic reconstruction that would involve the international order. Wealthier nations would have to help those that are poorer to have the means to generate electricity and purchase gas as well as to deliver them to their people at affordable rates. It will not be easy. Governments would also have to introduce strict and enforceable laws about the indiscriminate cutting down of trees.

Some of the problems could be solved by the use of irrigation and fertilizers. Irrigation would involve well-managed use of available water resources. The use of fertilizers would take care of the problems caused by the infertility of Africa's soil, because it would introduce nutrients where there were none before. It would also help with the issue of shifting cultivation. Instead of moving to another piece of land when one piece becomes infertile, the farmer could use fertilizers to reintroduce much-needed nutrients. And this is being done in many places. However, it is well known that these fertilizers have to be used with caution, since they might in their turn introduce chemicals that might affect the soil. It is well known, for instance, that some fertilizers make the soil more alkaline, which is bad for agriculture. The use of fertilizers is not, therefore, a perfect solution. There is, however, one attractive possibility in so far as the use of fertilizers is concerned. If proper arrangements are made for the disposal of human waste, it could be transformed into a very beneficial kind of fertilizer which would then be used to reintroduce nutrients into the soil. This would involve a very beneficial kind of circle, in which human waste becomes fertilizer, which in turn leads to the production of better food for human consumption.

Some attention would also have to be paid to population control. The notion that Africa can sustain a humungous population because of its size would have to be discarded. All these measures would need financial and manpower resources that might be beyond the reach of some countries. This is one of the reasons why the effort toward solutions has to be global.

References and suggestions for further reading

Agyei, Y. "Deforestation in Sub-Saharan Africa." *African Technology Forum* 8. Online at web.mit. edu/africantech/www/articles/deforestation.htm.

Anderson, D. 1987. *The Economics of Aforestation: A Case Study in Africa*. Baltimore, MD: Johns Hopkins University Press.

Bojo, J. et al. 1992. *Environment and Development: An Economic Approach*. Boston: Kluwer Academic Publishers.

Cole, N. H. A. 1986. "Environmental Problems and Policies in Africa." Pp. 31–52 in *Environment and Development Opportunities in Africa and the Middle East*. Conference Summary of the World Environment Center, September 25–27, 1985. Nairobi: UNEP.

Darkoh, M. B. K. "Desertification: The Scorge of Africa." Online at www.cru.uea.ac.uk.

Dixon, J. A. et al. 1988. *Economic Analysis of the Environmental Impacts of Development Projects*. London: Earthscan.

Erkholm, E., and L. R.Brown. 1977. *Spreading Deserts: The Hand of Man*. Washington, DC: Worldwatch Institute.

Leonard, Jeffrey. (ed.). 1985. *Divesting Nature's Capital: The Political Economy of Environmental Abuse in the Third World*. New York: Holmes & Meier.

Lewis, L. and L. Berry. 1988. *African Environments and Resources*. Boston: Unwin Hyman.

Nyang'oro, J. E. 2007. "Africa's Environmental Problems." Pp. 235–264 in A. A. Gordon and D. L. Gordon (eds.). *Understanding Contemporary Africa*. Boulder, CO: Lynne Rienner.

Okoko, T. "Scientists Move to Save Lake Victoria from Dying." Online at www.allafrica.com.

Stebbing, E. P. 1935. "The Encroaching Sahara: The Threat to the West African Colonies." *Geographical Journal* 85: 508–524.

Timberlake, L. 1986. *Africa in Crisis: The Causes, the Cures of Environmental Bankruptcy*. Washington, DC: Earthscan.

8   Religion in Africa

This chapter will be concerned with religion in Africa both in the past and the present. Although almost all the major religions are represented in Africa, we will concentrate on the three most important ones in so far as Africa is concerned: traditional religion, Christianity, and Islam. Religion has always been, and still is, a very important factor in African life. It is a very crucial aspect of African history and, in some respects, is closely tied to development. One major difference between the impact of religion in Africa and in other parts of the world is that it influences almost every aspect of the individual's life. It is very difficult to find an African, even in the present day, who will be prepared to say that he does not believe in the existence of a God or adhere to any religion, though some Western and university-educated individuals are claiming to be atheists. But even these individuals will attend the religious rituals of their relatives in times of celebration or sorrow, because they wish to remain a part of the community. Religion is one of the forces in Africa that give a sense of community.

Professor Mbiti, one of the world's greatest authorities on African religion, claims that Africans are "notoriously religious" (Mbiti, 1969, 1). Not everyone has shared this view. Some of the missionaries and early European travelers to Africa took back stories of pagan societies. In other words, since the Africans these travelers met were not Christian, they must be pagan and had no religion. These early travelers were not interested in finding out whether the Africans had any religion at all or in studying the nature of their religion. In fact, not only did Africans have their own religion, there are quite a few similarities between the Christianity that the European travelers practiced and brought with them and the religions of the Africans, as some writers have tried to demonstrate in their works. Chinua Achebe's *Things Fall Apart*, which is a presentation of traditional society and the relations of that society with the incoming Christians, shows, in a discussion between one missionary and a society elder, that both religions believe in the existence of a Supreme Being who made the whole world (*Things Fall Apart*, 179).

When Mbiti says that Africans are an intensely religious people, he probably means, not only that, in the traditional sense at least, Africans allow almost every aspect of their lives to be dominated by religion, but that they are determined to be obedient to their God in all respects and to accept the framework of morality created by the God's dictates. In many parts of Africa the religion was and is traditional religion. There has been considerable debate as to whether one should speak of "traditional religion" or "traditional religions" because there are differences among the systems practiced in many parts of Africa. Where we can talk about a central Christian or Islamic code which then became modified in various eras and in various places, we cannot do the same about a traditional African code, because the practitioners of African religions were not in contact

DOI: 10.4324/9781003111733-9

culturally and therefore are not practicing versions of one code. One of the problems here is that there is no common religious text or code like the Bible or the Qur'an. Some scholars prefer to use the term "traditionalism" when referring to African religions, but traditionalism implies much more than religion. There have been suggestions that we should talk of "African religions" because each code is more or less unique and complete in itself. However, in spite of the differences, there are many similarities among African religious codes and practices, and a scholar like Mbiti has suggested that we could talk of African religion while not being forgetful of the differences. This is the approach I will adopt in this chapter.

The research of scholars like Mbiti, Parrinder, and Moyo has established that although there are differences among the traditional religions in Africa, there are also numerous similarities. Here are the main ones: (a) belief in a Supreme Being; (b) belief in spirits and lesser gods; (c) belief in life after death; (d) religious personnel and sacred places; (e) belief in witchcraft/sorcery (see Moyo, 319). In addition, there is a common African "ontology," or the traditional African's perception of the nature and composition of the universe, which one must understand in order to understand traditional religions fully. According to this ontology, there is a hierarchical structure in the universe with the Supreme Being or "God" right at the top. As with other religions like Christianity and Islam, God is the source and sustainer of the whole of creation. Next in the hierarchy and below God the Supreme Being are the lesser divinities and spirits. It is probably unfair to the lesser gods to place them in the same category with the spirits because some of them, as we shall see, have enormous powers and are therefore more than mere spirits. There are three groups of spirits. There are those who are supernatural forces with innate powers that are much greater than those of human beings. Then there are the spirits of the ancestors, beings who died some time ago. Finally, there are the spirits of the unborn; that is, children who yet have to enter their mothers' wombs and be born. These two latter groups can also demonstrate extra-human powers. Right in the middle of the hierarchy comes man, or human beings in general. Next come the rest of biological life, animals and plants in other words. Right at the bottom are phenomena or objects without life. There is one more feature of this ontology that is extremely important. This is the existence of a vital force that permeates the universe. This force can be controlled or manipulated to bring about certain outcomes. God the Supreme Being is the ultimate controller of this force, but other beings in the hierarchy have or can acquire the ability to manipulate this force. The higher the being is in the hierarchy, the greater is its ability to manipulate the force. Thus God, who is the ultimate controller of this force, has a greater ability to manipulate it than spirits or the lesser divinities, who in their turn have greater ability in this regard than human beings. Of course, animals and plants and objects without life have no ability over this force at all. A lesser being, like man, can call on higher beings, like the spirits, to help him manipulate this force, and in the process can make use of the lesser objects like plants and animals. Now let us look at the various items of traditional African beliefs in turn.

God the Supreme Being

There is a common misconception that some traditional African societies believe in, not just one, but several gods. These are the so-called polytheistic societies, like ancient Greek or Roman society where there was a pantheon of several gods. The real truth is that even where there are several gods there is always a head God or supreme God. It is to this fact that one of the elders in Achebe's *Things Fall Apart* refers when he calls Chukwu the head God in the Igbo tradition. Chukwu's counterpart in the Yoruba tradition is Oludumare. The other gods are definitely lesser gods with much less power than the head God. In some traditions, like the Igbo tradition, they are assistants or helpers to the head God. This God, like the Christian or Islamic God, is omnipresent, omnipotent, and omniscient. Because he is so mighty, he is rather more distant from man than the other gods and in some traditions is supposed to live up in the skies. Although human beings can pray to him, they more often approach the lesser gods because they do not wish to keep on pestering the mighty head God, There are various names for this mighty God in the various societies, names that imply the most impressive attribute of the God. For instance the Gikuyu name for God is "the one who makes mountains quake and rivers overflow." The Ngambe name for God implies that God is immanent and is "the one who fills everything." Among the Shona of Zimbabwe God is Musikavanhu or "creator of humankind" and "Great Ancestor" (Moyo, 319). In traditional African religions this God is self-sufficient, having neither father, mother, nor child. He is generally good but can demonstrate tremendous anger if human beings offend him. It can be seen from this account that there are several similarities between traditional African religion's conception of God and the Christian view. The only major difference here is that the Christian God was supposed to have a son, Jesus Christ. But even here we know that the son was God himself who chose to come to earth to suffer for mankind. Some traditional African religions even have the doctrine of the Trinity, one of the most incomprehensible Christian doctrines. This has been brought to our attention by Emmanuel Twesigye as a result of his extensive research among his own people in Uganda. One of his informers told him that, before the arrival of the missionaries, his people had a very good conception of God whom they thought of as some kind of "eternally existing triplets" consisting of Nyamuhanga, the first one who made everything; Kazooba Nyamuhanga, the second brother who gave light to all human beings so that they will not stumble; and Rugaba Rwa Nyamuhanga, who takes what Nyamuhanga has created and gives it to the people as he wishes. The informant identifies these three brothers as being equivalent to God the Father, Jesus Christ, and the Holy Spirit. He also recognizes that the only difference the missionaries introduced was that Kazooba (Jesus Christ) was the son and not the brother of Nyamuhanga (Twesigye, 93). This very insightful statement tells us quite a lot about traditional African religion and its relationship with Christianity.

Belief in spirits and lesser gods

Lesser gods

The lesser divinities in traditional African religion are assistants to the Head God. They are specially designated by him to be in charge of certain areas of life like agriculture, or war, or lightning and thunder. For instance, Orunmila in the Yoruba pantheon is responsible for all knowledge, and Sango is the god of lightning and thunder, or power and energy. It is rather like a cabinet with each member being responsible for a particular department and answerable to the Head, even though each has tremendous laxity and freedom. As indicated above, it is unfair to put the lesser gods into the same classification as the spirits, because they obviously have much more power than most of the spirits. For instance, Ani, the goddess of the Earth in the Igbo pantheon, seems to be much more than a mere spirit. In the Yoruba pantheon the lesser divinities go under the collective nomenclature of Orisha. They include Obatala, Ogun, Sango, and Eshu, the well-known trickster god. Among the Igbo of Eastern Nigeria the head God is Chukwu, and the lesser gods include Ani, Ojukwu, and Ifejeoka.

Spirits

The spirits in African traditional religion include some supernatural creatures, extra-human entities with much less power than the lesser gods. For the most part, however, they are the spirits of the ancestors long departed. They are supposed to be intermediaries between the world of the living and the gods. Human beings therefore need to be in the good books of their departed relatives so that the latter could plead on their behalf with the gods. They therefore have to placate them with offerings and sacrifices. Apart from their proximity to the gods and their consequent ability to act as intermediaries, these spirits have powers that they could use to frustrate or advance the efforts of their descendants still living on the earth. My father never opened a new bottle of rum, whisky, or brandy without going to the front door and pouring a libation to the departed ancestors, thus invoking their favor. I remember a particular incident which is instructive in several ways. While constructing my house in Freetown, the capital of my native Sierra Leone, I invited a clergyman friend to say prayers, as was the custom, during the ceremony of laying the foundation stone. The minister was properly dressed in his Anglican robes and conducted a very Christian ceremony; he then pronounced the occasion over. However, my father, who was an excellent Christian, then came forward and said he was not finished. He called for a glass of water and started pouring libation to the departed ancestors, calling the names of people who had been long dead, and asking them to help in the execution of this mammoth task, the construction of a house. But he then ended it all with the usual Christian statement, "In the name of the father, and of the son, and of the holy ghost, Amen." This incident illustrates that no matter how Christian many Africans become, and no matter how educated, they still believe in the power of the ancestors and their ability to act as intermediaries with the Divine. They still observe the anniversaries of their ancestors' deaths with feasts and sacrifices. This is why in some quarters there is the misconception that Africans engage in ancestor worship. It is a misconception because Africans do not really worship their ancestors. While recognizing the place of the ancestors in the ontological hierarchy, the only being they worship is God. However, they revere and, in some cases fear, the ancestors and this is one of the reasons why they try to placate them.

In some traditional African societies there is the belief that before being born children existed as spirits and entered the mothers' wombs in order to be born. However, some of these spirits were rather naughty and, on coming into the world, did not wish to remain. They wanted to go back to the spirit world, and they did. But over and above that, they decided to taunt their mothers and would therefore re-enter the womb of the same mother, die again, and go back to the spirit world. They would keep doing this again and again. This kind of child is called the "abiku" child or spirit in the Yoruba tradition and the "Obange" in the Igbo tradition. The abiku is very well presented in one of Wole Soyinka's poems where he is haughty and arrogant and keeps mocking his mother and all those who would wish to keep him in the human world. This is obviously a spirit child. The Obange is well represented in Achebe's *Things Fall Apart*, but also in Ben Okri's novel *The Famished Road*. In the latter we see a spirit child who is quite different from Soyinka's haughty abiku. He is very insightful and quite sympathetic, and he is sorry for his mother who keeps on losing child after child. His problem is that it is his friends still in the spirit world who keep urging him to go back to them.

Most African religious traditions also involve spirits with supernatural powers, who are non-human, but are quite distinct from the lesser gods or divinities. Some are evil and others are good; some are mere tricksters. The evil ones are probably traditional religion's way of accounting for the presence of evil in the world, since most traditions have no concept of Satan. Bad things, in other words, are largely done by evil spirits. Humans can protect themselves against these evil spirits by the use of charms and amulets. Some people hang things given them by medicine men over their doors to prevent the evil spirits from going in. The Sierra Leonean "Ronsho" is one such evil spirit. Like the spirits of the ancestors, these spirits have the ability to influence the lives and fortunes of humans for good or for ill, and some humans have the ability to be in touch with therm.

Life after death

We have already seen that, as far as traditional Africans are concerned, immortality partly consists in being remembered after death, and there is no concept of heaven and hell, as in the Christian tradition. This does not mean that traditional Africans do not believe in life after death. Moyo states that in some traditions the dead are believed to be reincarnated, though it may be in other forms than they had in life. Thus, one could be reincarnated as an animal, and in that form one cannot be killed (Moyo, 323). The more common belief is that the dead become spirits and join the spirits of the ancestors. In some traditions the dead are buried with the items it is supposed they will need in this other world of the ancestors. Of course, the ancestors, as we have seen, remain in close communion with those still living in this world, especially their relations and descendants, and have the ability to influence their lives.

Religious personnel and sacred places

Because each religious tradition is unique to the area it serves and is complete in itself, African religions are not subject to the kind of centralized control that has become typical of Christian denominations such as Roman Catholicism or Anglicanism. Each area will have its priests who preside over the religious rituals and ceremonies. At times the priests are also elders in the community and have administrative functions, as in the stateless societies; at times the kings or rulers can also serve as priests or have religious duties. Traditional African religions do not have cathedrals like Christianity or mosques like Islam; however, there are shrines in holy places where the rituals are performed. The rituals are quite often related to the rites of passage like birth, coming of age, marriage, and death. The shrines are dedicated to particular deities, and they could be national shrines, village shrines, or household shrines. Apart from the priests and priestesses, there could also be oracles and diviners who have the ability to perceive and interpret the will of the gods, like the oracle of Agbala in Achebe's *Things Fall Apart*. The oracle is really a god speaking through a human being, usually the priest or priestess of the oracle, and using the human being to communicate with other humans. The communication might be a prophecy or an order. Whatever it is, it is regarded as sacrosanct. In order to communicate the message, the priest or priestess could be possessed by the spirit of the god and appear in quite a different light than usual. The diviner does more or less the same thing: interpret the will of the gods, or spirits; explain the nature of the present situation or the cause of the current problem; and suggest solutions. Unlike the oracle the diviner is seldom possessed, and he/she is trained to use objects like bones, water, nuts, and cowries to determine what is happening. The medium is rather similar to the oracle or the priest or priestess of the oracle, in that he or she communicates the wishes of the gods to the community. Where the oracle involves just one god or spirit, the medium can communicate with diverse gods or spirits.

Witchcraft

Most traditional Africans believe that witchcraft exists. In other words, they feel that there are some human beings who have some supernatural powers and can usually use these powers to do harm, like causing illness or even death; they are even capable of devouring other humans without physically touching them. There has been some controversy among scholars about the definitions of witchcraft, magic, and sorcery, and one can take one's pick among these scholarly definitions. For some, like Moyo, witchcraft is the use of certain powers for evil purposes, an absolutely destructive force. Magic, on the other hand, can be used for good or for evil (Moyo, 326). In that case, is there any difference between witchcraft and magic that is used for evil purposes? For Azevedo, sorcery is a willfully acquired power to cause evil in others. One might ask the inevitable question: how is this power acquired? Through training or contact with the gods? But Azevedo then goes on to describe the activities of sorcerers (traveling long distances by night; causing illness, death, injuries or bad luck) in much the same way as Moyo describes the activities of witches (Azevedo, 402). For Azevedo, witchcraft is an innate power to do evil. For some people the difference between witchcraft and sorcery is that witchcraft is done by women and sorcery by men. In other words, it is a question of gender. If you are a woman you are a witch; if you are a man you are a sorcerer. Unfortunately, it is virtually impossible to come to an accurate definition because all this is a matter of perception: how one perceives certain activities. There can't be any "facts" to prove one thing or another. Witches and sorcerers don't normally talk about their activities or the source of their powers. Most people would merely dismiss all these ideas as superstition anyway. In traditional Africa, however, witchcraft is taken seriously and does matter.

One feature that is common to all these attempts to explain witchcraft is a certain power or force. All witches or sorcerers or performers of "magic" have a certain power, and it is a tremendous power. The issue is: how do they get this power? We saw earlier that in addition to all the various categories of beings in the universe, according to African traditional belief, there is a vital power or force. The Supreme Being is the ultimate controller and sustainer of this force. However, some beings lower down the hierarchical scale, like spirits or human beings, can have or acquire the ability to manipulate this force for good or for ill. They can either manipulate it themselves or call on beings higher up the scale to help them manipulate it, and they can make this appeal by sacrifices or offerings or rituals. The manipulation of this force for good or for evil is apparently what witchcraft is. In this sense, witchcraft itself is neutral; it could be good or bad. Witchcraft is merely a superior ability or knowledge to manipulate the force either by oneself or with the assistance of beings higher up the ontological scale. Because of activities in Europe during the Middle Ages, the terms "witch" and "witchcraft" have acquired pejorative connotations. Witches were in all probability highly intelligent or perceptive women who had more abilities than others, particularly other women, were supposed to have. If they were men, they were hated as sorcerers. It is almost possible that some of his contemporaries saw Galileo as a witch or a sorcerer. During colonial days, some older people used to say that the white man is a witch. They were referring to the white man's apparent ability to invent things like telegraph, railways, and electricity. In other words, the "witch" may simply have been someone with heightened intellectual powers who was perceived by his or her peers to have derived these powers from some extra-natural source. The force, as has been suggested, can be manipulated for good or for evil. It could be used to destroy people; but it could also be used to heal people. Medicine men, who were quite often called "witch doctors," were among those who had the ability to invoke the spirits to aid them in manipulating the force to cure diseases. This is one of the reasons why a visit to the medicine man would start with his using all kinds of objects to invoke the spirits or even gods; he is asking for their assistance because he would have to manipulate the force to carry out acts of healing. Of course, witchcraft can also take disastrous forms and some of these powerful people could invoke the spirits to help them manipulate the force to carry out destructive acts.

African religious myths

Like all other religions, African religions have their myths and stories explaining the nature of the relationship between man and the Divine, as a number of scholars have demonstrated. Thus, almost every African traditional religion has its own unique creation story; that is, the story of how the world came into being, just like the Judaeo-Christian story in the Bible. There are also myths about how man became separated from God, just like the story of Adam and Eve eating the forbidden fruit and being thrust out of Eden, in the biblical book of Genesis. In the Yoruba tradition, which is about the most complex religious tradition in Africa, the supreme God, Olurun or Olodumare, gave permission to Obatala, a lesser deity, to create the earth. At the time, all the deities lived up in the skies. Olodumare was the ruler of the skies, while another lesser god, Olokun, ruled the waters below. Obatala is actually one of the three manifestations of the supreme godhead, just as Christ, in the Christian religion, is regarded as one of the three manifestations of God. It is actually Obatala who climbs down and creates the earth. He creates dry land, mountains, and valleys. Subsequently, Obatala becomes bored with his own work and he decides to make clay figures. He then asks Olodumare to breathe life into the figures, who then become perfect human beings. Obatala became the patron of mankind and he and the other deities were pleased with his work in creating the earth and mankind. However, Olokun became angry because he had not been consulted about all these developments. He therefore decided to cause a great flood which almost wiped out the creation completely. From that time all the gods take Olokun seriously.

We can see several similarities between this myth and the Christian myth of the creation, even though there are differences: the position of Obatala, who is the one who climbs down or descends to earth; the human figures created out of clay; Olodumare breathing life into the human creatures and making them perfect; and the gods being "pleased" with Obatalas's work. Although the flood is not part of the Christian creation story in the Bible, the details here are very similar to those of Noah's flood. Traditions among the Ahamba, Basuto, and Herero of Southern and Southeastern Africa say that God brought man out of a hole in the ground or the stem of a tree. A Herero myth suggests that God brought man and woman out of the mythical tree of life situated in the underworld. The tree of life is, of course, a very common archetype in the myths of many cultures. It is analogous to the tree in the Garden of Eden or the tree in the Garden of the Hesperides in Greek mythology. In some traditions, God is said to have brought man and woman to the world out of a vessel like a canoe. Some tribes along the Nile valley believe that God created man in heaven and then lowered him to earth.

Like the biblical story, many African myths suggest that man was originally innocent and pure. Some myths suggest that the original man and woman were so innocent that they did not even know how to have sex. Eventually, man became corrupted or separated from God. This was the coming of corruption, sin, and even death into the world. An Ashanti story says that originally man and the gods were not too far from each other. The gods lived in the sky, but at that time the sky was very close to man, as close as the ceiling of a house. As in the biblical story, it was the women who caused the problem. When pounding their millet in mortars, they kept hitting the sky with the pestles. At times they would even peel off bits of the sky to eat. The gods warned them to stop these anti-social practices, but they would not listen. In disgust the gods moved the sky as far away from man as they could. This was the separation of gods from humans. The Bambuti people of the Democratic Republic of the Congo believe that their main God, Sky Father, created man out of clay. He created black men out of black clay, white men out of white clay, and the Bambuti themselves (a pigmy people) out of red clay. The first people stole fire from a forest god, Tore. Tore chased them, but could not catch them, and when he returned home he found that his mother had died. He therefore cursed man and decreed that man, too, would die. This was the coming of death into the world. Tore himself became the god of death. In some myths, God placed a prohibition on man, as is the case in the Bible. In one, man was forbidden to eat of the fruit of the Taku tree; in another, man was forbidden to look at God. Of course, the prohibitions were discarded and man fell into a state of sin. Some peoples along the upper Nile believed that the Heavens were connected to man by a bridge made of rope, but a hyena accidentally broke the rope and thus separated man from God.

It is obvious, then, that the traditional peoples of Africa not only had religion, but in many cases their religion had many of the ingredients of the invading religions, Christianity and Islam. The main differences between these two new religions and traditional African religion are (a) that African religion has no concept of heaven or hell as a place where the dead go to answer for their activities on earth, and (b) African religion has no concept of salvation or redemption; that is, a redeemer coming down to earth to suffer for mankind, redeem man from his sins, and hold out the possibility of eternal life.

Christianity in Africa

John Mbiti suggests that Christianity in Africa is so old that it can rightly be described as indigenous, traditional, and African religion. (Mbiti, 1969). Christianity was established in Africa long before it came to most European countries like Britain and France. It goes back to the first century when it was established in Egypt. The main reason why North Africa became Christian so early is that the area bordered the Mediterranean and was therefore geographically close to those places in the Middle East and the Eastern Mediterranean where Christianity and other religions evolved. Christianity was brought to Egypt in the first century CE by the Apostle and Gospel-writer St. Mark. This was the beginning of the Coptic Church, which is still in existence today, though much diminished in numbers and influence. The Coptic Church is about the oldest church in the world. From Egypt Christianity moved southwards into Ethiopia. Some traditions maintain that it was St. Mark who continued the process of evangelization and took Christianity to Ethiopia, baptizing and converting a number of people, and establishing the foundations for the Ethiopian Orthodox Church, which also survives to this day and is one of the oldest and most powerful churches in the world (Azevedo, 404). In the Acts of the Apostles the Apostle Philip is reported to have baptized an Ethiopian eunuch. According to another tradition, therefore, it was this eunuch who returned to Ethiopia and started converting others, thus laying the foundations of the Church (Moyo, 328). What is absolutely certain is that in the fourth century CE the Emperor Ezanas proclaimed Christianity the religion of the state, and, as we have seen, it became a very powerful force in the land. From Egypt Christianity gradually spread westwards, during the second and third centuries CE, to the parts of North Africa occupied by the Romans, that is modern Algeria, Morocco, and Tunisia. It was thus embraced by the Berbers. According to Shillington, the Berbers, like the Egyptians before them, embraced Christianity probably as a reaction against the harsh realities of life in Roman North Africa (Shillington, 86). The Romans mercilessly persecuted the Christians in the areas under their jurisdiction in North Africa. Particularly revolting were the actions of the Emperor Diocletian under whom thousands of Christians were martyred. However, under the Emperor Constantine, Christianity was officially recognized throughout the Roman Empire in the fourth century CE and the persecution stopped.

Interestingly, the Church in North Africa was more vibrant intellectually than the Church in Rome and other areas. It produced a large number of theologians and theological philosophers who are still regarded as being among the most eminent thinkers ever. In this regard, the city of Alexandria was a leading light and some of its bishops were among the most learned and revered. One of these was Clement, another was Athanasius. Saint Augustine (not to be confused with Saint Augustine of Canterbury who converted the Anglo-Saxons to Christianity during the sixth century) is probably the most famous of these North African theologians. Born in 354 CE, he was a Berber who eventually became bishop of Hippo in modern-day Algeria in 396. He was an erudite scholar whose voluminous writings are still standard in the curricula of many universities. According to Moyo (328), his ideas on such issues as grace, original sin, and the kingdom of God shaped both Western Catholicism and the Protestant Reformation. This North African's reputation is now well established as one who left his mark on the Western intellectual tradition, as one of the greatest theologians of Western Christianity, and one of the world's intellectual giants of all time. He died in 430.

St. Athanasius Bishop of Alexandria (296–373), is probably best remembered because his name was given to an apparently difficult and incomprehensible creed of the Christian Church, "The Creed of St. Athanasius." The author of several influential works and a great father of the Orthodox Church, he is regarded as the greatest defender of the orthodoxy of the Church against the heresy of Arianism, which was started by Arius, who was also a theological scholar at Alexandria. Arianism revolves around the belief that although Jesus Christ is the son of God and possesses some divine attributes, he is not really a divine being. This is why Athanasius's creed asserts that Jesus Christ is also God. Other notable North African scholars and theologians include Tertullian, Cyprian, and Origen.

Synods and Councils of the Church were held in North Africa. Indeed, because of the intellectual vibrancy of the North African Church at this time, it was felt by some that the center of the Church would move from Rome to North Africa, and an inevitable tussle ensued between the two branches of the Church, with North Africa questioning Rome's superiority or authenticity. These and other events led to a weakening of the Church. One such event was the invasion of North Africa by the Vandals in 429 and the fall of the city of Hippo in 431. Augustine died during this invasion. However, the most important event that led to a weakening of the North African Church was the westward march of Islam. The Muslims believed in spreading their religion through jihads or religious wars. They also spread Islam as they traded with various countries. Within a very short time Islam was to dominate almost the whole of North Africa, though the Coptic Church still remained a force in Egypt and the Ethiopians stoutly resisted the march of Islam. The Ethiopian Church remained pure and lasts to this day.

The Portuguese and Christianity in Africa

When the Portuguese started coming down the coast of Africa in the fifteenth century their two main intentions, as we have seen, were to find a sea route to India and to participate actively in the gold trade, which was dominated by the Arabs. However, they also had religious motives. They certainly wished to contain the Muslim Arabs who dominated North Africa and were leaving their mark on the world. To contain them, the Portuguese had to find allies in Africa. They and other Europeans had heard of a legendary king of Ethiopia called Prester John and they wished to make his acquaintance and form an alliance with him. After rounding the Cape of Good Hope towards the end of the century, they were able to get to Ethiopia and come to an agreement with the reigning king. Unlike the North African Church, the Ethiopian Church had remained vibrant and the Portuguese were able to give it even greater vigor. Later in the sixteenth century the Portuguese effectively aided the Ethiopians to defeat a redoubtable Muslim army, thus saving Christian Ethiopia (Shillington, 129–130). Subsequent historians would question the wisdom of an African king inviting European powers to assist him against fellow Africans, particularly since the motives were mainly religious. Be that as it may, Christianity in Ethiopia and Ethiopia itself were saved by this Portuguese intervention.

It should be obvious that the Portuguese were also infused with an evangelizing fervor. The explorers who came down the coast of Africa and rounded the Cape of Good Hope were followed, not only by traders, but also by missionaries belonging to the Jesuit and Dominican orders, determined to spread the Christian faith. Some of them pushed inland and established missionary stations in Angola, the Kongo, Mozambique, Benin, Mwenemutapa, and Mombasa. In the Kingdom of the Kongo they converted numerous Africans and in 1506 intervened in a dynastic struggle that resulted in a Christian convert seizing the throne and ruling as Alfonso I (Shillington, 225–226). The king had thus assumed a "Christian," Portuguese name. Alfonso established communication with the Pope and referred to the king of Portugal as his "brother monarch." He even had one of his sons ordained as a catholic priest (Azevedo, 405). From Mozambique Jesuit missionaries, led by Father Gonzalo da Silveira went in 1560 to the great empire of Mwenemutapa, in what is now Zimbabwe. They converted the emperor to Christianity. Unfortunately, the mission ended tragically with the murder of Father da Silveira.

The Portuguese were therefore extremely active as missionaries during the fifteenth and sixteenth centuries in Central, Eastern and Southern Africa. However, their mission could not be sustained for several reasons. The first was their involvement in political matters like dynastic struggles in their attempt to establish control. This earned them the enmity of important sections of the population. Secondly, they did not always have the support and commitment of the Portuguese government at home. Thirdly, as Azevedo suggests, they failed to train and ordain indigenous clergy (Azevedo, 405). This further prevented the Church from reaching the real people. It was not enough to convert the leaders.

Christianity and imperialism

The next phase of Christianity in Africa was Christian activity in Sierra Leone and the rest of West Africa. Unlike previous Christian endeavors it was a continuous and uninterrupted process that led, as Moyo suggests, to the firm establishment of Christianity in Africa (Moyo, 330). We have seen that the decline of slavery towards the end of the eighteenth century was partly caused by the activities of Christian philanthropists like Wesley and others. There was support from the "back to Africa" movement and some Churches in America like the African Methodist Episcopal Church. Freetown in Sierra Leone, which had been designated as a haven for liberated slaves, was partly settled by freed slaves returning from America. These people brought with them the Christian religion to which they had been exposed in America. Of course, it was a Christianity that had been slightly modified by the African character of the slaves taken to the Americas. For instance, these people, known as the Creoles, brought with them religious songs called "shouts," that were quite different from the usual Christian hymns and psalms and are still sung to this day at funeral vigils in Freetown. Slightly later, some African American missionaries actually came to Freetown and worked in areas like education. One of them, the Revd. Edward Jones, became principal of Fourah Bay College. The entire Freetown enterprise was backed by the Church Missionary Society which was to have a powerful influence in Freetown and the rest of British West Africa.

Right from the start, therefore, the Christian missionaries had a firm footing and made an extremely important contribution in Sierra Leone, as they were soon to do in other parts of Africa as imperialism took hold. The first church in West Africa was built in Freetown. It was a Methodist church called the St. John's Maroon Church. Others, like "Zion on the Hill" and "Zion on the Level" soon followed. The first Anglican Church in West Africa, and probably in the whole of Africa, was St. Charles Church, in Regent village, a few miles outside Freetown. Both churches still stand to this day. Christian missionary activity in Sierra Leone was typical of missionary activity in the rest of sub-Saharan Africa once imperialism got under way. The missionaries took charge of education. They built both churches and schools. Quite often, the schools were attached to the churches. The missionaries saw that education was an infallible means of attracting Africans to the Church. Once imperialism got under way colonial governments preferred to leave education in the hands of the missionaries. The missionaries had more experience in these matters, and it was a less expensive approach. In 1827 the Church Missionary Society established Fourah Bay College, the first institution of higher learning in Africa south of the Sahara since the collapse of Timbuktu. It was originally intended as a center for the training of ministers of religion, but it soon became the place where all West Africans who wanted higher education went, unless they could somehow afford to proceed to Europe. Fourah Bay College thus became a most important bastion of education in the whole of West Africa, producing graduates who would eventually play an important role in the fortunes of all the British West African territories. In 1845 the CMS established the first secondary (high) school for boys in the whole of West Africa, the Sierra Leone Grammar School, and in 1849 it established the first secondary school for girls, the Annie Walsh Memorial School. Similar schools for both boys and girls were later established by the Methodists and the Roman Catholics.

It was from Sierra Leone that a number of religious personnel, like clergymen and others, were sent to help in the strengthening of the Church in the other West African countries. A famous one was Samuel Adjai Crowther, the first person to enroll as a student at Fourah Bay College, who was later ordained by the British as a bishop in Nigeria. Crowther was born in Nigeria in 1812 and was captured and taken as a slave, together with his entire family in 1821. However, slavery had been officially abolished by the British and Crowther was rescued and taken to Freetown, like a number of other Creoles, where he was converted to Christianity, baptized, and given the names Samuel Crowther. He eventually received a doctorate from Oxford University. Among other things, he began a translation of the Bible into his native Yoruba, translated the Book of Common Prayer into Yoruba, and compiled a Yoruba/English Dictionary. He was the first African Anglican bishop.

The Adjai Crowther story exemplifies several features of Christian missionary activity in Africa during the days of imperialism. Firstly, unlike the Portuguese missionaries, the new Christian Church in Africa was willing to make use of local religious personnel. It appointed local catechists and ordained local men as ministers, as long as they had the appropriate level of education, and it encouraged those who were willing to gain the required level of education in order to become clergymen. This was one of the reasons for the success of this new Christian activity in Africa. I can myself remember numerous ministers of both Anglican and Methodist Churches who were indigenous people and who rose to become canons, archdeacons, assistant bishops and bishops of the Anglican Church in West Africa as well as superintendents of the Methodist Church; I can also remember my mother and grandmother telling me about others, like the Venerable Archdeacon J. J. Thomas and Assistant Bishop T. S. Johnson. The Roman Catholic Church was, of course, slower in this regard; the main reason for this was the insistence on celibacy which was anathema to most African men. But even that Church had to make progress in the ordination of African men to the priesthood. Initially, the heads of the Churches, the bishops and other such senior personnel, were Europeans, but quite soon, as in the case of Adjai Crowther, indigenous people with the necessary qualifications began to be appointed. The missionaries' interest in education extended to themselves as they tried to learn as much as possible about the cultures of the people they served. They were interested in learning the local languages, in learning about the local social systems, and in compiling dictionaries. This enabled them to reach the people and mingle with them.

With the rise of imperialism and the growth of the evangelical movement, what was happening in Sierra Leone was repeated over most of Africa. The missionaries actually preceded the imperialist administrators, built churches and schools, converted the local people to Christianity, facilitated education, and showed their interest in local social systems and languages. They were also very active in the health arena, building hospitals and training local nurses and midwives. One example of this kind of activity was the Methodist hospital at Segbwema, a town in the interior of Sierra Leone. At the time it was regarded as the best hospital in Sierra Leone, performing what some regarded as miracles of healing. I know of people, some of whom had ghastly tumors, who were actually cured at Segbwema when the other hospitals had given up on them. The staff were actually highly qualified and excellent doctors and surgeons from Britain who had volunteered to go over as missionaries.

All this ensured that the Church in Africa was being built this time on firm foundations and it took hold. However, there has been very severe criticism from some quarters of the missionary activity in Africa during imperialism, and this must be examined. Some African nationalists accuse the missionaries of collaborating with the imperialists and even facilitating their operations. Since some of the missionaries knew the local languages and local customs, it was easy for the imperialist occupiers to use them as translators and in other capacities that would facilitate their imperialist takeover. We do know that in some situations the missionaries deliberately mistranslated documents containing agreements between the imperialists and the people, with the result that the people lost their lands. Furthermore, the imperialist occupiers used the presence of the missionaries as an excuse for their presence and the establishment of military posts. They claimed that they had to protect their nationals who were there serving as missionaries. It is a fact that some missionaries were killed by the local people. However, the need to protect missionaries was nothing more than an excuse, and we do know that many of the missionaries took the local people's part and were opposed to political annexation. Nevertheless, it is true that the very presence of the missionaries facilitated the military occupation and political annexation. Some Africans are of the opinion that the missionaries actually softened up and misled the local people and thus prepared them for political annexation. The introduction of the Christian religion was a kind of distraction to ensure that the people were unaware of what was actually happening and that their country was actually being take over. A famous story, attributed to Jomo Kenyatta and reproduced in various versions such as in Achebe's *Things Fall Apart*, relates that the missionary taught the African to clasp his hands and close his eyes in order to pray. He did so, but when he opened his eyes he discovered that his land had been taken by the imperialist.

The missionaries have also been accused of being indifferent or even hostile to aspects of African culture. Some of these missionaries had a "civilizing mission," and they were bent on transforming the African into a black European with European values. It was therefore part of their agenda to suggest that local culture was barbaric or even evil. In Sierra Leone, for instance, the masquerades, which were actually people wearing the masks of the ancestors, were referred to as "devils"; at least, that was what children were taught to call them. The masquerades came out regularly at festivals like Christmas, even though they were part, not of the Christian religion, but of traditional religion. In a country like Sierra Leone the children looked forward to seeing them, and Christmas was not complete if they did not appear. When the children saw the masquerades approaching, they would shout out, "The devils are coming! The devils are coming!" However, they did not use the word "devils" in a pejorative way as the missionaries originally intended the local people to use them. They loved the "devils," and were thrilled if they came into their compounds to dance. The missionaries who had intended to introduce the new religion of Christianity wanted the people to see aspects of their traditional religion as evil, as manifestations of the work of the devil. The missionary attitude towards African names is another instance of the insensitivity of some of them to aspects of African culture. It was good that the missionaries built schools and welcomed Africans to them, but before the Africans could enter the schools, in many cases, they had to be baptized and adopt "Christian names," as though they were nameless before this or the African names were bad or meaningless. In fact, we all know that most African names have meaning, while most European first names do not. This amounted to a tampering with the African sense of identity.

The missionaries' opposition to aspects of African culture and social organization like polygamy and female circumcision (also known in the West as female genital mutilation) elicited the accusation that they were not prepared to try to understand African culture and the reasons for the existence of these practices. Of course, the missionaries were opposed to polygamy because their Churches were, and in introducing Christianity they felt they had to insist on the "one man, one wife" concept. Some of their new members saw this as hypocrisy since they could read the Bible, or translations of the Bible, themselves and note that some of the biblical patriarchs, like Abraham and Isaac, whom the Christian missionaries lionized, were actually polygamous. The missionaries failed to realize that some of these issues had to be handled carefully and almost diplomatically. African creative works are full of representations of the clash between the missionaries and new Christians on the one hand, and traditionalists on the other, about these two concepts. The controversy brought about by these issues still rages today and there will be more about them later.

Yet, we must be careful not to judge missionary activity in Africa too harshly and be unappreciative of their remarkable contribution to the African story. Some of them might well have been arrogant, insensitive, and even deceptive in the sense that they were prepared to collaborate with the imperialists while pretending to be on the side of the African people. However, the vast majority were well intentioned, honest, disciplined, and selfless, and it was largely because of their generally laudable activities that the Christian Church became firmly established in Africa. We must never forget that some of them gave up the possibility of lucrative careers in their countries to help in Africa and spent their entire lives on the continent. David Livingstone was a case in point. He went out to Africa as a young doctor when he could have had a successful career in his native Scotland, and he spent the rest of his life in Africa, never returning home in the meantime. Quite a few others also served in the fields of education and health; without them education in Africa would never have been the same. Some of the very African nationalists who later criticized the missionaries got their early education at the hands of the missionaries. Many of the missionaries devoted themselves to studying African languages and cultures and translating works like the Bible into the local languages. A fair assessment would have to be, that although the missionaries made mistakes their efforts in Africa were highly successful and had a positive impact on the continent.

Largely because of the activities of the missionaries, the Church in Africa in the twentieth century went from strength to strength. It is inaccurate to say that all the major Churches were slow or unwilling to hand over power and authority to indigenous members. I was confirmed by a Sierra Leonean assistant bishop decades ago, and a few years later another Sierra Leonean was ordained as bishop of the diocese. The move towards the handing over of authority in the Anglican Church in West Africa actually started in 1951 when the archdiocese of West Africa was established and an archbishop of West Africa, the late Dr. Vining, was installed. He happened to have been an Englishman, but that did not matter as West Africans had their own archdiocese, and though the relationship with Canterbury was still strong, bishops and other clergy were now primarily responsible to the archdiocese of West Africa. Soon after this an African archbishop was installed. The Anglican Church in West Africa gradually became autonomous and the individual dioceses had their own constitutions. Similar developments were taking place in other areas like East Africa and other Churches like the Methodist Church. The Roman Catholic Church was rather slow in this regard, largely because of the paucity of African fathers for reasons we have already seen. However, even that Church soon fell in line and started appointing African Roman Catholic Bishops. The Roman Catholic Church in Africa is now so strong that at the time of the last papal election some observers suggested that it was time the Church had an African pope. Similarly, when the appointment of a new archbishop of Canterbury was recently being considered, some commentators suggested that there was no constitutional reason why the archbishop should not come from Africa.

Indigenous African Churches

One of the most important features of the Christian experience in post-independence or modern Africa is the rise of indigenous African denominations. They are regarded as being African and indigenous because their leaders have sought to give them an African complexion, whether it be in the nature of the ritual, leadership, doctrine, or outreach to the community. Some of these Churches started as revivalist movements within the established Churches, while others started because their leaders wanted to make a clean break and establish Churches that were more in accordance with African tradition and the general African situation. Some scholars suggest that the drive to establish "African" Churches could be ultimately traced to the activities of the Congolese woman Donna Beatrice who in 1700 claimed to have been possessed by the spirit of Saint Anthony (Moyo, 331). She gave up all her belongings to the poor and declared that Christ and his Apostles were black and that they lived in Angola. There are some clear "African" elements in the Donna Beatrice story. One of them is the fact that she claimed to have been "possessed" by the spirit of Saint Anthony. The concept of possession is part of African belief. Then there is the issue of a black Christ and black Apostles living in Africa. Donna Beatrice was suggesting that the usual image of a white Christ cannot be expected to appeal to most Africans and be relevant to their situation. Another early "African" Church was the Kimbanguist Church founded by Simon Kimbangu, also in what is now the Democratic Republic of the Congo. His movement was originally a revivalist movement that did not wish to make a clean break from the established Church. However, the religious authorities gravely disapproved of his movement and he was actually arrested, charged, convicted, and sentenced to death, although the sentence was commuted to life imprisonment. He died in prison in 1951. His movement became a powerful Church with branches in other parts of Africa like Zambia (Mazrui, 152–156).

There are several reasons for the rise of the independent African Churches. Though the established Churches had taken great strides in indigenizing the leadership and becoming almost autonomous, ritual and doctrine were still those of the Church in Europe. People still had to sing the same old Western hymns to the accompaniment of Western musical instruments, and the liturgy was in Western languages. Africans wanted to introduce features like clapping and dancing into the religious service. They wanted to hear the lessons read in the indigenous languages and they wanted to use African instruments like the drum. I can remember how adamant some of the leaders in the Anglican Church in Sierra Leone were in their opposition to the use of indigenous languages during the services and how ecstatic most people were when the Temne language was used in the cathedral for the first time. Up to the present moment the sermons in most Anglican churches in Sierra Leone are done in English and not in the indigenous languages. Many people in Africa did not like this and were therefore asking for features of the services and even the ritual to be Africanized.

The established Churches were not very good in pastoral work. This was unfortunate because if ever there was a continent in which pastoral work had to be emphasized it was Africa. Most Africans are poor and underprivileged. Many of them have experienced disasters such as illness, loss of family members, unemployment, and so on, and they therefore need all the comforting and attention they can get. This has to be one of the most important functions of the Church in Africa. Yet the Churches were found wanting in matters like visitation and concern for the poor and underprivileged. In the Anglican Church in particular, the clergy were too concerned about their positions in the church and exercising their authority. Some Africans found this unacceptable.

There was a feeling in some quarters that the leaders of the established Churches were too concerned with money. Too many homilies were about raising money or about members not living up to their financial obligations. There were situations in some countries where those who had not lived up to their financial obligations could not be given proper funeral services and burial by their churches. I can vouch that the practice existed in Sierra Leone until a forward-looking new bishop declared that no one who had been baptized could be refused a Christian funeral service in the Anglican Church. His bold decision might now have been rescinded.

At a time when most African countries were suffering under dictatorships and tyrannical one-party rule, it was felt that the established Churches could have taken a much stronger stance and spoken out boldly against injustice and oppression. A few did, but most were unwilling to offend the dictatorial leaders. (More reasons for the rise of indigenous African Churches are given in detail by Fashole-Luke et al. and Moyo.)

The rise of the African denominations, as we have seen, can be ultimately traceable to Donna Beatrice and Simon Kimbangu, but it gathered momentum just before and around independence. In Sierra Leone, for instance, there was the rise of a group led by a Nigerian "prophet" called Adejobi in the 1950s. He was associated with the Aladura Church. Moyo suggests that by 1960 there were about 6000 indigenous African Churches spread throughout Africa, and the trend continues. Some of the most important of the African Churches are the so-called "spiritualist" Churches. They are called "spiritualist" because their members believe that it is possible to be possessed or inspired by the Holy Spirit and to do marvelous things like "speaking in tongues" as the Apostles did at Pentecost, performing miracles, prophesying, and healing. We can see how deprived Africans could rush to churches where the leaders could heal them, or interpret their dreams, or prophesy to them about some unexpected good fortune. The so-called Pentecostal Churches constitute another variety of independent African Churches. Young people in particular flock to these Churches because they feel they can give them explanations for their misfortunes, whether these be unemployment, barrenness, or persistent illness. They also believe that these Churches can help them through prayer and other means to overcome misfortune. One can see how popular this kind of Church would be among people who are plagued by misfortune as many Africans are. It must be mentioned that some of these new Churches make as many financial demands on their new members as the established Churches. However, the new members are willing to meet these financial obligations because they are convinced these Churches will do much for them. There are also many cases where the new members still retain their membership of the established Churches because they would like their weddings or funerals to be held in the more prestigious established Churches. For regular religious observance, though, they go to the new Churches because they are more satisfying and minister to their needs as Africans.

Islam in Africa

Islam is one of the three major religions in Africa, all of them together constituting what Ali Mazrui would refer to as Africa's "triple heritage"; that is, the traditional, the

Christian, and the Islamic. One of the most amazing aspects of Africa's development is the rapid spread of Islam in Africa south of the Sahara since the collapse of Timbuktu. There are probably as many Muslims in Africa as Christians at the moment. Figures are generally unreliable; a 2020 Gordon Cornwell Theological Seminary estimate gives the figures as 49 percent Christian, 42 percent Muslim, 8 percent traditional and 1 percent other. Some other estimates put the figures at 49 percent Christian and 48 percent Muslim. There are Muslims in almost every African country, but they are particularly dominant in the Mahgreb countries in the north. Countries like Egypt, Tunisia, Algeria, Libya, Morocco, Mauretania, and Sudan are overwhelmingly Islamic, with Islam being regarded more or less as the state religion. But Islam is also extremely strong in West African countries such as Nigeria, Senegal, Guinea, Chad, Burkina Faso, Mali, and Niger. In the east, Somalia is predominantly Muslim, while Tanzania and even Kenya have large Muslim populations. Central and Southern Africa are the areas where Islam is not particularly strong, for reasons which will be discussed later.

Islam was established in the Middle East by the prophet Muhammad (570–632) in the early years of the seventh century CE. Largely influenced by both Christianity and Judaism to which it is clearly related, it offers its adherents a clearly defined way of life that is contained in its holy book the Qur'an, which Muhammad claimed was God's message communicated to him by the archangel Gabriel. Like Christianity and Judaism, it is a monotheistic religion, but its main difference from Christianity is its insistence that Jesus Christ was not the son of God, but a prophet like many others. Muhammad claimed that he himself was the last in that line of prophets. The Muslims also revere patriarchs like Abraham from whom they claim to have descended.

Having established themselves in the Middle East, the Arab Muslims set about the task of systematically subduing the Mahgreb world. Muhammad died in 632 and so the conquest of North Africa was undertaken by his zealous supporters. The methods used by the Muslims were largely trade and conquest. Even before Muhammad, the Arabs had engaged in trade with the Berbers of North Africa. The new Muslims also believed in what have come to be called jihads; that is, holy wars designed to bring about the expansion of Islam. As they traded with the Berbers they sought to convert them to their new religion, but they also used force. Their first target was Egypt which was under the tyrannical Byzantine Empire at the time. The people's suffering under the Byzantine Empire was one of the factors that made them welcome the Arab Muslims, and by 640 almost the whole of Egypt had succumbed to them. In 642 the Muslims were able to expel the Byzantines completely. The new religion further appealed to Egyptians because of its simplicity. It did not make many financial demands on its members although it stressed concepts like generosity and kindness. It did not have any complex creeds or doctrines and it was not ruled by a centralized or corrupt hierarchy. It only demanded that members affirm the belief in the one true God, pray five times a day, and observe the so-called five pillars of Islam.

From Egypt the Muslim jihadists moved westward into other parts of the Mahgreb, which was largely inhabited by Berbers who posed much stronger resistance to the new invaders than the Egyptians had done. The dominant religion in North Africa at this time was Christianity, but it had not really taken hold among the ordinary people and it was, in any case, weakened by internal schisms. All this facilitated the Muslim advance. The Christians were eventually defeated. The Muslims also intermarried with the Berbers and wherever they gained control tried to absorb them into their administration. This also facilitated the Muslim advance. The Muslims also had one great advantage denied to the Berbers: the use of the camel which was to have a marked impact on the development of North Africa. It has been said that wherever the camel could not go, the Arab Muslim advance stopped. The camel enabled the Muslim Arabs to start penetrating the Sahara and convert the Berber nomads of the Northern and Western Sahara to Islam. These converted Berbers would, in their turn, play an important role in the subjugation of the Western Sudan, North West Africa, and other parts of the Sahel to Islam.

The Almoravids

The Almoravids were among the Berbers who were converted to Islam. As we have seen in chapter one, the group arose because of dissatisfaction with the newly converted Berbers' commitment to and familiarity with the doctrines of the new faith. A Berber/Muslim scholar named Abdallah tried but failed to get them to change their ways, and, in disappointment withdrew to a monastery-like fortress on the coast of Mauritania where he was joined by faithful Islamic followers. This was the birth of the Almoravid movement, and some would claim that the Almoravids were largely responsible for the introduction of Islam to most parts of North Western and Western Africa, because they were ferocious fighters who believed in the spreading of Islam through jihads.

Islam and Western Africa

The conversion of most of the Western Sudan to Islam started with the capitulation of the great medieval empire of Ghana. There is a great debate among scholars as to whether Ghana was actually "conquered" by the Almoravids. Some claim that the rulers of Ghana were merely "converted" to Islam by a process of persuasion. The fact remains, however, that the Almoravids had been putting tremendous military pressure on the Ghana Empire for a considerable period, especially under the leadership of converts like the Umar brothers Yahya Ibn and Abu Bakar Ibn, and this largely led to the weakening of the empire at least. By the start of the eleventh century Ghana was completely Islamic. Some scholars like Moyo believe that the Islamization of the other West African empires and the rest of North West Africa south of the Sahara was brought about by peaceful means rather than by conquest, as was the case with North Africa (Moyo, 339). The spread of Islam was largely effected by merchants and traders following the old trade routes and establishing commercial and religious centers. It is therefore true that the merchants and traders played a huge role, but so did military force. Even if the Almoravids did not physically conquer the other parts of the Western Sudan, their success in Ghana, even if temporary, laid the foundations for Islam to spread to Mali and Songhay, as Azevedo says (Azevedo, 410). One must also not forget the roles of the kings and emperors who played a major role in the Islamization of these parts of the Sahel. Some of them, having been converted to Islam, made substantial efforts to convert their people, who had been largely traditionalists, to the new faith. Some of them, like Mansa Musa of Mali, made famous pilgrimages to Mecca. Some of them, like Askia Mohamed of Songhay, claimed that they deposed the previous monarch and took over the empire because they had the sanction of Islamic leaders who thought it was unacceptable for an "infidel" to occupy the throne. We thus see that Islam played a formidable role in the evolution of the medieval states of West Africa. It must also be noted that the Islamic conversion in general had an enormous impact on cultural and intellectual life. The oldest university in the world was established in Fez, Morocco, in 859. Amazingly for the time, it was established by a woman and is still in operation. Timbuktu in Mali was the first university in Africa south of the Sahara.

The further penetration of West Africa by Islam was effected by a combination of military and missionary activities. Traders and holy men continued to persuade individuals as well as rulers to convert from traditionalism to the new religion, but the jihads continued well into the nineteenth century. For instance, the Fulbe people of the Futa Jalon in Guinea were converted to Islam by Muslim traders but in 1725 they themselves rose in rebellion and fought a holy war against their rulers and other surrounding peoples and by 1750 they had conquered the whole region which they now brought under Islamic or Sharia law and created a Fulbe-dominated state (Shillington, 250). This inspired similar activities elsewhere in West Africa, particularly the exploits of a holy man called Usman Dan Fodio. Disgusted with the impiety, corruption and tyranny of Hausa rulers, he conducted a jihad against the king of Gobir in 1804 resulting in the defeat of the king, the conquest of several Hausa states and the creation of the mighty Muslim Sokoto caliphate. By the time of Usman's death in 1817 the caliphate had a population of 10 million people, the largest West African state up to that time.

The Muslims were less successful in extending their religion in the North East. North Sudan, because of its proximity to Egypt, became Islamized, but South Sudan was another matter. Christianity had been established in what was then Nubia as far back as the fourth century CE, and South Sudan stubbornly resisted the Islamic advance. This was to lead to grave political problems between the Muslim north and the largely Christian and traditionalist south which were only recently resolved by the secession of the south. Christianity had also taken deep roots in Ethiopia, which was one of the earliest countries to be Christianized. We have already seen how one of the Emperors called on the Portuguese for assistance against the Muslim "infidels." All this ensured that Ethiopia remained Christian and is Christian to this day. The Muslims were more successful further along the east coast of Africa. There is evidence that Arabs from the Arabian Peninsula had been coming down the Red Sea and had trading relations with the east coast of Africa even before the beginning of the Christian era (Azevedo, 411). The *Chronicle of Kilwa* informs us that by the eighth century, the century after the establishment of Islam, Arabs had definitely settled on the Somali coast and further along the east coast of Africa. Extensive trading between Arabs and the peoples of the east coast was certainly in progress by that time. The new traders established trading posts in places like Zanzibar and Mombasa and traded in goods like skins, cloves, gold, myrrh, cotton cloth, grains, timber dyes, and even slaves. Of course, they brought Islam with them and inevitably tried to convert the local people. They also intermarried with the local women, thus creating a new ethnic group. It was from this context that a new language emerged called Swahili, which derived from Arabic and local languages. Islam became a very important religion along the east coast.

However, the new settlers and traders did not penetrate into the interior, into places like Central Africa. They preferred to deal with African middlemen who brought the goods they wanted to them from the interior. Islam therefore did not penetrate into Central Africa and most areas of Southern Africa. Some scholars have accounted for this by suggesting that the new traders and settlers came as individuals and not as members of a crusading group bent on extending their religion. The nature of the terrain must also be given some credit for Islam's failure to penetrate further into Central Africa. After leaving the Sahel and the savannah area anyone wishing to penetrate further south would have to cope with the dense equatorial forest. Also, the Islamic crusaders who converted most of Northern Africa and the Sahel were aided by the Camel. However, the camel would be virtually useless in Central Africa and further south. As some scholars like Mazrui have suggested, Islam stopped where the camel stopped.

Islam has had a very powerful impact on the African continent. It is more dominant in some areas than in others, but there are probably as many Muslims in Africa at the moment as Christians. Several reasons account for the popularity of Islam in Africa. With comparatively few complicated doctrines it is simpler than Christianity. Its rituals are also simpler and less complicated. It is more in line with traditional African attitudes and customs. For instance, it permits the practice of polygamy since it allows a man to marry up to four wives, provided he can provide for them all and show no partiality. It is even tolerant of the practice of female circumcision. It does not frown on the use of charms and amulets and permits the practice of divination. Indeed, in some areas, the local medicine man to whom people go to explain strange matters and to have fortunes told is also the local imam. Islam is a much less expensive religion than Christianity and makes fewer financial demands on its members. For instance, its burial practices are simpler and inexpensive so that every Muslim can afford them. Unlike Christianity, it does not have a governing centralized hierarchical system.

Islam's success in Africa has also been partly due to the efforts of relatively new Islamic groups like the Ahmadiyya movement. This is a missionary movement devoted to assisting countries in areas such as education and health. In other words, they are doing for Islam in Africa what Christian missionaries did for Christianity in the past. They are particularly active in East and West Africa. Among other activities, they have translated the Qur'an into African languages and have taken measures to protect the position of women. For reasons such as this, other groups tend to consider them heretical, but there is no doubt that they are making a formidable contribution. The Islamic presence in Africa has also been strengthened by wealthy Islamic Middle Eastern countries such as Saudi Arabia who have poured money into African countries with large Muslim populations for the construction of schools and hospitals. To avail themselves of this financial help some African countries have been keen to declare themselves Islamic even though other religions might have a very strong presence in them.

In most African countries, Muslims and Christians live quite harmoniously together. The people have come to accept religious pluralism and show respect for the religion of others. In Sierra Leone, for instance, both Christians and Muslims celebrate all the religious holidays. Muslims celebrate Christmas almost as much as Christians do, and at Ramadan both Christians and Muslims join in the Ramadan Eve lantern parade which was one of the highlights of the Sierra Leonean year. However, there are some countries in Africa where religious differences have given rise to violence. In Nigeria, for instance, particularly in the north, there are often reports of Muslims attacking Christians and vice versa. The violence in the Sudan between Muslims and Christians has also been well reported. At times the violence is directed by Muslims against other Muslims, as in Algeria for instance, where the Muslim Brotherhood was locked in a struggle with other Muslims in the country for years, and was eventually prevented from forming a government, although all the signs pointed to the fact that it had won an election. Quite often these struggles and differences have been caused by politicians wishing to use religion for political ends.

Finally, we must confront the issue of Islamic terrorism and Islamic fundamentalism. These days, terrorism is almost always linked to Islamic fundamentalism in the minds of many Western people. It must be stressed that most terrorists are not even Muslims and there is quite a lot of home-grown terrorism in places like the United States which seems to regard Africa as a "breeding ground" for terrorism. Also, most African Muslims are not fundamentalists and do not support terrorism. They just want a decent peaceful life for themselves and their children. The fundamentalist Muslims in Africa are quite often motivated, not by religious reasons, but political, social, and economic ones. In other words, they see Western-type policies as having largely failed and are convinced that the introduction of purer and simpler fundamental Islamic rules would make for a better society. This is why these groups quite often call for the introduction of sharia law, the Muslim penal code. Boko Haram, the terrorist group that operates in Northern Nigeria and abducted 300 girls from their school on the eve of their school-leaving examinations in 2014, definitely believes in rejecting all Western notions. In fact, its name, Boko Haram, means that Western education is evil. This group is believed to be associated with al-Qaeda. Other Islamic fundamentalist groups such as al-Shabab have carried out attacks in Somalia. Most of the other terrorist groups are not linked to the major terrorist groups in the world like ISIS and al-Qaeda. Since the motives for their existence in Africa are social, political, and economic, the solution to the problem might well be not just the use of military force, though that is also necessary, but the elimination of the forces that gave rise to the terrorist movements and the acts of terrorism. In other words, political structures need to be created that will give rise to fair and just governments. Also, attention must be paid to the economic and other problems that have helped to create a class of young men so embittered that they are attracted to terrorist movements and the perpetration of acts of terrorism.

References and suggestions for further reading

Achebe, C. 1959. *Things Fall Apart*. New York: Anchor Books.
Alpers, E. 1973. "Towards a History of Expansion of Islam in East Africa." Pp. 172–201 in T. O. Ranger and I. Kimambo (eds.), *The Historical Study of African Religion*. London: Heinemann.
Azevedo, M. 2005. "Religion in Africa." Pp. 399–420 in M. Azevedo (ed.). *Africana Studies*. Durham, NC: Carolina Academic Press.
Baeta, C. G. 1968. *Christianity in Tropical Africa*. Oxford: Oxford University Press.
Brenner, L. (ed.). 1993. *Muslim Identity and Social Change in Sub-Saharan Africa*. Bloomington, IN: Indiana University Press.
Daniel, M. L. 1987. *The Quest for Belonging: Introduction to a Study of African Independent Churches*. Gweru: Mambo Press.
Evans-Pritchard, E. E. 1937. *Witchcraft, Oracles and Magic among the Azande*. Oxford: Clarendon Press.
Fashole-Luke, E., R. Gray, A. Hastings, and O. Tasie (eds.). 1978. *Christianity in Independent Africa*. London: Rex Collins.
Gehman, Richard. 1987. *African Traditional Religion*. Kijabi: Kesho Publications.
Gehman, Richard. 1990. *African Traditional Religion in Biblical Perspective*. Kijabi: Kijabi Printing Press.
Greenshaw, Martha. (ed.) 1994. *Terrorism in Africa*. New York: Macmillan.
Hastings, Adrian. 1976. *African Christianity*. New York: Seabury.
Idowu, E. B. 1971. *African Traditional Religion: A Definition*. Maryknoll, NY: Orbis.
Isichei, Elizabeth. 1995. *A History of Christianity in Africa from Antiquity to the Present*. Lawrenceville, NJ: Africa World Press.
Laqueur, Walter. 1999. *The New Terrorism: Fanaticism and Arms of Mass Destruction*. Oxford: Oxford University Press.
Lewis, M. 1980. *Islam in Tropical Africa*. Bloomington, IN: Indiana University Press.

Mazrui, Ali. 1986. *The Africans: A Triple Heritage*. Boston: Little Brown.

Mbiti, John. 1969. *African Religions and Philosophy*. New York: Praeger.

Mbiti, J. 1970. *African Concepts of God*. New York: Praeger.

Moyo, A. 2007. "Religion in Africa." Pp. 317–350 in A. A. Gordon and D. L. Gordon (eds.). *Understanding Contemporary Africa*. Boulder, CO: Lynne Rienner.

Nyang, S. 1981. "Sub-Saharan Africa: Islamic Penetration." Pp. 145–150 in P. H.Stoddard (ed.). *Change in the Muslim World*. Syracuse, NY: Syracuse University Press.

Parrinder, G. 1969. *Religions in Africa*. Baltimore, MD: Penguin.

Petersen, K. H. (ed.). 1987. *Religion, Development and African Identity*. Uppsala: Scandinavian Institute of African Studies.

Ray, B. C. 2000. *African Religions: Symbol, Ritual, and Continuity*. Upper Saddle River, NJ: Prentice Hall.

Trimingham, J. 1964. *Islam in East Africa*. Oxford: Oxford University Press.

Twesigye, E. 1987. *Common Ground: Christianity, African Religion and Philosophy*. New York: Peter Lang.

9 African economies

This chapter will deal with economic issues in Africa throughout the African experience, from the hunter-gathering stage right through to the present situation. It will therefore be concerned with the rise of agriculture, the development of internal and external trade, the impact of slavery on the African economy, the economy under imperialism, poverty and the post-independence malaise, the economic recovery of the nineties and the early twenty-first century, and the contemporary situation.

It is now generally agreed that the earliest economies in Africa were based on hunting, gathering, and fishing. The early Africans had to move from place to place in search of more food, and they were therefore in a sense nomadic, building dwelling structures that could be easily demolished when it was time to move. They used simple tools made from stone, bone and wood. However, with rising populations, the food got from hunting, gathering, and fishing became insufficient and it was necessary to move to another stage. About ten or eleven thousand years ago, Africans moved to the stage of agriculture or purposeful cultivation of crops and herding of animals for food. This change, which has been regarded as the beginning of civilization as we know it, took place in three main areas of the world, generally in places where there was abundant water supply: the Nile valley in Africa, the Tigris Euphrates valley in the Middle East, and South Eastern Asia. The move to agriculture is also generally associated with the Iron Age since metal tools were needed for tilling the soil, and it is generally considered a very important change in the history of the evolution of human society. It is very significant that Africa was one of the places where this momentous change took place. Africans were domesticating cattle and growing crops like corn, rice, millet, and sorghum. Of course, as we have seen, the rise of agriculture led to the rise of settlements and various other advances, such as trade. Trade results because some societies, usually the more efficient, produce surpluses which can be exchanged for things produced by other societies, initially by barter, but later for some form of currency like cowries. The production of surpluses also led to specialization since some people were now relieved from participating in agriculture and could do other things.

The trade was both within communities and among adjacent communities. Soon the trade became international or long-distance trade. Goods were carried over long distances, at times over difficult terrain like the Sahara. As we have already seen, gold from the countries of the Western Sudan was traded extensively for salt brought to the edge of the desert by people like the Berbers. The intervention of the Arabs only served to intensify this trade. Thus, even before external intervention long distance trade was taking place in Africa. In any case, it is certain that gold from West Africa was traded internationally as early as the eighth century (Fage, 15). Spices were also traded between Africa and the Middle East.

DOI: 10.4324/9781003111733-10

As we have already seen from our look at the medieval empires of West Africa, gold, salt, slaves, and many other products continued to be traded, during the Middle Ages, along the sub-Saharan trade routes connecting sub-Saharan Africa, especially West Africa, with Northern Africa (DeLancey, 110). There is also evidence that from about 150 CE Eastern Africa was engaged in trade with the Middle East and Asia (Austen, 59).

Long before the Portuguese started coming down the west coast of Africa in the 1400s, therefore, African countries were engaged in extensive international trade. The arrival of the Portuguese meant that African economies would now begin to interact with the economies of Europe. We have already seen that one of the main reasons why the Portuguese came down the west coast of Africa was that they wanted to have a major share in the gold trade and counteract the influence of the Arabs who, up to this point, dominated the trade. After rounding the Cape of Good Hope in 1497 and mastering the sea route to India, the Portuguese also became interested in the Indian Ocean trade between the African east coast, the Middle East, and Southern Asia, trade that had been going on since the second century CE, involving commodities like ivory, iron, mangrove tree poles, and slaves. This trade was dominated by the Omanis, but as from the early sixteenth century the Portuguese tried to wrest control.

Initially, the Portuguese were only interested in legitimate trade. They wanted to buy West African gold, which at the time had much more value for Europeans than for West Africans. They built a fort at Elmina in what is now Ghana, to protect their trading post and guarantee their access to the gold from the Akan goldfields. They traded copper, brass, and European cloth in exchange for gold (Shillington, 174). But they were also interested in other products. In the 1480s the Portuguese occupied the hitherto uninhabited islands of São Tomé and Principe in the Gulf of Guinea and Madeira further to the north. Some Portuguese settled on these islands and established sugar cane plantations which eventually became extremely successful (Shillington, 174). According to Shillington, São Tomé became the largest single producer of sugar for the European market in the early sixteenth century. However, to provide labor for their plantations the Portuguese used slaves from the African mainland, and the São Tomé plantation system was to become the model for plantation slavery in the Americas and the Caribbean (Shillington, 174).

The Portuguese, then, were engaged in what could be called legitimate trade. In the sixteenth century, however, this legitimate trade gave way to the abominable trans-Atlantic slave trade. The "discovery" of the Americas and the Caribbean towards the end of the fifteenth century led to the establishment of plantations in those places, similar to the ones the Portuguese had on the African islands. The work on plantations was exacting and the local populations proved to be completely unsuitable for this kind of work. Shillington states that "by the end of the first century of European contact 90% or more of the Amerindian population of the Caribbean islands had been wiped out" (Shillington, 176). Moreover, the Amerindians succumbed to diseases brought by the Europeans to which they had no immunity. But workers were needed to work on the plantations that produced lucrative crops like sugar cane and tobacco. The Portuguese, whose plantations in Africa had been enormously successful, knew that Africans could do the work and survive in the more or less tropical climate, so they went to Africa for slaves and the nefarious trans-Atlantic slave trade started.

The slave trade had a most devastating effect on the African economy which up to then was thriving. It greatly reduced the productive labor force, led to the stagnation of the African population for about three hundred years, caused a serious decline in agricultural production, and disrupted the established patterns of internal trade. The usual trade routes along which produce was carried were now dangerous because of slave raids. Also, some traders were now turning their attention away from the usual commodities to the traffic in slaves. The gold trade, for instance, peaked in the sixteenth and seventeenth centuries, largely because of the demand for slaves (Delancey, 111). The decline in agricultural production was partly due to the fact that even the workers who were available would not be able to farm regularly because of the threat of raids. It was also accelerated by the introduction of diseases by the incoming Europeans, like smallpox and cholera, to which Africans had no immunity.

The slave trade declined partly because of the rise of the industrial revolution, another event that had earth-shaking effects on the world's economies. Although the demand for slaves now gradually lessoned, Africa still remained in the forefront of the international economic system because its products were needed to fuel the factories of Europe. These factories needed commodities like cotton, cacao, palm oil, copper, iron, and rubber, and the success of the industrial revolution partly depended on the ability of European countries to get these commodities from Africa. The drive to get commodities from Africa for the European factories was one of the forces that led to the imperialist occupation. Let us now look at the African economy under imperialism.

African economy under colonialism

The most important economic aim of the European colonial powers, in so far as their African territories were concerned, was to get raw materials to stoke their factories. Commodities like peanuts, fibers, tobacco, coffee, and minerals were in great demand and Africa could supply them. Every colonial territory was therefore encouraged to concentrate on or even specialize in the production of certain commodities, or even one commodity, to the exclusion of other products. Thus, a country like Ghana emphasized the production of cacao, while Zambia concentrated on copper. This meant that the colonial powers did not encourage diversification of the economy, and that would have important consequences in the future. Furthermore, the beliefs and attitudes the Europeans colonizers brought with them affected economic enterprise. For instance, they had a very restrictive view of the kinds of activities that women should engage in. They felt that only men should be engaged in the production of these extremely important commodities, so the men were brought into the cash economy and the women were left out, although in the past women had been responsible for about 85 percent of agricultural activity. The women continued to grow the other crops and sell them in the markets. Generally, these included the crops that were needed for ordinary subsistence and were therefore important to the lives of the people, but the colonizers were not very interested in these. All this affected the position of women in Africa very gravely. In some countries, some men prospered from this demand for certain commodities. The case of palm oil is instructive, as can be seen in the documentaries on Africa made by Henry Louis Gates. Palm oil was, and is still, needed for the production of things like soap, other cosmetics, and margarine. Some Africans, particularly in West Africa, realized this and devoted themselves to establishing palm oil plantations, the harvesting of the palm fruit and the actual making of the palm oil. They knew what the Europeans wanted, and they provided it and became prosperous.

The concentration by some countries on mining and the production of metals meant that many young men were attracted to the mines or forced to go and work in them, and so there were new patterns of migration to these mining centers. This also affected the condition of the women who were left behind and who had to take on some of the tasks that used to be performed by men. It must also be stressed that the colonizers did not attempt to promote industrialization in their colonies, and the reason for this is obvious. Industrialized African countries would pose a threat to industrialized European countries. One of the main reasons for the European expansion into Africa was the need for overseas markets to sell the products of European factories and of the industrial revolution generally. Indeed, some European powers saw their colonies as one expanded common market, where they could sell their products. They could not sell these products if industrialized African countries were producing them. Let us take the case of cacao from what is now Ghana. Cacao was Ghana's most important agricultural product. Some people have asked why Ghana was not taught how to make things like cocoa and chocolates from their product, something that would have been comparatively easy. I can remember my father, who had a large compound with lots of trees, making his own cocoa and ground coffee from the cacao and coffee from his trees. It was not a very complicated process technologically; why could not an industry producing cocoa and chocolates have been developed in Ghana with the kind of scientific safeguards required to make the products acceptable to the international market? Instead Ghanaians, having exported their cacao, were forced to buy it back from the British in the form of cocoa and chocolates.

This leads to another very important aspect of the African economy under imperialism: the fact that Africans became not merely producers but consumers as well. A culture of consumption was created as Africans were encouraged to buy and consume things from Europe that at times they did not need: things like Western textiles; the latest Western fashions in ladies' styles and men's clothes, such as flare-bottom trousers, wedge-heeled shoes, and nylon shirts; liquors of all kinds; various kinds of cigarettes; crystal ware and so on. African workers were encouraged to see the possession of these things as a kind of status symbol, and in purchasing them they enriched the colonizing countries.

A very important aspect of the African economy under imperialism was that in some cases Europeans actually came to Africa and settled there with no intention of returning home. They made the African countries their home and thought they would have a better life as settlers in the colonies than in their countries of origin. Generally, they settled in those countries where the climate and vegetation were conducive for European habitation. The problem was that these European settlers took the best land from the Africans, more or less by force, and without any compensation. They established plantations, and since they had capital and some technical knowhow, they soon became eminently successful and wealthy. This happened in countries like Algeria in North Africa, Kenya in East Africa, and Southern Rhodesia and South Africa in Southern Africa. The settlers inevitably came to dominate economic life in these countries. Up to the time of independence they also dominated political life and their activities and attitudes were to cause a number of grave political problems in the future.

During the imperialist era, commerce was very largely in the hands of foreigners. Though some Africans were beginning to take an interest in commerce, as can be seen in the activities of those who dealt in palm oil, many lacked the capital to expand and were given little encouragement by the colonial governments. The major stores that sold imported European goods to Africans in Sierra Leone, for instance, were Patterson Zochonis, which was Greek; Genet and Co., which was French; Compagnie Française de l'Afrique Occidental (CFAO), which was French; G. M. B. Olivant, which was Dutch; and the United African Company, which was British. These companies were also the main purchasers of produce from the interior which was exported to Europe to fuel European industrial factories. Indians and Lebanese were also allowed to establish a major presence in the commercial arena and to engage, like the European companies, in the importation and export of goods. African participation was not encouraged.

On the whole, the economic set-up under imperialism did not benefit Africans. The system was intended to benefit the European imperialists and, by and large, it did so. Some would argue that Africans benefited from the modest infrastructure that imperialism created, but these, like the roads and railways, were designed to carry the produce that the imperialists wished to export to Europe from the interior to the harbors on the coast. In other words, they were intended to benefit the Europeans. In any case, this infrastructure was partly paid for with the new taxes that Africans were forced to pay. Africans were also forced to provide free labor for the construction of the roads and railways. As far as the imperialist economic system was concerned, the Africans were at the losing end.

The situation at independence

Most African countries gained their independence in the sixties. Some had to wait for the seventies and a few even for the eighties and nineties. With independence there was tremendous optimism for the future both among leaders and the general population. It was now generally accepted that imperialism had constituted a tremendous drawback for African development, and, with its end, the future would be bright, especially in the economic sphere. It is clear, however, that this optimism amounted to looking at the situation in Africa and the rest of the world through rose-tinted spectacles. To believe that the situation would be much bleaker than the leaders suggested is not even a matter of hindsight, for the facts and the signs were already present. After the euphoria and the rejoicing had subsided the leaders should have let the people realize that the road ahead would be long and extremely difficult and there were no easy solutions to the existing problems.

Let us consider some of the problems. Many African countries lacked the infrastructure that was necessary to enhance development or even enable the people to live comfortable lives. The roads, railways, telephone and water systems were inadequate and were dependent on Western assistance for maintenance. Some countries like Guinea and the Congo had to start right from scratch because the imperialist powers, the French and the Belgians, had done little to develop these countries and they had left in a pique, taking everything that could be carried with them. Building an adequate infrastructure would be an enormously expensive and time-consuming business. Secondly, attention had to be given to transforming the educational system to one that was geared to promoting African development. Math, science, agriculture, and African culture had to be emphasized, but all this meant more teachers, more schools, more equipment, and, therefore, much more expenditure and vision. Thirdly, there was a shortage of people who had been trained to operate at the managerial level, both in business and industry as well as the civil service. Many African countries had failed to really industrialize and diversify their economies. Most had concentrated on the production of a few commodities for the European market and had neglected other areas. One area that had been neglected was the production of subsistence crops for food, so much more attention had to be given to agriculture. Leaders should have realized that if they could only produce enough food to feed the people that would be half of the economic problem solved.

At the dawn of independence most African countries were not in a very good position relative to the former imperial power. Although on the surface some of the colonial powers seemed to be well-meaning and even generous in their attitude towards their former colonies, the latter were still in a position of dependence. Their imports mostly came from the former colonial power and they were almost obligated to sell their exports to that power. At independence a lot of aid was available, but most of the aid also came from the former colonial power and in some cases it was tied aid; that is, it came with certain conditions. France's relationship with her former colonies was particularly interesting. France has always sought, and still seeks, to maintain a very close relationship with her former colonies, and this can be seen in many areas, particularly in the fields of defense and the economy. With the exception of Guinea, France's former colonies used a currency, the CFA franc, that was very closely linked with the French franc. The name has been changed recently, but the currency is still closely allied to the euro, which is the currency now used by France. Furthermore, France required each former colony at independence to deposit a certain percentage of its reserves in France, and certain conditions had to be met before the reserves could be released. In effect, this amounted to all these former colonies pooling together their foreign and gold reserves in a common French account. Critics claim that both measures severely limited the countries' freedom of action in the economic sphere and this partly accounts for under-development. Furthermore, the link with the franc, and then the euro, led to an overvaluation of the CFA in the 1980s and to economic stagnation. The economic relations of these former colonies were with France, not with other African countries. They exported their products to France, and France's products were guaranteed easy access to their markets. On the other hand it can be argued that sharing the currency with a number of other countries and having it linked with a major currency imposed financial discipline, and this was one of the main reasons why the former French colonies experienced more economic growth and less inflation immediately after independence, and were less susceptible to the economic malaise that overtook Africa.

The economic relationship between Britain and her former colonies was quite different. After all the negotiations and struggles that led to independence, Britain seemed to wish to take her hands off her former colonies and to link her future with the European Union. Of course, there was still the Commonwealth of Nations, but this was now a rather informal association of sovereign states. Still, it was instrumental with regard to the giving of aid from the more developed countries like Britain, Canada, and Australia to the less developed members. Unlike the French, however, the British never insisted on the same binding economic relationship with their former colonies. The British respected the sovereignty of their former colonies and their right to freedom of action. Consequently, each former British colony had its own currency at independence and the results were not always good. The value of these currencies slumped on the market quite dramatically and this had a very adverse effect on the relevant economies. For instance, at independence the Nigerian naira, the Ghanaian cedi, and the Sierra Leonean leone all had the same value, two to the British pound. At the moment the leone is over 10,000 to the pound and the naira is several hundreds. It must also be noted that all the measures needed to promote development necessitated capital and heavy investment, but most African countries lacked the capital. They would have to depend on aid, which could only go so far, and investment from Western capitalist countries. This meant that they had to be on the good books of the former imperialists and other Western countries.

Let us now look at some of the initiatives adopted by African countries, individually or collectively, to promote economic development soon after independence. Some of them realized the importance of the agricultural sector and took measures to improve it. But for agriculture to be really successful some large-scale farming was necessary, and this demanded the use of heavy equipment such as tractors and sowing machines; heavy investment was therefore needed, and this was hard to come by. Some countries tried to place emphasis on industrialization and what was called "import substitution." The rationale was that local manufacture of certain products would drastically reduce the importation of these goods and save the country much-needed foreign exchange. But industrialization needed as much capital as agriculture for the purchase of tools and equipment and the building of factories and warehouses. There was also a tremendous shortage of skilled labor. Moreover, once the products were made one could not be sure that they were of a quality to prevent people yearning for the imported variety. Industrialization did not therefore always lead to a conservation of foreign exchange. There was also a new migration of workers from the rural areas to the cities where the factories were located. Industrialization therefore led, in some cases, to a neglect of agriculture.

We have already seen that, almost immediately after independence, some African leaders tried to introduce what they called Afro-socialism as the best way to promote economic development. The leading proponent of this was the highly respected president of Tanzania, Julius Nyerere, although other countries like Guinea, Senegal, and Zambia experimented with it. Nyerere's Afro-Marxism placed emphasis on the condition and participation of the people and the state. He therefore engaged not only in the redistribution of income to benefit the people and the nationalization of some of the country's main industries, but also in the collectivization of agriculture, which became the centerpiece of his program. He created "Ujama" villages where farms were collectively owned and run by the state, in the hope that this would lead to greatly enhanced agricultural production. In fact, it led to the opposite. There was a drastic decline in production largely because farmers could not devote themselves as intensively to working on farms that were collectively owned as opposed to working on farms they themselves owned. The nationalization policy also failed. It inevitably drove much-needed capital away. Fortunately, Nyerere was honest enough to admit the failure of his policies.

By the late 1960s African countries were beginning to grasp the real nature of the problems facing them in their drive for development and they started initiating collective programs of action. They named each decade a development decade and listed programs and goals that had to be achieved by the end of the decade. Thus, there was the 1960s development decade, the 1970s development decade, and the 1980s development decade. Many African countries were also among a group of 77 developing countries called the G77 at the United Nations, in the late 1960s, That drew up a program called the New International Economic Order (NIEO) with five main goals: (a) developed countries should set aside at least 0.7 percent of their GNP as economic aid to developing countries; (b) there should be ease of transfer of technology from the developed to the developing world; (c) there should be international agreements on commodities to ensure stability in the revenues of developing countries; (d) industrialization should be increased in developing countries to enable them to produce 6 percent of the world's manufactured goods by the end of the century; (e) developing countries should be able to get access to the markets of developed countries. It can be seen that these goals cover many of the problems we have discussed. This was roughly the situation at the end of the sixties.

The Organisation of African Unity had not been inactive during this period. In 1979 the heads of state of the Organisation adopted what has been called the Monrovia Declaration. This stressed, among other things, that in striving towards real development African countries should emphasize self-reliance and not merely depend on assistance from others. In April 1980, in collaboration with the United Nations Economic Commission for Africa, the Organisation of African Unity adopted the highly important Lagos Plan of Action. This plan indicated the steps to be taken in order to implement the Monrovia Declaration. The Plan stressed the importance of self-sufficiency in food production, which really meant the importance of agriculture, and it also urged countries to endeavor to be self-reliant in industry, transport and communications, human and natural resources, and science and technology (Delancey, 117). All these were noble goals perfectly consistent with the drive towards development that was largely based on the will and effort of the African people themselves. Unfortunately, many of the goals were unrealized and up to the 1990s most of Africa was confronted with an economic malaise and experienced dire poverty. By the end of the 1980s, therefore, about twenty years after the achievement of independence, many African countries were just as poor and undeveloped as they had been at the time of independence.

The causes and effects of poverty in Africa

We shall now look generally at the phenomenon of poverty in Africa. This means taking a detailed look at its causes and effects, and the solutions that were suggested or put in place to end it. Twenty years after the political liberation of the continent, Africa was considered the poorest continent; many would say that it still is. By poverty we mean the poverty of individuals living within the country as well as the poverty of the entire country itself. The definition of poverty has been hotly debated although we all know when an individual is poor and even when a whole country is poor. Some economists have suggested that the definition should relate only to financial matters and that only people living on less than one dollar a day should be considered poor. This has been hotly contested by others who realize that someone can have more than the dollar a day needed for existence and still not have many of the basics needed for a comfortable subsistence such as access to education, maintenance of good health, and tolerable transport facilities. Nor would this definition help much in so far as the state of the entire nation is concerned. Several other indices have therefore been adduced for the measurement of poverty, such as the acquisition of a certain level of education; life expectancy; infant mortality; access to reasonable health facilities; availability of a tolerable infrastructure including good water supply, a functioning energy system, and adequate transport and communications systems; attention to cultural matters; and attention to agriculture. The United Nations publishes annually what is called the Human Development Index which takes into account some of these indices, such as life expectancy, education, and per capita income, and uses them to compile a score which shows how the individual nations are doing. It then ranks the nations according to the scores they receive, thus showing the level of development. These are reasonable parameters.

Let us now look at how the countries are doing and how African countries performed in 1990, a relevant year for our purposes. Norway is on top as the most developed country with a score of .917 out of a total score of 1, followed by Switzerland and Ireland. The top 62 countries are categorized as having very high development with scores above .712. Only one African country falls into this category, and that is the 62nd, the

Seychelles. The next African country in the rankings is Tunisia at number 91, with a score of .569. Libya is 110 on the list, South Africa is 113, Gabon is 115, and Egypt is 116. These countries find themselves in a category referred to as countries with high human development. It must be noted that three are North African countries. Thirteen other African countries fall into the category of medium human development, but no less than 25 fall into the category of low human development. The poorest country in the world, according to this index, is Burundi with a score of .296. With the exception of Yemen, the poorest countries in the world are African. Admittedly, some African countries were doing comparatively well at the end of the 1980s, but at least 50 percent were on the low development list and were rated as poor.

It must be stressed that this poverty is by no means endemic. Africa has the potential of being the richest continent in the world, with resources that others, like Europe, would be grateful to have. Africa is very richly endowed with mineral resources, including the most precious, such as gold, diamonds, copper, iron, manganese, uranium, titanium, and others. Many countries in Africa have discovered oil. In spite of the environmental problems, Africa has tremendous potential for agriculture as most of the cultivable land is still untapped. With oceans and seas surrounding it almost completely, with numerous beaches, and with magnificent landscapes, there is great potential for tourism. Africa could also be an unparalleled supplier of seafood. In a sense, therefore, the continent has no reason to be poor, but it is still regarded as the poorest. What are the factors that have contributed to this state?

There are four main causes of poverty and the economic malaise that Africa has experienced. These are: (a) slavery and the colonial legacy; (b) environmental factors; (c) outside forces over which Africa does not have much control; and (d) the internal policies and attitudes of African authorities. Let us look at each of these in turn.

The effects of the slave trade on Africa in general have already been discussed. It is easy to see these as being merely short-term. However, the stagnation of an entire continent's population for three hundred years must have devastating long-term economic effects. The same applies to the forceful removal of the most able-bodied and creative segments of the population for the same length of time. It would take a very long time indeed for the continent to recover from the effects of such a loss. The disruption of the routes and even of the established patterns of trade must have led to financial and economic losses that were unrecoverable. If all this had not happened, the course of African economic development might have been quite different today. World history is littered with examples of countries and societies who, because of one momentous event, lost their position and prosperity for ever. The trans-Atlantic slave trade was such a momentous event, and it couldn't but have had an almost permanent effect on the continent of Africa. This is why one is inclined to accept Walter Rodney's powerful argument, in his ground-breaking book *How Europe Underdeveloped Africa*, that the slave trade considerably slowed down the technical innovation and economic advancement that had been going on in Africa up to the sixteenth century. Rodney justifiably argues that the poverty and underdevelopment characteristic of Africa in the middle of the twentieth century was a direct result of the slave trade. Besides, the slave trade paved the way for imperialism, since it considerably weakened African societies, and thus made them easy prey for the European invaders; and imperialism, of course, made matters even worse.

There could not be much debate about the adverse effect of imperialism on Africa's economic development. As we have seen, the economic structure under the imperialists was meant to benefit them, not the Africans. Commodity prices were fixed by the

Table 9.1 Human Development Index for African countries.

HDI Rank	Country	1990	2000	2010	2018
82	Algeria	0.578	0.646	0.73	0.759
149	Angola	..	0.394	0.51	0.574
163	Benin	0.348	0.398	0.473	0.52
94	Botswana	0.57	0.578	0.66	0.728
182	Burkina Faso	..	0.286	0.375	0.434
185	Burundi	0.295	0.293	0.402	0.423
165	Côte d'Ivoire	0.391	0.407	0.454	0.516
126	Cabo Verde	..	0.564	0.626	0.651
150	Cameroon	0.445	0.439	0.471	0.563
188	Central African Republic	0.32	0.307	0.355	0.381
187	Chad	..	0.298	0.374	0.401
156	Comoros	..	0.457	0.513	0.538
138	Congo	0.531	0.495	0.557	0.609
179	Congo (Democratic Republic of the)	0.377	0.333	0.416	0.459
171	Djibouti	..	0.361	0.446	0.495
116	Egypt	0.546	0.611	0.666	0.7
144	Equatorial Guinea	..	0.52	0.58	0.588
182	Eritrea	..	..	0.433	0.434
138	Eswatini (Kingdom of)	0.545	0.468	0.513	0.608
173	Ethiopia	..	0.283	0.412	0.47
115	Gabon	0.619	0.627	0.658	0.702
174	Gambia	0.328	0.382	0.437	0.466
142	Ghana	0.454	0.483	0.554	0.596
174	Guinea	0.278	0.335	0.408	0.466
178	Guinea-Bissau	..	..	0.426	0.461
147	Kenya	0.467	0.446	0.533	0.579
164	Lesotho	0.488	0.444	0.461	0.518
176	Liberia	..	0.422	0.441	0.465
110	Libya	0.676	0.728	0.757	0.708
162	Madagascar	..	0.456	0.504	0.521
172	Malawi	0.303	0.362	0.437	0.485
184	Mali	0.231	0.308	0.403	0.427
161	Mauritania	0.378	0.446	0.49	0.527
66	Mauritius	0.62	0.674	0.748	0.796
121	Morocco	0.458	0.531	0.618	0.676
180	Mozambique	0.217	0.301	0.396	0.446
130	Namibia	0.579	0.543	0.588	0.645
189	Niger	0.213	0.253	0.319	0.377
158	Nigeria	..	..	0.484	0.534
157	Rwanda	0.245	0.337	0.488	0.536

(Continued)

Table 9.1 (Cont.)

HDI Rank	Country	1990	2000	2010	2018
137	São Tomé and Príncipe	0.437	0.48	0.546	0.609
166	Senegal	0.377	0.39	0.468	0.514
62	Seychelles	..	0.712	0.762	0.801
181	Sierra Leone	0.27	0.298	0.391	0.438
113	South Africa	0.625	0.629	0.662	0.705
186	South Sudan	..	..	0.425	0.413
168	Sudan	0.332	0.403	0.471	0.508
159	Tanzania (United Republic of)	0.373	0.395	0.487	0.528
167	Togo	0.405	0.426	0.468	0.513
91	Tunisia	0.569	0.653	0.717	0.739
159	Uganda	0.312	0.395	0.489	0.528
143	Zambia	0.424	0.428	0.531	0.591
150	Zimbabwe	0.498	0.452	0.472	0.563

Source: Compiled from data at http://hdr.undp.org/en/data.

colonial powers and the cheap raw materials thus made available went to the factories of Europe to benefit European economies. One can say with some confidence that the ruthless exploitation of Africa's natural resources for the benefit of European economies was a major cause of poverty and underdevelopment on the continent. The profits from the exploitation of these resources were not ploughed back into the African economy to create wealth for Africans. The European colonizers failed to encourage African industrialization or the development of an education system that was conducive to economic development. One must also mention the artificial partitioning of the continent by the European powers at the Berlin Conference which gave rise after independence to vicious civil wars in places like Somalia, the Democratic Republic of the Congo, and the Republic of Nigeria, wars that certainly retarded economic development. It is not an exaggeration to say that the colonial legacy and slavery were partly responsible for the poverty and economic underdevelopment that characterized most of Africa at the time of independence and later.

Environmental factors also played a role in keeping Africa poor. The poverty of the African soil has had a marked impact on agricultural development. It led to shifting cultivation and eventually to more soil infertility. Much of the African soil consists of laterite which is no good for agriculture. Furthermore, there are large desert areas, both in the north and south, which are also unsuitable for agriculture. Climatic conditions have also led to drought in formerly productive areas like the Sahel, while, on the other hand, some parts of Africa, like Mozambique, have been devastated by the floods resulting from too much rainfall.

Some external factors over which African countries had no control also played a part in causing poverty in Africa. The newly independent countries of Africa were caught up in a world economic system which was not of their making and over which they had little control. We have already seen that at independence many African countries were locked in a culture of dependency on economic conditions largely created in the West, particularly dependency on the former colonial power. Besides, globalization was gaining steam, and success in a globalized economy required components that most African countries did not have at the time, such as capital, mastery of modern technology, and superb communication and advertising skills. A major factor was that the prices of the commodities that African countries produced and sold to the West were fixed, not by Africans, but by the Europeans. At one time the prices were determined by the General Agreement on Tariffs and Trade in which Africans played no part. This set of regulations had been created in 1947 and ratified in 1948 by 23 countries, but apart from Liberia, Ethiopia, and the special case of South Africa, no African country was independent by then. This meant that the European powers could fix the prices to their advantage and African countries received less than they should have for their commodities. Moreover, if the price of a country's main commodity fell, it could be plunged into poverty. When the price of copper, for instance, fell on the international market, the Zambian economy was plunged into chaos. Besides, the manipulation of the commodity prices could be done deliberately for purposes other than economic. If the European powers did not like the policies of a particular country, for instance, they could deliberately lower the price of that country's main commodity thus reducing revenue and causing suffering and chaos. It is generally believed that the drop in the price of cacao, one of Ghana's main exports, was deliberately engineered in the sixties to produce economic suffering in Ghana because some in the West did not like Kwame Nkrumah's Marxist drive. If that was the intention, it succeeded, because the subsequent tremendous suffering of the Ghanaian people led to the overthrow of Nkrumah in 1966. The unfairness of the GATT system was what the New International Economic Order was referring to when it asked for international agreements on commodities to stabilize the revenues that developing countries received from their exports.

The price of oil was another factor over which Africans had little control because it was dominated by outside forces. Many African countries have now discovered oil, but at this time, the two decades or so after independence, most African countries had to purchase their oil from outside. Oil was essential to the smooth running of these countries, because it was at the basis of everything: energy, transportation, the cost of goods, and therefore the cost of living. A sharp increase in the price of oil meant a comparable increase in the cost of transportation which some people would not now afford, frequent power outages, and an increase in the cost of everything including foodstuffs. It meant poverty. This was what happened to most African countries in the 1970s when the Middle Eastern countries, then the world's major suppliers of oil, decided to use the price of oil as a political weapon because of the Palestinian issue. The dramatic increase in the price of their oil had a blistering effect even in the United States, during the presidency of Jimmy Carter. I lived in Sierra Leone at the time and can remember not only the power outages and the queues at gas stations, but the students marching to town in demonstrations demanding "light now," because the shortage had caused an almost permanent power outage that was not conducive to academic work. The increased price of oil had caused outages because the government could not afford to purchase the amount of oil needed to keep the power system going. This was real poverty, and it was caused by forces over which Sierra Leoneans had no control.

The AIDS crisis is another factor over which, at the outset, most African countries had little control. It had a major impact on the economies of most countries. Although AIDS started making its presence felt in Africa in the mid- to late eighties when the economic malaise was well under way, it certainly had a major impact, if only because it slowed down or even stalled the progress that had been made in economic development. We can take as an example the country of Botswana in Southern Africa. Botswana had been doing extremely well economically largely because, unlike some other countries like Sierra Leone, it had properly regulated the diamond mining industry and was therefore getting very good revenues from it. The Botswana currency, the pula, was even stronger at the time than the South African rand. But then came the AIDS crisis which hit Botswana very hard as it did other Southern African countries, and the Botswana economy slumped. AIDS was an international epidemic which hit every country, though some were more afflicted than others. It was beyond the capacity of any country to prevent itself from being involved. AIDS hit every class of people, but its most devastating effect in Africa was on the younger and most productive segments of the population. This inevitably had a dramatic impact on the economy. Besides, resources that were badly needed to promote development in other areas had to be diverted towards dealing with the AIDS epidemic.

However, the economic malaise that overwhelmed most of Africa up to the nineties cannot be entirely blamed on slavery/the colonial legacy, environmental factors, and outside factors over which Africans had little control. A huge share of the blame must be laid on African authorities themselves because of their attitudes, policies, and actions. Outside factors certainly played a major role, but some would argue that African leaders should bear the greatest share of the responsibility for the malaise.

Although, as we have seen, the economic position inherited from the colonial powers at the time of independence was not the healthiest, the situation was not completely bleak, and in some countries there were some positive factors that could have been built upon and used as foundations for future development. Let us look at Sierra Leone as an example. At the time of independence in 1961 the country was self-sufficient in food production. This was a vital asset. Then, in spite of the fact that commodity prices were fixed outside the continent, some of the country's commodities, like palm oil and coffee, not to mention minerals, still commanded a reasonable price on the world market. The country's population was also low, and it stood to benefit from the general optimism and goodwill towards newly independent countries, as well as the availability of loans and aid. Thus, in spite of the obstacles and problems there were also some positive factors that could have been used as building blocks towards development. It is now clear that most of the advantages and opportunities wee squandered.

Let us now look at some of the policies and attitudes of Africans themselves that contributed to the economic malaise. We have already considered the effect of some of the Afro-Marxist policies adopted by some African leaders. Large-scale nationalization frightened off foreign investment and led to inefficiency and corruption, none of them conducive to economic success. A major factor was that African governments borrowed extensively from Western governments and financial institutions to finance various projects. It is clear that many of these projects were necessary and essential to development. There was a need for new and efficient infrastructure to replace the decaying ones left by the imperialists. There was also a need for better educational and health facilities, which meant the building of more schools and hospitals, not to mention the purchase of equipment. The governments had promised before independence that all these would be available, and they had to be seen to be living up to their promises. On hindsight, it might have been advisable if the projects had been "spaced" and African governments had not tried to do too much at the same time. But they had to be seen to be transforming their countries. In order to achieve all this, African governments had to get huge loans from the West. Thus began the piling up of the African debt which is still a huge problem today. Although the loans did not have to be repaid immediately or even in the near future, the interest had to be duly and regularly paid and, in many cases, most of the country's foreign exchange earnings, which could have been usefully applied to other development projects, went towards the servicing of the debt. It would not have mattered much if all these projects had the desired development and economic results. Of course, it would take a long time for some of the results to become visible. The problem was that many of the projects failed to have the desired results and made no contribution to development although the interest on the loans continued to be paid.

Let us take as an example the holding of the annual meeting of heads of state of the Organisation of African Unity (OAU). The OAU was established in 1963 with its headquarters at Addis Ababa, the Ethiopian capital. But up to very recently the meeting of heads of state was held in rotation among the various members of the Organization. The hosting country bore all the expenses, which included the cost of construction of accommodation like luxurious hotels and other buildings to house the thousands of people attending, since each head of state was usually accompanied by an entourage sometimes in the hundreds. At times new roads had to be constructed from the airport, and the entire capital city had to be made beautiful in order to impress the visiting heads of state during a meeting lasting only four days. The countries that hosted the OAU were sometimes the poorest, like Sierra Leone and Liberia. They gave as an excuse for hosting the meeting that the hotels and other buildings would be used for commercial purposes later and contribute to the economy. In the aftermath, this never really happened. The hotels remained empty, because certain factors had not been taken into account in their construction, and the houses were sold at rock-bottom prices to friends and relatives of members of the government. These governments borrowed heavily in order to host the OAU meeting, which could simply have been held every year at the headquarters. African governments later learned from their mistakes and decided to do just that: hold the annual meeting in Addis Ababa. However, in the meantime many African economies suffered terribly from hosting the OAU and in some cases, as with Sierra Leone and Liberia, this led to revolution and political turmoil. In the meantime, the interest on the loans had to be repaid.

In addition to having no tangible effect on the economy, some of the projects were much too grandiose and the amount of money spent on them could have been much more usefully devoted to other smaller projects with more tangible effects. For instance, the former president of Côte d'Ivoire, Felix Houphouet-Boigny, a Roman Catholic, decided to build an enormous church at his birthplace, a small village called Yamoussoukro. The church, called the Basilica of our Lady of Peace of Yamoussoukro, cannot even be called a cathedral because a cathedral is the center of the diocese and the seat of the bishop, and the diocese of Yamoussoukro already had a cathedral and a bishop less than 3 kilometers away. The basilica at Yamoussoukro is the largest religious edifice in the world, larger even than St. Peter's Cathedral in the Vatican, which, until the construction at Yamoussoukro, held the record of being the largest church in the world ever. Constructed between 1985 and 1989 at an estimated cost which varies from 175 to 600 million US dollars, it did not even have significant religious results because Yamoussoukro is too small a village to have significant numbers of people who worship at the Basilica regularly. Built to accommodate 18,000, Sunday worshippers run only into a few hundreds. The 175 or 600 million US dollars could have been used to finance other significant projects in a country in which most of the people are still desperately poor. The Yamoussoukro example also serves to illustrate the fact that some of the projects were wasteful prestige projects.

One of the major factors inhibiting development in Africa was the widespread corruption that prevailed in most African countries. It involved almost every level of government and administration. The fact that the head of state and his ministers were also involved in it provided insurance for functionaries lower down the ladder. Since a culture of corruption had been created, it was done without any shame or embarrassment as though it had become the accepted norm. Corruption took every form: bribery, nepotism, sheer theft, fraud, and embezzlement. The loans received from foreign governments and banks quite often went into the pockets and bank accounts of the members of the government. That was how they were able, within a few years or even months of their taking office, to build enormous mansions that at times cost a hundred times their normal salary. They appropriated most of the money intended to purchase essential equipment, and then used the small remaining balance to get shoddy second-hand goods that soon broke down.

Bribery was rampant. Foreign investors who wanted to set up enterprises in the country would be asked to give a certain sum of money to the relevant minister before the business would start. If they did, they would merely pass the extra cost onto the ordinary citizen thus helping to boost inflation. If they did not and went away in disgust, the country would have lost valuable investment and the establishment of an enterprise from which the whole nation would have benefited. Revenue from businesses and industries which should have been used to pay salaries and finance further development was squandered by individuals. Customs officials, for instance, would lower the duties some major businessmen had to pay on their imported goods in return for bribes, thus depriving the country of much-needed funds. Income-tax officials would do the same with regard to the tax due from many. While ordinary people paid the normal tax because it was automatically deducted from their salaries, extremely wealthy businessmen and others would pay less than 1 percent of the tax due from them. All these instances are not the result of hypothetical speculation but are actually scenarios that happened, as attested to at the commissions of inquiry that usually followed changes of government in many African countries.

At the time of independence aid was readily available for many African countries. There has been much discussion about the value of aid. Some argue that it perpetuates a culture of dependence, for if a country is sure of always getting aid, it might not be anxious to take the necessary steps to become self-reliant, and that would only perpetuate poverty. Others object to the aid being tied to some conditions. There was no doubt that African countries needed the aid, since their level of development at independence was relatively low and most of them did not have, or could not generate, the capital that was needed for development. The issue is not whether aid was good or necessary, but how it was used. Unfortunately, the aid, like the loans, mostly went into private pockets and bank accounts. As a result, the schools, hospitals, water systems, electricity systems, and roads the aid was supposed to provide were not constructed, or, if they were, were not of the required quality.

One of the major developmental problems in Africa was that some of the heads of government were the visible embodiment of the rampant corruption. Two cases are worthy of note: Siaka Stevens, long-term president of Sierra Leone, and Mobutu Sese Sekou, long-term president of the Democratic Republic of the Congo. Both men behaved as though the entire country was their private possession and they were at liberty to exploit its resources for their own personal benefit. Both were leaders of countries that were enormously rich in natural resources and therefore had the potential to be enormously rich and self-sustaining. Siaka Stevens virtually owned or had a major share in all the major enterprises. Furthermore, before one could establish any enterprise one had to get his blessing, which meant that a major share of the profits would have to go to him. He obviously had his own diamond mines that were not by any means accountable to the government and therefore outside the tax structure. Mobutu Sese Sekou also ensured that the profits from the country's major industries went to him personally. Both men became enormously wealthy. Within a short time, Mobutu Sese Sekou became a billionaire and was reputed to be one of the wealthiest men in the world. And this was a man who had virtually no education and started life as an ordinary soldier. If these men had ploughed the wealth accruing to them from the exploitation of the country's resources back into the country's economy, that would at least have been some atonement for their misdeeds. They would have created jobs and some revenue and reduced some of the people's misery. However, they sent their ill-gotten gains abroad, lodging them in banks in Switzerland. One of the most unfortunate aspects of this was that when they died, neither their descendants nor the country was able to get hold of the funds for all kinds of reasons. The money was left in Switzerland, and so there was the ironic scenario that these two African countries continued to be poor largely because of the crimes of their former presidents, while Switzerland, one of the richest countries in the world, became even richer.

The inadequacy of the educational system in most African countries was another major contributing factor to poverty. As we have seen, education is a very important component of the development process and the drive to reduce poverty. At independence, the newly elected African governments promised, and probably intended, to do quite a lot in the field of education, but, for the most part, they did not live up to their promises. More attention needed to be paid to math and science, to education for industry, to the preparation of skilled workers and managers, and to agricultural education. Some governments, such as that of Ghana, did as much as they could, but it was not enough. Illiteracy remained high, schools and colleges lacked proper equipment, teachers were not adequately paid, and targets for achieving free primary education were not met. The universities continued to turn out graduates in ever increasing numbers, but the new graduates discovered that there were few opportunities for getting employment in their areas of training. African countries therefore found themselves in the peculiar position of having thousands of employable but unemployed graduates, and there could be no better recipe for disaster in any country than having hordes of employable but unemployed graduates.

It must also be noted that one of the factors responsible for underdevelopment in Africa was the low level of savings. Most Africans were poor and could barely live on their wages and salaries. Only the elite had significant savings. With savings being poor there was hardly money for investment. There was therefore an almost total lack of investment by the citizens themselves and so, as far as investment in really meaningful business projects was concerned, African countries were almost totally dependent on foreigners.

A major factor contributing to the poverty of African countries at this time was that African governments spent a lot of money on the military. Some governments spent as much as 42 percent of their annual budgets on the military. This meant that much-needed money, which could have been spent on other areas that had a more direct bearing on development, was spent on the military. It can be argued that the military was one of the most unproductive segments of the country. Most African countries did not engage in wars with other nations, so there was no need for an army to defend the country against external aggressors. The army was, in fact, used as another police force, to keep order in the country. Dictatorial and one-party governments that had become enormously unpopular needed the military to keep the people down by armed force. Staying in power was often the government's first priority, and for this a well-equipped and satisfied army was necessary. Therefore, while other areas of the nation were starving, the army was pampered and had virtually everything it wanted. While ordinary people had to stand in queues for hours on end in order to purchase limited quantities of the main foodstuffs such as rice, the soldiers were sure of having their bags of rice safely delivered to their doors. The army was never short of gas or of electricity. The leaders of the army were given important concessions, like mining concessions, and they therefore had their own private businesses. Far from contributing to development, the pampering of the army, would, in fact, have all kinds of disastrous consequences for many African countries.

Finally, it must be stressed that political instability, which was characteristic of many African countries, was a major cause of underdevelopment and poverty. The political instability was largely caused by African governments themselves. The introduction of one-party states and of dictatorial regimes led, as we have seen, to instability because there was always the possibility that these regimes could be removed. Between 1963 and 2000 there were 88 successful military coups in 32 states in Africa. Some had more than one within a very short time. Some of the coups were followed by protracted civil wars. That kind of scenario scares off much-needed investment both from inside and outside the country. The political instability went hand in hand with a lack of accountability and these two are antipathetic to development. Investors do not like to pour their money into states that are unstable and where the governments are accountable to no one.

The signs of poverty

Let us look at the actual signs of poverty in African states. In other words, we'll be examining what actual poverty looks like. For the reasons discussed above, the typical poor African state would have been losing revenue, especially revenue derived from exports, which means there would be a lack of foreign exchange to purchase essentials from abroad, like food. This inevitably leads to drastic shortages of essentials. One of the first signs of poverty therefore is the endless queues of people anxious to buy things like sugar, rice, and even bread which has to be made from imported flour. Since there would not be enough money to purchase oil, there would be a tremendous shortage of gas; another sign of poverty therefore would be the long lines of cars at gas stations waiting to purchase limited supplies of gas. The shortage of gas means that the cost of transportation goes up drastically, so even those who do not possess cars feel the force of the shortage. If the cost of transportation, which also lies at the base of everything, goes up, the price of everything else goes up also, including goods that have to be transported from farms to the urban areas. People charge more for services because they have to compute the increased cost of transportation to get them to their places of work. Another important sign of poverty therefore is the greatly increased rate of inflation. In certain poor countries inflation could go up by hundreds of percentage points, as it did in Zimbabwe. Not only does the cost of everything go up because of the increased cost of transportation, the shortage of goods automatically drives up their cost. In other words, supply lags behind demand, which is always a sure cause of inflation. This in itself has the unfortunate consequence that people's salaries cannot keep up with the rate of inflation and even those who have employment find themselves joining the ranks of the poor.

Another infallible sign of poverty is the frequent power cuts. Many African countries rely on imported oil for generating electricity, and when oil is in short supply because there is not enough foreign exchange to purchase it there are bound to be outages. In Sierra Leone, for instance, the frequent demonstrations by students demanding the restoration of electricity was the surest sign that real poverty had struck. Of course, the lack of foreign exchange means inability to purchase equipment and materials for repairs and maintenance of systems like water systems or telephone systems. Another inevitable sign of poverty therefore is the breakdown of all kinds of facilities in hotels, in offices, at airports, and so on. Ali Mazrui masterfully documented all this in his brilliant documentary series *The Africans: A Triple Heritage*. Unfortunately, social services, such as health and education, are often the hardest hit. One can see this in the physical condition of the hospitals, in the lack of drugs, and in the rise of bribery and corruption as patients do whatever they can to get treatment. It can also be seen in the shortage of books and in school children experiencing real hunger in schools that lack desks, chairs, and other materials. These are not just matters of speculation, hypothesis, or even research; they are matters that people like Ali Mazrui, and myself, witnessed.

The debt burden as a cause of poverty

The debt burden has always been regarded as one of the foremost obstacles to the development of African countries. We have already seen some of the ways in which these countries came to accumulate such huge debts. However, in addition to borrowing for grandiose and unnecessary projects, they also borrowed to spend on essentials like oil for the provision of electricity and for transportation. Twice during the 1970s the price of oil on the international market went up drastically. Those African countries that were not producers of oil were very badly affected. They had to have the oil but did not always have the resources to purchase it. They therefore had to borrow money. We have also seen that the terms of trade, including the price that African countries got for the commodities they exported to the Western world, were not set in consultation with Africans. This was a matter over which Africans had little control, and the prices of these commodities could fluctuate considerably. In the 1980s the price of these commodities not only fluctuated, but fell considerably. In other words, African countries received considerably less foreign exchange than they needed to import essentials. They were therefore forced to borrow. In the 1980s also, foreign aid which had been plentiful at the time of independence began to dry up. This also affected the foreign exchange holdings of many African countries, thus enhancing the need to borrow.

It is felt in some quarters that debt in itself is not such a huge problem. After all, the United States, apparently the richest country in the world, is the greatest debtor in the world, with a total debt of over 22 trillion dollars, and the debt rises by a trillion dollars every year. Other rich countries also have huge debts. Surely, some people think, if the richest countries in the world can have such huge debts there can be nothing wrong with debt. The main difference between the developed and developing countries in this regard is that, generally, the former have the means of simultaneously servicing their debts while promoting development and doing all that they need to do with money.

The debt owed by developed countries is normally acquired from banks or as loans from other countries. China, for instance, is the source of the loans that constitute most of the American debt. Giving these loans is a kind of investment. For instance, the money that banks use to provide loans is the money put in the banks by ordinary people. This money could be their retirement benefits or their life's savings, and what they live on is the interest from this investment, not the capital itself. They are therefore quite happy for the capital to remain with the bank as long as the interest, which is their main source of income, is regularly paid. The important thing therefore, about debt, is that the interest must be paid. Lenders and investors are therefore happy to leave their capital where it is as long as they can get the annual interest, which normally is a percentage of the total loan or the total invested. Of course a problem will arise if the lender demands the capital back. If China, for instance, demands its trillions of dollars from the United States, the latter will be in a terrible bind.

Unlike the developed countries, most developing countries do not have the means of both servicing their debt and promoting much-needed development. Payment of the interest on the debt is mandatory in almost every case, so priority must be given to it. That means that money can be devoted to the development of health programs, educational programs, infrastructure, and water and electricity facilities only after the interest on the debt is paid. This leaves little for development. It is true that the percentage of GDP or the percentage of export revenues that African countries had to devote towards servicing the debt varied from country to country. In the case of Togo, for instance it was 2 percent while in Burundi's case it was 83 percent (DeLancey, 128). It is also true that much of the debt was owed to other countries and international organizations who were therefore not fussy about collecting the interest or the repayment of the loans. Some countries therefore defaulted on their debt payments. Even so, the arrears on the interest mounted and both the original debt itself and the arrears on the interest continued to hang on the shoulders of countries like an albatross. It is still quite true, therefore, that the debt burden is one of the foremost obstacles to development in Africa and should be regarded as a cause of poverty.

Although we have so far been concerned with the causes and signs of poverty in African countries in the period before the African recovery, it must be admitted that many of these factors still exist in quite a few African countries even today. Let us now concern ourselves with the measures proposed as solutions to the problem.

Solutions for the problem of poverty in Africa

Realizing that the debt burden was a major cause of underdevelopment and poverty, there were calls for debt relief, that is, reduction in the amount of debt owed, or for the debt to be written off completely. Consequently, France decided to cancel part or all of the debt owed to it by its former colonies. In 1996 the IMF and the World Bank decided to help the poorest and most indebted countries that were now designated "Heavily Indebted Poor Countries" (HIPC). However, the conditions imposed by these bodies for a country to qualify for debt relief were so stringent that few African countries were able to benefit. The conditions were somewhat relaxed under what was called HIPC-2, which required that in return for receiving debt relief these poor countries should pursue programs devoted to the reduction of poverty. In 2005 the GH8 leaders actually decided to cancel the debt of the world's poorest and most indebted countries, most of them in Africa. Still there were conditions attached. Absolute cancellation depended on these countries having fulfilled the condition imposed by HPIC-2; that is, the establishment of programs devoted to the reduction of poverty. This meant that a number of African countries were excluded from the cancellation initiative and, while progress has been made on the debt issue, it has not been finally resolved and only a small dent has been made on the contribution of the debt burden to the problem of poverty in Africa.

There have also been calls for the renegotiation of the terms of trade to enable poor African countries to get more revenue and foreign exchange from the export of their commodities, as well as gain access to the markets of Western countries. So far Western countries have been able to control access to their markets by the imposition of quotas and of tariffs. The renegotiation of the terms of trade therefore includes both the abolition of tariffs and better prices for African commodities.

As part of the drive towards solving the problem of poverty, there was now recognition of the need to update the educational system, making it conducive to development and the elimination of poverty. A heightened and well-managed educational system was essential for progress, not just in the economic field, but in all fields. Indeed, there was an increasing realization of the need for a holistic approach to development and the elimination of poverty. Attention needed to be paid not only to economic matters, but to fields like education, agriculture, and health. From now on governments stressed the need for improved agricultural production and various programs with fanciful names such as the "green revolution" were adopted by African countries with varying degrees of success. The Ghana plan, under the leadership of President Jerry Rawlings, was spectacularly successful. Quite significantly, there was a growing realization that, for development to proceed, there was a tremendous need for liberalization of trade. Nationalization and government monopolies had to be rejected. Up to this point some of the major financial institutions in some African countries had been nationalized and others, such as corporations and the so-called parastatals, were largely controlled by the government and run by government nominees. This led to corruption, nepotism, and low productivity. There was now a call for more privatization and a greater involvement by African countries in the global economy.

Most importantly, there were calls for the reform of the political system in order to create the political stability that was essential for economic progress and development. Up to the end of the 1980s most of Africa had been under dictatorial, military, or one-party rule with dire consequences for the economy. Africans throughout the continent were becoming tired with these dictatorial regimes which had not produced any development at all. If anything, the opposite was the case. Fortunately, this awareness coincided with the collapse of authoritarian and one-party regimes all over the world, especially in Eastern Europe which had been the bastion of this kind of political system. The Berlin Wall came down in 1989, and this was followed by the fall of communism all over Eastern Europe. African countries were therefore greatly encouraged in their drive to rid themselves of authoritarian regimes which they now saw as stifling development.

The structural adjustment programs

Perhaps the most important of the programs and solutions put forward for ending Africa's economic malaise were the so-called structural adjustment programs (SAPs). These were normally stipulated by international financial agencies like the World Bank and the IMF when countries with faltering economies applied to them for assistance in the form of loans. It could hardly be expected that the World Bank, in particular, would be very sympathetic and give the African countries seeking aid an advantageous deal. In 1981 it had published the famous Berg report which blamed African leaders for the economic malaise. However, both the IMF and the World Bank would express a willingness to provide assistance. But these bodies are not charitable institutions or mere aid granting bodies; they are financial institutions that expect their loans to be repaid. They therefore would want to ensure that the country in question would in future have enough foreign exchange to make repayment. They would therefore impose conditions that would guarantee an export-driven economy that would generate foreign exchange. Generally speaking the conditions would amount to cutting down on imports and domestic spending and boosting exports. The following are some of the conditions attached to IMF assistance:

a   *The devaluation of the currency.* The IMF (or the World Bank) would suggest that the country's currency was over-valued. Devaluation would mean that imports became more expensive due to the lowered value of the currency, while exports became cheaper. The assumption was that the country would therefore import less and export more; this would generate foreign exchange, strengthen the economy, and enable the country to repay its debts.

b   *Reduction of government expenditure.* The IMF would demand that the government in question shrink the civil service and cut spending even on things like education and health facilities. It is true that in some countries the civil service was bloated because of nepotism and the need to provide employment for proteges and hangers-on. This led to bloated expenditure. It could not be argued that the expenditure on education and health facilities was unjustified, but there were occasions when the amount of money spent on these was not used for the required purposes. It must also be noted that, in some cases, all the IMF asked for was a reduction in government expenditure, but the country interpreted this to mean a reduction of expenditure in all areas.

c   *Abolition of subsidies.* Some essential foodstuffs, like rice, had to be imported, thereby pushing up the cost considerably. This put them outside the purchasing power of the ordinary citizen. The same applied to an essential commodity like oil. The government would therefore decide to apply subsidies, thus artificially lowering the cost for the benefit of the ordinary citizen. However, this accounted for a huge percentage of government expenditure. Since the new program involved cutting down on government expenditure, the IMF would generally recommend the abolition of subsidies.

d   *Privatization.* The IMF insisted that major economic institutions should be privatized; that is, stripped of government control. Private investment in industry and the economy generally should be encouraged. This meant that the IMF was suggesting a return to the free-market economy.

e   *The free flow of capital.* The IMF would insist that capital be allowed to flow freely in and out of the country. This would mean, in effect, that there would be no inhibitions on investors who wanted to invest capital in the country, or who, at some point, wanted to take capital out.

They were called structural adjustment programs because they amounted to a restructuring of the economy. Some African countries accepted them because they had no alternative; others rejected them because they were concerned about the consequences of imposing such apparently stringent measures on their people. And there were a number of disadvantages as some of the countries that accepted them discovered. The devaluation of the currency inevitably led to increased inflation as necessary imports cost much more. The reduction in government expenditure might have saved the government some money, but it led to widespread unemployment. It also led to a cutback in social services such as health and education services, and this, in its turn, led to tremendous suffering. Some critics argue, in fact, that devaluation did not necessarily lead to more exports and therefore more foreign exchange because the amount of a commodity that a country could export was limited by the quota system. We are thus faced with a scenario in which the citizens of a country were paying much more for essentials like basic foodstuffs and gas, many were unemployed, and their health and education facilities continued to deteriorate. In some countries, the implementation of the SAPs did lead to economic discipline and some economic growth, but it was at the cost of great suffering by the people. Two countries that were supposed to have been highly successful in the implementation of the SAPs were Uganda and Ghana. Both are now among Africa's most prosperous countries. I can vouch for the prosperity of Ghana which I have visited several times. I witnessed the suffering of the people at the time that the implementation of the SAPs was at its height. But I have also seen the more recent prosperity. Perhaps the short-term disadvantages were necessary in order to ensure the long-term prosperity and success. However, in addition to the SAPs themselves discipline was needed for success.

Ghana's success was partly due to the iron discipline imposed by its then leader President Jerry Rawlings. We might deplore the fact that he took office after two coups, one of which was definitely bloody, and that he ruled for years as a dictator before converting himself to a civilian to contest the presidency in a democratic way. Nevertheless, it is true that he imposed discipline on the country and did his best, not only to promote agriculture, but to rid the country of corruption. It can be argued that the most important phenomenon that Africa needs in order to promote development and eliminate poverty is a complete change of mind-set by the population as a whole. Africa needs a mind-set that sees corruption as the greatest obstacle to development and prosperity. It is usual to say that the corruption has been carried out by the leaders who have therefore imposed suffering on their people. Of course, leadership is needed, and if leadership is uncorrupt, this will probably percolate down to the people. But in quite a few cases corruption has already taken over the entire population and it has become accepted as the norm. This acceptance occurs among those at the highest and those at the lowest levels. Africans must become aware that if corruption and bribery are eliminated, there will probably be enough revenue to pay adequate salaries to all, so that people will not need to indulge in bribery and graft in order to get the necessary funds to live. It must be admitted that corruption was at the heart of most of Africa's problems and this is what needs to be eliminated.

As we have seen, some countries accepted the SAPs with varying degrees of success, but others did not. The World Bank certainly thought the SAPs were generally successful. In 1989 it issued a report in collaboration with the UNDP that concluded that more than 30 of the sub-Saharan countries that accepted the SAPs were performing better than those who did not (DeLancey, 145). This would seem to be tremendous progress, but of course there were those countries that had not accepted the SAPs or disagreed with the World Bank's conclusions. So African countries themselves started drawing up more plans of action to rectify the malaise. They did so by themselves or in collaboration with bodies like the UN. The Lagos Plan of action was, in fact, one of the first such plans. Here are some others:

Africa's Priority Programme for Economic Recovery (APPER, 1986–90). This was part of the UN Programme of Action for African Economic Recovery and Development (UNPAARERD). The African countries accepted responsibility for the economic malaise and committed themselves to economic reform, but instead of merely accepting the dictates of the World Bank and the IMF they would design the restructuring themselves. Developed nations agreed to increase aid to Africa to US$46 billion.

African Alternative Framework to Structural Adjustment Programmes (AAF-SAP, 1989). This program suggested a list of actions for long-term development, as an alternative to the structural adjustment programs of the World Bank and the IMF. There was to be action on debt servicing, exchange rates, subsidies, expenditure on the military, and deficit spending.

Arusha Conference Declaration (1990). At a conference in Arusha, Tanzania, African participants declared that complete democracy was essential for full recovery from the economic malaise. They drew up a charter for Popular Participation in Development and Transformation, which stressed the need for political liberalization and freedom of speech and opinion.

New Partnership for Africa's Development (NEPARD, 2001) Probably the most important of the programs of action developed by African countries themselves, It was agreed on at the annual meeting of heads of state of the Organisation of African Unity. It stressed, among other measures, increasing domestic savings and investments, improving the management of public revenue and expenditure, improving Africa's share in global trade, attracting foreign direct investment, ensuring further debt reduction, and increasing capital flows. (All these programs are described in greater detail in DeLancey, 146.)

The OAU and regional groupings

The Organisation of African Unity, which became the African Union in 2002, played a very important role in the development of programs for the elimination of poverty and the recovery from the economic malaise. It also helped considerably in getting African nations to take responsibility for the malaise and to accept that solutions are only possible with huge participation by Africans themselves. The organization took the lead in the collaboration with relevant world bodies like the World Bank, the IMF, and the United Nations. Although one of its major aims was the creation of total unity among African states, it wisely realized that this would not be possible unless preceded by effective regional groupings in Eastern, Western and Southern Africa, and it fostered the creation of these groupings. The Western grouping, the Economic Community of West African States (ECOWAS) established in Lagos in 1975, has been able to foster economic cooperation between Anglophone and Francophone states; regulate currency requirements among the states; and promote ease of travel, communication, and transportation. The East African Community (EAC) was founded in 2000 as a grouping of Kenya, Tanzania, and Uganda. Rwanda and Burundi joined in 2007. Some regard it as "the most successful of African organizations for regional integration" (Shillington, 490). Although it has political objectives, it has concentrated heavily on economic matters.

The EAC is working towards the establishment of an East African common market and monetary union. The South African Development Community (SADC) was established in 1980 as the South African Development Coordination Conference (SADCC). It became the SADC in 1994. Before this the economy of most Southern African countries was dependent on South Africa which at the time was founded on apartheid. In 1980 Zimbabwe became independent with Robert Mugabe at its head, and this alone ensured that the dependence on South Africa would no longer be tolerated. With the collapse of apartheid and the election of Nelson Mandela as president in 1994, South Africa also joined the SADC. SADC has been very successful in coordinating transport, power, and telecommunications (Africa in Transition, 111).

The African economic turnaround

In the mid- to late 1990s the economies of African states started to improve. This improvement coincided with the march of African states towards democracy and liberalization of the political system, and several commentators even began to talk of an African renaissance which would include major progress in all areas. According to the Human Development Index, many African countries had made progress between 1990 and 2000, though African countries still came at the bottom of the development list. Thus, Rwanda had moved from .245 to .337, Tanzania from .373 to .395, Benin from .348 to .398, Malawi from .303 to .362, Guinea from .278 to .335, Mozambique from .217 to .301, and Mali from .231 to .308. A few countries had slipped and the movement was rather slow, but there was progress nevertheless. The IMFund reported that between 1995 and 1998 the economies of African countries grew on average to nearly 4 percent (World Economic Outlook, October 1999, 176). Over 20 African countries achieved quite high rates of growth. These included unlikely countries like Benin, Burkina Faso, Equatorial Guinea, Malawi, Mali, Mauritania, Niger, Rwanda, and Togo, as well as less surprising ones like Gabon, Ghana, Egypt, Ethiopia, and Tunisia. This did not mean that all Africans or African countries suddenly became rich; poverty was still widespread, but the economies were definitely improving.

Factors responsible for economic improvement

What were the factors responsible for this very significant improvement? Perhaps the most important factor was the liberalization of trade which went hand in hand with political liberalization and reform. There was now a drive for less state control, which meant denationalization of financial institutions such as banks. This, coupled with the political stability and the promise of accountability that went along with political reform, resulted in an increase in private investment. Foreign investors now felt more secure, but the new investment did not come merely from outside; investment by indigenous citizens now rose dramatically. In particular, there was a dramatic increase in the number of women who now became active in the economy, investing in small businesses as well as major ones. This was one of the most important aspects of the new trends. Hitherto, women had been marginalized in so far as the economy was concerned. Now they were playing a prominent role. Banks and foreign agencies were now more comfortable in giving loans to women.

Another major factor was the increased emphasis on agriculture. African governments realized that if they could ensure food security, a large measure of the struggle would have been won. Increased agricultural production was therefore seen as a top priority. In 2003 African leaders reached agreement on the Comprehensive Africa Agriculture Development Programme. This was a blueprint for moving towards agricultural transformation, and consequent food security and good nutrition, but it also recognized the role of agriculture in wealth creation and economic growth. It is noteworthy that some of the investment from outside even went into agricultural production. The Chinese, for instance, have been very active in agriculture in some African countries like Nigeria. This, in a sense, is welcome. However, leaders of countries where this kind of foreign investment is going on will have to ensure that the agreements reached with such outside investors are so watertight that they preclude the possibility of another kind of economic imperialism. With the emphasis on agriculture and the willingness of foreign investors to invest in it, the vast amounts of untapped arable land could now be utilized.

Another factor was the renegotiation of the terms of trade to which African countries had been subjected. There were now new terms of trade giving African countries more control in determining the prices of their exports and the conditions under which commodities could be exported. The new terms of trade also included improved access to Western markets. Most importantly, the new terms of trade, the new liberalization of trade, and the new emphasis on open markets led to greater cooperation between African countries and countries in Asia and Latin America, like India and Brazil, the so-called emerging markets. This diversification of trade was highly beneficial to African countries.

Africa still has enormous reserves of mineral resources that are still in demand all over the world. This attracted foreign investment and African governments also followed the example of a country like Botswana and paid attention to the proper regulation of the exploitation of mineral resources to ensure that their countries benefited from them. Finally, the economies of African countries benefited immensely from the improved handling of the AIDS crisis, which had played havoc with the economies of many African countries such as Botswana, Lesotho, Zambia, and even South Africa. With assistance from Western countries, such as the USA, the crisis was brought under control even though no cure has been found for AIDS.

As a result of all this, bodies like the World Bank, the United Nations, and the IMF can now declare confidently that many African countries are now among the fastest growing economies in the world. For instance, Ethiopia and Rwanda were among the five fastest growing economies in 2019. In 2018, six of the world's fastest growing economies were in Africa: Ghana, Ethiopia, Côte d'Ivoire, Djibouti, Senegal, and Tanzania. The projection is that the five fastest growing economies in the world for the period 2019 to 2024 will be Rwanda (7.7 percent), Bangladesh (7.5 percent), Senegal (7.3 percent), Ethiopia (7.0 percent), and Myanmar (6.8 percent). Three of the five are in Africa and the top country will be Rwanda. The cynical might say that it was inevitable that these countries should grow fast seeing that they manifested low development to begin with. There is some truth in that, but the progress is real nonetheless. The development has not been without its bumps; it stalled for a bit round about the middle of the first decade of the millennium, to the extent that some commentators avowed that the renaissance was over. However, the progress picked up again and has been sustained since. The improvement has been so significant that knowledgeable commentators like Fareed Zakaria, the host of the CNN program the *Global Public Square*, could say confidently that Africa is the continent of the future.

African leaders continue to take action and draw programs designed to ensure continuing development. For instance, in 2019 the Francophone countries in West Africa announced that the name of the currency they have been using since independence, the CFA franc, will be changed to the eco. The currency will still be tied to the euro to ensure financial discipline and stability, but, most importantly, the Francophone countries will no longer be required to deposit 50 percent of their foreign reserves in the French treasury. This finally removes a very controversial relic of French imperialism which limited the freedom of action of the Francophone countries in the arena of development. The creation of the eco was taken within the framework of ECOWAS, and it seems very likely that the eco will actually become the common currency of West African states because three Anglophone countries, Ghana, Nigeria, and Sierra Leone, have indicated that they intend to join the eco area. The eco actually came into effect in 2020.

Perhaps the most important action taken by African countries in the arenas of economics and development was the creation of the African Continental Free Trade Area (ACFTA) which came into effect on May 30, 2020. If there is any one entity that is likely to make the greatest contribution towards making Africa an economic powerhouse, it is this. It will be a common market consisting of 1.2 billion people. It will account for $4 trillion worth of international trade. Fifty-four of the 55 African countries signed the agreement; only Eritrea has yet to sign. The objectives of the ACFTA include the creation of a single market and enhancing economic integration; establishing a liberalized market; facilitating the movement of people and capital and thus investment; movement towards the establishment of a continental customs union starting with the removal of tariffs on at least 90 percent of goods; the establishment of sustainable economic development and of gender equality; enhancing the competitiveness of member states within Africa and in the global market; and encouraging industrial development, agricultural development, and food security. The United Nations Economic Commission for Africa estimates that the agreement will increase intra-African trade by 52 percent by 2022.

In 2013, the fiftieth anniversary of the establishment of the Organisation of African Unity, the heads of state of the African Union drew up an agenda, called simply "Agenda 2063: the Africa we Want," with a list of objectives to be achieved by the year 2063, which will be the hundredth anniversary of the founding of the OAU. The agenda set goals for inclusive and sustainable development by 2063. One must note that the COVID-19 pandemic introduced an element of uncertainty into the African economic framework, since it affected international trade and the growth of all countries. However, it is significant that the pandemic ravaged Africa much less than other continents, and there are signs of an imminent recovery. In general, African countries seem to have realized that the capacity for achieving real development and prosperity lies in their own hands and they seem to be taking the necessary steps towards their achievement.

References and suggestions for further reading

Alden, C. 2007. *China in Africa*. London: Zed Books.
Amin, S. 1972. "Underdevelopment and Dependence in Black Africa: Origins and Contemporary Forms." *Journal of Modern African Studies*, 10, 4: 503–524.
Austen, R. 1987. *African Economic History: Internal Development and External Dependency*. London: James Currey.
Challenor, H., M. Humbert, C. Spradlin, and D. Tyree. 2000. *Africa in Transition*. Atlanta, GA: Southern Center for International Studies.

Chife, A. 1997. *The Political Economy of Post-cold War Africa*. Lewiston, NY: Edwin Mellen Press.

Cooper, F. 2002. *Africa since 1940: The Past and Present*. Cambridge: Cambridge University Press.

Davidson, B. 1972. *Africa: History of a Continent*. New York: Macmillan.

DeLancey, V. 2007. "The Economies of Africa." Pp. 109–154 in April Gordon and Donald Gordon (eds.). *Understanding Contemporary Africa*. Boulder, CO: Lynne Rienner.

Fage, J. 1959. *Ghana: A Historical Perspective*. Madison, WI: University of Wisconsin Press.

Fieldhouse, D. K. 1986. *Black Africa 1945–1980 Economic Decolonization and Arrested Development*. London: Allen & Unwin.

Herskovits, M. and M. Harwitz. 1964. *Economic Transition in Africa*. Evanston, IL: Northwestern University Press.

International Monetary Fund. 2005. *Regional Economic Outlook: Sub-Saharan Africa*. Washington, DC: IMF.

Katsouris, C. and N. K. Betsi-Enchill. 1995. "Africa Under Pressure from Falling Aid, Rising Debt." *Africa Recovery* 9(June): 1–12.

Neumark, D. 1964. *Foreign Trade and Economic Development in Africa: An Historical Perspective*. Stanford, CA: Food Research Institute, Stanford University.

Neumark, D. 1977. "Trans-Saharan Trade in the Middle Ages." Pp. 127–131 in Z. A. Konczacki and J. M. Konczacki (eds.), *An Economic History of Tropical Africa*. Vol. 1London: Frank Cass.

Rodney, W. 1972. *How Europe Underdeveloped Africa*. Washington, DC: Howard University Press.

Shillington, K. 2019. *History of Africa* (4th edn). London: Red Globe Press.

Todaro, M. 1989. *Economic Development in the Third World*. New York: Longman.

Todaro, M. 2005. *The Millennium Development Goals Report, 2005*. New York: United Nations.

United Nations Development Program. 1999. *Human Development Report*. New York: United Nations.

United Nations Development Program. 1990. Human Development Index. New York: United Nations.

United Nations Development Program. 2000. Human Development Index. New York: United Nations.

Van der Veen, R. 2004. *What Went Wrong with Africa: A Contemporary History*. Amsterdam: KIT Publishers.

Wickins, P. *Africa 1880–1980: An Economic History*. Cape Town: Oxford University Press, 1981.

10 Women in Africa

The received opinion seems to be that the condition of women in Africa is quite deplorable. Women, according to this view, are absolutely subjugated by their husbands who are indisputably the heads of households and whose position as the law giver whose will must be obeyed remains unchallenged. Women have less access to education and consequently fewer opportunities for gaining employment, particularly in the positions that really matter. Women work extremely hard, much harder than men, because in addition to raising the children, they have to look after their husbands, do the cooking and the cleaning, while at the same time holding down some of the most unpleasant jobs. But they get no credit or gratitude for this because society expects it of them. African women are sometimes subjected to the most barbaric physical practices, such as female genital mutilation, and sometimes married off before it's time to much older husbands they may not like. They have no property rights, hardly any political rights, and after years of labor and helping their husbands to improve their positions in society they could be divorced or thrown out of their homes by their husbands without any compensation. The list can go on. Some of these accusations are quite true; others, however, amount to an exaggeration of the actual situation. Such views do not take into account that the condition of women in Africa can vary from country to country and region to region. It has also varied from era to era. One must therefore be cautious in making generalizations. Moreover, although a lot still needs to be done to improve the African woman's condition, considerable progress has been made during the last 30 years or so because African women have taken their destiny into their own hands and have been agitating for reform. One must also assert that in traditional Africa woman was very highly regarded, and it will be the main argument of this chapter that the condition of women in Africa has been largely due, not so much to the inherent attitudes and actions of traditional African society, but to outside forces such as Islam, Christianity, and imperialism, and that though much still needs to be done, progress is at last being made in the improvement of women's lives. This chapter will start by looking at the condition of women in traditional Africa and then go on to consider the impact of Islam, Christianity, and imperialism. We will then go on to discuss the present condition of the African woman and explore what still needs to be done.

Woman in traditional African society

In traditional Africa women played roles in society that were just as important as, if not more important than, those played by men, even though they may not have been at the top of the political structure in most cases. The fact is that what obtained in traditional

DOI: 10.4324/9781003111733-11

Africa was a division of labor and a division of roles, rather than women playing a subordinate role and performing inferior tasks. Certain things were done by men and others by women, and the duties performed by women were just as arduous and important as those performed by men. Men were generally the hunters and fishers and fighters, although, as we shall see, women participated physically in warfare in many cases. Women were the ones who grew the food that was necessary for subsistence although men played some part in this area as well. Very importantly, it was the women who bore and cared for the children who would continue their husbands' lines and ensure their immortality. Quite often, the woman did very arduous work, like hoeing the soil or pounding grain in a mortar, with the child strapped to her back. Indeed, a certain mystique attached to woman because she gave life to children and continued to ensure their existence until they were grown. She also cooked the food for both her children and her husband. In other words, she was both provider and nurturer, something that could hardly be said about her husband. Women could not be hunters and gatherers because the children had to be nursed and looked after, something the men could not do. However, in some nomadic societies, it was the women who built the dwellings and took them down again when the clan had to move to another area. In many traditional African societies it was the women who repaired the houses or decorated them. There is an African story, related to the beginning of the world, that at the creation God, having created the world and man and woman, had to decide which of them to place in charge of the four elements: earth, air, fire, and water. In the end he gave earth to woman, and so woman had the responsibility for making sure that the earth was properly farmed and produced enough to feed people; he gave water to woman, so woman had the responsibility for collecting water; he also gave fire to woman, so woman had the responsibility, not only for collecting wood and making the fire, but also ensuring that the fire never went out. And did God give air to men? No! He kept air for himself. Woman therefore was in charge of three of the four most important elements in the world.

The story suggests the very high regard in which woman was held in traditional African society. She may not have been in charge politically in most cases, but even the men who were in charge politically revered and respected woman. We can see this copiously illustrated in works of art and in literature. For instance, in Chinua Achebe's novel *Things Fall Apart* we have the important saying "mother is supreme" (*Things Fall Apart*, 133). Man might be in charge politically, but mother is still supreme. This is why in many traditional African societies a man will never swear by his father; but if he swears by his mother one had better take him seriously. One never takes the name of a mother in vain. One can "curse" someone's father, but the greatest insult one can direct towards anyone is to "curse" his mother.

The existence of matriarchal and matrilineal societies is a testament to the importance of women in the traditional African past. As we have seen, the matriarchal societies were those in which women were in charge politically. There were examples of these in traditional Africa, but they were not many. However, there were several matrilineal societies. The matrilineal societies were those in which people traced their ancestry through the mother's and not the father's line. Even more importantly, inheritance of property and even rights of succession were determined by one's relationships through the mother's line. Perhaps the best-known matrilineal society in traditional Africa was the kingdom of the Ashantis in what is now central Ghana. The Ashantis placed such tremendous importance on the mother because they believed that the mother's blood played a very important part in the making of the individual. Every individual was made out of the mother's blood and the father's spirit (McFerson, 445). In other words, if one is going to talk about "blood relationship," the relationship that determines issues like inheritance and succession, it has to be the mother's blood that is relevant. One therefore inherits property not through the father's line, but the mother's line; and a man leaves his property, not to his own sons, but to his sister's sons. The extensive research done by scholars like Professor K. A. Busia (later prime minister of Ghana) has demonstrated the very complex ways in which the principle operates. Thus, a man's potential successors are, not his sons, but his brothers in order of age, his mother's sister's son, his sister's son, and so on. The mother–child bond is the strongest in this kind of society. The mother is really supreme.

The social and political structures of traditional African society ensured that women were consulted in most things. In many traditional African societies there was a very powerful woman who had the ears of the men at the very top of the political structure. This ensured that the female perspective was represented. In at least two regions in traditional Africa, Ashantiland in West Africa and Lesotho in Southern Africa, the exalted position of queen mother existed and still exists. The queen mother was a very powerful woman, one of whose duties among the Ashantis was to play the leading role in the selection of the next Asantehene or king when the ruling king died. At times she was referred to as the "kingmaker in chief." She was well placed to perform this task because she was regarded as the authority on genealogical matters. She was also the embodiment of the society's spirituality. Among the Ashantis she did not have to be the mother of the reigning king. She could be the king's sister or aunt. This suggests that her position was not dependent on her being the mother of the king. She was a leading member of the nation, belonging to the royal family, and she owned independent wealth, which probably accrued originally from the Ashanti gold mines. She was a very powerful member of the king's court, and, during meetings of the council, she sat immediately to the king's left. This suggests how powerful she was politically. Often, she had her own court. The queen mother was consulted on all matters of state as well as domestic issues. Each smaller political entity, like the towns and villages, had its own "queen mother," who generally supervised all the women in that entity. The queen mother's position in Lesotho was similar. In Lesotho's case, she was usually the mother of the reigning monarch and, if anything, she played a stronger role in the selection of the next king. It is interesting that the position is called "queen mother" and the king himself is not referred to as "king father." Maybe it is just to distinguish her from the "queen," but the fact that the expression "mother" is used suggests that the intention is to point to the mothering and nurturing role of women in general and the "queen mother" in particular.

Among the traditional Yorubas in Western Nigeria there is a woman who is called the "iyalode." The position is not necessarily hereditary nor does the iyalode have to be a relation of the ruler who is generally called the Oba. She is just a very powerful woman who has been appointed to the position she holds by virtue of her admirable social, moral, and political attributes. Although she is not called "queen mother," she represents the women's perspective and is one of the oba's leading advisers. The position of "iyalode" is best illustrated in Wole Soyinka's tragic masterpiece *Death and the King's Horseman*. In that play we see the tremendous power and influence the iyalode exerts. Both men and women listen to her and she is about the only one who can tell the king's horseman, one of the leading chiefs in the area, the blatant truths about his nature and his duties. These two formal positions show that even in areas in traditional Africa where women did not hold the absolute political power, there were women who wielded very powerful political influence.

Several women in traditional Africa actually held the highest political office, that of reigning monarch or reigning queen. Whenever some people think of an African reigning queen, their minds go back to Cleopatra, Queen of Egypt. Some would argue, however, that Cleopatra was not really African, having descended directly from the Greek Ptolemy, the general of Alexander the Great who took over the Egyptian section of the Greek Empire after Alexander's death without an heir. Even if we exclude Cleopatra, there were at least two other female reigning monarchs of Egypt. One of them was Hatshepsut, the fifth pharaoh of the Eighteenth Dynasty and the second female pharaoh, the first being Sobekneferu. Hatshepsut was certainly much more successful and effective than Sobekneferu. Her name means "foremost of noble ladies." She was born around 1508 BCE. When she was barely 12, she married her brother who succeeded to the throne as Thutmose II. The marriage of brother and sister, especially in the royal family, was quite common in order to secure the purity of the line. Hatshepsut thus became queen, but her husband/brother died before she was 30 and she became queen in her own right in 1478 BCE. Actually, she was supposed to be regent to her very young stepson, but within a short time she assumed the full powers of a pharaoh. Officially, she was co-ruler with the stepson, but there was no doubt about who actually wielded the real power. During her reign Egypt flourished. She paid great attention to economic matters and expanded trade with other nations. She also constructed many temples and monuments. One of her most famous actions was the trading expedition she made to the land of Punt, situated to the southeast in the Horn of Africa, coming back with riches such as gold, ivory, and myrrh trees. In some of her statues she is portrayed with a beard. This was deliberately done in order to let the world know that, though a woman, she had the full authority of a male pharaoh. Although her reign was generally peaceful, she also engaged in military campaigns, sending military expeditions to neighboring places like Byblos and the Sinai Peninsula. She died in 1458 BCE.

Queen Amina of Zaria, in what is now Northern Nigeria, gained the reputation of being a Hausa warrior queen around whose personality legends have been constructed. She was born in 1533, the same year as Queen Elizabeth I of England. On the death of her father in 1566 her brother succeeded to the throne and she became a leading figure in her brother's highly respected cavalry, gaining a tremendous reputation for her military prowess. Some of the praise songs about her refer to her as "a woman as capable as a man." Her brother died in 1576 and Amina became queen in her own right. During her reign of more than 35 years she greatly expanded the borders of her kingdom, resolutely waging war throughout the period against neighboring states. Her army was one of the most powerful that Africa had ever seen. She subdued surrounding populations, defended Hausaland against invading Fulani armies, conquered Nupe and Hausa towns, and fortified them by building massive earthen walls around them. She used massive military force and the labor of war captives in the building of the walls, which survived until the British conquest of Zaria in 1904. However, some of the walls survive up to this day. The walls and fortifications she built are collectively known as "Amina's walls." She died in 1610.

Queen Nzinga ruled the kingdoms of Ndongo and Matamba, in what is now Angola, during the seventeenth century. In order to protect her kingdoms she waged a tireless guerilla war against the Portuguese and kept them at bay. Born in 1583 (some sources say 1581) she was highly respected for her great intelligence and for her political and diplomatic skills. She not only had to navigate the tangled web of political intrigue in her own country, but she also had to engage in complicated negotiations with the Portuguese and the Dutch, playing one against the other. When her father was alive, he had encouraged her to take great interest in state affairs and to observe how he governed the kingdom. He also took her with him to battle, so she got useful training as a warrior. On the death of her father, who had been king, her brother, the new king, directed tremendous hatred towards Nzinga because he feared that Nzinga's son, a mere baby, would eventually dethrone him. The brother had the baby killed and Nzinga herself was in disgrace. However, the brother soon had to swallow his hatred because he needed Nzinga's reputed skills. For one thing she was literate in Portuguese. He appointed her ambassador to the Portuguese and charged her with the task of negotiating with them. This was the time when the Atlantic slave trade was at its height and the Portuguese wanted to control it. In order to do this, they needed to have as much influence as possible within Africa itself. One of the most famous stories about Nzinga relates to her meeting with the Portuguese governor of Luanda. He had provided chairs for all the Portuguese officials, but only a mat was provided for Nzinga. This was deliberately done to show, not only the superiority of the governor to Nzinga, but also the superiority of the Portuguese to mere Africans. Nzinga recognized the insult and immediately ordered one of her entourage (some say it was her maid) to crouch on all fours. She used the crouching individual as her chair throughout the meeting and thus showed that within her country she had greater power than the Portuguese. She was able to negotiate a very favorable treaty, but the Portuguese never adhered to it and continued taking Nzinga's people as slaves. On the death of her brother in 1624 she became regent to her nephew, the legitimate king. However, it is reported that she had her nephew killed and she herself assumed the full powers of the kingship. For most of her reign she waged relentless war against the Portuguese. She was brilliant at guerilla tactics which the Portuguese could not understand. She won some spectacular victories, but the Portuguese won others. However, she continued to resist them until the latter were forced to give up their claims to Ndongo. A peace treaty was signed in 1657. Because of the internal resistance to her rule and the existing prejudices against a woman on the throne, Nzinga decided to assume the qualities and attitudes of a man during the 1640s. She personally led her army in battle and was a very deft warrior herself. She practiced polyandry, taking multiple husbands whom she got to dress in women's clothes. In spite of several attempts by the Portuguese to assassinate her she lived to the grand old age of 80 and died peacefully.

Madame Yoko was a queen of the Mende people in the southeast of Sierra Leone during the nineteenth century. The previous king had been her husband, so she was not really in the line of succession when her husband died. However, her superb intelligence and unmatched political skills enabled her to outsmart her male rivals and she succeeded to the throne. For the rest of her reign she had to use those skills to outmaneuver, not only domestic political opponents, but also the British colonial administrators. Like Hatshepsut and Nzinga who had to assume male qualities and attributes in order demonstrate their authority, Madame Yoko had to have her uterus removed, according to some reports. She is still a revered figure in Sierra Leone.

Apart from the reigning monarchs there were other formidable women in traditional African society, most of whom mobilized their people against oppressors and invaders and are regarded as heroes even today. Queen Mother Yaa Asantewaa of Ghana (1849/60–1921) was appointed to the position of queen mother (some say by her brother who was a powerful ruler) in the 1880s. As the British sought to consolidate their hold on the then Gold Coast towards the end of the nineteenth century after the fateful Berlin conference, they captured the reigning Asantehene, Prempeh I, in 1896, and exiled him to the Seychelles. The conflict had been exacerbated by the British representative's heinous act of sitting on the Golden Stool which was the symbol of the Ashanti nation. One of the queen mother's duties was to be the guardian of the Golden Stool. Therefore, while other leaders hesitated and debated on the course of action to be taken, Yaa Asantewaa mobilized the Ashanti people, particularly the Asante regiments, and led them in a fierce rebellion against the British, starting in 1900. She is reputed to have declared that if the men would not do anything then the women would do the fighting instead. She was herself eventually captured and exiled to the Seychelles. She never returned home to witness the burgeoning tide of resistance that would result in total independence, but she is to this day regarded as a great hero of the struggle against imperialism.

The Berber prophetess Kachina played a great role in holding back the Arab invasion of North Africa in the eighth century. Similarly, the prophetess Nehanda of what is now Zimbabwe led her people in spirited resistance to the British imperialists under the leadership of the notorious Cecil Rhodes. Nehanda was a spirit medium. In other words, she claimed the ability to communicate with a particular spirit, in her case an ancestral spirit called Nehanda. Her spirit had instructed her to lead her people in rebellion, and this she did. She was eventually captured and executed by the British, but she is still revered in Zimbabwe as a hero of the long resistance against imperialism which culminated in an independent Zimbabwe.

As we have seen, some women played a major role in warfare; they did not merely leave it to the men, even though, according to the division of roles, men were supposed to be the warriors. The men were the warriors because women were better equipped to take care of and nurse the children, not because they were too weak or easily terrified to be any use in warfare. When the situation demanded, women could also rise to the challenges of war. There were female armies in traditional Africa. The best known female army was the army of Dahomey, now the Republic of Benin, which consisted entirely of women. Some say that they were all wives of the king. This is quite possible, but most of them could have been wives in name only, since the army consisted of thousands of women. They were about the most ferocious army in the history of Africa and they wreaked havoc among the Portuguese and French invaders. They are reported to have been absolutely fearless and highly disciplined. There were also ordinary individual female soldiers who fought as well as men, particularly in attempts to repel invaders. One of the most gripping vignettes in Ali Mazrui's documentary series *The Africans: A Triple Heritage* is of a Somali woman soldier, a Somali "Joan of Arc," as Mazrui calls her, who goes on fighting even though pierced in the breast by an arrow.

It will be noted that many of these women have a spiritual mystique associated with them. It probably derives from an awareness of the woman's duties and role in society. Spirituality is extremely important in traditional Africa and, quite often, it is the woman who is the embodiment of this spirituality. Quite often it is the woman who is the medium, oracle, priestess, prophetess, soothsayer, or spirit figure. Many of the gods in traditional African religion are women. Chinua Achebe has brilliantly demonstrated that among the Igbo of South Eastern Nigeria the most powerful god is the goddess Ani, Goddess of the Earth. She is the goddess responsible for making the earth produce, thereby staving off famine, hunger, or even death. She is the goddess who must not be disobeyed, for fear of unleashing these terrible catastrophes on the people.

In traditional Africa, then, there is abundant evidence of the way in which the female principle was interwoven into the fabric of the system and how it manifested itself. Woman was revered as provider and nurturer, with responsibility for fertility, life, and even death. She was responsible for protecting the earth and making sure that it produced abundantly through her arduous activities in agriculture; she was also responsible for collecting water and preserving fire. But when the need arose, she could also be a fierce warrior, strenuously defending her people from oppression.

The impact of Islam

Islam was to have a significant impact on the African people, particularly on the condition of women. Without being judgmental, one must affirm that Islam came with its own views about women and their place in society. It had definite attitudes about the relationship between husbands and wives, about women's attitudes towards their husbands, about the place of women relative to men and their husbands in general, about how women should appear, about the kind of activities that women should not engage in, and so on. It seems that a stricter level of conduct was required of women who were expected to be modest and respectful, but who were also to be revered. However, they should earn this reverence by their own modest conduct. In many Muslim societies up to the present day (and these are not the most extreme), women are still expected to dress in certain ways. Only recently have women been allowed to drive in Saudi Arabia. I know from my own personal experience that Muslim women are not allowed to shake hands with men at certain times. They are also not allowed to go to the graveyard during a funeral and witness the burial. During ceremonies in the mosque, women and men sit separately. I have attended Muslim weddings in Sierra Leone where the bride and the groom were in separate compartments of the building and never came together during the ceremony. The groom sat with the men in one compartment and the bride sat with the women in another. During the betrothal, the imam passed the ring which had been given to him by the bridegroom through a small cubby hole to the godmother, who was in the other compartment with the bride. It was the godmother who actually placed the ring on the bride's finger. During my adolescence, I lived in a majority-Muslim community and in adulthood I have had numerous Muslim friends and relations and thus attended many Muslim weddings and funerals. I am therefore writing from personal observation and experience. I know, for instance, that at some weddings, the imam giving the address would admonish the bride to give "the best part of the pot" when she cooked to her husband. Without being judgmental, one can say that all this suggests that Islam had certain views about the ways in which women should comport themselves in society and how they should behave to their husbands and other men.

The Muslim holy book is the Qur'an. Let us look at a passage from it that suggests the Islamic attitude towards women in so far as their place relative to men is concerned. Surah 4, verse 15–16 says, "If any of your women are guilty of lewdness, take evidence of four (reliable) witnesses from amongst you against them; and if they testify, confine them to houses until death do claim them, or Allah ordain for them some (other) way. If any men among you are guilty of lewdness, punish them both. If they repent and amend leave them alone; for Allah is oft-Returning. Most merciful." It will be noted that the offense is the same, "lewdness." (It does not really matter whether it is fornication or unnatural sexual desires.) However, the women's punishment seems much more severe. The text is not specific about how the men should be punished. Then there is the coda that if they amend or repent they should be left entirely alone. On the other hand, the guilty women are to be imprisoned for the rest of their lives. This surely suggests that a much higher standard of conduct was required of women. It is inevitable that these strict rules and these attitudes would permeate through to the Africans whom the Muslims converted and would significantly affect the condition of women.

The influence of Christianity

Christianity also brought with it certain set attitudes about the condition of women in society and their place relative to that of men. Basing most of its attitudes on the activities in the Garden of Eden where God created Eve out of one of Adam's ribs, and Eve succumbs to Satan's temptation and then persuades Adam to eat of the forbidden fruit, Christianity has traditionally seen woman as a being that is subordinate to man and must be kept in check by man. It is even more blatant than Islam about the need for this subordination. That women should submit themselves to their husbands is good Pauline theology. Until recently, the liturgy used for the marriage ceremony in most churches required the woman to vow to honor and obey her husband. Even Queen Victoria, who was the most powerful woman in the world at the time and the head of the greatest empire the world had ever seen, had to promise, during her wedding ceremony, to obey her husband. The Church was extremely slow in allowing women to occupy prominent positions in the Church. Not until recently could women become priests and bishops in the Anglican Church, and many Anglican churches still do not permit women to sing in the choir. Of course, the Roman Catholic Church still does not permit women to become priests. They therefore cannot become bishops and cardinals.

The impact of imperialism

Imperialism, which came to many parts of Africa at about the same time as Christianity, had similar attitudes. The European imperialists came from the same Christian European countries as the Christians and it was therefore inevitable that their attitudes should be similar. From their experience in Europe, the European imperialists held not only that women should be subordinate to men, but that their proper place should be in the home. The middle-class European woman was expected to be docile, passive, generally sharing her husband's views and having few of her own. The typical European woman of the nineteenth century was David Copperfield's mother in Charles Dickens's novel of the same name: absolutely docile and submissive, absolutely passive, having no views of her own and always submitting to whatever her husband required, even if it meant misery for her son. The eighteenth- and nineteenth-century Englishwoman had little control over money. Even if she brought money into the marriage it immediately passed into the possession of her husband who could use it as he pleased. She played little or no part in politics, although she could exert some influence in the background. She played no part in business or industry and could not even attend university.

It was this view of womanhood that the European imperialists brought to Africa, and it had a marked impact on the condition of the African woman. One of the ways in which the imperialists tried to profit from their colonialist occupation was to encourage the growing of cash crops for export to fuel the factories of Europe, and, naturally, they thought that this very important enterprise should be placed in the hands of men. They felt women would not be up to such important activity, even though women had, in the traditional past, been responsible for more than 80 percent of the agricultural work. Men were thus brought into the global cash economy and women were relegated to simply growing the subsistence crops which they proceeded to sell in the markets. The men were therefore placed in an advantageous position relative to the women. In the traditional past, land had been owned communally and anyone who intended to farm was able to get land. Now the best land was given to men for the growing of the all-important cash crops, and this meant that women lost their right to certain lands. The land was apportioned to individuals and women lost their right of automatic access. The imperialists also wanted to extract Africa's rich mineral deposits and they needed men to work in the mines. Numerous men thus left their homes to do so. Their wives and children could not join them, and so the women were left behind to do the work that should have been done by the men. This affected their position adversely, because they were now doing much more and receiving much less, while the men were being gradually brought into the cash economy.

Imperialism affected the traditional African woman's political position very adversely. As we have seen, several African women held important political positions. The imperialists were blind to the kind of political influence the women wielded and the positions to which they could aspire. From their own experience, only men should be in the political arena. They therefore ignored women when it came to making certain appointments to certain positions. When they decided to appoint the co-called warrant chiefs, for instance, it was men who were appointed. The court messengers were men. When the imperialist started appointing consultative councils or "native" authorities, it was men who were appointed. This led to a complete silencing of the woman's voice and a complete elimination of the woman's perspective.

It is possible to conclude, then, that the condition of African women in the modern period has been largely the legacy of these three essentially outside forces: Islam, Christianity, and imperialism. This is not to say that the traditional African situation was perfect, or that forces in modern African society have not contributed to the African woman's condition. It is merely to state the nature of the situation and to say that these outside forces should bear the greatest share of the responsibility. Since independence, various African countries have been taking measures to improve the condition of women. There have been some spectacular successes, but a lot still needs to be done. Let us look at the areas where the situation might still be considered unsatisfactory and then consider those where progress has been made.

The current situation of the African woman

The issue of polygamy still remains. In a sense this has only been a problem because it seems, to some, to devalue the woman, and it can create problems within the polygamous household. Polygamy will be difficult to eradicate because it has always been a part of the fabric of African life. It was part of traditional African life and was not the importation of Islam. As we have seen, one of the reasons why Islam was acceptable to many African communities was that it also endorsed the practice of polygyny which had been an aspect of traditional African life for centuries. Many African women, including some modern educated ones, accept the practice of polygamy. Although a country like Côte d'Ivoire now has laws against it, it has now been generally accepted that this is not a matter for state action, but of individual choice, and it will probably resolve itself. As Africans become more educated or more exposed through the media to the practices of other people, they might move away from polygamy. Most modern educated Africans living in the urban areas are abandoning polygamy, if only because the expense and pressures of modern living make it impracticable. The custom of bridewealth also still exists. Giving money or other material things to the bride's family has been seen to amount to buying a wife, thus reducing the woman to the level of an object or commodity that could be possessed. However, it is now generally agreed that giving material things to the bride's family really suggests that the woman is highly valued by both her family and her prospective in-laws. In various societies it takes various forms, some of them symbolic, thus heightening the suggestion that the emphasis is on how the woman is valued.

Although African governments genuinely intended to transform educational systems at the time of independence in order to enhance development, the economic woes that later plagued the African continent prevented them from spending as much on education as they should have done, and women were more adversely affected by this reduction in the expenditure on education than men. Even in the modern era it is still true that if there is insufficient money in the family to educate all the children, preference would be given to the education of boys than to girls. Although more women are attending university than before, there are still many more men than women at this highest level of education. The situation is even worse at the primary and secondary levels. Indeed, in so far as education is concerned, the situation of the African woman is most deplorable in the rural areas where, according to a World Bank Report, only 20 percent of girls are attending school. Generally, only 25 percent of African girls are in school. Studies have shown that for every 100 boys in primary school there are only 81 girls, and for every 100 boys in secondary school, there are only 72 girls. Obviously, this situation needs considerable improvement. Because of poverty, millions of girls in Africa never attend school at all. Of those that do, some are withdrawn and married early to older men. Some become pregnant and are expelled. Tanzania and Sierra Leone are two countries with severely discriminatory rules about pregnant girls in school. In almost every case they are forced to leave and are not allowed to continue their education after giving birth.

Apart from these setbacks, progress has been made by many African countries in many areas, progress that is quite often not acknowledged. The progress is partly due to the activities of the Organisation of African Unity which later became the African Union. Although the OAU/AU has no power of enforcement, the fact that year after year the annual meeting of the heads of state discussed and passed resolutions on the need for gender equality and improvement in the position of women in Africa led to heightened awareness and action. Also, activities in the world in general propelled African governments to action. For instance, there was the International Year of the Woman, January 1 to December 31, 1975, which then became the International Women's Decade, 1976 to 1985. There was also the memorable United Nations' World Conference on Women held in Beijing, China, in 1995. All these focused on gender inequality and the problems women face throughout the world, and African governments could not help but take notice.

In the last 25 years or so several African countries have passed laws designed to improve the condition of women quite significantly, thereby moving towards gender equality. April Gordon, referencing Dei, Sow, the Center for Reproductive Law and the World Bank, lists some of them (Gordon, 310). In the 1990s Ethiopia, Ghana, and South Africa passed laws affirming the equality of men and women in their new constitutions and prohibiting gender discrimination in areas such as property ownership, employment, and marriage rights. Ghana stipulates in its constitution that women have a right to maternity leave. The constitutions of Ghana and Ethiopia prohibit practices like female genital mutilation. Côte d'Ivoire has laws against polygamy and bridewealth. Senegal has laws ensuring that women cannot be married off without their consent, men can only take additional wives if the first wife consents, and only a judge can grant divorce. In 1985, Ghana passed the very important succession and property laws stipulating that all customary marriage and family property should be registered and that there should be a distinction between acquired and family property. Where previously, in the matrilineal areas of Ghana, a man's property could be inherited by his relatives on his mother's side leaving his wife and family with next to nothing, the law now stipulates that if a man dies without a will his wife and children get three-quarters of his property. A Zimbabwe law stipulates that when a man dies his wife and children are automatically his beneficiaries, and the matrimonial home and all the household goods belong to the wife. These are all measures enacted by African governments which, if properly enforced, will have a significant impact on the African woman's condition, and they are all the result of an awareness that gender equality and attention to the problems facing the African woman are essential for development.

Women in politics

One area in which significant progress has been made in the last 25 years or so is the arena of politics. Immediately after independence, and for some time after that, little attempt was made to give women the place they deserved in politics and government. The old colonial view that political leadership was entirely a male preserve still prevailed, in spite of the fact that women had played a very significant role in the struggle for independence and in the liberation struggles in places like South Africa, Zimbabwe, and Kenya. They had very strenuously supported their men. Yet, their role immediately after independence was still a supporting role. Women like Funmilayo Ransome-Kuti of Nigeria and Constance Cummings-John of Sierra Leone tried to break the glass ceiling, but were not entirely successful. Funmilayo Ransome-Kuti, the mother of the famed singer and performer Fela Ransome-Kuti, was a redoubtable activist and fighter for women's rights who was described at one time as the "Lioness of Lisabi." She was instrumental in the formation of the Nigerian Women's Union and the Federation of Nigerian Women's Societies, and on one occasion she led marches of thousands of women protesting against the excesses of the alake of Abeokuta, forcing the alake to abdicate temporarily in 1949. Constance Cummings-John formed the Sierra Leone Women's Movement and was the first woman to be popularly elected to the Sierra Leone parliament, which she did even before independence. However, rival male politicians brought what many considered to be an unfounded election petition against her, and she was deprived of the seat in parliament. She however succeeded in becoming the first female mayor of Freetown. Both women were very active politically but never made it into their country's parliament.

The situation began to change dramatically in the late eighties and early nineties. In the South African election of 1994, which coincided with Nelson Mandela's accession to the presidency, women won 25 percent of the seats in parliament (Gordon, 304). They were able to do so because the ruling African National Congress (ANC) had taken a decision to ensure adequate female representation of women on the list of candidates.

Uganda also revised its constitution in 1995 to include a stipulation that one-third of all the seats in local government were to be reserved for women. This set the stage for other countries in Africa to enact laws and regulations to ensure adequate representation of women in parliament. The 14 member countries of the Southern African Development Community (SADC) agreed to achieve 30 percent representation of women in their parliaments. From then on the news is of steady progress. The inter-Parliamentary Union, which tracks the number of women elected to parliament every year throughout the world, reported in 2019 that in 2018 women occupied 23.7 percent of seats in African parliaments. Djibouti, which had no women in parliament in 2000, now has 15 women or 26.2 percent of the total number. Rwanda has not only the highest percentage of women in parliament in Africa, but in the whole world. This was largely because its constitution stipulated that at least 48 percent of the seats in parliament should be reserved for women. The percentage of women in the Rwandan parliament in 2017 was 64 percent and in 2018 61.3 percent. Rwanda has a bi-cameral legislature, and its constitution requires that 30 percent of the seats in both houses should be reserved for women. There are several other African countries with a fairly high percentage of women in the legislature. They include Namibia (46.2 percent), South Africa (42.7 percent), and Senegal (41.8 percent). Some African countries also have provisions for a minimum percentage of seats on local councils and municipalities to be occupied by women.

Women have also made advances in their representation on the executive. Several African countries have a fairly high percentage of women occupying ministerial positions. Rwanda has 51.9 percent, South Africa 48.65, Seychelles has 45.5 percent, Uganda has 36.7 percent, and Mali has 34.4 percent. Up to the recent past the ministerial portfolios usually given to women were the so-called "soft" ones like women's affairs, children's affairs or, perhaps, education. Now women are filling ministerial positions traditionally held by men. There are 30 percent more women ministers of defense than in 2017, 52 percent more women ministers of finance, and 13.6 more women ministers of foreign affairs. African women have also been able to achieve the highest political position in the land, that of president, where leading Western countries, like the United States, still have to elect a woman as president. In 2005 Ellen Johnson-Sirleaf became the first woman to be elected president, not only in Liberia, but in the whole of Africa. She handsomely defeated her rival, a famous male soccer player, by 19 percentage points. She went on to serve for two terms as president and, for her efforts in restoring Liberia to normalcy after a vicious civil war, she was awarded the Nobel Prize for Peace. Joyce Banda of Malawi became president on the death of the substantive President Bingu Wa Mutharika, since she had been serving as vice-president. In 2018 Sahle-Work Zewde became president of Ethiopia, having been unanimously elected by the parliament. It is true that she is a ceremonial president without executive powers, those powers being exercised by the prime minister who is head of government. Nevertheless, Ms. Zewde is head of state, which is in itself a great achievement. In March 2021 another woman, Samia Suluhu Hassan, who had been Vice President of Tanzania, became President on the death of President Magufuli. Of course, there are still prejudices and structural barriers operating against advances by women in the political arena. Women still lag behind men in getting access to the best education facilities, which means they are still at a disadvantage in getting access to the best jobs, including the political jobs. Nevertheless, with figures such as those above, how can we say that there has not been progress? Moreover, every African country is now pledged to achieving sustainable development goals which include gender equality, and to empower all women and girls.

Table 10.1 Women in African national parliaments as of 1 February 2019.

Rank	Country	Lower or Single House				Upper House or Senate			
		Elections	Seats*	Women	% W	Elections	Seats*	Women	% W
1	**Rwanda**	03.09.2018	80	49	61.3%	26.09.2011	26	10	38.5%
2	**Cuba**	11.03.2018	605	322	53.2%	—	—	—	—
3	**Bolivia**	12.10.2014	130	69	53.1%	12.10.2014	36	17	47.2%
4	**Mexico**	01.07.2018	500	241	48.2%	01.07.2018	128	63	49.2%
5	**Sweden**	09.09.2018	349	165	47.3%	—	—	—	—
6	**Grenada**	13.03.2018	15	7	46.7%	27.04.2018	13	4	30.8%
7	**Namibia**	29.11.2014	104	48	46.2%	08.12.2015	42	10	23.8%
8	**Costa Rica**	04.02.2018	57	26	45.6%	—	—	—	—
9	**Nicaragua**	06.11.2016	92	41	44.6%	—	—	—	—
10	**South Africa****	07.05.2014	393	168	42.7%	21.05.2014	54	19	35.2%
11	**Senegal**	30.07.2017	165	69	41.8%	—	—	—	—
12	**Finland**	19.04.2015	200	83	41.5%	—	—	—	—
13	**Spain**	26.06.2016	350	144	41.1%	26.06.2016	266	98	36.8%
14	**Norway**	11.09.2017	169	69	40.8%	—	—	—	—
15	**New Zealand**	23.09.2017	120	48	40.0%	—	—	—	—
"	**Timor-Leste**	12.05.2018	65	26	40.0%	—	—	—	—
17	**France**	11.06.2017	577	229	39.7%	24.09.2017	348	112	32.2%
18	**Mozambique**	15.10.2014	250	99	39.6%	—	—	—	—
19	**Argentina**	22.10.2017	255	99	38.8%	22.10.2017	72	30	41.7%
"	**Ethiopia**	24.05.2015	547	212	38.8%	05.10.2015	153	49	32.0%

Source: http://archive.ipu.org/wmn-e/classif.htm.

* Figures correspond to the number of seats currently held in parliament.
** The figures on the distribution of seats in the upper house do not include the 36 special rotating delegates appointed on an ad hoc basis and all percentages given are therefore calculated on the basis of the 54 permanent seats.

Women in business and the economy

Reading some of the literature on the present participation of women in the African economy and in business generally one might form the impression that the situation is still quite bleak. Although women are still responsible for about 85 percent of agricultural activity, they still operate under tremendous disadvantages. In many places they still do not have right of ownership to land, which is generally owned by their menfolk. When their husbands die they may not even be able to inherit the land, and their participation in profitable, larger-scale agricultural enterprise is therefore severely restricted. Women farmers, who operate in rural areas, get little help from their governments or international agencies, because when investments are made little goes to rural development, and that mostly goes to the production of cash crops which is, of course, under the control of the men (Gordon, 301). Women get little aid, in any case, because, in order to receive assistance, the farmers have to produce their titles to the land, which the women could not do because the land is often registered in the husband's name. Because of the gap in education between men and women, women generally do not have access to the training required for the vital jobs in business and other areas, and the problem has been exacerbated by the reduction in government spending on education due to the economic meltdown. "Discriminatory laws and cultural practices make it difficult for women to compete successfully in agriculture, wage jobs, or business. Typically, women have little access to ownership and inheritance of property or to bank credit" (Gordon, 303).

All this is probably true of the situation at the start of the millennium, and there is no doubt that much work still needs to be done, but the fact is that the African woman's participation in business activity has now improved considerably. This is attested to by United Nations reports. The improvement is due both to the African woman's determination to achieve her best potential in all areas and also to the realization, which we have seen, by agencies such as the African Union, the United Nations, the African Development Bank, and even the World Bank, that development in Africa is impossible unless women are empowered and given the resources to achieve their full potential. Of course, the African woman has always been a sagacious entrepreneur. The African market woman, for instance, is well known in places like Nigeria, Ghana, and Sierra Leone for pursuing her trade energetically and making significant profits. I once had a messenger in my department in Sierra Leone who thought that his only responsibility towards his family at the end of the month was to provide a bag of rice, the staple food. Everything else had to be provided by the wives, from the rest of the food for the family, to paying bills and the children's school fees. The wives did this most successfully by their efficiency at their trade. The African woman had the potential and the capacity to be highly successful in business; she just needed more financial resources or investment to do bigger things. By the end of the last millennium it was clear that the assistance was beginning to arrive. African women were moving into bigger enterprises than merely selling their goods in the markets. They were owning and operating gas stations (which can be very important in Africa as Ousmane Sembene's movie *Faat Kine* demonstrates) and running fisheries businesses. They were opening restaurants and controlling fashion empires. This improvement has continued unabated, and it is partly due to the encouragement and assistance from the above-mentioned agencies and other donors.

The African Development Bank, for instance, launched the African Women in Business Initiative (AWIB). This was a very detailed plan designed to bolster the role of women in business and to empower women entrepreneurs through better access to finance. Other agencies have been doing similar things. For instance, in Ghana Esther Ocloo and 14 other women founded an international financial institution to service women entrepreneurs through the establishment of a branch of the American-based Women's World Banking (McFerson, 457). All over Africa discriminatory laws and regulations, such as those relating to land tenure, inheritance, property, and ownership, that militated against women's participation in business are being reviewed and, in many cases, repealed, in accordance with the views and decisions of bodies like the African Union. Women now have much greater access to bank finance. We now constantly hear of the success stories of African women entrepreneurs in African countries such as Nigeria, Kenya, South Africa, Ghana, Malawi, and so on. According to Africa.com the ten top female business leaders in Africa in 2019 were Njeri Rionge of Kenya, Isabel Dos Santos of Angola, Folorunsho Alakija of Nigeria, Sibongile Sambo of South Africa, Divine Ndhlukula of Zimbabwe, Bethlehem Tilahun Alemu of Ethiopia, Tabitha Karanja of Kenya, Haja Bola Shagaya of Nigeria, Salwa Akhannouch of Morocco, and Bridget Radebe of South Africa. The African women entrepreneurs are in information technology, oil, mining, and other areas, and they are definitely breaking the gender stereotypes. To talk about the activities of a few of them: Njeri Rionge of Kenya has been described as one of the women pioneer investors in the information technology sector in Africa. She co-founded Wananchi Online, East Africa's first mass-market internet service provider. She owns lots of other businesses including Ignite Consulting, which is a business consultancy. Isabel Dos Santos of Angola has an estimated net worth of $3.3 billion and is regarded as the richest woman on the continent. She has interests in the oil, diamonds, banking, and communications sectors. Sibongile Sambo of South Africa started her own aviation business after she was rejected for a job as a flight attendant with South African Airways because she was below the minimum height required. She is now the founder and managing director of SRS Aviation, the first black-female-owned aviation company in South Africa. Bethlehem Tilahun Alemu of Ethiopia is the founder of SoleRebels, an eco-friendly footwear company which is one of the largest footwear companies in Africa. It has acquired world-class status with stores in Taiwan, Spain, Switzerland, Austria, the US, Singapore, and Japan.

All these women have been able to create hundreds of jobs for their fellow Africans, and they have done so both because of their own determination and competence and also because the climate for the participation of African women in business has been made much easier. However, these are only those right at the top. Below these are hordes of other successful African businesswomen. Women in the once-neglected rural areas have formed cooperatives and bonded together, making it easier for them to receive loans and grants. Some of these groups are also financial self-help groups. For instance, in many parts of Africa there is the existence of the arrangement known as the "tontine" in some places, and "osusu" in others. According to this arrangement, a group of women (maybe ten, 12, or 24) deposit a certain amount of money each into the common pot each month. At the end of each month one of them collects the whole pot, but she keeps on depositing her own share each month until all the others have each taken the contents of the whole pot. Then she collects again. So if there are 24 women in the group and the monthly amount each deposits is $100, each collects $2400 when her own turn comes and will not collect again until the other 23 have collected theirs. It is a kind of savings scheme. It enables each of the women to have a substantial amount of money once every two years which could be devoted to expanding her trade or any other activity she wishes to devote it to. We must therefore acknowledge the progress that women have made recently in so far as participation in business and the economy is concerned, even though there is still a lot to be done.

Female genital mutilation

The practice of female genital mutilation (FGM) is a very controversial issue in Africa. FGM, or female circumcision as many Africans would prefer to call it, is the practice of excising parts of the female genitalia. It is still widespread in Africa although it is also carried out in certain parts of Asia. Indeed, some people believed at one time that it was sanctioned by Islam, and efforts are now being made to educate people into realizing that Islam does not necessarily sanction the practice. FGM takes various forms depending on the area in which it is being practiced. It could be infibulation, or excision of one or other parts of the female genitalia. How or why the practice started is not clear. Some believe that it was intended to ensure that women remained pure until marriage. Others, especially some Western feminists, believe that it was due to a masculine urge to curtail women's sexual pleasure and the female sexual libido and thus render females faithful and subservient to their male partners. Others suggest that it was intended to remove any part of the female genitalia that resembled the male's. There is no real evidence to support any of these claims. What is undeniable is that it is a very painful and traumatic experience for the young girls who are subjected to it, usually at puberty. It also has some devastating health consequences. FGM could affect the female's reproductive capacity, in some cases, permanently. It could also lead to cysts, infertility, chronic discomfort, and diseases of the bladder and the urinary system. At times it could lead to death. It could also lead to the communication of sexually transmitted diseases because the woman carrying out the practice usually uses the same instrument on all the girls involved.

One would expect that if the practice originated because of the wish of men to curtail women's sexual pleasure and keep them subservient, then men would be the most vociferous in arguing against its abolition. In effect, however, it is women in Africa who are most opposed to abolition. Many women in the traditional areas oppose abolition because they claim FGM is part of their tradition. It is only one aspect of a rite of passage during which the young girl is educated in the duties of a wife and mother and thus enabled to take her rightful place as a fully developed female member of society. One can see this, for instance, in Ousmane Sembene's movie about FGM, *Moolaade*. In some countries women use all kinds of derogatory expressions to refer to women who have not gone through the practice. Going through the practice means automatic membership of some of the most important female secret societies in traditional Africa. And yet, it is a harmful practice which many human rights activists and enlightened people feel ought to be abolished. Activists see it as a terrible infringement of the young girl's human rights and make it a human rights issue. Of course, feminists see it as a conspiracy by men to curtail the feminine libido and exert control over women. It is beginning to seem as if the way to succeed with abolition is to convince everyone, particularly the women, about the manifest health hazards, and not merely to adopt the Western feminist slant that it is a masculine-engineered practice intended to curtail women's sexual libido and keep them subservient. That line of attack would only antagonize the men whose help is needed in order to secure abolition. One must recognize that FGM is part of a time-honored rite of passage with significant importance in the cultural life of the people. That must be acknowledged. Then, perhaps, it might be possible to suggest that a symbolic act could replace the harmful physical practice, while retaining all the other aspects of the rite of passage. The countries that have concentrated on educating the people about the health hazards are precisely those where the drive towards abolition has succeeded. As of 2015, 25 African countries have enacted laws banning FGM. These include Benin, Burkina Faso, the Central African Republic, Chad, Côte d'Ivoire, Djibouti, Egypt, Eritrea, Ethiopia, Gambia, Ghana, Guinea, Guinea-Bissau, Kenya, Mauritania, Niger, Nigeria, Senegal, Somalia, Sudan (only in some states), Tanzania, Togo, Uganda, Zambia, and South Africa. Of course, passing a law does not necessarily result in immediate conformity with or enforcement of the law. However, considerable progress has been made and the trend is towards complete abolition.

Impact of structural adjustment programs, AIDS, and conflicts

Even while the improvement in the African woman's condition was gaining steam three things happened which threatened to impede the progress being made. These were the structural adjustment programs, the AIDS crisis, and civil wars and conflicts. The structural adjustment programs imposed by bodies like the World Bank and the International Monetary Fund (IMF) on certain African countries towards the end of the last millennium affected women disproportionately. These policies resulted in cutbacks in social services, like health and education, and women suffered more from these cutbacks. Women's access to health facilities in areas like pre-natal and post-natal care was severely reduced. Cutbacks in education always affect women more than men because families who are forced to choose which child to educate, given the high cost of education, always choose boys, and girls either do not attend school at all or have to drop out. With the cutback in subsidies and the higher cost of food it is women who have to scramble and see how food could be put on the table. The AIDS epidemic also affected women disproportionately, largely because of the power relations between men and women. African women have much less power to resist the sexual advances of their men. Generally, they also seem to lack the ability to persuade their men to use condoms. Several girls were forced by poverty to resort to prostitution, thus exposing them to the AIDS virus and further complicating the situation. Also, with several of their men dying, African women and girls were forced to become heads of households and take on additional burdens. Young girls were forced to care for their siblings and, in some cases, to resort to prostitution to do so. It is not surprising that, in Africa at least, all the statistics show that the AIDS epidemic affected women more than men.

As we have seen, there have been numerous civil wars and conflicts in Africa, and these have had a disproportionately adverse effect on women. As with the effect of the AIDS virus, the absence of their men meant that women had to take on additional burdens and be the sole providers. But even more devastating was the abduction of thousands of young girls by the rebels and dueling parties. Some of these women were forced to be soldiers, but others became sex slaves used to satisfy the sexual desires of the male soldiers. The personalities and characters of these girls were thus transformed forever. Even more repellent was the fact that rape was now used as an instrument of war to strike terror into the hearts of several populations. This is one of the reasons why rape is on the increase in Africa and several women activists are demanding that African governments enact laws to punish offenders. This is now going on in a country like Sierra Leone.

In summary, the African woman had a perfectly respectable place in society and held important positions before the arrival of outside forces like Islam, Christianity, and imperialism. These forces arrived with their own peculiar notions of womanhood, and these adversely affected the condition of the African woman. This situation continued even after independence. However, largely because of the need for development and the awareness that the utilization of the woman's potential was essential for this development, there has been a steady improvement in the African woman's condition and this has been spearheaded not only by the women themselves, but also by bodies like the African Union and the United Nations.

References and suggestions for further reading

Achebe, C. 1959. *Things Fall Apart*. New York: Anchor Books.
Aidoo, A. A. 1981. "Asante Queen Mothers in Government and Politics in the Nineteenth Century." In F. Steady (ed.). *The Black Woman Cross-culturally*. Rochester, NY: Schenkman Books.
Bauer, G. 2006. "Losing Ground without Mandatory Quotas." Pp. 85–110 in G. Bauer and H. Britton (eds.). *Women in African Parliaments*. Boulder, CO: Lynne Rienner.
Bauer, G. and H. Britton. (eds.). 2006. *Women in African Parliaments*. Boulder, CO: Lynne Rienner.
Britton, H. E. 2006. "South Africa: Mainstreaming Gender in a New Democracy." Pp. 59–84 in G. Bauer and H. Britton (eds.), *Women in African Parliaments*. Boulder, CO: Lynne Rienner Publishers.
Boserup, E. 1970. *Women's Role in Economic Development*. London: Allen & Unwin.
Brown-Radcliffe, A. E. and D. Forde. (eds.). 1950. *African Systems of Kinship and Marriage*. London: Oxford University Press.
Busia, K. A. 1954. "The Ashanti of the Gold Coast." In D. Forde (ed.). *African Worlds: Studies in the Cosmological Ideas and Social Values of African Peoples*. London: Oxford University Press.
Carney, J. 1988. "Struggles Over Land and Crops in an Irrigated Rice Scheme: The Gambia." Pp. 59–78 in J. Davison (ed.). *Agriculture, Women, and land: The African Experience*. Boulder, CO: Westview Press.
Cutrufelli, M. 1983. *Women of Africa: Roots of Oppression*. London: Zed.
Dei, G. 1994. "The Women of a Ghanaian Village: A Study of Social Change." *African Studies Review* 37 (September): 121–145.
Gordon, A. 1996. *Transforming Capitalism and Patriarchy: Gender and Development in Africa*. Boulder, CO: Lynne Rienner.
Kabira, W., and E. Nzioki. 1993. *Celebrating Women's Resistance: A Case Study of Women's Group Movement in Kenya*. Nairobi: African Women's Perspective.
Kivane, M. 2004. *Women and Development in Africa: How Gender Works*. Boulder, CO: Lynne Rienner Publishers.
Langley, P. 1983. "A Preliminary Approach to Women and Development: Getting a Few Facts Right." Pp. 79–100 in G. Ssenkoloto (ed.), *The Roles of Women in the Process of development*. Douala: Pan African Institute for Development.
Lovett, M. 1989. "Gender Relations, Class Formation, and the Colonial State in Africa." Pp. 23–46 in J. Parpart and K. Staudt (eds.), *Women and the State in Africa*. Boulder, CO: Lynne Rienner.
McFerson, H. M. 2005. "Women in Africa." Pp. 443–464 in M. Azevedo (ed.), *Africana Studies*. Durham, NC: Carolina Academic Press.
Mikell, G. 1997. "Conclusions, Theorizing and Strategizing About Women and State Crisis." Pp. 333–348 in G. Mikell (ed.). *African Feminism: The Politics of Survival in Sub-Saharan Africa*. Philadelphia: University of Pennsylvania Press.
Nwomonoh, J. 1995. "African Women in Production: The Economic Role of Rural Women." Pp. 171–181 in V. James (ed.). *Women and Sustainable Development in Africa*. Westport, CT: Praeger.

Pankhurst, D., and S. Jacobs. 1988. "Land Tenure, Gender Relations, and Agricultural Production: The Case of Zimbabwe's Peasantry." Pp. 202–227 in J. Davison (ed.), *Agriculture, Women, and Land: The African Experiencer*. Boulder, CO: Westview Press.

Staudt, K. 1987. "Women's Politics, the State, and Capitalist Transformation in Africa." Pp. 53–76 in I. Markovitz (ed.), *Studies in Power and Class in Africa*. New York: Oxford University Press.

Steady, P. (ed.). 1981. *The Black Woman Cross-Culturally*. Rochester, NY: Schenkman Books.

Sweetman, D. 1984. *Women Leaders in African History*. Portsmouth, NH: Heinemann Educational Books. 1989.

World Bank. 1989. Sub-Saharan Africa: From Crisis to Sustainable Growth: A Long-Term Perspective Study. Washington, DC: World Bank.

World Bank. 1990. Women in Development: A Progress Report on the World Bank Initiative. Washington, DC: World Bank.

11 Africa's health issues

Health is a very crucial factor in development. The state of the people's health is normally taken into consideration in evaluating a government's progress in development, and whether the people are healthy or not actually affects development, since illness affects productivity. Africa has had and still has a number of health issues, and success at tackling these and finding solutions has been impeded by the continent's economic problems and other forces like conflicts and apathy. This chapter will look at the major health issues affecting Africa. It will consider the health infrastructure that has the responsibility for delivering adequate healthcare to the African peoples, and it will also discuss the major diseases. These diseases will include those that have been eradicated or almost eradicated, those that had been eradicated or were near eradication but have made a comeback, and those that are still major forces to be reckoned with. In this connection, AIDS will feature prominently. The chapter will then look at the role of traditional medicine within the health infrastructure.

The health infrastructure

A very important aspect of the health infrastructure is the availability of properly trained and competent medical personnel such as doctors, nurses, specialists, and dentists. All the evidence suggests that these are in short supply in Africa. A UNDP report of 2002 gave the physician/population ratio in sub-Saharan Africa as 1/60,000; one doctor for every 60,000 people, in other words. Although a more recent estimate gave the ratio as 1/15,000, this almost certainly refers to the situation in the urban areas. It is a fact that in certain parts of sub-Saharan Africa a Western-trained doctor could not be found for 50 to 100 miles. All this suggests that in spite of the expansion in health services that took place in Africa during the period of economic renaissance in the nineties, there is still a desperate shortage of competent and well-trained medical personnel. For certain kinds of medical treatment, which means consulting certain specialists, patients from some African countries have to travel to other African countries with a more advanced infrastructure, or to the United States or Europe if they can afford it or can procure the necessary visas. Before independence, most African countries got their doctors either by bringing them from Europe or the United States, or training their own local people to become doctors in European or American universities. After independence, however, many African countries established their own medical schools and started training their doctors themselves for several reasons, such as the high cost of higher education in the West, and the need to expose doctors in training to the kinds of medical conditions they would have to grapple with in Africa. In general, this was a good idea, but the establishment of local medical schools involved great

DOI: 10.4324/9781003111733-12

expenditure for equipment and medical knowhow which many of these countries, given the economic situation at the time, could not afford. One could not therefore be sure about the quality of the medical personnel turned out by these medical schools, although there are some excellent schools in places like Ghana, Nigeria, Egypt, and Senegal. The medical personnel in any country have to be superbly competent because the health issue is a matter of life and death.

For the health infrastructure to be adequate money has to be spent, not only on the training of medical personnel, but also on physical structures like hospitals and clinics and on equipment like testing kits and diagnostic machines. However, the economic malaise that hit most African countries prevented governments from spending as much as they should have on health services. The situation was further exacerbated by the structural adjustment programs stipulated by world financial bodies, because these policies involved cutting back on social services like health and education. One constantly hears horrible stories of things like hospital beds and even bed linen being in short supply and of some very sick patients being refused admission. The infrastructure also involves the availability and affordability of drugs. No matter how competent the doctors are in diagnosing the illnesses and prescribing cures, their efforts will be in vain if the necessary drugs are unavailable or prohibitively expensive, as is the case in many parts of sub-Saharan Africa even at the present moment. African governments must do something to regulate the drug business in their countries. One often hears of fake or inferior drugs being sold, even in the pharmacies. This is dangerous. A patient who needs to take a certain anti-biotic to cure his condition but takes, instead, a capsule filled with chalk, will not recover. This is something that actually happens.

To ensure adequate delivery of health services the infrastructure must also include the attitude and outlook of the medical personnel, particularly the doctors and the nurses. We know that doctors take the Hippocratic oath to be compassionate and caring towards their patients. However, it is amazing how many doctors fall short of this in sub-Saharan Africa. I have actually witnessed a doctor shouting at a patient on at least two occasions. And the nurses could be worse. I have been present on one occasion when a nurse turned a patient in pain out of the ward because the latter could not find the money to buy the drugs her doctor had prescribed. In her view, the patient was wasting her time and occupying a bed that could have been more usefully occupied by another patient. Quite a few doctors in Africa treat their calling as a business. Many of them were trained at the taxpayer's expense and are actually government employees receiving government salaries, but they still insist that the patients should pay their heavy fees before they would have anything to do with them. Medical personnel in Africa need to think first about their patients if they are to be competent and successful providers of healthcare. This point needs to be stressed even though it is unpalatable. We must also note that many African countries still do not have programs to ensure that their citizens have access to adequate health services when needed, either through a viable insurance scheme or through government-run arrangements avail-able to all the people. The result is that many of those who need medical attention have to consult doctors privately and pay exorbitant fees. Good healthcare is therefore not afford-able for many citizens. This is one major problem that needs to be tackled.

The major diseases

It is believed in some quarters that Africa is a fertile breeding ground for diseases because most of the continent is hot and humid, and the climate is thus conducive for disease-causing microbes and parasites to breed and infect people (Zewde, 515). Whether Africa is more conducive than other continents for the breeding of diseases is debatable. Perhaps one can only say that it is more conducive for the breeding of certain diseases. Certainly, Africa has had and still has its own share of diseases. Fortunately, some of these diseases have been eradicated, thanks to the research of scientists both outside and within Africa. Three such diseases are smallpox, yellow fever, and polio. Smallpox was a worldwide disease that was almost always fatal, but is now totally eradicated. Yellow fever was more tropical since it was one of those diseases carried by the mosquito, and there was a time when travelers in Africa had to carry with them a vaccination certificate showing that they were currently vaccinated against certain diseases including yellow fever. It is now almost completely eradicated, although yellow fever vaccination certificates are still necessary to enter countries. With polio the story is slightly different. Up to very recently, it was believed that polio had been eradicated and its elimination was one of the greatest public health success stories. A target date of 2000 for the elimination of the disease was set by the World Health Organization and it was then extended to 2005. An aggressive vaccination campaign was carried out, although there were reservations in some countries for religious and other reasons. Nevertheless, Africa eventually seemed free of the disease. However, it seems that a new outbreak has been caused by a mutation of the virus contained in one of the vaccines used for preventing polio. A resurgence of polio has thus appeared in three countries including the West African country of Nigeria. The new strain is called wild poliovirus, or WPV. Fortunately, it is reported that there have been no cases of WPV in Nigeria for the last 33 months and that the African region will be declared WPV free in 2020.

An outstanding success story is the eradication of river blindness, or onchocerciasis. The eradication or near-eradication of this scourge is a demonstration of the success that could be achieved by determined international cooperation. River blindness is one of the water-borne diseases, since it is caused by a parasitic worm that thrives in rivers or in fertile, well-watered lands. The parasitic worm attaches itself to individuals who come into contact with the water in which it thrives; it could be by a simple process such as swimming in the river. The parasite then lays eggs which hatch and breed in the human body. An insect called the black fly helps in the transmission of the infection by biting and sucking the blood of infected people and then passing the parasite to other people it bites. The infection causes irreversible blindness. Just before the campaign to eradicate the disease started, it was estimated that 18 million people were affected in West Africa alone, particularly in Cameroon and Nigeria. Some North African countries, like Tunisia, were also affected. Some administrations, in an effort to contain the disease or prevent people from being infected, decided to move large populations away from the well-watered areas where the parasite was thriving. However, this meant the abandonment of very fertile land that could have been used for agricultural production. The eradication of the disease was therefore top priority. In the early seventies, the United States Agency for International Development (USAID) in collaboration with the World Health Organization and several African countries launched a program to eradicate river blindness completely. It was eminently successful and by 1995 the disease had been eradicated from Ghana, Burkina Faso, Mali, Benin, Guinea Bissau, and Sierra Leone (Zewde, 520). Chad, Cameroon, Nigeria, Sudan, and the Democratic Republic of the Congo were freed from it by 2002.

Let us now look at some diseases that were thought to have been completely eradicated but have returned to Africa with a vengeance. Measles is a contagious disease which causes blistering rashes on the skin, but the disease is actually caused by a virus and it could be fatal or lead to blindness. It affects people worldwide, but it mostly affects children, and is indeed considered one of the leading causes of death amongst children. The World Health Organization reports that in 2015 134,200 people died from measles worldwide, most of them children under the age of 15. Over the years, strenuous attempts have been made internationally to contain the virus through wholescale vaccination. A very effective vaccine was developed in 1963 and the number of deaths from measles began to plunge. In fact, the figure of 134,200 deaths in 2015 was still part of a remarkable decline because between 2000 and 2015 measles vaccination led to a 79 percent drop in measles deaths, from 651,000 worldwide. The year 2015 had been set as the target year for the eradication of measles. In 2015 85 percent of the world's children had been vaccinated by their first birthday. During the period 2000 to 2015 it is estimated that vaccination prevented 20.3 million deaths. The *Los Angeles Times* reported that between 2000 and 2017 deaths plunged by 80 percent and many believed that the disease would soon be eradicated. Indeed, Zewde, writing in 2005, claimed that Africa had largely rid itself of the scourge of measles. However, around 2017 measles reared its head again. The disease can only be contained by the vaccine, and the vaccine is very effective. Therefore, if every child is vaccinated, one can be certain that within a short time the disease would be eradicated. However, for various reasons some people failed to have their children vaccinated. Also, government vaccination programs were either delayed or did not happen in some years. This is why there is a new outbreak. A resurgence in Uganda occurred in January 2018 and in less than two years 3440 measles cases had been confirmed including nine deaths. Other countries like the Democratic Republic of the Congo were also affected. By September of 2019 Africa had about 44 percent of the world's cases of measles. Of course, the measles resurgence was not confined to Africa; it happened even in the United States, but Africa was suffering the most. It is hoped that with heightened awareness most people will have their children vaccinated and the disease will soon be totally eradicated.

When I was growing up in Sierra Leone tuberculosis was unfailingly a fatal disease. To be diagnosed with it was to be under a death sentence. Besides, it carried the kind of stigma that AIDS was to carry later, and since one could get it by being in the same room and breathing the same air as a person who had been diagnosed, those infected tended to be shunned. The Sierra Leonean name for it was "dry cough." It was really a terrible disease which tended to afflict the young mostly. Then came antibiotics and other drugs. Furthermore, effective vaccines were also discovered and the disease was almost completely contained. Towards the end of the last century, however, it broke out again and this time it was more virulent than before. The new outbreak has been associated with the rise of the AIDS pandemic. Tuberculosis is one of the diseases the human body is subject to when the immune system is greatly weakened, as happens in the case of AIDS. Of course, Africa, which was the region most affected by the AIDS pandemic, was most affected by the resurgence of tuberculosis. *The New England Journal of Medicine* reports in an article by Richard Chaisson and Neil Martinson that although in the period 1990 to 2005 Africa had 11 percent of the world's population it carried 29 percent of tuberculosis cases and 34 percent of related deaths. The World Health Organization estimates that the average incidence of tuberculosis in African countries more than doubled between 1990 and 2005 from 140 to 343 per 100,000 of population, while the rates in other regions were declining. Mali and Togo had incidence greater than 300 per 100,000. The situation is not hopeless, however. Though the new strains of the disease were resistant to the drugs used in the past, new drugs are now in existence. Provided the disease is diagnosed early and the patients are regularly treated for six to eight months with the cheap but highly effective drugs, and their progress regularly monitored, there is hope that eradication will actually happen and happen soon. All African governments have pledged themselves to achieving this goal.

Let us now turn our attention to those diseases that are still major problems, largely because eradication seems a long way off, although considerable advances have been made in treatment. When one talks about the really major diseases in Africa at the moment, people generally assume that one is going to discuss AIDS and AIDS only, because that is the disease that has devastated the continent and that most people know about. And yet there are several other major diseases, some of which now pose an even greater threat than AIDS. Worthy of note are the so-called water-borne diseases. These are the diseases that are largely caused by people coming into contact with contaminated water or with parasites that have been bred in water, or by ingesting contaminated water. River blindness can therefore be regarded as a water-borne disease. So is malaria which will be discussed later. Furthermore, there is a whole slew of deadly diseases that are caused by the ingesting of contaminated water. These include hepatitis A, typhoid fever, cholera, salmonella, roundworms, diarrhea, schistosomiasis, and dysentery. These diseases are mostly caused by people drinking water that has been contaminated by pathogens, handling food that has come into contact with contaminated water, or even touching people who have come into contact with contaminated water. If the water is used for preparing food that has not been properly cooked, people eating that food could be affected. Contaminated water is the problem. The fact is that many people in Africa, especially those in the rural areas, do not have access to clean, properly treated water. Instead of getting their water from pipes and faucets, they have to get it from streams, pools, and rivers. At times it is the same streams and rivers that people bathe in. Such water is bound to be polluted. One of the most powerful vignettes in Ali Mazrui's documentary series *The Africans: A Triple Heritage* shows a couple of women getting brown-colored water from a dirty stream. That is all the water they have access to. That is the water they and their family would drink and that they would use for cooking. Some parts of Africa are arid anyway, and water is in short supply. People therefore have to make do with the water that is available. One of the United Nations Millennium Development Goals was to get countries to manage their water resources in ways that would ensure adequate drinking water for the people by 2015. Sub-Saharan Africa failed to meet these goals although most of North Africa had almost done so. In sub-Saharan Africa, 40 percent of the people had no access to safe drinking water. Piped-in water is non-existent in the poorest 40 percent of households in sub-Saharan Africa. In 1990 it was estimated that only 32 percent of people in rural areas had access to safe drinking water. This was usually in the form of wells. Indeed, some people are turning to the construction of wells in order to get safe drinking water, and in others authorities have arranged for pipe-borne water to be conveyed to central areas where people can go to get their water. The wells have become absolutely essential because even those people who have indoor plumbing and pipe-borne water run short when the authorities turn off the water because of scarcity. However, even the wells have problems. Pathogens can get into them and make the water unsafe unless it is properly treated. Also, the water that seeps out and accumulates around public wells and pipes can become fertile breeding ground for mosquitos. Furthermore, some of the wells and other systems fail because of lack of resources to keep them functioning properly. It is estimated that over half of such systems have failed.

The problem is complicated by poor sanitation. Many people in Africa have no indoor plumbing and no access to proper sanitation. In 1990 it was estimated that only one in five people in the African countryside had access to adequate sanitation. The United Nations Millennium Development Goals had also set goals on sanitation to be achieved by 2015. Reports showed that only 34 percent of sub-Saharan households had reached the development goals by the target date. This means that many Africans have no access to the WCs that are available in the West. Some make use of outdoor latrines, but many lack access even to these. This means that many Africans merely use the bushes as a toilet, an activity known as open defecation, or simply throw out their waste openly. This is a completely unsanitary activity that can have a marked impact on the environment and on the people's health. Untreated human waste that is simply thrown out or left in the open can seep into the water supply and contaminate it. Even where there are outdoor latrines or toilets the waste material can still seep into the water supply unless the latrines are very well constructed. It has been estimated that about 80 percent of all diseases in the developing world is caused by drinking contaminated water. Waterborne pathogens kill 3.4 million people every year and account for one-third of all deaths in developing countries, including those in Africa. Four thousand children die each day as a result of ingesting filthy water. It is estimated that 115 people in Africa die each day from diseases related to poor sanitation, poor hygiene, and contaminated water.

Let us look at some of these water-borne diseases. Cholera is a vicious disease caused by a bacterium called the vibrio cholera. It affects the small intestine and can lead to excessive vomiting and even diarrhea. The symptoms appear between two to five days after exposure, and, if diagnosed early, the disease can be cured; if not, it can lead to a very painful death. It can be easily transmitted from person to person and it therefore usually comes, not so much as an individual infection, but in outbreaks involving thousands of people at times, leading to hundreds of deaths. The disease is also usually caused by contact with or consumption of food or water that has been contaminated, usually by feces. Eating seafood which has not been properly cooked also causes it. There is an effective cholera vaccine, but it is extremely painful, and it only lasts for six months. Fortunately, it can now also be given orally. The best treatment is oral rehydration, since the vomiting and diarrhea which accompany the disease usually result in dehydration, and it is this that causes death. It is estimated that cholera affects between 3 and 5 million people annually and leads to between 28,800 and 130,000 deaths, most of them in sub-Saharan Africa. Hepatitis A is a disease of the liver that is caused by the hepatitis A virus and spread by eating food that is contaminated with feces, usually feces carried in contaminated water. As with cholera, it can also be spread by eating under-cooked seafood. Unfortunately, it can lead to acute liver failure if not treated early and properly. The only way in which the disease can be contained is through vaccination, there being no real cure, except, perhaps, a liver transplant. Also, proper sanitation, proper hygiene, and cooking food thoroughly will go a long way. About 114 million cases of hepatitis A occur every year, mostly in areas with poor sanitation. Schistosomiasis is a snail-borne illness that can also be water-borne. It is endemic to certain parts of Africa and is rare in places like the United States and Europe. It affects the liver, the intestinal tract, and the urinary tract and can also cause anemia. It is usually caused by people getting into infected water; that is, water that has parasitic worms, urine, and feces. The pathogens usually enter the bloodstream through the skin. If untreated, it can lead to liver failure.

Diarrhea and dysentery have always been perennial problems in Africa, particularly among children. It is estimated that in households without proper sanitation, the children have a 60 percent higher chance of dying than in households which have. What a lot of mothers in rural Africa do not know is that they could alleviate the situation by giving their children a simple solution of boiled water with some salt in it. It is the dehydration caused by excessive defecation that causes death and what is needed is adequate rehydration.

Malaria

Malaria is one of the deadliest diseases affecting Africans today. It could be regarded as a water-borne disease since the little insect that spreads it breeds in shallow water-places. It is a very debilitating disease which significantly affects productivity and therefore the economies of several African countries, since millions of people suffer from it every year. There are four major plasmodium parasites that cause the malaria infection. The most dangerous is the plasmodium falciparum, and it is this that causes the vast majority of the infections in Africa. The parasite is spread by a vector, the little mosquito insect. In Africa, the most common vector is the anopheles mosquito which is very widespread in Africa and is the most difficult to control. These are some of the reasons why Africa is the continent most affected by malaria. The mosquito needs to feed on human blood to strengthen its eggs. It therefore bites humans and draws their blood. Mosquitos make a most annoying noise when they are near humans, going mostly for the ears. Their bite is most vicious and painful. In fact, they transfer the parasite from human to human as they bite. After the parasite enters the human blood it goes to the liver and there it multiplies. The parasite invades the red blood cells, which are essential for carrying oxygen, and multiplies to such an extent that the red blood cells burst. It then continues to multiply. A malaria attack can easily cause anemia, liver diseases, kidney failure, blood clots, jaundice, diarrhea, and headaches. Worst of all it can enter the brain and cause cerebral malaria, which can be fatal in a few days.

Africa, as we have seen, is the continent most affected by malaria, largely because climatic and other conditions are very conducive for the breeding of the mosquitos and the survival of the parasite. According to a World Health Organization Report of 2002, 90 percent of all malaria deaths in the world occur in sub-Saharan Africa. It was also reported that one million people in Africa died from malaria each year and most of these were children under five (WHO Report, 2002). The most recent (2018) figure for deaths in Africa is about half a million each year. It is possible for some people to develop immunity to malaria over the years, but the immunity does not really kick in until they become adults. Children are more susceptible because they would not have acquired the immunity. The figure of half a million deaths a year in Africa alone shows that, in spite of efforts at eradication, malaria is still a formidable threat, especially in Africa. There are anti-malaria drugs that can cure the disease, but this can happen only after someone has been infected and shows symptoms. In order to eradicate the disease people must be prevented from being infected. This means exterminating the mosquito vector, which seems unlikely at the moment, or making the parasite inactive in the human body, which means vaccination. The problem is that, so far, there is really no effective vaccine. There are certain prophylactics that can be taken to prevent infection, but these do not last for a long time. For instance, one of them must be taken every week. Travelers to countries susceptible to malaria are advised to begin taking these drugs long before they even set foot in the relevant country. The use of mosquito nets has proved very effective. The nets prevent the mosquitos from entering and biting individuals. However, they must be kept in perfect condition. The Bill and Melinda Gates Foundation has been enormously helpful in providing mosquito nets for susceptible countries. They have also devoted enormous resources to research in the drive to find not only cures but also an effective vaccine. Insecticides can also be very useful in killing the mosquitos, but there is increasing opposition to their use because of their effect on the environment and on agriculture. Until a very effective vaccine is developed, malaria will remain a formidable threat to Africa's development.

AIDS

Of all the diseases that present a challenge to Africa, AIDS has been, perhaps, the most devastating. Strictly speaking, AIDS, which is caused by the HIV virus entering the human blood system, is not itself a disease; rather, it is a condition which renders the individual susceptible to a whole range of diseases, most of them deadly. The letters AIDS stand for acquired immunodeficiency syndrome and refer to a condition or state in which the human body has lost almost all its immunity. The individual is therefore liable to attack from several diseases like cancer, tuberculosis, and diarrhea, and it is these diseases that lead to death. So far there is no known cure, which means that once individuals are infected the virus cannot be removed from their systems. However, some very effective anti-retroviral drugs have been perfected which can contain the disease and ensure that, as long as individuals take their medications and are monitored regularly, they can continue to live normal healthy lives.

AIDS is a global issue which affects every corner of the world and every demographic bloc. However, there is no doubt that Africa has been and is still the hardest hit, especially Southern Africa. AIDS has had the most devastating effect on the economy of Africa. The first cases were actually found, not in Africa, but in the United States, when in the early seventies some young men showed signs of an inexplicable rash or skin cancer. The disease was later diagnosed as AIDS. Soon the number of cases multiplied, and young men started to die. Because of the virulence of the disease, because it soon became apparent that it was related to sexual activity, because most people knew nothing about it, and because at the time diagnosis was almost certainly a death sentence, some myths and misconceptions developed around it, and it acquired a stigma which led to an unwillingness by some to be tested and thus to the disease becoming more widespread. Pratap Rhugani has dealt with most of these in his article "Love in a Time of Hatred."

Let us look at some of these misconceptions. The first is that we do not know a lot about the AIDS virus. In actual fact, professionals and scientists then knew and now know quite a lot about AIDS and the virus that causes it. For one thing, it is now known that the disease is not contagious. The late Princess Diana, who on one occasion was actually photographed cradling a young child with AIDS in her arms, was influential in demonstrating this. Another feature we definitely know about the virus is that it cannot survive for long outside the human body. This is very important information for those who come into contact with contaminated human blood. If that blood has been outside the human body beyond a certain period of time it is no longer infectious. In fact we have a lot of information about how the disease is spread and how infection takes place. The virus is spread by the exchange of bodily fluids such as blood, semen, or mother's milk. This is why it is largely spread by sexual activity, but infected mothers can pass the disease on to their children through their milk and it could also be communicated by blood transfusion if someone receives the donated blood of an infected person. The reuse of a needle that has been used by or on an infected person can also cause infection since microscopic amounts of the infected person's blood might still be on it. There is little evidence, so far, that it is spread by saliva, so kissing an infected person will not spread it.

Another major misconception with serious consequences was that HIV/AIDS was a gay plague that only affected homosexual men indulging in certain sexual practices. This had serious consequences because those who did not belong to that demographic continued to indulge in the kind of sexual practice (like having unprotected sex) that could lead to AIDS. In fact, as far as Africa is concerned, HIV/AIDS is largely a heterosexual disease affecting more women than men and largely transmitted through heterosexual intercourse. It does not discriminate with regard to gender, color, race, or nationality. As long as one has been exposed to unprotected sex one is liable to get it.

Although details remain unclear, one theory is that the disease started in Africa and was then transmitted to the United States by tourists who had been to places like the Democratic Republic of the Congo or East Africa. The theory is that the virus was originally present in animals, like the chimpanzee, but since some Africans are fond of eating animals like the chimpanzee which they call "bush meat," the virus might have been passed on to them via this process. One must say that the jury is still out on this. Although certain forms of the disease exist in some animals, like cats, for instance, there is no evidence, either that it started in animals, or that humans contracted it through eating animals. Some might feel that this kind of debate is irrelevant anyway since our main preoccupation should now be the containment or elimination of the disease.

People started to take note of AIDS in Africa from the middle to the late eighties. Before this, many Africans who had heard of it assumed that it was a disease plaguing the developed world; that is, Europe and North America. April Gordon, quoting Chin, asserts that statistics published by the WHO in 1990 then estimated that 10 to 12 million people were infected by the virus and that, although sub-Saharan Africa had only 10 percent of the world's population, it had 25 to 50 percent of people infected with AIDS (Gordon, 223). This, of course, was early days with the statistics, in so far as Africa was concerned, and it is almost certain that the numbers were grossly underrated. In 1994 WHO gave the worldwide number of sufferers as 15 million of whom 10 million, or two-thirds, were living in Africa. In 1999 WHO gave a figure of 34 million people living with HIV/AIDS worldwide of whom over 24 million were living in Africa. In 2002 the number of AIDS sufferers worldwide was 42 million and 70 percent of those were living in Africa. By 2011 when most African countries were beginning to get a grip on the AIDS crisis Africa still had 69 percent of all people suffering from HIV/AIDS and 70 percent of all deaths. The latest figures available are those for 2018 by the UN, and, according to those figures, 37.9 million people worldwide were infected with the AIDS virus and of those 25 million were in Africa. The figures for individual countries show that countries in Southern Africa were hardest hit. In 2003 Botswana had 3,330,000 people affected with HIV/AIDS (37.5 percent of its population) and 33,000 deaths; for Lesotho the figures were 300,000, 28.9 percent and 22,000; for Namibia 200,000, 21.3 percent and 16,000; for South Africa 5,100,000, 21.5 percent, 570,000; for Zimbabwe 1,600,000, 24.6 percent and 170,000; and for Ethiopia 1,400,000, 4.4 percent and 120,000. The difference between the occurrence in Southern African countries and a Northern African country like Ethiopia is striking. South Africa had and still has the highest number of people with HIV/AIDS in the world, although Botswana has the highest percentage of the entire population suffering from the disease. The figures show quite incontestably that Africa was the region hardest hit by HIV/AIDS. The question that needs to be answered is why.

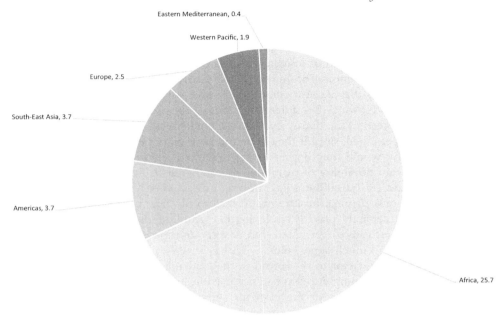

Number of People Living with HIV by WHO Region in 2019 (in millions)

Figure 11.1 Number of people living with HIV by WHO region in 2019 (in millions).
Source: Data compiled from https://apps.who.int/gho/data/view.main.22100WHO?lang=en

Some commentators think that a major reason why Africa was the hardest hit region is that there is a very high occurrence of pre-marital and extra-marital sex in Africa, which many Africans yet have to confront (see Gordon, 223). While it is true that many Africans still have to accept the fact that the level of pre-marital and extra-marital sex in Africa is higher than supposed, it is debatable whether sex outside marriage is more common in Africa than on other continents, such as Europe and North America. A much more obvious reason is poverty. It has now been established that whenever there is a pandemic the poorest areas suffer the most because of the lack of an infrastructure and resources needed to cope with the outbreak. In the case of AIDS, African countries were almost universally too poor at the time to afford the diagnostic procedures that were needed. If sufferers were not diagnosed they would not know they had the disease and would thus continue infecting others. Even if the disease was properly diagnosed most Africans lacked the resources to afford the very expensive medications that would help them avoid death and, as some believe, reduce the viral load in their bodies to such a level that they would not infect others. It must also be noted that poverty caused some people in Africa, particularly young women, to indulge in practices, like prostitution, which enhanced the spread of the disease. Many parts of Africa, especially Southern Africa, are very attractive and popular tourist areas visited by tourists from all over the world. The temptation to indulge in prostitution to service the tourists must be very great indeed for young people some of whom normally earn less than a dollar a day.

The cost of treating the disease once it is diagnosed is worth dwelling on. It has been estimated that it costs about $15,000 a year to treat an AIDS patient; this includes the cost of medications, doctor's visits, and testing, and this is if the patient is covered by insurance which covers most of the cost. Actually, the cost for some people might be much more because some of the medications are ridiculously expensive. The pharmaceutical companies seem to be exploiting people's misery and making a killing. HIV drugs like Truvada and Triumeq actually cost $3000 for a month's supply; that is, $36,000 a year. The right kind of insurance will cover most of that, but the patient still has to spend a substantial amount of money, which a lot of Africans did not, and still do not, have. Let us note that we are talking of a time when there was not yet much assistance from the West for AIDS sufferers in Africa. The availability and cost of treatment affected the spread of the disease because some people who knew they were at risk did not bother to get tested, since if they were found to be positive there was no way to get treatment. Why would they bother to get tested and endure the stigma of having AIDS if there was no possibility of treatment? It was better to live in blissful ignorance. The fact is that most Africans did not have access to the kind of health provisions, like an insurance scheme or a national health system, that would take care of the cost of their treatment. Apathy certainly played a role in the spread of the disease because some people simply did not care to get tested, but poverty and the exploitative nature of the drug companies played much larger roles.

Another contributing factor to the spread of the epidemic in Africa was ignorance. In the eighties in particular, most Africans had not even heard of the disease or they did not know much about the causes or the grievous consequences. Most of those who had heard of it thought that it was a Western disease that mostly affected Western gay men. They quite wrongly thought they were living in an environment where homosexuality was not a problem and so there was no threat to them. There were even some gay men in Africa who thought that the disease was confined to the Western world and it had not got to them, nor would it ever do so. Ignorance led to a kind of denial and therefore a lack of awareness of the need for programs to educate people about the disease. In order to prevent the spread of AIDS, education, particularly of the young, is needed on the causes and consequences and the means of prevention. This education inevitably involves talking about sexual matters. However, it is well known that at the time of the outbreak of the epidemic discussion about sex was virtually taboo in many African societies. There were very few schools that included sex education in the curriculum. It was simply not done, and this had a marked impact.

We have already mentioned the stigma that attached to AIDS. This was probably due to the fact that the disease was largely contracted through sexual activity and there had always been, in Africa at least, a kind of subtext that regarded sexual activity as something shady or even obscene. However, the stigma had some terrible consequences. It meant that anyone who was known to have AIDS or the HIV virus was also stigmatized and shunned. It was also highly likely that the person would be ostracized from his society and from all the groups he belonged to. If one were tested, therefore, one ran the risk of being found to be HIV positive and therefore of being ostracized completely from one's society. Hordes of people were therefore reluctant to get tested, even when testing became available. They also knew that if they were tested and found positive, they could only look forward to a painful death as treatment at the time had to be ruled out.

Another factor that must be considered is the fact that many Africans believe that all misfortunes have a supernatural cause. A simple matter like an individual hitting his big toe against a rock and having to endure great pain would elicit the explanation that the individual might have antagonized his ancestors or that the ancestors might be trying to warn him of some impending disaster. Nothing happens without a supernatural cause in many parts of Africa. In this kind of environment AIDS is regarded as having been caused by witchcraft. The individual is ill because he has an enemy who wishes him dead. This kind of attitude is likely to preclude consideration of the real causes of the diseases and the methods of prevention.

Indeed, some social factors influenced the spread of AIDS in Africa. Apart from the traditional attitudes which give supernatural explanations for AIDS, and the unwillingness in some African societies to discuss sex publicly, the polygamous structure of many African societies might also enhance the spread of the disease. Husbands who feel they have a right to as much sex as they want, whether it is within or outside marriage, might have sex with women other than their wives, contract the disease, and then infect their wives. This would be even more serious if the family is polygamous, because the husband might infect all his wives. We have also referred to the impact of the power relations between men and women in Africa. Most African women seem either unable or unwilling to ask their partners to use condoms, which is one of the safest ways of preventing transmission. There were also some areas where it was believed that having sex with a virgin was a definite cure for AIDS. This, of course, would merely serve to spread the disease even further.

We have already looked at some of the economic causes, poverty being the main one. The activities of some migrant workers also helped to complicate the situation. In Southern Africa, especially, some men who were in search of a more secure economic position, left their wives and families in order to go and work in the mines. They had to leave their families behind because families were not allowed in the camps where the workers were given accommodation. Prostitution inevitably grew around these camps of migrant workers, who would then spread the virus on their return home. But it was not just the migrant workers who helped spread the disease by consorting with prostitutes; some professionals also, like teachers, doctors, lawyers and even professors, had to be away from their homes and families at times, perhaps attending conferences. They too would consort with prostitutes, contract the virus, and proceed to spread it. Then there were also the activities of the long-distance truck drivers. A look at the map of Africa will show that there are a few landlocked countries in Africa and some of them are in Southern Africa, like Botswana, Zimbabwe, Zambia, and Lesotho. These countries have to convey their exports to the coast by using enormous trucks driven by specially trained drivers. These drivers have, at times, to drive hundreds of miles, passing through other countries. It is a very arduous job. Of course, there are rest stations where they pause to rest, and there they are met and entertained by prostitutes.

We must also not ignore the political causes for the spread of the virus and the disease. Some African political leaders refused initially to admit that their countries were affected by the virus because it would be bad for tourism, and they needed the revenue from tourism. Also, if it became widely known that HIV/AIDS was prevalent in their countries this would be a blow to their national pride, and they would feel degraded in the eyes of the world. The most egregious example of this was Tambo Mbeki who succeeded Nelson Mandela as president of South Africa in 1999. Tourism is extremely crucial to the South African economy. Tambo Mbeki refused to accept that AIDS was present in his country. Indeed, he went down on record as declaring that AIDS was not caused by the HIV virus. In speech after speech he claimed that the main threat to Africa was poverty, not the virus. This attitude alone was completely damaging because it prevented people from being tested and treated. But it led to even more serious consequences. It was widely known that mothers could pass the virus on to innocent children through mother's milk. However, it had also been established that if the mother had been diagnosed in time (even while pregnant) and adequately treated with certain drugs, the virus would not be transmitted to the child. This was an extremely important aspect of prevention, yet Mbeki prevented expectant mothers from being tested and treated. Hordes of South Africans contracted the virus who should not have done so, and many of them are dead. It was only after Mbeki left office that the new president, Jacob Zuma, took the opposite stance and South Africa engaged in a vigorous anti-HIV campaign.

Impact of AIDS on African society

Let us now look at some aspects of the impact of HIV/AIDS on African society. There were enormous social consequences. One of the most important is the condition of the so-called AIDS orphans. These are children who have lost both parents to AIDS. These children have no one to provide for or care for them, and it is usually left to the eldest child to act as surrogate parent. This often means that that child drops out of school and is forced to take menial jobs. If the eldest child is a girl, she quite often resorts to prostitution to provide for her younger siblings. If their home was a rented property they are usually evicted; but even if it was owned by their parents they are often forced out of it by grasping relatives, with the claim that it was family property. The children are therefore virtually homeless. They are also usually ostracized not only by the community but also by their family, largely on the unwarranted suspicion that they too might have the virus. The situation of the AIDS orphans is therefore very bleak indeed. A UNAIDS report of 2002 put the figure of AIDS orphans worldwide at 11 million. Most of these are in Africa, many in Southern Africa. Here are some figures for the AIDS orphans in some countries: Botswana, 120,000; Ethiopia, 720,000; Lesotho, 100,000; Mozambique, 470,000; Nigeria, 1,800,000; South Africa, 1, 100,000; Uganda, 940,000; Zimbabwe, 980,000. These figures are obviously staggering. Obviously, the AIDS situation causes a breakdown in the extended family system. Normally, these children should have been cared for by their relatives, but the fear of contracting the virus and the stigma attached to it make relatives distance themselves from the orphans. These factors also often cause relatives to distance themselves even from adults living with the disease.

Most devastating, perhaps, were the economic consequences. HIV/AIDS attacked the most productive segment of the population, people between the ages of 15 and 49 who were at the height of their capacities. This is not surprising, since the disease mostly affects those who are sexually active. Worldwide, it was estimated that more than 50 percent of infections occurred in people between the ages of 15 and 24. In one South African university it was estimated that 25 percent of the students were infected. As we have seen, the disease was non-discriminating. It affected management, doctors, lawyers, teachers, professors, ministers of government, engineers, and relatives of ministers. In fact, it hit the professionals particularly hard because they are usually the most mobile segment of the population and therefore likely to travel and be exposed to the disease. A World Bank report of 2000 estimated that, at that time, per capita growth in half of the countries in Africa was falling by between 0.5 and 1.2 percent each year as a result of HIV/AIDS (Global Fund, "Fighting AIDS). One of the most unfortunate countries in this regard, as we have seen, was Botswana in Southern Africa. It was doing extremely well until HIV/AIDS struck, and the country was badly affected. At one time, it had the highest percentage of the population affected by AIDS, over 37 percent. That is more than one in three people. Of course, its economy stagnated. However, because of the measures adopted by the government, the country is once more on the road to full recovery. The AIDS crisis hit every sector of African countries' activities. Apart from the economy and the social system, it hit education, because professors and students died and some schools had to be closed. It was estimated that in one country maybe a third of the teachers were infected. It hit agriculture because farm workers died or were too sick to work in the fields. It hit the health sector which, in most cases, had been inadequate anyway and was now stretched to breaking point; UNAIDS reports of 2000 and 2004 estimated that between 19 percent and 53 percent of all health employee deaths in Africa were caused by HIV/AIDS.

The AIDS crisis in Africa, and indeed in the whole world, has now eased considerably because of measures adopted by governments and a number of world agencies. In particular, African leaders, who for economic and other reasons were in denial and were slow to admit that the virus had hit their countries, were now forced to take action. As a result, the number of people living with the AIDS virus worldwide and in Africa has declined somewhat. It has not declined dramatically, because once an individual is infected with the virus, it remains in his system indefinitely, since no cure has as yet been discovered. In other words, it is not yet possible to remove the virus completely from the human system. Those who are infected therefore remain infected, although, thanks to the discovery of the so-called anti-retroviral drugs, they can go on to live normal healthy lives. The number of new infections, however, can be drastically reduced by the use of condoms and the adoption of safe-sex procedures. Most importantly, the number of deaths has been drastically reduced because of the availability and use of the new drugs. An HIV/AIDS diagnosis, therefore, is no longer a death sentence. One striking success story is that of Uganda which was, at one time, one of the countries hardest hit in Africa. The disease was diagnosed there in 1982 and the national infection rate was 18.3 percent. It is reported that whole villages were decimated because the government at the time was in denial and failed to take action (Zewde, 530). Under the leadership of a new president, Uri Museveni, the country admitted the presence of the HIV virus and decided to combat it by grassroots mobilization. It also asked for and received help from the international community to pursue prevention and treatment policies. At the core of the Uganda campaign was the so-called "ABC strategy": abstinence, be faithful, condoms. In other words the authorities were suggesting to Ugandans that they abstain from sexual activity until marriage, that they be faithful to their partners and avoid promiscuity, and that they use condoms during sexual activity. The government also quite rightly saw that in order to combat HIV/AIDS successfully a multi-faceted or even multi-disciplinary approach was needed, which would bring together the expertise of several sectors. It thus established the Multi-Sector Approach to Control AIDS (MACA) which brought together the efforts of various government departments. The government also established the Uganda AIDS Commission. Uganda's efforts were so successful that by 2002 the rate of infection had been reduced to 4.1 percent. Other countries decided to follow Uganda's example and adopt similar or comparable measures. Zimbabwe also encouraged delaying sexual activity, avoiding promiscuity, and using condoms. By 2007 the rate of infection dropped from 23 percent of the population to 20.5 percent. Among women aged 15 to 24 it dropped by half, and among men aged 17 to 29 it dropped by 25 percent (Gordon, 227). Senegal acknowledged the role of prostitutes in spreading the disease and decided to control their activities by issuing all prostitutes with a government card and allowing them to work legally (Gordon, 227). They were thus brought from underground and could be provided with condoms and be adequately supervised. They are tested monthly for STDs and every six months for HIV. Those who test positive are given adequate counseling (Gordon, 227). Senegal has one of the lowest infection rates in Africa. South Africa, which was once in denial about AIDS, has developed the Mobile Task Team (MTT) approach, largely spearheaded by the University of Natal. It is a program which is devoted to educating people generally about HIV/AIDS and to the intensive training of medical personnel who are treating AIDS patients.

Ironically, while it is thought that female circumcision might help spread the virus, it seems that male circumcision might help to control it. Male circumcision involves the removal of parts of the male genitalia, and it is thought that these parts, the foreskin in particular, might harbor the virus, and their removal might therefore reduce the possibility of its remaining on the human body. It has been established that the incidence of HIV is less among circumcised men than among the uncircumcised, and some countries are actively promoting male circumcision as a means of containing the virus.

There were quite a few international agencies that gave assistance to African countries in their bid to stem the advance of HIV/AIDS. These include UNAIDS (United Nations Program on HIV and AIDS), USAID (United States Agency for International Development), and the Global Fund. The Global Fund was established in 2002 by Kofi Anan the then Secretary General of the United Nations to fight AIDS, tuberculosis, and malaria. He asked various countries, including the United States, to contribute to a target of 10 billion annually to combat these diseases. That target has never really been achieved, although some countries and individuals contributed generously. The Bill and Melinda Gates Foundation, for instance, has been exemplary in making donations to the fund and in expanding resources devoted to the improvement of the health of Africa in general. In 2003 the Foundation donated $1 billion to the fund. Most surprising was the response of the United States. It was during the presidency of President Reagan that HIV/AIDS began to rivet itself on the world's attention. The United States had been severely criticized for doing very little either domestically or on the international scene to combat the epidemic. The view held by most right-wing supporters of the Reagan government was that it was a gay plague, and it was probably a punishment by God on those involved for their wayward lifestyle. In 2002, however, President George W. Bush responded very positively to Kofi Annan's request. Some still believe that this was one of the best things done by the Bush administration. He had pledged only $200 million initially, but in 2003 he pledged $15 billion over five years. He also committed the United States to ensuring adequate treatment for 2 million infected people. The promise about treatment was particularly important and welcome because, as we have seen, the anti-retroviral drugs were extremely expensive and African countries would only be able to give their patients the much-needed treatment if they received substantial help from the developed world. Support from the United States went a long way. As we have seen, the pharmaceutical companies were exploiting human misery and making a killing. In fact, cheaper brands of the anti-retroviral drugs were being produced in places other than the United States and Europe. One such place was Brazil, and some African countries, like South Africa, attempted to get the cheaper brands for their people. The pharmaceutical companies (one of them at least) brought legal action against South Africa for infringement of patent. In other words, these companies were prepared to let people die as long as they made their profits. Fortunately, the South African government won the case and cheaper drugs became available to a number of countries. This also went a long way, but the Bush initiative was also a life-saver for many.

Of course, President Bush was also severely criticized for insisting that 30 percent of US aid should go towards promoting abstinence as the most effective means of preventing HIV/AIDS. In this, he was responding to some of his Republican fundamen-talist backers who were against condom use for religious reasons. They felt that the use of condoms was a means of birth control which they opposed. They also felt that encoura-ging the use of condoms was tantamount to encouraging promiscuity. The problem is that to insist on abstinence is to be unrealistic. Some people might take the advice, but there would be hordes of others who would not, and denying them assistance amounts to saying that they must be left to die. By insisting on abstinence, the fundamentalists were intent on imposing their own moral and ideological beliefs on other people, many of them for-eigners. Some might say that the US was right in imposing conditions since it was giving the aid, aid which came from the taxes paid by its people. This might be acceptable in normal situations, but the HIV/AIDS situation was not normal, because people were dying. The aid should have been given for humanitarian reasons, without pre-conditions, to prevent unprecedented suffering. The encouragement of abstinence was also part of Uganda's strategy, and that country was also severely criticized for it. Indeed, some believe that the abstinence component was the least effective aspect of the Uganda strategy. The use of condoms and the avoidance of promiscuity were more realistic, more achievable, and much more effective. Most countries have simply ignored the abstinence component. Because of the measures adopted, advances have been made in the treatment and preven-tion of HIV/AIDS in Africa although it is still a problem in most countries and the virus has not been eliminated.

Mention must be made of COVID-19 which is currently ravaging the world. Inter-estingly, it has been least virulent in Africa, which seems to have been spared the trauma other continents have experienced. The reasons for this may have been that Africa is much warmer than other places, and that Africans spend much more of their time out-side. We still don't know much about the virus. As more research is conducted, attention will undoubtedly be given to these aspects of the disease in Africa.

Traditional medicine

Any survey of the health situation in Africa must discuss the role of traditional medicine. There are people who still regard African traditional medicine as nothing but superstition and mumbo-jumbo. This is probably the worst misconception about Africa. These people fail to realize that Western medicine came to Africa only towards the end of the nineteenth century and Africans must have been tending to their sick in all the centuries before that, enabling some people to live very long lives. Even in the contemporary era many Africans might be a hundred miles and more away from the nearest hospital or Western doctor and are therefore dependent on the traditional medicine man, who is really a "medicine man" in the sense that he is engaged in the practice of medicine, though not trained in Western medicine. Even when he is called a witch doctor, as some people would pejoratively like to call him, the nomenclature is not altogether inap-propriate because, as we have seen, witchcraft in Africa can be both positive and nega-tive, and the term witch doctor suggests someone with heightened powers who engages in the practice of medicine. The fact is that the traditional medicine man is engaged in an activity that is quite scientific. He knows about diseases and what he must use in the attempt to cure them. He knows about herbs and the properties of leaves, roots, and the barks of trees. He might not know the chemical names for the substances they contain, but he knows about the effects of these substances and what he must do to extract them; some have to be squeezed, some must be boiled, some must be dried in the sun, and so on. Those who are skeptical might remind themselves that before the development of drugs like chloroquine, the best cure for the deadly malaria was quinine, which was got from the bark of the chinchona tree. Getting medicines from barks and leaves is therefore quite scientific. The traditional medicine man knows that the best cure for malaria today is the leaf of the ojuologbo tree. He collects the leaves, boils them in water, and gives the potion to the patient to drink. It is particularly effective for cerebral malaria. I can remember my father telling me about a particular case where a delirious malaria patient was given the hot drink from the boiled ojuologbo leaves, and he recovered completely in a few days. This is African science of which there is a lot, and the African medicine man has competence in it. Before he begins to practice his craft he normally goes through a long period of apprenticeship, and he generally has the trust and confidence of the people he serves. The services of the traditional medical practitioner are crucial even in the urban areas where people have greater access to hospitals. Many people go to traditional medicine because the local hospitals are overcrowded, under-staffed, or under-equipped; because they can afford the charges of the traditional practitioner; and because they feel the traditional medicine man knows and understands their problems much better.

These traditional medicine men and women are performing miracles of healing. They are particularly good at mending fractures and broken bones. When the patient goes to them, they might try to give the impression that their craft is mystical and that they derive their power from the spirits or the supernatural. They might actually believe that this is the case. To this end they might recite some verses designed to invoke the spirits and ask for their assistance. But the rest of their activities are actually science-based. They might prescribe a potion derived from leaves, roots, or barks that would cure the patient. My information suggests, for instance, that a young patient who goes to the medicine man with a fractured or broken leg might be asked to bring a white cock. After treating the young patient's foot the medicine man might then proceed to do various things with the cock, including breaking its leg, but he does not kill it; he lets it go, but will watch it carefully during the ensuing weeks. He assumes that when the cock is perfectly healed again it will be time for the patient's foot also to be perfectly healed and he must remove the wrappings and other things he had used. The cock is therefore used as a device for gauging when the patient's foot would have healed completely.

The traditional healers are also extremely competent at treating insanity or nervous breakdowns. They are in a position to understand the psychology of the African in a way in which the Western-trained doctor does not. I am aware of at least one case of a young man who had apparently gone quite mad but who was cured by a traditional healer. If his relatives had taken him to the local psychiatric hospital with its bad reputation, he would have languished there for the rest of his days. Instead, they took him up-country to be treated by a traditional healer. When he returned to the city it was obvious that he was completely cured. He was rather shaky on his legs, because the treatment was apparently quite harsh, but he was cured, and he subsequently got a good job, got married, and now has several children and probably grand-children.

Indeed, the most astonishing example of the competence of the traditional healers happened quite close to me. As a young college professor in Sierra Leone I had a steward, as they were called, a young man of about 20, who did the housework. On one occasion this young man went to the local hospital to have a tooth extracted. The government dentist who was in attendance extracted the tooth, but in the process he fractured the young man's jawbone. Days after the extraction, the young man was in great pain. He could hardly eat and could barely open his mouth to drink water. I sent him back to the dentist with a note pleading with the latter to treat the fractured jawbone, but the dentist either would not or could not do it, and the young man continued to suffer horribly. In desperation he decided to go home to Guinea, which was his original home, to be treated by local medicine men. Three weeks later he returned perfectly cured. A local medicine man had cured his fractured jawbone. This was something I witnessed at first hand.

The traditional midwives are particularly splendid. They are the ones who deliver the vast majority of African babies. They are very skillful at both pre-natal and post-natal treatment. They know which herbs and other medicines to use before and after child-birth. They know what the mother must and must not do. They are performing a very useful service indeed.

Fortunately, most African governments are now acknowledging the importance of tradi-tional medicine in the national health-care system. They recognize that the national Wes-tern-type system is underfunded and overstretched, and that traditional medicine has some answers for some of the diseases and epidemics that have attacked the African continent, and that Western medicine sometimes does not. They are therefore trying to integrate traditional medicine and the activities of the traditional healers into the national system. The African Union has encouraged this trend. At their annual meeting held in Lusaka, Zambia in 2001, the heads of state of the AU agreed to get their countries to investigate the ways in which traditional medicine could be incorporated into national health systems and thus become an important part of the drive to meet the health challenges of a modern African continent. They decided to launch the 2001–2010 Decade of Traditional Medicine. In particular, emphasis was to be placed on research into traditional African cures and traditional medi-cines, and all the evidence suggests that this is yielding good results.

Africa thus faces numerous health challenges. In order to confront these, substantial resources need to be devoted to healthcare and some of the resources will inevitably come from international agencies. The governments and peoples of Africa need to adjust their attitudes on certain issues. Emphasis must also be placed on the incorporation of traditional medicine into national health systems. All the evidence suggests that all this is going on now.

References and suggestions for further reading

Abdullahi, A. A. 2011. "Trends and Challenges of Traditional Medicine in Africa." *African Journal of Traditional, Complementary and Alternative Medicine* 8 (55): 115–123.

Centers for Disease Control. 2002. HIV/AIDS Special Surveillance Report NO, 5 HIV Testing Survey. Washington, DC: Department of Health and Human Services.

Chaisson, R., and N. Martinson. 2008. "Tuberculosis in Africa: Combatting an HIV Driven Crisis." *New England Journal of Medicine* 356: 1089–1092.

Dervarics, C. 1999. "Uganda Beats Back HIV/AIDS." *Population Today* 27 (November): 5.

Gordon, A. 2007. "Population, Urbanization, and AIDS." Pp. 203–234 in A. Gordon and D. Gordon (eds.), *Understanding Contemporary Africa*. Boulder, CO: Lynne Rienner.

Gregson, S., B. Zaba, G. Garnet, and R. Anderson. 1998. "Projections of the Magnitude of the HIV/AIDS Epidemic in Southern Africa." Pp. 27–60 in A. Whitehouse (ed.), *Implications of AIDS for Demography and Policy in Southern Africa*. Piertermaritzburg: University of Natal Press.

Guest, E. 2001. *Children of AIDS: Africa's Orphan Crisis*. Sterling, VI: Pluto Press.

Lemoine, M., P.-M. Girard, M. Thursz, and G. Raguin. 2012. "In the Shadow of HIV/AIDS: "Forgotten Diseases in Sub-Saharan Africa: Global Health Issues and Funding Agency Respon-sibilities." *Journal of Public Health Policy* 33 (4): 430–438.

Loewenson, R., and A. Whitehouse. 1998. "HIV and AIDS in Southern Africa." Pp. 13–26 in A. Whitehouse (ed.), *Implications of AIDS for Demography and Policy in Southern Africa*. Pietermaritzburg: University of Natal Press.

McNeil, Jr., D. 2005. "A Path to Cheaper AIDS Drugs for Poor Nations." *The New York Times*. Online at www.nytimes.com (January 26).

Miller, N. and R. Rockwell (eds.). 1988. *AIDS in Africa: The Social and Policy Impact*. Lewiston, NY: The Edwin Mellen Press.

Rhugani, P. 1993. "Love in a Plague of Hatred." *New Internationalist* 250 (December).

Stillwaggon, E. 2002. "HIV/AIDS in Africa: Fertile Terrain." *Journal of Development Studies* (August): 1–22.

UNAIDS. 2002. Report on the Global HIV/AIDS Epidemic. Geneva: UNAIDS.

UNAIDS. 2005 "AIDS Epidemic Update December 2005 Sub-Saharan Africa." Online at www.unaids.org.

United Nations Development Program. 1996. Development and the HIV Epidemic: A Forward Looking Evaluation of the Approach of the UNDP HIV and Development Program. New York: UNDP.

Walker, L., G. Reid, and M. Cornell. 2004. *Waiting to Happen: HIV/AIDS in South Africa*. Boulder, CO: Lynne Rienner.

Whitehouse, A. (ed.). 1998. *Implications of AIDS for Demography and Policy in Southern Africa*. Pietermaritzburg: University of Natal Press.

World Bank. 1993. *Better Health in Africa: Experience and Lessons Learned*. Washington, DC: International Bank for Reconstruction and Development.

World Bank. 2000. *World Development Report 1999/2000: Entering the 21st Century*. Washington, DC: World Bank/Oxford University Press.

World Health Organization. 2002. World Health Report 2002: Reducing Risks, Promoting Healthy Life. Geneva: World Health Organization.

Zewde, A. 2005. "The Health of Africa and the Diaspora: Confronting Crisis and Charting New Directions." Pp. 513–537 in M. Azevedo (ed.), *Africana Studies: A Survey of Africa and the African Diaspora*. Durham, NC: Carolina Academic Press.

12 Education in Africa

One of the most widespread misconceptions about Africa is that it was the imperialists who brought education to Africa when they occupied the African continent towards the end of the nineteenth century. Before that, the assumption goes, Africans could neither read nor write and therefore had no access to the wealth of knowledge that was available in other parts of the world, especially Europe. Nothing could be further from the truth. Even if one accepts the fallacy that education simply refers to the ability to read and write, it must be acknowledged that there were several literate societies in Africa before the arrival of the Europeans, and quite a few of the languages, like Mende among the Mendes of Sierra Leone, Amharic among the Ethiopians, and Arabic among the North Africans, were written languages. Some of those who claim that there was no education in Africa prior to colonialism think of education only as a formal, structured activity with children going to school to be taught by trained members of the community. Of course, this amounts to a gross simplification of the concept of education. But even if one accepts this fallacy, one would have to acknowledge that there was formal structured educational activity in many parts of Africa before the advent of colonialism. There was the great medieval university of Timbuktu to which students and scholars went from many parts of Africa. The texts used by these students are still available for examination today. One would also have to point out that the oldest university extant in the world is not Oxford or Cambridge or Bologna or Paris, but Fez in Morocco, which goes back to the ninth century. A lot depends on how one defines education. One definition that is universally acceptable is that education is the process whereby individuals are given the skills necessary for them to be acceptable, well-adjusted, and contributing members of their society. If that definition is accepted, then it should be clear that education could be both formal and informal and that every society must have its system of education; that is, its system of grooming its members to become acceptable, well-adjusted, and contributing members of the society. This certainly applies to every African society. Long before the advent of the Europeans, structures were available in Africa for ensuring that the young were taught the values of the society and were properly equipped to become valuable contributing members.

The nature of traditional education

Let us therefore begin this chapter by discussing the nature of education in traditional African society. This is a topic that is increasingly attracting the attention of those interested in education, like Mbiti, Fafunwa, and Chrispen Matsika of Zimbabwe whose interesting book, *Traditional African Education*, is a useful survey of the subject. I owe

DOI: 10.4324/9781003111733-13

many of the insights contained in this chapter to all three. In traditional Africa, education was the process whereby the young were equipped with the skills, attitudes, and other forms of behavior that were of positive value to the society. It was also the process whereby knowledge was disseminated or handed down and the culture of the society transmitted so that it could be perpetuated and sustained and there would be a guarantee that the entire society would move forward in a rational direction (Fafunwa, 11). For his part, Mbiti stresses the collective and formal nature of traditional African education. As we have seen, traditional African education could also be informal, but Mbiti is certainly right in stressing that it is also both formal and collective. We shall soon be looking at its formal nature. Let us stress at this point, as Mbiti does, that it is collective in the sense that it responds to and provides for the needs of the entire society and therefore has intimate ties with social life. Although it is concerned with the development of the individual, it concentrates more on the needs of the society as a whole than those of the individual. Indeed, in Fafunwa's view, traditional education becomes the means whereby individuals lose their isolation and proceed to become fully integrated members of the community or the entire society. Like education in other societies, it is a gradual process with various stages that match the physical, emotional and mental development of the individual.

The aims of traditional education

The aims of traditional education in Africa are broadly similar to those of other educational systems although there are some differences. They have been aptly summarized by Matsika:

a   To understand that all life is joined, and that everything relates to all other things in a physical and metaphysical way;
b   To make everyone understand their bloodline in the family, the clan, and the tribe as whole;
c   To acquire the various skills necessary to become a contributing member of society;
d   To be an expert in at least one profession;
e   To educate in analytic skills and the application of knowledge to life situations;
f   To develop will power, asceticism, stoicism, and self-control;
g   To develop character;
h   To teach the value of respect for elders and those in authority.(Matsika, 128)

In spite of the similarities, there are some differences between the aims of traditional African education and those of other systems. The major differences are that other systems might not emphasize awareness of the cosmic bonds that exist among all things in nature, suggesting that man is intimately linked to nature, including the animal and the plant worlds, and to the world of the spirits. Also, other systems might not give such high priority to the ability to recognize one's place in the family or to showing respect for elders or those in authority. These are important in traditional African society because of the nature of the African worldview. Otherwise, it is clear that traditional African education has roughly the same aims as other educational systems.

Formal and informal education

As already stated, education in traditional Africa can be carried out both informally and formally, with the informal going on continuously. Girls in Africa do not learn to cook by reading recipes or by being given lessons in cooking, although that is now being done in home economics classes in the formal sector; they generally learn to cook by observing their mothers. This is one of the reasons why, in contrast to what happens in the West, they are always expected to assist their mothers during the cooking process. Boys learn how to look after animals by being with their fathers in the field and observing what their fathers do. As they observe they might not even be aware that an educational process is going on, but it is going on all the same. It is not structured or written down, but it is education all the same, and it is just as important as formal education. It is what might be called "hands-on" or "experiential learning," or "learning beyond the classroom," as some would say. As Matsika says, informal education has often been held to be inferior to formal education and has not always been given the attention it deserves (Matsika, 140). However, it is every bit as important, in the African context anyway, as formal education. It is education through exposure to everyday life experiences or life activities and it could therefore be rightly said that its classroom is the world environment.

The informal "curriculum"

Even with the informal situation, there is what might be called the curriculum; that is, what the young are expected to learn. Firstly, there is what might be called the common curriculum, consisting of the things that both boys and girls are expected to learn. Here are some of them:

a   ability to communicate effectively;
b   ability to give appropriate treatment, including respect, to family and clan members;
c   ability to use common tools and instruments effectively and economically;
d   ability to keep family and clan rules;
e   ability to identify one's position in the family and the clan;
f   ability to carry out instructions and to convey messages effectively;
g   ability to identify family possessions and to protect and value them;
h   ability to withstand reasonable difficulties without complaining.(Matsika, 150–151)

   Then there is a girls' curriculum containing matter that only the girls are expected to learn, and here are some of them:

a   ability to draw water from the well or fountain;
b   ability to plaster house floor and walls with mud and other special soils;
c   ability to recognize and collect vegetables/herbs for food from the fields;
d   ability to care for babies or infants;
e   ability to grind or pound grains like rice or sorghum;
f   ability to collect firewood and carry it home on one's head;
g   ability to dress appropriately, and sit or bend oneself decently.(Matsika, 153–154)

   There is also the boys' curriculum containing matter which only the boys are expected to learn, and here are some of them:

a   ability to look after animals;
b   when and how to clap hands when receiving something, before eating a meal, or when enquiring after the health of the elders;

c   respect for other people's wives and property;

d   reasoning in dispute and playing special games to sharpen their reasoning skills;

e   hunting and looking after the family's livestock;

f   how to behave in the presence of in-laws;

g   ability to withstand hunger for a reasonable time;

h   ability to detect an animal's disease or discomfort;

i   ability to span oxen and plough the fields;

j   ability to defend oneself and protect the animals in one's charge.

(Matsika, 152)

There were some other very important aspects of knowledge that were acquired through the informal system. On the surface, it might seem impossible for the ability in mathematics to be acquired informally. And yet, in traditional Africa, people apparently acquired this ability without going through the formal structured system. They had to have arithmetical ability in order to be able to count their cattle, chicken, sheep and goats, fruits and even vegetables, and engage in commercial transactions. They certainly had to master addition, subtraction, and multiplication, and they mastered these through the informal system. In other words, they did not acquire this ability by being taught by a trained person outside the family, as would be the case in a structured formal system. Many were probably helped to master these activities by their fathers and mothers. Many learned to count as they learned the language, just as one would learn to count in a metropolitan language today if one were learning the language. The ability was enhanced by playing games such as traditional versions of chess and hopscotch. All these proved effective because people in traditional Africa were and still are numerate. I have often marveled at the efficiency with which illiterate market women counted the money they received from their customers and were able to give accurate change. No matter how much money they made and had in the bank they were aware of the total amount and it was impossible to defraud them.

The oral tradition and the informal system

The oral tradition played an extremely important role in the traditional educational system in Africa, particularly in the informal system. The oral tradition in every African society is vast. It includes oral literature, oral history, oral medical information, and so on. Children would learn about the history of their society and their own genealogy from what knowledgeable elders told them. Of particular importance, however, was oral literature, which was also vast. It consisted of epics, legends, myths, poetry, folk tales, riddles, and proverbs. The folk tale and the proverb can be said to encapsulate the values and mores of a particular people to a greater extent than any other form of oral literature. Therefore, when a grandmother gathered her grandchildren around her, after the elders had gone to the farm, and proceeded to tell them stories, it was not only to entertain them, but to begin the process of inculcating into them the values that the society held dear. The characters in the folk tale were generally animals, but they were given human characteristics, and even the children realized that the tales were really about human beings and human behavior. In the tales values like generosity, kindness, bravery, and honesty were applauded and anti-social attitudes and qualities like fraud, dishonesty, deceit, greed, and arrogance were rejected. Although they were told in an informal setting, the tales gave moral and social instruction to the young. So did the proverbs.

Collectively, a particular people's proverbs give an accurate representation of that peo-ple's character, values, mores, and attitudes. Children who constantly hear their elders recite certain proverbs get to know about their society's beliefs, values, attitudes, and character. They are therefore being schooled informally to acquire these. With regard to the riddles, they were told to get the young to sharpen their thinking skills. All this was part of a very effective informal sector of the African traditional education system.

Vocational training

There was an area of the traditional education system that seemed to have components of both the informal and the formal sectors. This was the area of vocational training. It was extremely important in traditional Africa because it involved a number of trades and crafts like traditional healing, working in leather, building, training to be a blacksmith, or training to be a griot. The individual who wanted to have a career in any of these spe-cialties was apprenticed to an expert for a certain length of time during which he learned all the aspects of the trade or craft. In a sense, therefore, it was a formal arrangement because the young individual had a master who was an expert in the area, he had to report for work regularly and punctually, and his completion of the program had to be certified by the master. There were quite a few other rules that had to be adhered to. However, it had some aspects of the informal system. The apprentice learned largely by observation, not through formal lessons, even though the master might tell him from time to time how to do certain things. As in the informal system, this was "hands-on" "experiential learning" whereby the apprentice learned the details of the trade or craft by being actively immersed in it. It was like a traditional internship, and it had been going on in Africa long before the advent of colonialism. In certain parts of Africa even girls had to go through some forms of apprenticeship. Among the Creoles of Sierra Leone in West Africa, for instance, girls were sometimes apprenticed to a "sewing mistress" after they left the formal school but before getting married. Ostensibly, the girls were apprenticed to the sewing mistress in order to learn how to sew. However, very few of them actually became seamstresses. They were actually being prepared for their lives as wives and mothers, because in those days that was the only occupation open to young women in Creole society. For that kind of career they would need to be able to sew and make their own curtains, cushion covers and bedclothes, as well as the clothes of their young children. In fact, their activities at the sewing mistress's went beyond learning to sew. The sewing mistress would often send them to the market to purchase groceries, so they would learn how to bargain and haggle for the goods they wanted to purchase. She also taught them how to cook well. In every sense of the words, then, the girls were being prepared for married life. My own mother had some very interesting stories to tell about her experiences with her sewing mistress and the other girls at the time of her apprenticeship during the early 1930s.

Formal education in traditional Africa: "initiation academies"

Of course, there was also a formal sector in the traditional African education system. In every sense of the word it was a formal system because the young went through the experience for a certain length of time, the activity happened in a specific place at a specific time, the young were taught by experts who did not belong to their families, and these experts actually gave instruction to the young and examined them. It was as formal an activity as anything that happened under the colonial education system. The formal education system involved the initiation activities that marked the transition from childhood to full adulthood in the tribe. They constituted an extremely important rite of passage and were generally conducted by the secret societies associated with the tribe. The purpose was to ensure that before the young individuals became adults they were equipped with the knowledge that every adult member of the tribe ought to have and they knew how to comport themselves, act responsibly, and do all the things that adult members of the tribe were expected to do. In other words, this was the apex of their training in order to become responsible contributing members of their society. The initiation rites and activities, therefore, were educational in every sense of the word. The connection with education is so pronounced that someone like Matsika has referred to their ambience as "initiation academies."

The initiation process is designed to make the youths aware of the behavior, attitudes, and abilities that the society requires of its members in order that they would become fully integrated contributing individuals. They are also designed to reinforce the connection between human beings and nature as well as the world of the spirits and the ancestors. At a certain time of the year, youths who have reached the appropriate age are taken into the forest and secluded from other members of the society. There are different academies for boys and girls. While they are in these camps in the forest they are supervised and instructed by eminent or heroic members of the society appointed by the leaders. These instructors have the responsibility for showcasing attitudes, practices, and behaviors that are socially acceptable and deploring, controlling, or censuring those which are not. Every member of the society is expected to go through the initiation experience because the knowledge that they acquire during the process would not be available to them if they did not.

One of the most important activities during the initiation process is the ritual of circumcision. The world concentrates so much on the circumcision of girls that it seems to forget that in Africa boys are also circumcised. For the boys the act of circumcision is both a physical process involving the removal of parts of the male genitalia that are considered unnecessary, and a symbolic or even spiritual one emphasizing the interconnectedness between humans and the world of nature and the ancestors. During the procedure the young boy's blood is allowed to drip onto the ground, and this represents a merging of the living individual with the earth or the soil from which he came and to which he must return; it also links him with the ancestors buried in that earth and therefore with the living dead and the spirits. The fact that the boy is supposed to become merged with the earth and with nature is extremely important. This largely explains the sense of connection with and belonging to the land, especially the land where circumcision blood was spilt or the umbilical cord was buried. The connection is a spiritual one that many Western people do not understand, since in Western society people move often and therefore do not feel a spiritual or even sentimental connection to the land or the place where they were born. The African has an almost spiritual connection with land or with the earth, which is one of the reasons why he gravely resented this land being appropriated by the colonizer in some cases like Kenya or what is now Zimbabwe.

The circumcision is only a part of a very comprehensive and largely educational process during which the youngster is introduced to all aspects of responsible adult life within the community. The whole process represents entry into adulthood and acceptance of the privileges and responsibilities associated with being an adult. The boys' courage and capacity for endurance also have to be tested and, in a sense, this is one of the things that the circumcision itself achieves. The supervisors cast very wary eyes over all the boys to see how each responds during the process. In traditional African society in the past, courage was a vital quality because enemies must be confronted and defeated and the security of the community maintained. Therefore, every male was expected to demonstrate courage and stoicism. Courage was often tested in other ways. In some societies the boys were expected to demonstrate that they could face and kill wild animals. In other societies where this was not practicable an artificial monster was created, unbeknownst to the boys, and the supervisors watched to see how the boys would react to its roaring. Mock invasions or mock cattle raids would be staged. The boys were also taught the basic skills of rhetoric, warfare, philosophy, and economics and were also instructed in religion and law. The boys would also have practice in the art of debate and argument, thus sharpening their rhetorical skills. They would be taught the significance of proverbs and examined on the meaning of riddles and puzzles. They would go on hunting expeditions, learn relevant songs, and encounter symbolic obstacles. They would engage in activities that suggest their relationship with the ancestors or with the living dead. One of the aims of the initiation was to teach the boys to become responsible fathers and husbands, so they were given instruction in matters of sexuality and responsible manhood.

The initiation of the girls was similar. The intention was to prepare them for entry into full womanhood and responsible adulthood. By the end of the initiation process they should be ready to be responsible wives and mothers, and the training and instruction were geared to that end. Unlike the boys, they were not expected to know the arts of warfare or the basics of rhetoric, or the principles of law. They were supposed to know how to look after their husbands and their children, how to cook, collect water and firewood, and keep their environment clean and attractive. Like their menfolk they also were instructed about their duty to the community, about the capacity for hard work, and about self-respect and respect for established authority. As with the boys, the actual act of circumcision, though painful, potentially harmful, and traumatic, was only a part of this very comprehensive and largely educational process. This explains why many African women are opposed to abolition. Fortunately, solutions are being increasingly implemented whereby the harmful physical act is abandoned while the largely instructional aspect is retained.

At the end of the initiation process, which can last up to several weeks, there is tremendous rejoicing and something like a graduation celebration. The initiates receive gifts from relatives and friends, and, in the case of the girls, there is dancing through the streets of the village or town. The female initiates are usually gorgeously dressed, some of them even in Western clothes and shoes. It is a kind of "coming out" party, and as they parade through the town it is obvious that they are proud of their achievement. Young eligible bachelors normally see this as a splendid opportunity for selecting their preferences for brides.

Formal education in North Africa

The above account largely presents the situation in sub-Saharan Africa before the advent of the Europeans. In North Africa, formal education had been going on all along, and it was closely connected with religion and the Qur'an. The invading Arabs thought that one of the ways of spreading the Islamic religion was to get people to be able to read the

Qur'an, which meant they had to be literate in Arabic. The Muslim invaders therefore set up Qur'anic schools to teach boys and girls the Qur'an and Arabic. The process involved copying verses from the Qur'an on to tablets that could be washed and used over again. The verses were then recited by rote. It was not the best pedagogy, but it worked. As a result of this, many Africans became literate in Arabic, even if they were unable to read in the metropolitan languages. The Qur'anic schools still exist today.

Education under imperialism

As we have seen, the missionaries took the lead in education in Africa during the period of imperialism. The colonial governments were not particularly anxious to see Africans becoming educated because that might lead to challenges to colonial authority. Imperialism was meant to benefit the Europeans, not Africans, and the education of Africans would not have been conducive to the continuation of the colonial grip on African territories. Even when the colonialists began to show an interest in African education it was largely because they needed a cadre of Africans who would man the lowest levels of the administration and thereby help advance the colonial effort. The missionaries preceded the imperialist administrators, and their main intention was to spread Christianity. They saw the education of Africans as a tool in this process.

The first thing the missionaries usually did was to build a church, but they also built a school either as a basement of the church or adjacent to the church. Indeed, the school was used as a means of luring Africans to the church. On the arrival of the missionaries, Africans realized that acquiring the white man's education would be a valuable asset in the future. As we can see in the novels of Chinua Achebe and Ngugi Wa Thiong'o, Africans wished to acquire this new knowledge because it would help them understand and negotiate with the white man and because they realized that the Africans who would be influential in the future would be those who had this knowledge. They therefore wanted to go to school and to send their sons to school. But the missionaries insisted that in order to go to their school the Africans must also become members of their church. Furthermore, they must adopt Western names or "Christian" names. This is the reason why, until recently, the forms that Africans had to complete asked for their "Christian" names, rather than their "first" names. The missionaries were also interested in training local "catechists," as they were called, who would help them in their relations with the locals and help spread the word to other areas and people that the missionaries themselves could not reach. Obviously, these catechists had to have some education.

Although the missionaries have been criticized in modern times, it must be acknowledged that they played a very important role in education in Africa. Without them it would have taken very much longer for Western education to be introduced to Africa, since colonial governments, as we have seen, were not very interested. Many of the missionaries were passionate, sincere, and dedicated. Of course, the education they offered initially was of a very limited kind. Many of them were supported by religious organizations back in Europe, but even so money was in short supply and there were millions of Africans that this education simply could not reach. The curriculum was almost basic, rather similar to what the missionaries themselves had been accustomed to at home. There was some social science (history and geography), but the main emphasis was on religious knowledge and the so–called three Rs: reading, writing, and arithmetic. The intention was not to turn out highly educated individuals, but good Christians who would also be useful in teaching other Africans in the primary schools and in serving as clerks in the lower levels of the colonial civil service. Religious knowledge was sometimes called religious and moral instruction, and it was taught, not only in the schools, but at Sunday school after church on Sundays and in evening Bible classes during the week. There were also evening classes for adults, separate ones for men and women.

As more Africans received education, the missionaries were able to use local teachers, particularly in the primary schools. Later they would even be used in the secondary schools. The use of local teachers went hand in hand with the introduction of corporal punishment into the educational system. With a few exceptions, the white missionaries never used the cane themselves, but they allowed local teachers to administer it. It was generally accepted even by the children's parents. The church sanctioned it because of the biblical statement: "Spare the rod and spoil the child."

The curriculum was limited not only with regard to the range of subjects taught, but also the nature of those that were taught. Thus, there was hardly any science and no physical education, and in the case of the British territories, geography was Western geography, the geography of Europe and the British Isles; history was European history and the history of the British Isles; literature was European literature and British literature. There was no African history and no African geography. Children who were required to know the date of the Battle of Hastings knew nothing about Sundiata or about their own ancestors. This tendency was even more pronounced in the Francophone countries because the French had an educational policy deliberately designed to create black Frenchmen and Frenchwomen out of their colonial peoples and to embrace as many of them as possible within the wider ambit of French culture and civilization. Ultimately, it proved impossible to achieve this drive completely, but it had some success, with disastrous consequences. It resulted in the alienation of many of those who were exposed to the French educational system. These men and women discovered that as a result of their education they had been alienated from their roots in the African tradition. In the Anglophone countries the missionaries actually made attempts to decry aspects of African culture and tradition. They tried to teach that African religions amounted to paganism; that to cultivate an interest in African masquerades, in which most of their students took delight, was tantamount to having interest in the devil; that polygamy was irreligious and immoral. In other words, they tended to look down on various aspects of African culture. It is largely for this reason that the missionaries in Anglophone Africa have come under attack. Fortunately, Anglophone Africans developed the uncanny ability to profit from missionary education while still retaining and appreciating the basics of their culture.

The missionaries advanced both primary and secondary education in Africa. In 1845 they established the first secondary school for boys in sub-Saharan Africa: the Sierra Leone Grammar School which was established by the Church Missionary Society and is still one of the best secondary schools in Sierra Leone today. This was followed in 1849 by the establishment of the first secondary school for girls, the Annie Walsh Memorial School, which is also one of the best secondary schools in Sierra Leone. Similar schools followed in other parts of Africa such as Nigeria and East Africa. In 1827 Fourah Bay College was established for the training of local ministers of religion. It became affiliated with the University of Durham in England, a university with theological leanings, and in 1879 started awarding degrees of the University of Durham.

The French, like the British, left education largely in the hands of the missionaries, although a small number of state primary schools were established. Most of them, like the William Ponty School established in 1903, were in Senegal. The intention was to train low-level local functionaries such as teachers, medical assistants, interpreters, and clerks. It became a rather celebrated school, the only one of its kind in French West Africa, and no less than five eventual presidents of Francophone countries are numbered amongst its alumni (Shillington, 401). The missionaries went on with their activities, establishing both primary and secondary schools. At the end of their secondary school careers the successful students had the opportunity of proceeding to France for further education.

In the 1920s the British political authorities started taking some interest in the education of Africans in their colonies. This was partly due to the report of the Phelps-Stokes Commission of 1921, which was actually an American commission set up to investigate and make recommendations on the education of African Americans. However, it also considered the education of Africans in the British colonies. It suggested that more attention and resources should be devoted to the education of Africans, but quite unsurprisingly it also implied that since Africans lived mostly in rural communities they would need only basic literacy and numeracy and vocational training in areas like agriculture, building and carpentry (Shillington, 401). In other words, it did not foresee a situation in which Africans would become as educated as people in the Western world and aspire towards running their own affairs and promoting the development of their countries. They would be under British or French domination forever. Be that as it may, the British started establishing government secondary schools in some of their colonies. The Prince of Wales School was established in Freetown, Sierra Leone in 1925 and similar institutions were established in other parts of British West Africa, East Africa, and Southern Africa. The curriculum was still rather limited, with not much attention given to science. Indeed, in the whole of Sierra Leone only one secondary school, the Prince of Wales School, gave attention to the teaching of science right up to the early 1950s, and students from other schools who wanted to become doctors or engineers had to transfer to the Prince of Wales after their first school-leaving certificate. There were now two streams of schools, so to speak: mission schools and government schools. Eventually, the British established a unified teaching service, so that whether teachers were employed in government schools or mission schools they had the same conditions of service. This was essential because the missions could no longer afford to pay the salaries of the teachers in both primary and secondary schools. Still, the mission schools only became government-assisted rather than government-supported schools.

Although the curriculum under imperialism was rather restricted and although education was confined to only a few, the standards were fairly high. The missionaries were not the only British teachers in Africa; numerous other highly educated British men and women joined the cohorts of teachers. Some came to have experience of Africa, some were looking for adventure, and some were genuinely interested in spreading education to areas where there were under-privileged people. Whatever their motives, they usually did a very competent job. Also, the school-leaving examinations taken by the students in both the Francophone and Anglophone territories were uniform. Students in all the British territories, whether they were in West Africa, East Africa, Southern Africa, or the West Indies, took the Cambridge School Certificate Examination after five years of secondary school. The examination was the same for all. The papers were set in Cambridge, England, and the written scripts were graded in Cambridge. Those who wanted to, or could, then went on to sixth form for two years and then took the Cambridge Higher School Certificate Examination. If they got the required level of passes, they could then go on to university in Britain, because the examinations were of exactly the same standard as those taken by students in Britain. In the Francophone territories, students took what was called the *baccalauréat*. The *baccalauréat* became a dreaded phenomenon. Success or failure in it made the difference between a flourishing career in the professions or condemnation to a very low-level or even menial job.

During this period the local African teacher was highly respected. He was one of the most literate people in the entire community and he had partaken of the white man's knowledge to such an extent that he was now able to impart it to others. Even if he was a primary school teacher, he was looked up to with something like reverence. He even became something like a sage, and the designation of "teacher" became almost a title. He was also usually a prominent figure in the church. Indeed, most of the ministers of religion were also teachers. Teachers were a substantial proportion of the group that led the drive towards independence and liberation. Several of the independence leaders, like Nkrumah, Mugabe, and Nyerere, were teachers at some time or other. In fact, Nyerere was given the honorific title of "Mwalimu," which means "teacher."

Education in an independent Africa

With the achievement of independence came some real changes in education in Africa. The new leaders realized that under imperialism the system was not really set up to benefit Africans. Illiteracy was still widespread, and there was a desperate shortage of skilled personnel in all fields. Certain vital areas like agriculture and science had been neglected. Substantial development was needed in Africa and the educational system therefore had to be geared towards this development. In other words, the emphasis had to be on education for development. African governments thus committed themselves to the achievement of universal literacy which meant universal free primary education. There was to be a new emphasis on science, math, and agriculture, since agriculture was the mainstay of the economies of most African countries. Africans also had to be made aware of their real identity, and so there was to be a new emphasis on African history, African geography, and African literature. The entire curriculum was redesigned. Africans took control, not only of the curriculum, but also of the standards and the examinations. In British West Africa, the West African Examinations Council was established and took control of the syllabi and the two main school leaving examinations, the West African School Certificate and the West African GCE "A" levels. Similar developments took place in other parts of Britain's former African possessions. The same trend was going on in the Francophone countries. The *baccalauréat* became more Africanized although high standards were still maintained.

In the immediate post-independence period, then, African governments set themselves some very laudable goals in the area of education. However, many of these goals were not achieved. The economic malaise which set in in the seventies and eighties, and the structural adjustment programs that some countries adopted in order to stem the malaise, ensured that fewer resources were devoted to education than was necessary. The field of education was one of the hardest hit by the adjustment policies as governments had to abolish subsidies that would have enabled the schools to purchase equipment and, in some cases, provide scanty meals for the youngest children. In some cases, there was even a reduction in the number of teachers, when there should have been an increase, and the salaries of teachers remained ridiculously low. In general, morale in the educational field was very low during this period of economic decline. Where teachers in the past had been highly respected, they now lost their dignity because they were so poorly paid and were employed in a field that was hardly supported financially.

One of the first casualties of this lack of financial support for education was the drive towards universal free primary education. African leaders kept pledging to achieve it by certain dates which kept being moved further and further. In 2000 the United Nations had adopted the Millennium Development Goals, one of which was to ensure that by 2015 children all over the world would have achieved at least primary education. Not to be outdone, African countries meeting in Dakar, Senegal, adopted the so-called Framework for Action, committing themselves to achieving universal primary education by 2015. The sense of urgency was partly caused by a UNESCO report that suggested that only 57 percent of African children of primary school-going age were actually enrolled in primary school. However, very few African countries met the target. One of them was Ghana which had achieved universal free primary education long before that date, largely through the policies of the country's first president, Kwame Nkrumah. One of the problems involved in the move towards universal free primary education was that the drive resulted in an explosion in the number of school-going children, particularly at the early levels. This explosion also required a substantial increase in the number of trained and qualified teachers. It required the construction of new school buildings and the purchase of more equipment. It was calculated that in order to reach the target by 2015 sub-Saharan Africa would need 1.2 million more teachers. African countries simply did not have the financial resources to provide all these. Some countries tried passing laws that, in theory, made primary education free and mandated all children of a certain age to attend school. However, the notion that primary education was free was really an illusion. It was free in the sense that there were no fees, but the children had to purchase numerous other things like uniforms and books, and their parents had to make contributions to the parents' associations. Some of these were too expensive and beyond the reach of many students who therefore had to drop out of school. Up to the present moment the goal of universal free primary education has not been achieved by all African countries.

The economic malaise hit other areas of education. In some countries, scholarships were abolished. The basic fees were high and sending one's child to secondary school became almost a luxury. Equipment, such as stationery and chalk for writing on blackboards, was in short supply. There was also a desperate shortage of books, since, at that time, most of the books came from the Western world and had to be purchased with foreign exchange which was also in short supply. A common feature in African cities at the time was empty bookstores. One heard desperate stories of teachers who had to teach texts where only about three out of about 30 students owned the texts. Of course, libraries were desperately under-stocked. In some cases, there were not enough desks and chairs for the students, some of whom had to sit on the floor during their classes. There was also a shortage of trained teachers and those who were in the teaching service were severely underpaid. Some had to wait for weeks to get the salaries they had earned. Because of the low level of salaries, some teachers had to take on other jobs to make ends meet. Some were reduced to growing their own vegetables in their backyards. Some had to give private lessons in order to make extra money. The situation led to numerous students dropping out of school and some teachers leaving the profession or joining the brain drain; that is, seeking careers outside their own countries.

With the improvement in the African economic situation and the reinstatement of democratic government that started in the nineties, funding for education also increased, but the situation at the moment is still far from ideal. There has been an explosion in the number of school-going children, largely because of the efforts at universal free primary education. The number of teachers has also increased, largely because many new graduates (whose numbers have also increased) cannot find ideal jobs outside the field of education. With a few exceptions, there has not been much of an improvement in the situation of teachers, many of whom are still badly paid. Many countries continued to institute reforms to take their educational system further away from the colonial arrangement and make it more responsive to the needs of modern African states. For instance, in former British West Africa, there has been a change from the system that compelled students to start specializing at a very early stage of their education. Up till recently, students had to choose as early as the third form (about eighth grade) whether they were going to specialize in arts subjects or science subjects. This happened at a time of their lives when students were hardly in a position to decide on a career. Now, with the three–three–four system (three years in junior secondary, three years up to the school-leaving certificate, and four years at university) students can decide much later. The system is common to all Anglophone West African countries and it also includes Liberia. Books are still a problem, but in most countries there is a thriving local publishing industry that directs its efforts to the production of textbooks for schools. The textbooks are written by local authors who understand the African situation, and they are generally much cheaper than those that used to be imported from abroad. The number of girls attending school is still less than the number of boys. The problem is that education is still relatively expensive and families who have to choose which child to give secondary education almost always choose the boy. However, with encouragement from bodies like the African Union, many countries are doing their utmost to change this situation.

Higher education

Let us now look at the situation in higher education. One of the major misconceptions about Africa has to do with this area. Many Europeans would be surprised to hear that there were universities in Africa before the coming of the white man and the establishment of imperialism. As we have seen, the oldest extant university in the world is in Africa, the University of Fez. Evidence suggests that there were other communities of scholars in North Africa who regularly taught students coming from far and wide. The reason for this was probably that Northern Africa was connected with the Islamic Middle East which was then a bastion of learning. Then there was the great university of Timbuktu which flourished at about the same time as Oxford and Cambridge in England, Bologna in Italy, and Paris in France. It was the first university in sub-Saharan Africa. In a sense, the coming of the Europeans put a stop to the developments in higher education that had been going on in Africa. On the arrival of the Europeans and the onset of imperialism, Fourah Bay College in Freetown, Sierra Leone, was established in order to train local ministers for the Christian ministry. As we have seen, education then was largely in the hands of the missionaries who, in fact, preceded the imperialists. Fourah Bay College was later affiliated to the University of Durham in England and started awarding degrees of the University of Durham in 1879. Fourah Bay College became the center of higher learning in West Africa and even in Africa. To this college came students who wanted higher education but could not afford to go to England. Later, similar institutions were established in other parts of Africa such as Makerere in Uganda. The curriculum was very restricted because the original purpose of the founders of these institutions was not to prepare Africans for independence or to enhance African development. In the case of Fourah Bay College it was to spread the Christian religion. Also, the curriculum was largely modeled on those in Britain and France where it was also limited anyway during the nineteenth century. It focused on the arts or humanities: Latin, Greek, literature, and history. Though mathematics was taught and economics was later added, there was no agriculture, engineering, law, or medicine. These had to be added much later. Fourah Bay College, for instance, started teaching science only in the fifties, and engineering came much later.

It was only after World War II that the British began to realize the importance of higher education in the development of Africa and started establishing more universities in their colonies. Thus, the University of Ghana was established in Legon, Ghana, and Ibadan, Nsukka, and Ahmadu Bello universities were established in Nigeria. With the coming of independence and its achievement there was real change in the nature and purpose of the universities in Africa. The curriculum was now significantly expanded to include disciplines such as rural development, agriculture, education, geology, engineering, home economics, medicine, and law. There was now real emphasis on African history, African geography, and African literature and culture. In other words, African universities were now responding to the real needs of modern African states.

Like other aspects of the education system, African higher education was adversely affected by the economic malaise, though the extent of the suffering varied according to the state of the country's economy. Though sanctions imposed during apartheid hurt a bit, the South African universities continued to do quite well, as did the North African universities. The deprivation was worst in the Anglophone universities, particularly those in Anglophone West Africa. To run universities efficiently great expenditure is needed, particularly in order to keep standards as high as they are in other parts of the world. Many African governments simply did not have the resources to maintain their universities at that level, and of course, at the time, almost all African universities were supported by governments. The experience at the University of Sierra Leone can be taken as typical of the Anglophone West African universities. The first casualties of the inadequate funding were the scholarships which had enabled almost all students who qualified to study at universities. When I joined the faculty at Fourah Bay College, all the students were on scholarships. Within a short time the scholarships were only awarded to very few, mainly those whose parents were supporters of the government. All the students had lived in dormitories on campus in single rooms. Within a short time there was not enough accommodation on campus for students, mainly because of lack of funds for the construction of new dormitories, and those who lived on campus had to share rooms. The dormitories themselves were badly in need of repair, as were the houses for professors on campus. The telephone system broke down completely. There was tremendous shortage of water on campus, mirroring the shortage in the country as a whole, and the same thing happened to the electricity supply. There was also a desperate shortage of equipment and materials such as chemicals and other equipment for the labs, desks and chairs in the classrooms, stationery for the secretarial staff, and, of course, books. The bookstore was a shadow of its former self and ultimately closed down completely. The reference to a teacher teaching a text to a class that had only three copies of the text was really to myself who at one time taught E. M. Forster's *A Passage to India* to a final-year class of 30 with only three copies of the novel in the class. However, there was such dedication and such a tremendous passion for knowledge among these students that they worked out a successful system whereby each of the 30 students got to read the text eventually.

Perhaps the saddest aspect of higher education during this period was the condition of the professors. They were badly underpaid and many of them, like the teachers in the high schools, had to do other things to make ends meet. Many of them could hardly afford cars and had to walk like their students or use public transport when it was available. Before this, professors were almost revered because of their learning. Now there was a diminution in their status because it seemed as if knowledge was no longer at a premium; it was the possession of wealth by whatever means that was highly regarded. Many of them could no longer attend international conferences to keep their information up to date because their universities could not fund their participation at such meetings. Their universities could not always afford subscriptions to the international journals that disseminated new trends in their fields. One consequence of this, though, was that African professors were forced to interact much more with each other within the continent. Increasingly, more conferences were being held on African soil and journals were being published in Africa. This helped professors to keep on top of their disciplines and enhance the development of African ways of looking at things.

One of the reasons for the diminution in the status of professors was the hostility of governments to universities and the higher education framework in general. It was in the interest of African governments to control the universities because, at this time of dictatorships and one-party rule, the universities were the last bastions of opposition and freedom of speech. Usually, one of the first things that African presidents did on coming to power was to get themselves installed as chancellors of their universities. The chancellor was actually the head of the university though not the operating head. The university court was usually the ruling body, rather like a university system board of regents in the United States. Since the chancellor could not be involved in the actual running of the university, he usually appointed a chairman of the university court to represent him and act on his behalf. That way, however, the chancellor/president could control the university, since it was the university court that determined policy, including the appointment of the vice-chancellor/president of the university, who was usually a government nominee. At this time also, most of the universities had been established by the government and were almost exclusively funded by governments. African governments therefore had the means of controlling universities and they often did. This means they often sought to control the appointment of faculty and even the admission of students. I recall a situation in Sierra Leone when the government, under Siaka Stevens at the time, tried to impose a faculty member on my department without going through the normal process of advertising, shortlisting, and interviewing. It must be mentioned that some of the faculty were always in collaboration with the government because they saw that as the only means of advancement. One would suddenly see a faculty member with whom one was suffering during the privation of the times, quit the job, become a member of parliament under the one-party system, and be appointed a member of the government. President Siaka Stevens of Sierra Leone used to boast that he had the PhDs in his grasp because they all had their price or they could be bought for two a penny.

Many African governments were also hostile to universities because of the actions of the students. During this period of autocratic rule the students were about the only people who could actively demonstrate against the governments, and they did so in country after country. In Nigeria demonstrations happened with tremendous frequency and some universities were closed by the government for long periods of time. In Sierra Leone, the students at Fourah Bay College, which had become part of the University of Sierra Leone, staged a fearless demonstration in 1977 against the dictator Siaka Stevens who was about to declare a one-party state. In retaliation, Siaka Stevens sent his All People's Congress (APC) thugs to attack the university. They beat up several of the students, destroyed several buildings, particularly the dormitories, and severely mauled the warden of students. The university was then closed down for quite a long period. All this—the terrible economic situation and the increasing autocratic rule of governments—led to a massive exodus of professors from the continent, commonly known as the "brain drain." They went to countries like the United States, Britain, and Germany, although a few of them also went to other African countries where the conditions were better. The brain drain had a very adverse effect on African universities and on the educational system of Africa as a whole. Whole departments were decimated and properly qualified replacements could not be found. This led to a decline in quality and standards.

One of the ways in which African universities had kept standards high was the use of the external examiner system. This system was mainly used in the former British countries because it was a very important part of the British system itself. According to this system, a university would appoint external examiners for all departments. The external examiner came, not only from outside the university, but usually from outside the country, and he was well noted in the discipline. After the faculty within the university set the tests, they were sent to the external examiner so that he could vet them and certify that they were adequate and comparable to tests from similar institutions. After the students had taken the papers, the external examiner actually came to the university and read samples of the written scripts to ensure that the grading of the internal examiners was fair and consistent. He played a major role in deciding the results for the students. This was an excellent system which served as a kind of accreditation for the universities, ensuring that their standards were roughly comparable to those existing outside the country and even outside the continent. But it was very expensive and, as economies worsened and the financial position of African universities became precarious, it was abandoned altogether, or the universities started to rely on external examiners from within the country. This also led to a decline in standards.

With the return to democratic rule and the improvement of the economies of Africa, the situation of the universities has improved. In some countries like Nigeria and Ghana, the salaries of professors have been increased considerably and some professors who had left during the brain drain are now returning.

One major feature of the present higher education situation in Africa is the explosion, not only in the number of universities, but in the number of private universities, or universities not supported by the government financially. Some of these have been established by religious organizations, some by wealthy individuals. However, they are responding to a real need. The government universities could not cope with the explosion in the number of students wanting higher education. With the explosion in the number of universities, the problem still remains of maintaining standards that are universally acceptable. This still has to be solved. There is still the problem of the availability of suitable books, but the effectiveness of the web and other sources of information has helped considerably in this regard. African governments still have to do more in giving their universities adequate financial support. Many African universities still have to provide adequate housing for the students and the faculty, more equipment in classrooms and labs, and better libraries. More also has to be done in promoting fairness on the part of the faculty and eliminating harassment. Generally speaking, however, African universities are doing fairly well at the moment. *The Times Higher Education* lists the top three African universities as the University of Cape Town, Witwatersrand University, and Stellenbosch University, all in South Africa. Several other South African universities make it into the top ten and are very well ranked internationally. There are some excellent ones in all regions of Africa like Legon in Ghana, the University of Tanzania, and Cairo University. In most African universities there are dedicated students and faculty doing relevant research designed to enhance the condition of Africans.

References and suggestions for further reading

Ajayi, J. F. A., Lameck, K. H. Goma and G. Ampah Johnson. 1996. *The African Experience with Higher Education*. Accra: Association of African Universities.

Bowan, J. 1994. *Theories of Education*. London: John Wiley & Sons.

Brickman, W. 1963. "Tendencies in African Education." *The Educational Forum* 27 (4): 399–416.

Brock-Unte, B. 2000. *Whose Education for All? The Recolonization of the African Mind*. New York: Falmer Press.

Brown, G. M. and M. Hiskett. 1976. *Conflict and Harmony in Education in Tropical Africa*. Rutherford, NJ: Fairleigh Dickinson University Press.

Buchert, J. 1994. *Education in the Development of Tanzania, 1919–1990*. Oxford: James Currey.

Callaway, H. 1976. "Indigenous Education in Yoruba Society." In G. N. Brown and M. Hiskett (eds.), *Conflict and Harmony in Education in Tropical Africa*. Rutherford, NJ: Fairleigh Dickinson University Press.

Carnoy, M. and J. S. 1990. *Education, Social Transformation and Transition States in the Third World*. Princeton, NJ: Princeton University Press.

Erny, P. 1981. *The Child and his Environment in Black Africa: An Essay on Traditional Education*. New York: Oxford University Press.

Fafunwa, B. 1967. *New Perspectives in African Education*. London: Macmillan.

Fafunwa, B. 1974. *A History of Education in Nigeria*. London: Allen & Unwin.

Kamara, M. 2005. "French Colonial Education and the Making of the Francophone African Bourgeoisie." *Dalhousie French Studies* 72: 105–114.

Matsika, C. 2012. *Traditional African Education*. Gweru: Mambo Press.

Mbiti, J. 1989. *Introduction to African Religion*. Oxford: Heinemann Educational Publishers.

Nwauwa, A. 1997. *Imperialism, Academe and Nationalism: Britain and University Education for Africans, 1860–1960*. London: Frank Cass.

Ociti, J. P. 1973. *African Indigenous Education*. Nairobi: East African Literature Bureau.

Okafor, N. 1971. *The Development of Universities in Nigeria*. London: Longman.

Shillington, K. 2019. *History of Africa*. London: Red Globe Press.

United Nations. 2010. "Millennium Development Goals Goal 2 Fact Sheet." www.un.org. September: 3–16.

Whitehead, C. 1987. "The 'Two-Way Pull' and the Establishment of University Education in British West Africa." *History of Education* 16(2): 119–133.

Windel, A. 2009. "British Colonial Education Policy in Africa: Policy and Practice in the Era of Trusteeship." *History Compass* 7(1): 1–21.

13 African technology, music, and art

It is in the fields of technology, music, and art that the misconceptions about traditional Africa, and even about modern Africa, are most glaring. The view is very widely held that Africans cannot use Western technology successfully, and were incapable of devising any technology of their own before the arrival of the Europeans. In the field of music there is the view in some uninformed quarters that Africans are incapable of complex musical expression and composition, and can certainly not handle the kind of music associated with Handel, or Wagner, or Scott Joplin. In other words, they cannot handle classical music or jazz. In art, there was the view that Africans are incapable of producing three-dimensional or realistic works. Yet, it is arguably in these fields that African ingenuity, both in the traditional past and in the modern era, is most powerfully displayed. It is the purpose of this chapter to illustrate this. The chapter will start with a look at technology in Africa in the past and the various ways in which Africans devised technological systems in order to overcome the most daunting obstacles and achieve the most stupendous objectives. It will then go on to look at music in Africa and attempt to illustrate not only the nature of traditional African music, but also the ability of many Africans to handle Western musical forms and to blend both the traditional African with the Western in order to create unique new African styles. The chapter will then end with a look at some aspects of African art in order to illustrate similar points.

Technology in Africa

This section will look at various aspects of technology in Africa. It will start with a detailed look at the technological achievements of Africans in the past and in traditional Africa. It will then go on to consider the ways in which Africans have used or failed to use Western technology. Africans have always been ingenious in devising technologies that are appropriate to the unique African situation, sometimes referred to as "appropriate technology," and this will also be considered. Finally, the section will consider what Africa has to do in order to keep on moving in the twenty first century with technology, both Western and African.

Technology in the African past

In some earlier chapters, we have already seen the stupendous achievements of Africans in the past in the area of technology. We will first look at the pyramids of ancient Egypt, those magnificent structures that are still among the wonders of the world. The first point to be stressed is that these were constructed by Africans, not people from Arabia or

DOI: 10.4324/9781003111733-14

the Middle East. The first pyramids were built as early as about 2600 BC, long before people from the Middle East started to move to Africa. The first pyramid was the pyramid of Saqqara, which was built for the Pharaoh Djoser (2650–2620 BCE), the first king of the third dynasty. As is well known, the pyramids were intended as tombs for the pharaohs, and Djoser intended his pyramid to be the largest structure ever built. The Pharaoh Khufu (2545–2525 BCE) of the fourth dynasty constructed what has come to be regarded as the first perfect pyramid, the famous pyramid of Giza, which became the largest and tallest man-made structure in the world until the construction of the Eiffel Tower in 1889. Other notable pyramids were that built by Khufu's son Djedefra who built his pyramid near Memphis, and that of Khufu's brother and successor Khafra, who also constructed the Sphinx. Khafra deliberately built his on higher ground, so that it would look larger than their father's, but it looks decidedly smaller.

The pyramids are marvels of engineering. They were built with huge blocks of stone each weighing at least a ton. Khufu's pyramid, according to some estimates, consisted of 2.3 million blocks of limestone (Shillington, 39). The blocks of stone were actually quarried several miles away, and therefore had to be transported along the Nile River to the area of construction. This, in itself, was a tremendous engineering feat requiring expert technical knowledge at a time when the tools available to us in the modern age were not in existence. The blocks then had to be cut to the appropriate size and shape, with particular attention being given to getting the angles of the pyramid exactly right. This required expert knowledge of mathematics. Some scholars suggest that the pyramids were constructed in such a way that the rays of the sun would strike them at certain points at certain times of the year. This required expert knowledge of astronomy. The ancient Egyptians were, of course, experts in astronomy and mathematics. They were the ones who developed the world's first 12-month calendar of 365 days. Of course, perfecting the art of pyramid building was not accomplished in a day. It was the result of years and even decades of experimentation and of trial and error, which in themselves illustrate the African capacity for inventiveness, adaptability, and the ability to devise systems to solve the challenges posed by their own objectives. The builders had to ensure that the pyramid did not collapse under its own enormous weight and that it did not start sinking into the soil like the Leaning Tower of Pisa.

The ancient Egyptians were not the only African people with the ability to construct pyramids and other massive stone buildings. There were also the pyramids of Meroe. They were built between 300 BCE and 400 CE, about one thousand years after the Egyptians had stopped building pyramids. These pyramids were smaller than the Egyptian pyramids, but they had their own distinctive features. There were also the very impressive "stelae," the tall stone structures built by the people of Axum in what is now Ethiopia. Each of these structures was built out of one block of solid stone, with beautiful carvings on it. They date from about 300 CE, and the tallest weighed about 700 tons and was 33 meters high. The medieval kingdom of Great Zimbabwe is also noted for its construction of great stone walls and massive stone buildings. It is amazing that these were constructed without the use of mortar, yet some of them are still standing. These Great Zimbabwe stone structures must be also regarded as marvels of engineering. Finally, there are the huge "cathedrals" hewn out of the solid rock in the mountains near Lalibela, Ethiopia, and built by King Lalibela himself (1185–1225).

From what we have seen so far, it is clear that Africans, even in the distant past, had considerable knowledge and skills not only in engineering, but also in astronomy, and mathematics, and some of their structures combined these areas of knowledge. Another extremely impressive structure that demonstrates Africans' competence in these areas in the past goes back to almost the prehistoric period, thousands of years before the Egyptians built their pyramids. This is what is called the "Nabta Playa" in the Nabta basin in the Nubian Desert. Located in Southern Egypt about eight hundred kilometers south of Cairo, it consists of a circle about four meters in diameter with several pairs of huge upright stones on the circumference. There are two rows of smaller stones in the center. The stones are very carefully aligned with each other. The structure is similar to Stonehenge in England where there are also huge slabs of stone placed perpendicularly. However, the Nabta Playa is at least one thousand years older than Stonehenge, going back to 6000 to 6500 BCE. It has now been determined that the structure is a prehistoric observatory or calendar designed to indicate the time of the summer and winter solstices.

As we have seen, Africans' competence in astronomy is indicated in the Egyptians being the first to develop a 365-day 12-month calendar by the observation of the stars. This competence can also be demonstrated by an examination of manuscripts from the medieval university of Timbuktu. These manuscripts tell us of those scholars' involvement with astronomical science. They made use of the Julian calendar. There are diagrams of the orbits of the planets and it is clear that they were capable of complex mathematical calculations. They recorded astronomical events including a meteor shower of 1583. They were the ones who developed algorithms. Some other African peoples were gifted in astronomy too. Indeed, Askia Mohamed, one of the emperors of Songhay, was an astronomer.

The oldest known mathematical artifact in the world is the Lebombo Bone which was found in the Lebombo mountains between Swaziland (now Eswatini) and South Africa. It dates back to about 35,000 years, some say 43,000. It was made out of the fibula of a

Figure 13.1 Nabta Playa.
Source: Raymbetz - Own work, CC BY-SA 3.0,
https://commons.wikimedia.org/w/index.php?curid=7525976

baboon and consists of 29 equally placed notches, so it is rather like a prehistoric rule or slide rule. The 29 notches suggest that it must have had something to do with the lunar month, probably to mark phases of the moon. This has led some commentators to conclude that it might have been related to marking a woman's menstrual cycle, since measuring that cycle has something to do with the phases of the moon. Others suggest that it might have been related to rituals. Whatever it was used for, it is a remarkable artifact that suggests that Africans, even that far back in time, were capable of devising a tool that helped them measure phases and the passage of time fairly accurately.

The ability to work with and shape metals, particularly iron, has always been regarded as an index of advancement. This is why one of the most important eras of civilization has been called the Iron Age. During this period humans learned not only to work with iron, but also to blend it with other metals such as copper or tin, thus producing alloys like steel or bronze that were stronger than iron or could be used for various purposes. The competence with metals such as iron became the basis for the foundation of states, kingdoms, and empires, and led to an expansion of trade. There is evidence that as early as the first century CE iron was one of the major items of trade between Africa and other areas such as the Middle East. Indeed several countries in Africa are rich in iron ore deposits. However, the iron originates as an ore, that is an iron-bearing rock, and the iron itself has to be extracted from the rock by a complex technological process known as smelting. There is evidence that Africans had mastered, not only the art of smelting, but also that of converting the iron into steel, some 2000 years and more ago, long before the process was available in Europe. This happened in sub-Saharan Africa, in areas between Lake Chad and the Great Lakes in Eastern Africa. The process was carried out in iron furnaces dug below ground or in circular clay structures above ground. Bellows were used to provide oxygen and keep the temperature high, and lime from sea shells was also used to aid the smelting process. The ability to work with metals resulted in some outstanding examples of works of art in many parts of Africa as we shall see later. The most famous of these are the world-famous Benin bronzes made in the kingdom of Benin which is now part of Western Nigeria.

It is possible to believe, from reading some books and reports in the press, that in the traditional past the only buildings Africans were capable of constructing were mud huts. Yet there were marvels of architecture in traditional Africa. Architecture is, of course, linked to technology since the form and design of the building have to take into consideration whether it would stand and how it could be constructed. One such marvel of architecture and construction is the Great Mosque at Djenne in medieval Mali. It is the largest adobe building in the world and is as large as many Western cathedrals. It was a tremendous engineering feat to construct such a huge building which was still standing when the French explorer Rene Caillie "discovered" it in 1827. The mosque had been built in the thirteenth century, and from Caillie's report we know that it was in a state of disrepair, largely because in the desert's heat the plastering has to be continually renewed. However, the report still suggests a most impressive building. The mosque was substantially rebuilt between 1834 and 1836, and again in 1907. On both occasions the original design was largely retained, and the original materials largely used, so that the mosque today looks substantially as it must have done in the thirteenth century. It has been named a UNESCO Heritage Site. One of its most impressive aspects is that although it is almost in the middle of the desert, the materials used render the interior quite cool.

African ingenuity and technological ability were also displayed in the field of medicine, in the accomplishment of tasks that would today be possible only with the help of modern technology. The ancient Egyptians were extremely competent in medicine. We know that the Greek historian Herodotus commented on the skills of the Egyptian doctors and even mentioned that there was a high degree of specialization among them. They were extremely good with diseases of the stomach and intestinal tract, the heart, the lungs, and the head. Also, evidence derived from the examination of bone remains suggests that the Nubians used tetracycline between 350 and 550 CE. This is hardly surprising since some of these drugs were and still are extracted from herbs and plants and the traditional medicine men had mastered the technology of extracting them from the herbs though they might have used other methods than those used today and called these drugs by different names.

African skill in medicine was not confined to the Egyptians and North Africa. There was an astonishingly high level of development in the medical field south of the Sahara also. For instance, European travelers in the Great Lakes region around Rwanda and Uganda observed caesarean sections being performed, and they were performed quite regularly and successfully. The people who performed these made use of an anesthetic derived from banana wine. From the surviving texts that were used at the University of Timbuktu, we know that the Malians also had remarkable medical skills. They knew about malaria and its causes and they could perform surgical operations like the removal of cataracts. Traditional Africans also had mastery of the technology used in preserving human and other corpses. We know, of course, that the Egyptians were masters of this art, but other Africans were as well. David Livingstone's very loyal African followers were able to preserve his body as they traveled with it for ten months to reach the coast. I know of at least two occasions when the relatives of the dead person used traditional methods to preserve the corpse for several days before burial because they could not afford the cost of using the mortuary or the funeral home. The preservation is usually done by hunters, and one can understand why hunters in traditional Africa would need to know how to preserve flesh. They might be hunting several miles away from home and the animals they kill would have to be preserved until they return.

Textile technology was another area in which traditional Africans had mastery. We know this from the excellent Kente cloth made by the Ashanti people of Ghana. Finally, some Africans were experts at marine technology and proved this in naval battles. In 1260 the first portable hand cannons loaded with explosive gunpowder was used by the Egyptians at the battle of Ain Jabut. The ancient Phoenicians were particularly adept at maritime technology.

Breakdown in Western technology in Africa

In sum, then, Africans had mastered various aspects of technology and were capable of achieving the most stupendous technical objectives long before the arrival of the Europeans and the imperialists. As happened in so many areas, imperialism actually stifled the development that had been going on. Africans were then introduced to Western technology, and though they first took to it and used it fairly well, a period of deterioration set in. This was roughly contemporaneous with the economic and political decline of the seventies and eighties. One of the most remarkable moments in Ali Mazrui's documentary series *The Africans: A Triple Heritage* was that in part seven, "A Garden of Eden in Decay," which illustrates how aspects of Western technology were breaking down all over the continent. These included water supply and plumbing systems, electricity systems, telephone systems, railway systems, and so on. I was teaching at the University of

Sierra Leone at the time and can attest to the accuracy of this report. The elevator in the seven-story Kennedy Building on campus did not work for several years (and is probably still not working), because electricity was in short supply. Even if the power came on from time to time, people refused to use the elevator because the power could go off suddenly and they would be stuck in the elevator. The telephone system also broke down completely and remained broken for several years. The water supply system could be off for a whole week, and one had to store water in containers and bathtubs whenever it came on. Of course, the railway system was so bad in some places in Africa that it was discontinued altogether.

Let us now look at the reasons for this almost total breakdown in the use of Western technology. It is certainly not that Africans did not know how to use Western technology. Many Africans received training in its use in Europe and other places and on their return home proved very competent. The main problem was the lack of resources in many African countries during the seventies and eighties. Money and foreign exchange were in short supply both to train enough people in the use of Western technology and to purchase spare parts or new equipment. This proved decisive. Technology all over the world will break down sooner or later and will either need to be replaced or repaired. For this, financial resources are needed, and African countries were lacking in this regard at the time. Another important factor was the widespread corruption that prevailed. At times, money would be voted by a concerned parliament, aid would be obtained from a helpful foreign donor, or a loan might be obtained from an international agency to repair the system or install a new one. However, most of the money found its way into private bank accounts and very little was devoted to the purpose for which it was obtained: the repair or replacement of deteriorating technology. In Sierra Leone for instance, ferries were normally used to transport travelers from Freetown across the estuary of the Sierra Leone River to the airport and vice versa. On one occasion almost all the ferries broke down and money was obtained for replacements. However, most of the money disappeared, and, instead of new ferries, very shoddy, second-hand ones were purchased. Of course these also broke down within a very short time, thus causing tremendous inconvenience to travelers and great harm to the economy.

There is another important factor affecting Africans' successful use of Western technology, which has seldom been considered. This is the concept of exactness. Experience has shown that many Africans accept approximation rather than exactness, maybe because of traditional beliefs and attitudes. In the traditional arena many Africans will not be able to tell when exactly they were born, or when exactly a relative passed away. They will tell you that it was at the time of the full moon or when the great famine occurred. This has often been used to demonstrate that Africans have no sense of time. That is incorrect. It is not that Africans have no sense of time; it is simply that many don't consider that exactness is crucial. Unlike the practice in the West, it does not seem to be the African way to measure the passage of time exactly by clock and calendar. However, a sense of exactness is necessary in order to operate Western technology successfully. If a necessary spare part for a car needs to be three-quarters of an inch in diameter, it has to be three-quarters of an inch in diameter or it will not work successfully. However, a well-intentioned African mechanic will tell you that although he was unable to get the three-quarters of an inch item, he was able to get one that was five-eighths of an inch and he would try that one. Of course, he will try it, it will get the car going and it will work for a time, but the car will subsequently break down again. Fortunately, with education and other kinds of training, the need for exactness is being slowly inculcated.

The mechanic's willingness to try the five-eighths of an inch diameter item and Africans' general acceptance of approximation should not necessarily be criticized, because it is related to something positive about the African's attitude to technology in general, and that is the capacity for improvisation. Africans are extremely good at improvisation. In certain circumstances certain things might be in short supply, but Africans always demonstrate a remarkable ability to devise other things to be used instead. This is another index of African ingenuity. I can remember the time when I was very young and Western toys were not available. My brothers and friends and I were very good at making our own toy cars out of wire and wooden thread reels. We also made little boats out of paper and Plasticine. The capacity for improvisation reached its zenith during the Biafra/ Nigerian Civil War of 1967 to 1970. Most of the Western nations supported Nigeria and were therefore unwilling to supply ammunition to Biafra. Biafran scientists proved very adept at making their own ammunition, particularly the very effective bombs called "onuwigwe" which wreaked havoc on Nigerian forces.

Appropriate technology

Africans have always been very good at devising a technology that is appropriate to African conditions. The conditions might be financial or climatic. We have already seen the example of the Great Mosque at Djenne in ancient Mali, where adobe or mud was used because it was readily available and it helped to cool the mosque's interior. There are many smaller examples of appropriate technology in Africa. In many countries, water for drinking is kept in what are called "country pots." These are large earthenware pots made of porous clay. There are also smaller ones called "coolers." The general intention is to keep the water cool in areas where there were, and still are, no refrigerators, and the water is definitely kept cool. Apparently the principle used is about the same as that used in an actual refrigerator. It has to do with latent heat. The porosity of the clay means that the water in the pot somehow has to escape or even evaporate. In order to do this, it uses the heat latent in the water and the water's temperature is reduced.

All over Africa today there are ovens and stoves designed to use charcoal or wood because of the unavailability or unreliability of electricity. One of the most fascinating is the small local iron or "goose" as it is called, which is used for ironing clothes. Charcoal is put in the goose made of iron, and the charcoal is lit. There are holes in the side to let in air or oxygen and keep the coals red hot. Finally, in some parts of the continent ingenious systems have been devised for filtering unclean water by passing it through sand and pebbles.

Africa and technology in the twenty-first century

In order to promote development in the twenty-first century Africa will have to come to terms with Western technology. Of course, there will be advances in the field of appropriate technology and Africans will have to investigate ways in which traditional African technological expertise can be modified and utilized to meet modern demands. However, the demands of globalization and a global environment will surely dictate that Africans become comfortable with Western technology or they will fall behind. Africans will still need working telephone systems, electricity generation systems, and water storage and distribution systems. There will still be a dire need for medical technological systems developed in the West. However, the area of Western technology that will probably be most needed and have the greatest impact is information technology. The effect that computers can have on African development is almost unimaginable. Computers will be invaluable in the field of medicine, with African doctors being able to have immediate contact with their colleagues in other continents and compare notes on diagnosis, treatments, and the nature of diseases. Computers will also be invaluable in business and, above all, in the field of education. With a continuing shortage of qualified teachers and of books, computers will be a tremendous source of information and knowledge for students. One can easily imagine situations in which courses that are unavailable at the students' school or college can be taken online with another institution. It should be possible for African students to take online courses offered from another continent. Of course, cell phones are already being widely used in Africa, because of the breakdown of the landlines. In some African countries, almost everyone, from market women to students, possesses a cell phone, and they have become invaluable in many areas of activity.

The successful use of technology, whether it be indigenous or Western technology, will require enormous financial resources. Putting a check on corruption, as many African governments are presently trying to do, will surely help. It will mean that funds for acquiring or repairing the technology infrastructure will be used for that purpose and the technological decay that was characteristic of the 1970s and 1980s will be avoided. There will be a continuing need for the training of personnel to operate this technology successfully, but provided the funds are available, this should not be a problem. African resilience and adaptability have already made it possible for many Africans to acquire such expertise. However, there will also have to be significant changes in attitudes and an awareness of the problems that might arise from an uncritical adoption of some aspects of Western technology. Africans, while retaining their capacity for improvisation and inventiveness, might have to be more alive to the concept of exactness and realize that certain things have to be done precisely as the designers or manufacturers intended. They will also need to be aware of the dangers of information technology. Not all the sources of information are reliable and one has to acquire the ability to discriminate among "the good, the bad, and the ugly." This particularly applies to the so-called "social media" which can be misused and abused and is sometimes used to disseminate misinformation. Africans must also be aware that it is possible to become addicted to certain aspects of information technology, such as video games, and lose that very African quality, the ability to communicate with other people and consolidate relationships. Provided these caveats are borne in mind, Africans should be able to move fairly smoothly in the twenty-first century with technology, particularly Western technology, and the evidence suggests that this is already being done in some countries. African ingenuity and inventiveness are reasserting themselves. It was announced recently that the Ugandans have succeeded in creating a car brand making use of entirely African materials and African technical knowhow. The South Africans are also making use of their innate ingenuity and coming forward with all kinds of inventions. For instance, in 2001 Ken Hall perfected the charcoal briquette stove. This can be regarded as appropriate technology because the stove uses charcoal, which is readily available, rather than gas, electricity, or paraffin, which are more expensive and can cause fires. It is particularly useful in the rural areas. In 2005 Mulalo Doyoyo invented a paint made out of recycled industrial waste. Provided the right attitudes are adopted, the prospects for technology in Africa are bright because ingenuity and the capacity for inventiveness are certainly present.

Music in Africa

This section is entitled "Music in Africa" because it discusses not only African music, traditional and contemporary, but also African attitudes to Western music, particularly classical music, and the role that this plays in Christian societies in Africa. Indeed, the section will start with an overview of classical music in African society and then go on to discuss traditional African music and modern African popular music.

The Christian influence on music in Africa

Many people in the West will be amazed to hear that there are numerous people in Africa who are quite comfortable with Western classical music. Yet, in many parts of Africa, Western classical music is part of the musical scene. This is largely due to the influence of Christianity. The Christian missionaries brought, not only a doctrine, but the music that was associated with that doctrine. Converts were taught to sing Western hymns to Western tunes. Eventually choirs emerged, particularly in the Anglican, Methodist, and Roman Catholic churches. Many individuals learned to read music and many also learned to play the organ and become organists in churches where the service became more and more elaborate. Many of these African churches adopted exactly the same liturgy and rituals that were used in the parent churches in the West, and so Africans learned to chant the psalms and canticles like the "Venite." Organists led their choirs in the singing of "anthems" in exactly the same way as they would be sung in the West. My father was born in a village in Sierra Leone in 1909 and was baptized into the Anglican Church. He found the congregation in the Anglican church in this village singing psalms, hymns, and anthems accompanied by a small organ called a harmonium. He started singing in the choir himself even before he entered his teens and eventually bought the harmonium from the church when they sold it for a bigger organ. He told us a lot of stories of brilliant Sierra Leonean organists who could perform on massive organs just as competently as Western organists. I can confirm the truth of this as I also knew some of these organists and heard them perform. The amazing thing about these organists was that they were not professional musicians, in the sense that they had not studied music at college or other musical institution. They had other careers and took up music in their spare time. But they became so proficient that some of them played as competently as modern Western organists who have studied music at university. The same was true of the choristers. In fact, some of them could not even read music, but they learnt their parts by heart and were able to participate in the singing of some very complex pieces. The congregations too were quite proficient. Not only did they join in the singing of the hymns, most of which they got to know by heart, they were also very good at the singing of the psalms and canticles, which is not an easy thing to accomplish.

It was easy for organists and their choirs to move from simpler religious music to more complex pieces by Bach, Mozart, Mendelssohn, Haydn, Handel, and others. For instance, some of the better choirs might choose to sing a chorus like Handel's "For unto Us a Child is Born" as the anthem on Christmas Day. The choirs not only sang anthems and excerpts from major works by these composers, they also performed the entire works: cantatas, oratorios, and masses. Most of the choirs observed what was called "choir Sunday" during which the choir was on display and was expected to perform a major work by one of the great classical composers. Handel was particularly popular, largely because of *The Messiah*, but the other oratorios, like *Israel in Egypt*, were performed as well. Musical societies were formed in major African cities, like the Free-town Choral Society, which performed Handel's *Messiah* in its entirety in 1991 to commemorate the two hundred and fiftieth anniversary of the oratorio's composition. Similar things were happening in other Anglophone countries like Ghana, Nigeria, Kenya, Uganda, and so on. Christianity was therefore largely responsible for the intro-duction of Western classical music to Africa and many Africans proved responsive to it. With the expansion of African universities, departments of music are springing up that include traditional African music as well as Western classical music in the curriculum. It must also be noted that Africa has produced some excellent performers on the piano. The performances of the Nigerian Akim Euba are almost legendary. Indeed, Africa has produced some excellent professional musicians who are proficient in classical music. The Nigerian Fela Sowande is a case in point. Though steeped in his native musical tradition, he became world famous for composing music in the classical tradition. Born in 1905 to Christian parents (his father was a priest and a music enthusiast) he joined the choir of the Cathedral Church of Christ in Lagos as a boy. His compositions in the classical tra-dition have been performed all over the world. He died in 1987.

Traditional African music

The first point to make is that there is great diversity in so far as traditional music in Africa is concerned. In the first place, the music of the North African countries like Egypt, Tunisia, and Morocco is quite different from that of most of Africa south of the Sahara. The music of these Northern countries is much more like that of Middle Eastern Arabic-speaking countries. But there are differences even among the sub-Saharan coun-tries, in spite of similarities. It is possible to tell the difference, for instance, between West African music and Southern African music. The late Professor Kwabena Nketia, the world's leading authority on African music, in discussing the main characteristics of sub-Saharan African music and the commonalities that exist, implies that the basic differential of African music is a matter of rhythm. In other words, African music leans towards rhythm, especially a particular kind of rhythm, in ways that other kinds of music do not. I once heard Professor Nketia demonstrate that by adding a different rhythm to the famous carol "Good King Wenceslas" one could transform it from a European to an African song. He famously introduced the use of 6/8 time as opposed to triplets in duple time as the basic method of transcribing African music. But though Nketia laid stress on the commonalities, he was also aware of the diversity of African music. He referred to the diversity of expressions that African music accommodates, a diversity arising from different applications of common procedures and usages. He saw the music of Africa as being "ethnic bound" with each society practicing its own variant. So there are com-monalties, but each society also has its own mode of expression. Some other common-alities of African music are the content of songs and the role of musicians. This section will look at songs and singing in traditional Africa and then go on to consider African musical instruments and instrumental music. The discussion of songs and singing will also include dancing.

African songs

Africans are very fond of singing, and singing is a very important aspect of African music. Africans will break into song for any excuse and on all occasions, whether they have good voices or not, and they will sing lustily and full-throatedly. As with other forms of African art, songs almost always have a purpose. The singing might be personal, in what Roderic Knight and Kenneth Bilby refer to as "personal music" (Knight and Bilby, 254). This is music in which only one person is involved, or, in the case of singing, only one person is singing. It may be a mother singing a lullaby to her child; it may also be a woman spontaneously breaking into song as she pounds rice or millet in a mortar, or as she grinds corn on a grinding stone. However, there is one kind of song in traditional Africa that is done by only one person, but it is intended for the ears of others, so there is more than one person present, although only one person is singing. This is the performance of the "griot" who is a trained professional. The griot is an artist in West Africa who goes through a period of training that may last up to seven years. Usually, he learns the history of the tribe and memorizes epics and other stories about the exploits of legendary ancestors, and he is expected to recite or perform these from memory on special occasions and on the orders of the king or other authority. But he does not merely recite the stories; he "sings" them, in a kind of chanting mode, to the accompaniment of musical instruments. The griot could also, on occasions, sing the praises of members of the audience, particularly the person who has commissioned his performance.

Songs can also be sung by an entire group. It may be a group of children singing together while playing a game. It might be the entire community singing to celebrate a harvest or a wedding or at a funeral. It might be initiates who have just graduated from the initiation academy singing together in celebration. One of the most impressive demonstrations of the beauty of African music happens when the members of the female Bundu secret society in Sierra Leone sing and dance through the town with the beautifully dressed initiates accompanied by a variety of musical instruments and often breaking into delightful harmony.

Choral music, in the sense it is known in the West, is not very common in traditional Africa. However, this is not to say that Africans are incapable of practicing polyphony, or breaking into two or more distinct parts. As we have seen, the members of the Bundu society in Sierra Leone do so with perfect ease, although in this case only women are involved. However, polyphony reaches heights of perfection and complexity among the Bambuti and Babenzele of Central Africa in the Democratic Republic of the Congo. These are the people otherwise known as the pygmies, and it is amazing that people who have been regarded by some as being primitive are the ones who can achieve heights of polyphonic complexity unknown even in the West. They have the ability of spontaneously breaking into song and dividing into seven or eight parts. Knight and Bilby suggest that they could break into as many parts as there are people, and some of the performers at times are children (Knight and Bilby, 259). All the parts are in the same key and the gradations among them are absolutely accurate. The whole thing merges into beautiful harmony.

As can be seen from the foregoing discussion, there are various kinds of songs in traditional Africa, depending on the content and purpose. Apart from those mentioned above, there are also work songs, cult songs, and praise songs. Work songs are often made up spontaneously by groups of men or women engaged in a common activity. A group of men cutting the grass outside a building or a group of women loosening the earth with their hoes on a farm could break into spontaneous singing. They might sing old songs that they all know, or they might just as easily make the songs up spontaneously as they work. The song's rhythm will almost certainly correspond to the rhythm of their movements as they work. Cult songs are used by members of a cult or secret society as part of their rituals. It might be only the leader or celebrant who recites or sings the song; or it might be all the members together.

The most common kind of traditional African song is the praise song. As seen in the discussion of the role of the griot, the praise song is often sung by one individual in praise of a leader or hero or someone who has performed some tremendous feat. The subject of the song is usually an extremely important person. The singer usually improvises as he goes along, enumerating the qualities or actions of the subject. It is not only humans who are praised; at times, people might sing the praises of their cattle or other animals if those animals are doing well. However, the praise song can also be inverted to denounce or expose someone who has been behaving badly. It can thus be used for the purpose of satire in order to affirm the values of the tribe. It has to be noted that certain kinds of songs that are common in the West are not found in traditional Africa. There are hardly any love songs. This is probably because the concept of romantic love was late in coming to Africa. Also, ballads, or the telling of a story in song, verse by verse, are also rare. Most cultures, however, have epics, which can also be sung.

A very important feature of traditional African singing is what is known as "call and response." This is usually done by a group, but there is always a leader who sings out the "call" or opening statement. The rest of the group then responds with a refrain. The leader can then change the call, and the "chorus" similarly changes the response. The leader's position gives him tremendous flexibility and opportunity for improvisation. This singing style has had a marked influence on the music and poetry of other cultures. It is an important feature of African-American poetry and helped to influence the rise of jazz in the United States.

There is no concept of copyright in so far as traditional African music is concerned. The music is supposed to belong to the group or people as a whole and therefore personal ownership of the music is almost unknown. Traditional African music is always transmitted orally and neither the words nor the music are written down.

African dance

There are dances for almost every occasion in traditional Africa. There are festival dances, dances to celebrate a successful harvest, initiation dances, wedding dances, and funeral dances. Some people in the West might be amazed to learn that Africans in the traditional scene dance at funerals. They do so because they are celebrating the life of the deceased and the dancing is an expression of gratitude for a life well spent. It is significant that the practice goes on even today among Africans in the diaspora. At a recent Sierra Leonean funeral in Tampa, Florida, there was a party-like atmosphere the day after the funeral, with lots of dancing; the deceased was over a hundred years old.

Dancing in traditional Africa is usually gender specific. The Western practice whereby a young man engages a young woman to dance with him is hardly known. Women generally dance by themselves in a group, and the men do the same. However, in some cultures there are some dances in which both men and women participate, though not as partners. The dances for the men are usually energetic. The dances for the women are less energetic and characterized by very graceful movements of parts of the body, like the hips, and intricate movements of the feet. A typical dance for women is the Sierra Leonean "Goombay" dance, a dance performed at weddings in which the women dance by themselves to the accompaniment of drums. The women generally engage in friendly competition to show who can perform the most graceful movements of the body or the most intricate movements of the feet. Masks often dance by themselves, like the "hunting" mask of the men's hunting society in Sierra Leone, whose dance is extremely energetic but also includes very intricate footwork. Dancing, often accompanied by singing, can be done by the group or by individuals. One of the most beautiful individual dances is that done by the "Sampas" of the Susu tribe in Sierra Leone, Guinea, and Senegal. This dance is usually done by a young woman suitably attired for the occasion and bedecked with beads and an attractive head-dress. It is a very energetic dance in which the dancer performs the most amazing contortions with the skill of a gymnast. Some group dances can be skillfully choreographed. One example of this is a very virile dance done by the Chopi men in Mozambique to the accompaniment of the Timbila (Knight and Bilby, 254).

African musical instruments

Many in the West know of only one African musical instrument, the drum. Yet there are several indigenous African musical instruments, and the whole gamut of categories of instruments is represented. There are string instruments, wind instruments, percussion instruments, and instruments that provide rhythm. The African xylophone, otherwise known as the Balafon, is very similar to the Western xylophone. It is a fairly large instrument made up of strips of wood securely bound together. These are the keys, like the keys of a piano. Under each of the strips of wood is a gourd. The gourd resonates when the player strikes the key above it and the size and nature of the gourd determines the nature of the note. Because of its similarity to the Western xylophone, some skeptics have suggested that the African xylophone was introduced to Africa by the Portuguese. However, there is indisputable evidence that this instrument was in existence in Africa as early as the fourteenth century; that is, at least a century before the Portuguese started to arrive. It is mentioned in the writings of the Arab traveler Ibn Battuta.

The kora is a stringed instrument combining features of the Western harp and lute. It can be of various sizes. It usually has a long wooden neck which is attached to a gourd that has been cut in half. The gourd is then covered with leather to produce a resonator. Twenty-one strings are then attached to the neck and extended along the entire length of the instrument. The music is produced by plucking the strings. This instrument which goes back to the sixteenth century is particularly popular in West Africa. Another instrument that one plucks is the mbira, which could also be circular or rectangular. Quite often, the main body of the instrument is a tin can, but it could be made out of other materials. Slender strips of metal are attached to the main body and the player plucks them to make the music as he walks along. The player usually sings as he plays.

There are also flutes of all the varieties known in the West: vertical, transverse, and oblique. The flute is usually made out of the hollow stem of a plant. A slit is cut in the side, and one end is blocked as the player blows through the other, thus producing the sound. Other musical instruments include single note trumpets made out of antelope horn, elephant tusks, or wood; castanets; rattles; and scrapers. The last three are part of the rhythm section.

Of all the traditional African musical instruments the best known and, perhaps, the most popular, is the drum. The drum is now played all over the world, but it is native to Africa. The drum is basic to African music because it is almost always present in the background producing the main beat or rhythm. It is difficult to think of a musical activity in Africa that does not include drums. There are various kinds and sizes of drums.

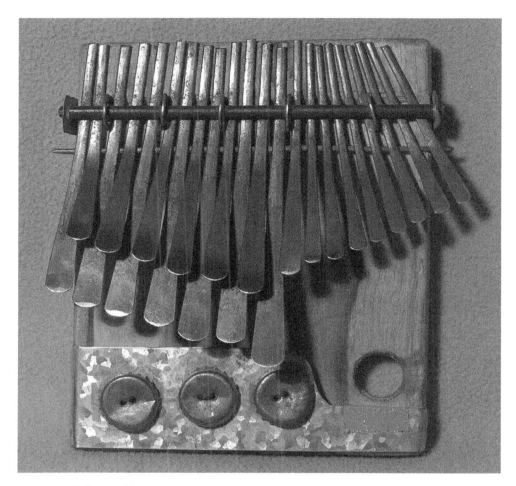

Figure 13.2 African mbira.
Source: By Alex Weeks, CC BY-SA 3.0,
https://commons.wikimedia.org/w/index.php?curid=965892

The most enormous are made out of the trunks of great trees or out of wood. Smaller ones are made out of the trunks of smaller trees or gourds. All are usually covered with hide. There are drums for women and drums for men. There can be solo drums, meant to be played individually and producing a very loud sound or setting the rhythm in the background, and there could be drum ensembles, consisting of several kinds of drums, each with its own rhythm. The main beat is given by the biggest drum, and one of the smaller ones, usually beaten by the leader, establishes the main rhythm or produces the main "theme" and its variations. The most fascinating drum is arguably the "talking

Figure 13.3 African xylophone.
Source: By Didierwiki - Own work, CC BY-SA 4.0,
https://commons.wikimedia.org/w/index.php?curid=55092568

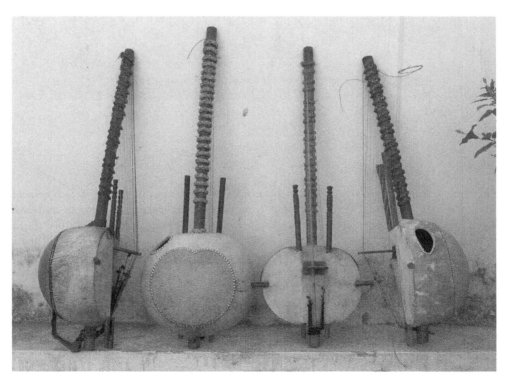

Figure 13.4 Koras.
Source: By Mathaz - Own work, CC BY-SA 4.0,
https://commons.wikimedia.org/w/index.php?curid=55597414

drum." This plays a prominent role in Chinua Achebe's classic novel *Things Fall Apart* where it is used to communicate the news of the death of an elder to the whole clan, some of whom are several miles away. It is an enormous drum called the ekwe, and parts of it could be beaten in such a way that it produces the sounds of the language. Most of the members of the clan can therefore understand the message being communicated.

It is possible to have an ensemble consisting entirely of African musical instruments. Knight and Bilby mention the drum ensembles of the Ewe of Ghana (Knight and Bilby, 258). Although they call this a "drum ensemble" it actually consists of several instruments, not just drums. Apart from the drums there are iron bells and rattles, which, incidentally, can play a major role in establishing the rhythm. Scrapers can also do the same. I was fortunate to be present at a performance given by a purely African orchestra at the 1977 Lagos Festival of African Arts and Culture (FESTAC). There were over 20 musicians in the orchestra and the musical instruments they played were entirely African. The total effect was extremely beautiful and very effective.

Modern African popular music

There is a thriving industry in African popular music with several musicians emerging after the World War II, many of whom have gained a world reputation. Generally speaking, these "pop" musicians have succeeded in blending elements from the traditional with modern influences arising largely from the West. In their songs the traditional elements are unmistakable. The nature of the songs—content, rhythm, and tune—is purely African. What derives from the West are the use of certain musical instruments, like the guitar and the clarinet, certain musical styles like jazz, and the ambience created when these performers are on stage. The use of Western decor, a Western lighting system, and even Western choreographic movements is apparent. While the Western influence is marked, the traditional influence generally predominates. Some notable names are Miriam Makeba from South Africa (1932–2008); Joseph Shabalala, the director of Ladysmith Black Mambazo, also from South Africa (1940–2020); King Sunny Adé from Nigeria (b. 1946); Manu Dibango (1933–2020) from Cameroon (b. 1936); and Fela Ransome-Kuti from Nigeria (1938–1997).

Miriam Makeba can be regarded as the "Queen" of African popular music. She was one of the very first African musicians to be recognized not only in the West, but throughout the world, and she must be credited with bringing African music to the Western world's consciousness. Her flawless performance in songs such as "Malaika" and "Pata Pata," and her commanding stage presence and great vocal range would have done that anyway, but she caught the world's attention even more because of her strenuous and courageous stand against apartheid in South Africa and the oppression of black peoples throughout the world. Indeed, she shot to fame when she starred in the anti-apartheid movie *Come Back, Africa* in 1959 and her second husband was Stokely Carmichael, a leader of the Black Power movement in the United States. Many of her songs are a blistering denunciation of the apartheid system. For this reason she was not welcome in apartheid South Africa and spent most of her time in Europe and the United States. The South African government even prevented her from returning home to attend her mother's funeral in 1960. With the end of apartheid, she returned to South Africa and her international reputation was consolidated. She became a United Nations Goodwill Ambassador in 1999. In all, she released more than 30 albums and received a Grammy Award in 1966. In her songs we see the distinctive feature of African popular music. Her songs blend elements from the traditional, like township tunes, with elements from the West like jazz and even Christian hymns.

Joseph Shabalala, who passed away recently, was the founder and director of the group Ladysmith Black Mambazo, which his obituary in the *Guardian* referred to as "the most popular vocal group Africa has ever produced." The group released 50 albums and won five Grammy Awards. The group started out by capitalizing on traditional folk songs, but they later added Western elements like Christian hymns and other Christian tunes. Their rendition of "Swing Low, Sweet Chariot" became a hit and was used as England's theme song in the Rugby World Cup. The group performed for the Queen at the Royal Albert Hall in 1996 and was invited by Nelson Mandela to accompany him to Stockholm in 1994 to receive the Nobel Peace Prize.

King Sunny Adé (real name Sunday Adeniyi Adegeye) is regarded as the greatest exemplar of Nigerian "juju" music, which suggests his debt to the traditional. Juju music has itself been described as a fusion of traditional Yoruba vocal forms with Western rock and roll. In 1967 Sunny Adé formed his own band, the Green Spots, and later renamed it the African Beats. He launched his own record label in 1974. He always sings in his native Yoruba, and he and his band achieved fame with hits like "Synchro System," "Merciful God," "Samba, "Appreciation," "365 is My Number," "Solution," and "Ariya."

Manu Dibango, who also passed away recently, was a Cameroonian saxophone player whose style was a blend of jazz, funk, and traditional Cameroonian music. He was a member of the Congolese rumba group African Jazz. His first big hit, "Soul Makossa" (1972), had a profound influence on other popular musical hits and other musicians, including Michael Jackson, whom Dibango accused of stealing from the song in the composition of his own "Wanna Be Startin' Somethin'." Dibango was nominated for a Grammy Award and won several other honors.

Fela Ransome-Kuti of Nigeria is perhaps the best known, and was certainly the most exuberant, of all the African popular musicians. He was once described as "Africa's most challenging and charismatic music performer." He was born into a very distinguished Nigerian family, his father being a minister of religion and school principal, and his mother a well-known political activist and feminist. His first cousin was the world-renowned writer and Nobel Prize winner Wole Soyinka. Fela himself gave up the study of medicine in England to study music at London's Trinity College of Music. On returning to the newly independent Nigeria he established his own band, Koola Lobitos, but it was while on a visit to Ghana that he conceived his own personal musical style which he called "Afrobeat." This was a combination of jazz, highlife, funk, salsa, calypso, and traditional Yoruba music. Fela renamed his band, consisting of both males and females, Africa '70, and he established his own musical village in Lagos in which the entire troupe lived. The village was a kind of commune which he called the "Kakatua Republic," and he famously on one occasion declared the "Kakatua Republic" independent from Nigeria. As the years went by his songs became famous for their political and social comment, particularly their attacks on the Nigerian dictatorial regime. For this reason, the "Kakatua Republic" was frequently raided by the government, in one of which raids his mother was killed and the commune was completely destroyed. Fela was well known not only for his showmanship, but also for his remarkable stage presentations which deployed all the accoutrements of modern show business. His instrumentalists were extremely deft, and his songs, some of them in Nigerian pidgin, were quite obviously from the Nigerian tradition. He was particularly adept at the "call-and-response" technique, in which he would make the "call" and the entire troupe would come in with the "response." This can be seen in a song like "Lady." His albums include the famous *Zombie*, *Lady*, and *Beasts of No Nation*. When he died in 1997 his funeral was attended by one million people at the site of the old "Shrine."

African art

Up till very recently, the West did not have a very favorable opinion of traditional African art. One of the main reasons for this was that up to the twentieth century African art consisted mostly of sculpture and carvings, and painting was relatively absent. In the West, on the other hand, art has almost become synonymous with painting. Ever since the great achievements of artists like Giotto, Botticelli, Michelangelo and Leonardo da Vinci during the European Renaissance, painting has tended to dominate the art world, even though sculptures like "David" and the "Pietà" are considered to be amongst the world's most remarkable works of art. In the West, painting, not sculpture, has been regarded as the highest form of art, and, whereas some remarkable works of sculpture have been made in Africa throughout the ages, there were very few remarkable paintings.

African art was also considered to be inferior to Western art because it seemed to be unrealistic and un-naturalistic. A good many of the carvings and sculptures, like those worn by traditional masks, seemed distorted and fragmented. Heads, in particular, seemed almost geometrical and teeth were elongated and too large. On the other hand, artists in the West had, since the Renaissance, sought to do naturalistic representations, particularly of the human body. This, of course, was a consequence of the work on perspective and three-dimensionality done in the early Renaissance. However, the practice of African artists in this regard must be placed in its cultural context. If traditional African artists did not do naturalistic representations of heads and of the human figure in general, it was not because they were unable to or were incompetent. We will soon see examples of African art which show that traditional Africans were able to do naturalistic representations. If they did not do so in some cases, it was because of spiritual and philosophical beliefs. Many African cultures believed that the head was the most important and the most powerful part of the human body. This largely explains why the head features so prominently in traditional African art. There was also the belief that in representing the head it was necessary to show its power and the awe it inspired. It was this essence that had to be presented. This is why many African masks, apart from being large, are also awe-inspiring, There are also traditional African societies that believe that it is almost sacrilegious to represent the individual as he really is. To do so almost amounts to capturing the person's spirit with possible dire consequences. This is one reason why some Africans refused to have their photographs taken.

However, there has been a change in the West's attitude towards the un-representational nature of traditional African art. This is partly due to the activities of modern Western artists like Pablo Picasso and Georges Braque who have used these elements from African art in their work. Indeed, it can be argued that the modern style of Cubism is directly due to African art. In the paintings of Picasso we have the same absence of naturalistic representation, fragmentation, and abstraction that are present in some examples of traditional African art, and this time connoisseurs commend it highly and the works are very valuable.

The concept of art in traditional Africa includes much more than painting. It includes sculpture, textiles, pottery, jewelry, furniture, household objects, and architecture. It can be seen that it embraces all areas of human life. In traditional Africa art, like music, is functional. The artists devote a tremendous amount of skill to producing objects of beauty, but these objects are intended for a purpose. They may have been used originally for rituals like birth, initiation, coming of age, marriage and funeral ceremonies; they may have been used for festivals like harvest, New Year or New Yam; they may have been used at the installation of a new king or for heightening the ceremonies in the king's palace; they may have been used in the practice of medicine; they may simply have been used in normal religious ritual to establish communication between human beings and the world of the spirits and ancestors. When individuals put on the awesome masks of the ancestors they believed they were imbued or possessed with those spirits and could therefore perform special tasks. The works of art are therefore intertwined with the life and experience of the people: spiritual, political, educational, and economic.

The most common material used in traditional African art was wood, largely because wood was plentiful, particularly in West and Central Africa. However, areas where trees were more sparse used other materials like terracotta. Brass and bronze, in the use of which Africans had developed skills quite early, were also used, particularly in the courts of kings.

African rock paintings

Let us now look at some outstanding examples of African art. We will first consider the oldest, the rock and cave paintings in South and North Africa. The ones in Southern Africa are to be found in South Africa itself and in Botswana. Carbon dating suggests that the ones in Tsodilo, Botswana, go back 27,000 years and are at least 7000 years older than the rock paintings in Lascaux, France. They were done by the San, otherwise known derogatorily as "bushmen." It is ironic, however, that these paintings, supposedly done by "primitive" people, show a capacity for reproducing rounded, naturalistic figures. The paintings depict human hunters, but they also depict the animals being hunted; and those animals are reproduced in all their fullness, force, and power. There are rhinos and giraffes, and the giraffes look like real giraffes. A famous South African site is the one at Bamboo Hollow in the Drakensberg Mountains in Natal Province. Some of the figures are abstract, but others, like those of the bulls, look like a convincing attempt at naturalistic representation.

One of the best examples of North African rock art is to be found in the Niger Plateau in Algeria. These are engravings and paintings that were done between eight and twelve thousand years ago, at a time when the Sahara was greener and not as arid as it is now, because some of the animals depicted normally live in savannah rather than desert-type terrain. There are crocodiles with their young and naturalistic representations of life-sized giraffes, elephants, and cattle. The hunters with their arrows look real. These rock paintings give us a glimpse into the kind of life that these people lived about 10,000 years ago, during the hunter-gathering stage of human existence. They also categorically show that Africans have been quite capable of naturalistic representation when the situation required it.

Ancient Egyptian art

The ancient Egyptians were expert at making all kinds of artifacts, and their wall paintings were also quite impressive. While the latter are not as naturalistic as some people might desire, they nevertheless render the physicality of the subjects adequately. The Egyptians were also very good at the use of varieties of color, thus realistically showing

Figure 13.5 African cave painting at Game Pass Shelter in South Africa showing an eland.
Source: By Alandmanson - Own work, CC BY 4.0,
https://commons.wikimedia.org/w/index.php?curid=63098315

the color differences among the subjects of the paintings and confirming the view that
the ancient Egyptians, like the Nubians, were people of color. This can also be seen in
their clay sculptures, with their realistic representations of color, muscular tone, and eyes.
Many of these sculptures can still be seen in the Great Museum in Cairo. Above all, the
Egyptians were masters at the art of making artifacts of brass, bronze, and even gold, as
can be seen in the numerous objects they made to be buried with the pharaohs in their
tombs. The fabulous treasures discovered in the tomb of Tutankhamun, particularly the
magnificent funeral mask in solid gold, are a testament to this.

Nok culture

The Nok culture flourished in West Africa between 500 BCE and 200 CE. It was based in
the Jos Plateau of what is now Northern Nigeria, just north of the confluence of the
Niger and Benue rivers. The Nok people perfected the technique of working in iron,

but they are best known for their sculptures of human heads made out of terracotta. These remarkable heads are more than life-size, with prominent eyes, flaring nostrils, and open mouths. They reinforce the importance conferred on the head in traditional African cultures, and were probably used in religious rituals. The Nok sculptures most probably influenced the creation of the later Ife and Benin bronzes.

The masks of Ife and Benin

The Yoruba kingdoms of Ife and Benin are well known for the extremely beautiful sculptures made out of bronze, copper and brass, and sometimes of ivory. The sculptures are mostly of heads, probably the heads of kings and queens. Although many of them are stylized in the sense that they appear more beautiful than the originals probably were, they are nevertheless very realistic, even to the extent of reproducing the tribal marks on the cheeks. They would have done great credit to any modern Western sculptor. The artistry is even more impressive because it must have involved expertise at the casting of metals and alloys such as copper, brass, and bronze. These masks, which were probably commissioned by the king and done by the king's workmen, were housed in the palace of the oba (as the king was called) and were probably used for ceremonial purposes. The walls of the oba's palace were also decorated with elaborate plaques showing the oba's military activities or those of his ancestors. There are therefore several military figurines. Interestingly, there are carvings of Portuguese soldiers and merchants, which must have been done after the Portuguese started arriving in the fifteenth century. The Portuguese figurines have led some skeptics to suggest that this mask-making art was introduced to the people of Ife and Benin by the Portuguese. However, carbon dating has proved that many of these artifacts go back to the thirteenth century or even earlier, whereas the Portuguese started to arrive in Africa only in the fifteenth. The artists of Benin also made numerous artifacts out of ivory like salt cellars, and they were also very good at making terracotta and wooden figures. Unfortunately, the remarkable artifacts in the palace of the oba of Benin were looted or destroyed by a punitive expeditionary British force in 1897.

Architecture: the Great Mosque at Djenne

The Great Mosque at Djenne in medieval Mali illustrates the ability of Africans in the traditional period to device an architectural framework that takes into account both the climatic conditions and the nature of the available materials. It was a remarkable building that was constructed to suit North African conditions. This mosque and others like it in the Sahel are quite different from mosques in the Middle East. As we have seen, it is made of mud or adobe bricks, and the construction takes into account the need to keep the interior cool in the heat of the desert. It is a testament to African ingenuity, creativity, and expertise.

African art during colonialism

During the colonial period traditional African art stalled, largely because the imperialists adopted a very unfavorable attitude towards it. As we have seen, the imperialist experience actually put a stop to a lot of the development that had been going on in Africa. Some of the missionaries encouraged local artists in places like Zimbabwe, Kenya, and Nigeria, to the extent of finding work for them and even staging workshops that helped

Figure 13.6 Ancestral head of an oba (a king).
Source: Benin bronze in Bristol Museum Uploaded by NotFromUtrecht, CC BY-SA 2.0,
https://commons.wikimedia.org/w/index.php?curid=12656070

them improve their skills. However, the missionaries encouraged the locals as craftsmen and artisans, rather than as budding artists. They could not bring themselves to regard these locals as artists that could be discussed and evaluated in the same way as Western artists. They found them useful for constructing the elegant doors of churches and beautifully carved altar pieces. To these missionaries, the local artists were little more than glorified carpenters. Therefore, although there was some encouragement, it was of a very limited kind. Around the time of independence, the educational authorities started paying attention to art as a discipline in the schools, and some students started offering it as a subject. However, the teachers were Western people hired from Europe and the notions of art that they taught were Eurocentric. Nevertheless, there were some European teachers and art administrators who were genuinely interested in producing a generation of trained and competent African artists. Kenneth Murray who worked for the Nigerian educational system as an art instructor and administrator played an influential role in furthering the careers of some later artists. The German Ulli Beier was instrumental in the establishment of the Mbari cultural group at Ibadan, a group interested not just in the promotion of literature, but also the promotion of African art. Some of the African students these people taught or encouraged were very interested in art and performed brilliantly. They obtained scholarships to study abroad in places like Britain, the USA, and Germany, and, on their return to Africa, they were in a position to take control of the direction in which art in Africa would proceed. These are the people who became the modern African artists.

Modern African artists

Nigerians seem to dominate the modern African art scene. This is probably because of that country's rich traditional artistic heritage, as we have seen in the case of the Ife and Benin Bronzes and the Nok culture, but also because of the existence of notable schools of art in places like Ahmadu Bello University, which started as the Nigerian College of Art, Science and Technology. Notable names in the African art world are Aina Onabolu and Ben Enwonwu, both from Nigeria, but there is also Miranda Burney-Nicol from Sierra Leone. These artists are painters, sculptors, and graphic artists. They all studied in the West, and are therefore quite familiar with the Western aesthetic. They are in a position to interpret it to their students in their studios. However, they are also steeped in the African tradition and the African aesthetic and are therefore also in a position to explain that to the West. It is interesting that some of them own studios in which they not only practice their art, but also teach students apprenticed to them. Some are also university professors.

Ben Enwonwu (1917–1994) is a case in point. His father was a carver in the traditional Igbo style. When his father died, Ben inherited his tools and went on to follow in his footsteps. He studied fine art at both secondary schools he attended and was particularly influenced by Kenneth Murray who was the colonial British officer in charge of art in Nigeria. He later studied at the Slade School of Art in London. On returning home, he went on to teach art at various schools in Nigeria and eventually became the first professor of fine arts at the University of Ife in 1971. He created some famous paintings and sculptures. One was a bronze statue of Queen Elizabeth II, and his famous portrait of an African princess called "Tutu" was auctioned for almost 1.5 million dollars. He did several portraits of distinguished Nigerians and his works have been exhibited all over the world. These modern African artists cannot be said to attempt to blend the traditional with the modern. Having mastered both, they elect to use whatever style they choose for each particular work.

References and suggestions for further reading

Atwood, R. 2011. "The Nok of Nigeria." *Archaeology* 64 (4) (July/August): 34–48.

Beaumont, P. B., and R. G.Bednaric. 2013. "Tracing the Emergence of Palaeoart in Sub-Saharan Africa." *Rock Art Research* 30 (1): 33–54.

Beier, Ulli. 1968. *Introduction: Contemporary Art in Africa*. New York: F.A. Praeger.

Berliner, P. F. 1978. *The Soul of Mbira*. Berkeley, CA: University of California Press.

Bourgeois, J.-L. 1987. "The History of the Great Mosques of Djenne." *African Arts* (UCLA James S. Coleman African Studies Center) 20 (3): 54–92.

Breunig, P. 2014. *Nok African Sculpture in Archaeological Context*. Frankfurt: Africa Magna.

Breunig, P. et al. 2005. "New Studies on the Nok Culture of Central Nigeria." *Journal of African Archaeology* 3 (2): 283–290.

Brown, E. 1966. *Africa's Contemporary Art and Artists*. New York: The Harmon Foundation.

Coulson, D., and A. Campbell. 2001. *African Rock Art: Paintings and Engravings on Stone*. New York: Abrams.

El Daly, O. 2007. *Egyptology: The Missing Millennium. Ancient Egypt in Medieval Arabic Writings*. New York: Routledge.

Dark, P. 1973. *An Introduction to Benin Art and Technology*. Oxford: Oxford University Press.

Edwards, I. E. S. 1991. *The Pyramids of Egypt*. London: Penguin.

Garlake, P. 2002. *Early Art and Architecture of Africa*. New York: Oxford University Press.

Knight, R. C. 1984. "Music in Africa: The Manding Contexts." Pp. 53–90 in G. Behague (ed.), *Performance Practice: Ethnomusicological Perspectives*. Westport, CT: Greenwood Press.

Knight, R., and K. Bilby. 2005. "Music in Africa and the Caribbean." Pp. 253–283 in M. Azevedo (ed.), *Africana Studies*. Durham, NC: Carolina Academic Press.

Lehner, M. 1997. *The Complete Pyramids*. New York: Thames & Hudson.

LeQuellec, J.-L. 2004. *Rock Art in Africa: Mythology and Legend*. Paris: Flammarion.

Manley, B. 1996. *The Penguin Historical Atlas of Ancient Egypt*. London: Penguin.

Merriam, A. P. 1982. *African Music in Perspective*. New York: Garland.

Nketia, K. 1974. *The Music of Africa*. New York: W.W. Norton.

Shillington, K. 2019. *History of Africa* (4th edition). London: Red Globe Press.

Vogelsang, Ralf, et al. 2010. "New Excavations of Middle Stone Age Deposits at Apollo 11 Rockshelter, Namibia: Stratigraphy, Archaeology, Chronology and Past Environments." *Journal of African Archaeology*. 8 (2): 185–218.

Wendorf, F., and R. Schild. 1998. "Nabta Playa and its Role in Northeastern African Prehistory." *Journal of Anthropological Archaeology*. 17: 97–123.

Wilkinson, T. 2010. *The Rise and Fall of Ancient Egypt*. London: Bloomsbury.

Willett, Frank. 1985. *African Art: An Introduction*. New York: Thames and Hudson.

14 African literature

In this survey of African literature, this chapter will discuss both traditional African literature and modern African literature and will attempt to demonstrate that the roots of modern African literature lie partly in various aspects of traditional African culture, especially the oral tradition. African oral literature will be thoroughly discussed, and the chapter will then move on to illustrate that modern African literature is, in a sense, a hybrid which has drawn from both indigenous sources and influences as well as trends and influences from the outside world.

The story of African literature begins with the very considerable body of African oral literature which has been going on from time immemorial. There are various categories of African oral literature or folk lore. These include prose, folk poetry, and epigrams. We will look at each category in turn and into the forms into which they can be further subdivided.

Prose folk lore

Myths

Oral literature in prose consists of relatively long pieces that can be chanted, narrated, or recited. These pieces can be further subdivided into myths, legends, and folk tales. Some epics are also in prose. Myths can be defined as stories that attempt to explain or illustrate the relationship between human beings and the supernatural forces in the universe, and almost every culture in the world has its own myths that attempt to define man's place in the universe and man's relationship to the extra-human forces. The research of scholars like Professor Northrop Frye and Joseph Campbell have demonstrated that many of these myths have archetypes in common because they spring from a universal desire embedded in the human psyche to define man's relationship with the gods or with the divine. Thus, there are creation myths in most cultures explaining how humans came into being and there are also myths demonstrating the separation of man from the gods. African cultures have their own creation myths which tell how the supreme being or the gods created human beings or how human beings annoyed the gods and became separated from them, just like the story of Adam and Eve in the biblical book of Genesis, which leads to the crime of the first two humans, their expulsion from Paradise, and the whole concept of "original sin." As we have seen in the chapter on religion, most African cultures believe in the existence of a Supreme Being and it is not surprising that they have their own myths defining the relationship between humans and the divine.

DOI: 10.4324/9781003111733-15

Legends

While myths deal with man's relationship to the gods, legends are almost exclusively about human beings. Legends recount the exploits and activities of extremely important and impressive ancestors of the tribe or the nation. These characters are always larger than life, and, unlike the situation in epics, which are similar, their exploits and activities are often exaggerated and the feats they perform border on fantasy. The purpose of the legend is to capture the admiration of the audience by setting the subject apart as a most extraordinary individual. Because of the similarity between epics and legends, legends have arisen around figures like Shaka Zulu and Sundiata, who are also the subjects of epics.

Folk tales

By far the most popular form of prose folk lore is the folk tale. In the world of the folk tale the various orders of beings in the universe can intermingle. Some tales have humans, animals, and spirits; some have humans and spirits; some have only animals; and some have only humans; but animals clearly predominate. However, even when there are only animals in the tale, those animals are given human characteristics and it is clear that the story is not really about animals at all, but about humans and their relationships with each other. The animals display the characteristics of humans and those characteristics are quite often stereotypical. Some animals display courage; some display a kind of low cunning; some display greed; some display stupidity. The moment, therefore, that an animal appears in a tale the audience can be sure about the quality it represents. The lion and the elephant usually display stupidity; the rabbit, the hare, the spider, and the tortoise almost always display a kind of low cunning which is nevertheless attractive because, in spite of their size, they end up outwitting much bigger animals. They are the so-called "trickster" characters. In West Africa the rabbit is called "cunny (cunning) rabbit," and the nomenclature "brer" is often added to the spider and the rabbit, so they become "brer spider" and "brer rabbit"; this is an affirmation of their cleverness.

Generally speaking, the smaller the animal in the folk tale, the cleverer it is, and large animals are generally more stupid. Thus, the elephant, the lion, and the hippopotamus are extremely stupid. This can be seen in a tale featuring the enormous lion and the small dog. Dog had got tired of hearing Lion being referred to as the "king of all the animals," so on one occasion he rebelled and went about shouting that he did not regard Lion as his king. The other animals urged him to keep quiet because Lion the king had many spies who would go and report his comments, with terrible consequences. However, Dog was adamant and went further to say that he was, in fact, more powerful than Lion, and if he wished he could ride Lion like a horse. The other animals were flabbergasted and once more warned Dog to be quiet, but Dog merely repeated what he had said. So some of Lion's spies went and reported Dog's comments to their king, Lion. As was expected, Lion was mad with rage and ordered the animals to return to Dog and command him to appear in his court. He would accuse him, judge him, condemn him, and proceed to eat him in punishment. The other animals dutifully returned to Dog and repeated Lion's commands, adding that they had warned Dog about the consequences. But Dog was clever. He knew what would happen, so before the animals arrived, he had rubbed himself all over with oil, as the sick often do, and taken to his bed, pretending to be seriously ill. So when he heard Lion's commands he said he was willing to comply but, as the other animals could see, he was gravely ill and unable to walk. However, as soon as he recovered, he would comply with Lion's orders. The other animals returned to Lion and told him what Dog had said. However, the enraged Lion declared that he was going to get Dog to the court for trial that very same day, even if he had to bring him himself. So Lion raced in fury to Dog's house. When Dog repeated the explanation he had given, Lion shouted that he would take Dog to the court himself and ordered Dog to jump on his back, which Dog did. Lion then started racing to the court with Dog on his back. But as he sped along, the clever Dog took out a white handkerchief and started waving it as he rode on Lion's back. The astonished animals started murmuring, "So it is true; look! Dog is riding Lion like his horse." It took the stupid Lion some time to realize what was happening, but at that moment, Dog jumped from his back and ran into the forest. That is why there has always been enmity between Lion and Dog. It must be noted that at the end of the tale, there is an explanation. The circumstances narrated explain why there has always been enmity between Lion and dog-like creatures, like the hyena, for instance. The actual narration of the tale, as we shall see later, would be much more dramatic than has appeared here. There would be much more direct speech and more questions and answers.

The tales are told for various reasons. Firstly, they are told for entertainment. We must remember that these were societies where the radio, television, and movie screen had not yet infiltrated, and telling tales was one of the means of entertainment available to the people. After a hard day's work on the farm the family would gather round the hearth, or the village as a whole would gather in the village square to hear the talented tell the tales. The tales were also told in order to explain certain phenomena in a humorous way, as can be seen in the tale about the lion and the dog. Thus, one tale explains why the tortoise has a reticulated shell; another explains why the spider has such a tiny waist; another explains why the baboon has a shiny bottom; and another explains why the lizard is always shaking his head. Some of the tales pose riddles or problems which the members of the audience are asked to solve. The intention is to test the intellectual capacities of the audience and get them to think, an activity that is particularly helpful for the young. For instance, there is the story of a man who marries three wives. The man dies suddenly while they were all traveling on the wayside, and the grief-stricken wives wish to bring him back to life. One has powers of clairvoyance and sees that in a distant town there is a medicine man who could bring their husband back to life. The other has a magic carpet and claims to be able to fly on it to the medicine man's town and bring the latter back to resurrect their husband. The third promises to stay by the side of the husband and prevent anything bad happening to the body, like its being eaten up by wild animals. So the first two wives fly on the magic carpet and bring back the medicine man, who then proceeds to bring the husband back to life. The puzzle is, which of these three wives is the best? If the husband were to have only one wife, which would it be?

Most importantly, the tales are told for the purpose of moral instruction, especially for the young. Most of the tales stress moral lessons, castigating vices such as greed, ingratitude, jealousy, and treachery, and applauding virtues such as generosity, courage, loyalty, and respect for truth. Taken together, the tales generally encapsulate the values and the mores of the society, and they are an excellent tool in the educational process.

The telling of a tale is a highly dramatic activity. It is, in fact, a performance by the teller. The teller is not expected to tell an original tale, one that he himself has made up. He usually takes the tale from the corpus of his people's oral lore, but he retells it in such a way that he makes it peculiarly his own. This is one reason why there are so many versions of one tale. The teller can add or subtract and modify the tale as he pleases. In his narration he tries to present dramatic scenes to the audience. He certainly gets the audience involved by asking them questions. He can get them to clap or sing or even dance. He would make a call and get them to respond with a kind of refrain. He himself makes use of what are called para-linguistic devices; that is, devices over and above the spoken word. He uses facial expressions and gestures and special movements of the eyes and other parts of the body, such as his arms and hands and legs. My father was an expert at telling tales. In the telling of the tale about the tortoise, the elephant, and the hippopotamus, where the tortoise outwits the two much bigger animals after challenging them to a tug-of-war contest, he could tighten the muscles of his arms and biceps in such a way that one could feel the tension in the rope and in the muscles of the two large animals as they battle in the tug of war. It is in ways like this that the teller of the tale shows his artistry, ingenuity, originality, and creativity, and makes the inherited tale peculiarly his own. Some of the tales are short, some are so long that they could easily be regarded as novellas, with a beginning, complications and conflicts in the middle, and the resolution at the end.

The epic

The epic could be either prose or poetry. Like the legend, it usually revolves around the exploits of heroic figures in the past, but while the legend could be about just one individual and might be confined to one anecdote or story, the epic might involve several heroic figures, though there is usually one major figure, and it might consist of several anecdotes or stories strung together. The epic is a grand lengthy narrative involving heroic exploits and set against the background of an entire civilization. It usually involves the march of civilizations or the clash of civilizations. The African epic, like the epics in other cultures, was the loftiest form of literary endeavor. Whether in prose or in verse, it was usually recited or chanted to the accompaniment of one or more musical instruments by a trained professional called a griot, who had spent years of apprenticeship memorizing the epics and other historical material from his people's history and culture. He also had to master the nuances of the process of recitation. The griot was usually attached to the king's house and could be called by the king on special occasions to recite or perform the epic.

The African epics were every bit as complicated as Western epics. Some were so long and elaborate that they took, not hours, but days to perform. Some even involved other folkloric forms like song, proverbs, and poetry, if the main epic was in prose, and prose, if it was in verse. Well-known African epics include the *Sundiata* epic and the epic of Emperor Shaka Zulu. The *Sundiata* epic is about the legendary founder of the medieval empire of Mali. Although originally oral, it has been transcribed and written down, and has been translated into several languages. *Shaka Zulu* is about the exploits of the great Zulu leader who established the South African Zulu kingdom and strenuously resisted British imperialism. Perhaps the two most famous African epics are the *Ozidi* epic from Eastern Nigeria and the *Mwindo* epic from Zaire. The *Ozidi* epic is an epic of the Ijaw people of Eastern Nigeria and involves the heroic exploits of an ancestral hero. Its performance usually takes several days, and it is therefore infrequently performed. The performance has the air of a festival which involves the entire community participating in the singing, dancing, and general celebration (Owomoyela, 7). The *Mwindo* epic is an epic of the Nyanga people of Eastern Zaire. Owomoyela suggests that only fragments of it are now generally performed because of its extreme length. When it was last performed in its entirely in 1954 for the benefit of researchers, the performance lasted for 12 days (Owomoyela, 7).

Oral poetry

The body of African oral poetry is quite considerable, and it has had quite an impact on modern African poetry. There was a time when some scholars thought that the complexity of modern African poetry largely derives from modern Western poetry; that is, the poetry of people like W. B. Yeats, T. S. Eliot, and Ezra Pound. Further research has demonstrated, however, that the complexity and density of texture of the poems of authors like Soyinka and Okigbo derive as much, if not more, from traditional African poetry which can be just as complex. Since this is poetry that often has to be committed to memory, it is characterized by pleasant rhythms, but also by recondite images and symbols whose significance is known to only a few. In the traditional context, poetry, like so many other forms of African art, is functional. It is meant to be used for specific purposes and in specific situations. Poetry is usually chanted and could be used for the following purposes:

a   in rituals, as part of the rites of various cults and secret societies;
b   in the practice of medicine;
c   in divination;
d   in incantations;
e   as dirges or praise poems.

Cultic chants

These are the songs chanted by members of a cult or secret society as part of the rituals of that society. Usually, the intention is to invoke the protection or aid of the god who is the patron of the cult by enumerating the qualities of that deity. The songs would normally be chanted by the priests and his assistants, but at times by all the members of the cult. The songs and chants would be known only to members of the cult, and to keep the songs and their meaning secure, the significance if the references, symbols, and images would normally be known only to the members. These symbols and images are therefore often obscure and very private.

Medicinal chants

Poems are chanted in the practice of medicine in order to invoke and ask for the assistance, not only of the spirits and gods, but also of the various forces latent in the universe which might be in a position to help. Such forces include trees, leaves, and streams.

Poetry of divination

This is a very important branch of African oral poetry. Divination involves probing into the forces of the universe in order to find out what has happened or what will happen. Thus it can be used to reveal what kind of man a new-born baby will become, or why a particular individual is haunted by bad fortune, or what the individual must do in order to become more fortunate or achieve certain objectives. The divination is normally done by the priest of the oracle, as was the case in ancient Greece. There are various oracles in traditional Africa, the most famous of which is arguably the Ifa Oracle of the Yorubas of Western Nigeria. The priest of the oracle is called the Babalawo, and he does the divining. When an individual goes to the Oracle in order to divine his fortune, the Babalawo consults the Ifa text which he has committed to memory. The text, which is called the Odu, consists of 16 heads or sections. Each head is then further subdivided into 16 subsections. The Odu therefore consists of 256 subsections, each a fairly long poem which could consist of as many as 40 lines. The Ifa priest would have gone through a period of apprenticeship and would therefore have committed the entire Odu to memory. When the individual goes to the Babalawo to find out his fortune, the latter searches his memory to see which of the 256 subsections fits the supplicant's situation. It is really a question of searching for precedents; specifically, the precedent that fits the supplicant's situation. The Babalawo then recites the relevant subsection or precedent and tells the supplicant what he must do. The subsection usually starts with a traditional salutation, then a statement of the problem or request, then an account of what was done in the past when there was a similar problem and therefore what the supplicant must do, and finally a description of the result. It can easily be seen that committing the entire Odu to memory must have been a tremendous feat.

Incantations

Incantations were used not only in the practice of medicine, but generally to invoke the forces that control the universe and which can be manipulated or implored in the service of man. The incantation could be done for a specific purpose or generally as part of a ceremony or religious ritual. The incantation could take the form of an invocation to a favorite god or spirit.

Dirges and praise poems

Dirges were chanted at funerals, and praise songs, as we have seen, were chanted to sing the praises of worthy individuals. There are quite a few poems, for instance, in praise of Shaka and quite a few also of spirits and gods. The situation can be reversed and the praise song inverted to satirize a reprehensible individual. The praise song can also be used to laud not just individuals but also animals and possessions that do one credit, like one's cattle, for instance. Praise poems are the most common form of poetry and are vital to traditional African life.

Epigrams

The final category of African oral literature to be discussed is epigrams, which consist of proverbs and riddles. Proverbs are wise pithy sayings that encapsulate the ancestral wisdom of a people, while epigrams are short statements or questions that are intended to test the individual's intellectual capacity. African cultures are rich in proverbs. As Chinua Achebe says in his novel *Things Fall Apart*, "Proverbs are the palm-oil with which words are eaten." This suggests that in Africa proverbs are used to lace conversation and argument and make them more beautiful and compelling. Because the proverbs are a kind of summary of the ancestral wisdom, it is possible to get some idea of the nature and main characteristics of a particular people by a study of their proverbs. Let us take, as an example, the case of the Creoles of Sierra Leone in West Africa. Here are two of their favorite proverbs:

If your yams are white, you must cover them.
The mother of a cowardly child never mourns.

Yams in Africa are huge and when they are cut after the harvest, they could be either absolutely white or slightly darker. The best ones are those that are white. The proverb is exhorting the audience not to gloat if they discover that their yams are white. Of course, the statement is metaphorical and means that one should not gloat or brag about one's fortunate circumstances. Modesty, in other words, is the best policy. The second proverb counsels restraint. The mother will never mourn because the child is "cowardly" and will not take the kind of risks that will lead to death. The proverb suggests that the Creole man or woman does not take risks. They would rather leave their money in the savings bank and get a return of 5 percent a year, than invest it in dubious ventures promising 10 percent a year that will lead to considerable losses. The average Creole man or woman believes in caution, restraint, and modesty.

As we have seen, one of the most important characteristics of proverbs is that they are a distillation of the wisdom of the people over the ages. Therefore, the old are the ones who are most familiar with them. Generally, it is only the elderly who use proverbs. In fact, it is considered impertinent for a young person to use them. We can see this reflected in some of the novels of Chinua Achebe, where young people are, at times, sarcastically rebuked for their pretentiousness in using proverbs. Another major characteristic of proverbs is that they are very useful tools in argument or debate. In Achebe's novel *Arrow of God*, the author presents great set debates among the leaders of the community in which these leaders try to get the better of each other and win the argument by a skillful use of well-known proverbs. Proverbs are also effective rhetorical tools because they involve the use of powerful illustrative imagery. When, for instance, someone says "The fowl that does not hear 'shee' will hear the stone," we see an actual picture of an adamant chicken refusing to pay heed as an individual tries to "shoo" it away using the expression "shee," but it is suddenly forced to fly away when the individual picks up a stone and hurls it at it. The picture effectively illustrates the point that anyone who does not respond to words of warning will inevitably have to do so when faced with graver consequences, or will endure graver consequences. Proverbs also enable the speaker to make very effective points indirectly. They therefore enable people to be tactful or sarcastic. Take the situation, for instance, where an individual is boasting about his achievements, something that is normally not done. A member of the audience might want to tell him that he knows he is lying, but he does not want to do so directly, because that would be impolite, so he uses a proverb: "The eunuch always claims to have fathered many children, but only in distant lands." The speaker has made a very telling point indirectly. He has told the individual that he is lying and he has also insulted him by calling him a eunuch, but he has not done so in so many words.

Unlike proverbs, riddles are not used to spice conversation, but they are, nevertheless, a very important part of the oral tradition and of oral literature. They pose problems or ask questions that people must solve in order to demonstrate their capacity for thinking and their intellectual abilities. One very good example is "A house in which one does not turn around." Although the person who poses the riddle does not ask the question,

"What is it?" the question is implied and the audience proceeds to attempt to answer or solve the riddle. The answer is the coffin or the grave.

The corpus of African oral literature, therefore, is vast and complex, and it has had a profound influence on the development of modern African literature. We can see this, for instance, in some of the poems of the Nigerian Christopher Okigbo. In the poem "Idoto," he is obviously using a traditional form, the incantation, as he calls on his favorite goddess to inspire him. We can also see how some of these forms of oral literature modulate into written literature and the ways in which some of the early practitioners of modern African literature incorporate the oral tradition or oral literature into their own works. As we shall see, Achebe makes extensive use of proverbs and folk tales in his novels; Amos Tutuola composes his *Palm-Wine Drinkard* by stringing together versions of folk tales from his people's oral tradition to create a narrative that seems to have many of the characteristics of the African epic; Fagunwa writes his story, later translated by Wole Soyinka as *Forest of a Thousand Demons*, in his native Yoruba, incorporating tales and other details from the oral tradition and really presenting the framework of an African oral tale; and both Soyinka and Okigbo actually incorporate elements from African oral poetry into their own poems. It is not an exaggeration to suggest that African oral literature lies at the root of modern African literature.

Early African written literature

Written African literature was largely the consequence of the European intervention into Africa and the rise of imperialism. It was largely the missionaries who introduced literacy to most parts of Africa and it is therefore not surprising that the earliest African written works had a heavy religious content and manifested the Christian ideology. These early practitioners had attended mission schools, had been born of Christian parents or had become Christian, and had been imbued with Christian doctrine. Thomas Mofolo, of what is now Lesotho in Southern Africa, published three novels, *The Traveller of the East* (1906), *Pitseng* (1910), and *Chaka* (1925). J. E. Casely Hayford of what is now Ghana published *Ethiopia Unbound* (1911), and R. E. Obeng, also of what is now Ghana, published *Eighteen Pence* (1943). It is remarkable, however, that Mofolo wrote his novels, not in English, but in his native Sesotho. This suggests that in spite of their Christian devotion there was tension going on in these early writers between the new religion and culture to which they and their people had been introduced and their traditional affiliations. Indeed, throughout the development of African literature, we'll see this tension between the new ideas and attitudes brought by the imperialists on the one hand, and the African people's own traditions and impulses, which is a genuine part of their identity, on the other. One might almost say that modern African literature emerges out of this tension. The tension was present in various forms in many of the newly occupied territories throughout the early years of the twentieth century. Mofolo was obliged to reflect Christian attitudes, but he also felt bound to assert his own individuality and his true African identity. In fact, he encountered some resistance from the publishing world. His first novel, *The Traveller of the East*, has echoes of Bunyan's *The Pilgrim's Progress*; however, his second, *Chaka*, which was written in 1908, was about the legendary Zulu warrior and terror of British imperialism, and it did not sit well with the British missionaries. Mofolo was steeped in his people's history and culture and was attracted to the figure of Chaka. The detailed presentation of traditional beliefs and actions, like the activities of seers and medicine men, was anathema to the missionaries, and the novel was not published until 1925.

At this time there were also the pioneer poets like Dennis Osadebay of Nigeria, and Crispin George and Jacob Stanley Davies of Sierra Leone whose work also reflected Christian attitudes and the Western poetic practice. Here is a typical stanza from a poem by Crispin George entitled "Let Wisdom and Modesty Guide Us":

> Be not so foolish as to boast,
> Save only on his might
> He only is the Lord of Host
> Who doth all things aright.

The tone, the meter, and the meaning are all those of English hymnology. There was one Sierra Leonean poet, however, who could be described as a kind of rebel. Although Gladys Casely-Hayford (1904–1950) used Western metrical patterns in her poetry, she infused them with a definite African consciousness. Even when she writes a Christian poem about the nativity, she envisages the Christ-child and his mother as black. Mary places her black baby on a "deer-skin hide" and wraps him with an African "lappa." Casely-Hayford also calls rousingly on her fellow black people to take pride in their blackness:

> Rejoice and shout with laughter,
> Lay all your burdens down
> If God has been so gracious
> As to make you black or brown.

The poetics might be rather simplistic because she is using simple English metrical forms, but the black and African consciousness is unmistakable.

Of all these early African writers it is probably the Nigerian Chief D. O. Fagunwa who most clearly illustrates the tension in the emerging African written literature between traditional African and Christian European attitudes, or, rather, the attempt by some to see whether the two could be reconciled. Fagunwa was a Christian and a highly educated education officer in Nigeria. His works generally reflect a Christian attitude, but they are also populated by extra-natural beings, such as spirits, who also figure in Yoruba mythology, especially in the folk tale. Moreover, his works were written in his native Yoruba. The most famous was translated into English by Wole Soyinka and entitled *Forest of a Thousand Demons*. It can be argued that in Fagunwa's works there is a super-imposition of a Christian perspective on what is otherwise a Yoruba mythological world, like the super-imposition of a Christian outlook on an otherwise pagan Scandinavian world in *Beowulf*.

This tussle in early African written literature between influences from the European and those from the traditional is continued by the Nigerian Cyprian Ekwensi, in novels like *Jagua Nana* and *People of the City*. Ekwensi was educated in the Western tradition and was familiar with the novels of English writers like Charles Dickens. But he was also very familiar, not only with traditional oral literature, but also with the very popular tradition of Onitsha market literature. These were very popular stories or chapbooks about low life in the urban areas of Nigeria. The aim was entertainment, and they were hastily written and hawked in the markets in the urban areas. Ekwensi's racy and very fascinating novels derive from this tradition, but they also owed something to the novels of English writers like Dickens. In a sense we see, in the novels of Ekwensi, the process of the African novel struggling to be born. Ekwensi stands in the same relation to the African novel as the English writer Daniel Defoe stands to the English novel. Just as Defoe makes use of popular and hastily written materials as he gropes his way towards the creation of the English novel, so Ekwensi makes use of the popular Onitsha market literature in the progress towards the modern African novel. But he is also using techniques derived from his knowledge of the Western novel.

It can be seen, then, that in the evolution of modern African literature a major concern was how to reconcile influences derived from the African and traditional with those from the European. Both are very important influences which cannot be discounted. Many of the writers were educated in the Western tradition and were familiar with numerous aspects of Western literary practice. But they were also steeped in their native traditions, especially the oral tradition. Moreover, there were certain trends emanating from the Western world, like Christianity or imperialism, that these writers had to react to, or even reject. One way or the other, the emerging literature had to reckon with influences, or even attitudes, from the West.

Negritude

One of the most important trends in the emerging literature that was a reaction to forces emanating from the Western world was the concept of "Negritude." Put simply, Negritude means complete recognition and assertion of being black, or consciousness of and pride in being black and African. It was a reaction to Western attitudes towards African life and culture and had everything to do with the assertion of a genuine African identity. Specifically, it was a reaction to the consequences of French colonial policy. We have already seen that while the British generally practiced the policy of indirect rule, thus leaving most aspects of traditional life and culture intact, the French practiced the policy of assimilation with the intention of including as many of their colonial subjects as possible within the bigger ambit of an all-embracing French civilization. The situation was exacerbated by the fact that many of these Francophone youngsters were later sent to France and put through a thorough French system of education, resulting in their almost total alienation from their roots in African culture. And yet, these Africans, while they were in France, did not get the impression that they were totally accepted as being French. There was thus a crisis of identity. It was for this reason that some African intellectuals like Senghor and Diop, together with others from the French West Indies, who were going through similar experiences, embraced the concept of Negritude. The movement was actually started by black intellectuals in French West Indian colonies like Martinique, who spearheaded the movement because they had, in a sense, been subject to a double alienation. Not only had they been translated from their original environment in Africa to the West Indian Islands, but they had also been further translated to France and were therefore in a cultural limbo. Indeed, the first significant publication of the Negritude movement was the long poem *Cahier d'un Retour au Pays Natal* or *Return to my Native Land* by Aimé Césaire from Martinique.

The Negritude movement was therefore pivotal to the beginnings of modern African literature. It gave rise to a remarkable body of poetry that sought to assert the true nature and identity of the black African. This poetry was very much about a genuine African identity; it was about how others saw Africans and how Africans saw themselves. It was poetry and literature born out of reaction against others' perception of the African. The first publication of the movement was a one-issue student journal by French Antilleans in

Paris in 1932. The journal was followed two years later by *L'Etudiant Noir* on which Africans like Senghor, Diop, and Ousmane Soce collaborated. It was in that journal that Césaire first used the term "Negritude." *Presence Africaine*, a very influential journal which presented the poems and ideas of members of the Negritude movement, was published by Alioune Diop in 1947. In 1949 Léopold Sédar Senghor brought out his monumental and ground-breaking *Anthology of the New Black and Malagasy Poetry*. The French philosopher and writer Jean-Paul Sartre contributed a preface which propelled Negritude into the realm of international intellectual discourse and has been generally regarded as the best description of the Negritudists' intentions.

Let us now look at the characteristics of Negritude as displayed in the poetry. First, there is the insistent embrace of Africa and the celebration and glorification of African values. We see this in David Diop's "Africa" (Moore, *Penguin Book of Modern African Poetry*, 328) and Senghor's "Night of Seine" (ibid., 314). "Night of Seine" also reveals another characteristic of Negritude: the glorification of the African woman who is seen as a nurturing and protective force, a potent symbol of fecundity. The African woman is almost conflated with Africa herself, Africa that is now seen as "Mother Africa." In the poem "Black Woman" by Senghor, the African woman becomes the Savannah "shuddering beneath the East Wind's eager caresses, the Promised Land."

The negritude poets are also noted for their celebration of various aspects of African culture such as African music and African musical instruments. African musicality is, in fact, central to Senghor's conception of negritude and to his assertion of the nature of the African personality. Not only does he celebrate the power of African music in his poetry, some of his poems are meant to be recited to the accompaniment of specified musical instruments. By the same token, in many of these poems we find a veneration of African masks, the masks of the ancestors, which symbolize the continuity between the world of the living, the world of the dead, and the world of the unborn, an extremely important aspect of African ontology. We can see this, for instance, in his "Prayer to Masks."

The celebration of African values by the negritude poets also involved, in some cases, an attack on, or at least, a critique of Western values. In a sense, this was inevitable since the West was seen as the home of capitalism and the perpetrator of imperialism. African values were seen to be superior to Western ones. While the West was seen to be materialistic, addicted to technology and individualism, and characterized by lovelessness and lack of emotion, African civilization, on the other hand, was seen to be infused by spirituality, a sense of community, and a love of nature and the natural. The best example of the exploration of this theme is probably Senghor's poem "New York" (Moore, *Penguin Book of Modern African Poetry*, 318).

Amos Tutuola and the rise of the African novel

The publication by the Nigerian Amos Tutuola of his *The Palm-Wine Drinkard* in 1952 has been taken by some to herald the dawn of modern African literature. Others might regard this as rather arbitrary, but it is still clear that it was one of the momentous events that happened around this time suggesting that a new literature was emerging. Tutuola wrote his work, not in standard English, but in the kind of West African English with which he was familiar, There has been a lot of controversy as to whether he was deliberately bending the English language to suit his own artistic purposes. It is now generally agreed that Tutuola wrote as he did, not because he was trying to demonstrate the malleability of the English language and his ability to get it to do whatever he wanted, but because that was the only way in which he knew how to write. His education did not proceed beyond what is the equivalent of the fourth grade. However, it is extremely important that he felt confident enough to write his long fictional narrative in a language of his own choice in order to express his own particular vision. The work is very African in its inspiration. It is interesting that his publishers first thought they should make considerable corrections to Tutuola's grammar, style, and use of language. However, they soon realized that if they did so, they would end up with a work that was not Tutuola's and did not reflect his voice, so they left the work as Tutuola wrote it, and it is fortunate that they did so.

The Palm-Wine Drinkard is a long fictional narrative consisting of several tales from the Yoruba oral tradition that are strung together to form a continuous whole and tell the story of a hero who journeys to the land of the dead to retrieve his palm-wine tapster. Of course, he cannot bring back his tapster, but he learns some very useful lessons and returns with some extraordinary boons. There has been tremendous debate as to the kind of work Tutuola was trying to write. Was he trying to write a novel based on traditional mystical life like Fagunwa, but this time in a form of English? Must we regard this work as the first real African novel? We can be sure that Tutuola did not deliberately set out to write a novel. Given his level of education he could not have read many novels and he probably did not wish to model his work on the English novel. He was, of course, familiar with long African oral narratives in prose, like the African epic, He was also familiar with the African oral folk tale. In composing his long fictional written narrative, therefore, he decided to string together several oral tales into one continuous whole, telling a continuous story, and sounding rather like an African epic. The similarity between *The Palm-Wine Drinkard* and the epic form is extraordinary. It has so many of the qualities and the archetypal figures, characters, and events that appear in epics. Also, like most other epics, the work was composed by stringing together narratives that already exist in the people's oral tradition. The similarity is such that some have suggested that Tutuola must have read the ancient Greek and Latin epics like the *Iliad* and the *Aeneid*. We know, however, from Tutuola's level of education, that he could not have done so. He only needed to have heard his own culture's epics and oral tales. Like other African writers of the time, Tutuola is, perhaps unconsciously, moving towards the African novel form: a long, written, fictional narrative. He has not quite got there yet, but in composing this long fictional narrative he uses models with which he is familiar. As we have seen, *The Palm-Wine Drinkard* is rooted in African culture and is very African in its inspiration. The accents of the African storyteller can even be heard in the accents of Tutuola's narrator. Tutuola would go on to write several more works in the same vein, but none would capture the world's attention like *The Palm-Wine Drinkard*. They include *My Life in the Bush of Ghosts, Simbi and the Satyr of the Dark Jungle*, and *The Brave African Huntress*.

Chinua Achebe and modern African literature

It is the work of the Nigerian Chinua Achebe that most clearly demonstrates that the African novel in particular, and modern African literature in general, arose partly in response to forces emanating out of the West. It was definitely a reaction to certain Western attitudes to African life and culture. In a sense, it was Africa "answering back." Modern African writers were trying to reassert and proclaim the true African identity and to refute the representation of Africa in the Western media by celebrating various aspects of African life and culture. Achebe was central to this enterprise. Achebe was born and educated in Nigeria, but in the British academic tradition. He was familiar with the novels of Jane Austen, Charles Dickens, George Eliot, Thomas Hardy, and D. H. Lawrence and with the poetry of W. B. Yeats and T. S. Eliot. All these must have influenced him. But he was also steeped in his Igbo people's cultural traditions, particularly their religion, mythology, and folk lore. Most importantly, however, he was aware of the existence of certain attitudes about Africa among Western peoples. Let us take our minds back to the date of publication of Achebe's first novel *Things Fall Apart* in 1958. Intensive research into African history and culture was just beginning. This was the time when a respected historian like Hugh Trevor-Roper, Regius Professor of Modern History at Oxford University, could make the astonishing statement that Africa has no history, and that "the African past was nothing but the unrewarding gyrations of barbarous tribes." The Western audience had had their fill of the sensational in Africa presented by such propagandists as Rider Haggard and Henry Morton Stanley, and the Western media delighted their audience by presenting Africa as a dark, disorganized, benighted, and backward place inhabited by dirty, lazy, pagan peoples incapable of rational thought or of participating in certain disciplines, and needing to be rescued from the consequences of their own barbarism by imperialism.

In particular, Achebe was stung into writing his first novel by the views and attitudes of two other novelists, Joseph Conrad and Joyce Cary. The naturalized British novelist Joseph Conrad had originally been a sailor and had made a journey up the Congo River into the heart of Africa in 1890. As a result, he wrote a now famous novella entitled *Heart of Darkness*. The title itself speaks volumes about Conrad's view of Africa, since "darkness" could suggest, not just the unknown and unexplored or a place associated with the dark peoples, but also barbarism or even evil. Although Conrad exposed the evils of imperialism in Central Africa in this novel, especially King Leopold II's brand of imperialism in the Congo, he also concentrated on the barbaric practices, including cannibalism, that the Africans perpetrated, as he claimed, and even suggested that the protagonist, Mr. Kurtz, was an idealistic and highly intelligent European who was corrupted by the Africans. Many African intellectuals, including Achebe, saw Conrad as presenting a racist and completely distorted picture of Africa and Africans. Indeed, in a well-known article entitled "An Image of Africa: Racism in Conrad's *Heart of Darkness*," Achebe published a celebrated riposte in which he accused Conrad openly of racism. Joyce Cary was an Irishman who worked for the British colonial administration in Northern Nigeria and published a series of novels based on his experiences. One of these was *Mister Johnson*, which presented the activities of a deluded and comic Nigerian character who blindly sought to imitate British mannerisms and lifestyle and is cruelly ridiculed in consequence. Achebe felt that both Cary and Conrad had presented caricatures of the African and a false picture of traditional African society. He therefore sought to set the record straight and write a novel presenting a real African gentleman and a genuine picture of African society. The result was *Things Fall Apart*. In Umuofia, Achebe presented a genuine traditional African society and in the protagonist Okonkwo he presented a genuine African gentleman.

Achebe always saw himself as a teacher, teaching not only non-Africans but even Africans themselves about the true nature of traditional African society. The picture he presents of this society is quite objective. He is not out to merely glamorize or glorify traditional African society as some of the Negritude poets had done, but to present both the strengths and weaknesses of this society. He also presents both the strengths and the glaring weaknesses of his African gentleman, Okonkwo, who emerges as a truly tragic character. As he himself said on one occasion, he was not going to gloss over inconvenient facts.

After *Things Fall Apart*, Achebe wrote *No Longer at Ease* which is set in contemporary Nigeria and presents the activities of the generation that would lead Nigeria to independence. The protagonist is Obi Okonkwo, the grandson of the protagonist of *Things Fall Apart*. Achebe uses him and his circle to present the decadence of a more contemporary Nigeria. His third novel, *Arrow of God*, returns to traditional Nigeria and presents the clash between traditional elements and the new religion after the arrival of the English missionaries and administrators. His fourth novel, *A Man of the People*, was published about five years after Nigerian independence and presents the corruption and incompetence of the Nigerian government formed by indigenous Nigerians. Achebe thus sets a novel in traditional society alternating with another set in more contemporary society. At the end of the fourth novel there is a coup, and Achebe was therefore regarded as a prophetic writer because a coup actually happened in Nigeria in January 1966. His first four novels, therefore, can be said to present the story of Nigeria, or even the recent story of Africa, involving colonialism, the move towards independence, the achievement of independence, and the consequences of independence.

Achebe's first novel was published at the time when African nationalism was gaining steam. Ghana had just achieved its independence in 1957 after a determined struggle, the first black African country to do so. The activities of writers like Achebe and the Negritude poets can be regarded as the cultural counterpart of the political nationalism that was driving through the continent. They, like the politicians, were determined to assert the inherent dignity of the African, the validity of African institutions, the ability of the African to take charge of his own affairs, and the wrong-headedness of any attempt to oppress him or to suggest he had no essence of value and to try to impose an alien identity on him. It was for this reason that many of the works written at this time, whether in poetry, the novel, or drama, sought to assert, not only the inherent dignity of African life, but the stupidity of the attempt to change it, suppress it, or impose anything else on it. Inevitably, this led to a presentation of the clash between traditional African values and the alien values that the European imperialists or Westerners in general would like to impose. We see this in plays like Soyinka's *The Lion and the Jewel* and *Death and the King's Horseman*; in Achebe's *Things Fall Apart* and *Arrow of God*; in Ama Ata Aidoo's plays *Dilemma of a Ghost* and *Anowa*; in T. M. Aluko's novels *One Man, One Wife* and *One Man, One Matchet*; in Mongo Beti's *The Poor Christ of Bomba* and *Mission to Kala*; and in Ferdinand Oyono's *The Old Man and the Medal* and *Houseboy*. It becomes a very important theme in African literature.

Achebe is justifiably regarded as the doyen of African letters. It can be said that he was the one who showed others how to write the African novel, the one who perfected the form, and his *Things Fall Apart* has become the archetypal African novel. Using a basic form to which he had become accustomed from his study of European literature, he showed others how to Africanize it, largely by incorporating elements from the African oral tradition. One of the areas in which Achebe led the way is that of language in African literature. We have seen that modern African literature more or less emerged out of the drive to assert the validity, the beauty and the dignity of African life, culture, and identity. Language is a very important aspect both of culture and identity. The issue is this: in writing African literature can we use an alien language like English or French, a language which is, moreover, the language of the imperialist oppressor? Would that enable Africans to express a genuine African identity? African writers found out that they had to use one or other of the metropolitan languages because most African languages were not written and in order to find publishers and reach a wide audience they had to use the metropolitan languages anyway. But should they use these languages as native speakers would? It was Achebe who showed the way out of the impasse. He showed that the African writer could use the English language, for instance, but he could also bend it to suit his particular purpose and reflect a genuine African environment. However, he could bend this malleable language only if he was proceeding from a position of strength, not from a position of weakness. In other words, he must have achieved mastery of the language before proceeding to put it through interesting hoops. This was Achebe's practice. He incorporated elements from the oral tradition and used proverbs and direct statements from the Igbo language. He also contrived different registers for different groups and classes of people. He was thus able to create a genuine African atmosphere in his novels.

Wole Soyinka

One writer who followed in Achebe's footsteps in so far as language is concerned was the brilliant Wole Soyinka, the first African to win the Nobel Prize for Literature, which he did in 1986. Like Achebe, Soyinka mastered the Western literary tradition and was also very much at home and steeped in his native Yoruba culture and mythology. He had his university education both at Ibadan University in Nigeria and at the University of Leeds in England where he studied English language and literature. While at Leeds he wrote a now famous essay on the African conception of tragedy. This shows that from a very early age he was prepared to vouch for the authenticity of the African literary tradition. His association with the London Royal Court Theatre, which specialized in the staging of the so-called avant-garde plays of writers like Beckett, Osborne, Wesker, and Arden, got him acquainted with the dynamics of contemporary Western drama. On his return home to Nigeria he was able to blend elements from the traditional Yoruba with those from the modern Western drama. This has been the hallmark of his drama. He uses techniques like multiple levels of stage, ingenious lighting, flashbacks, and so on, but he takes the content from the myths and beliefs of his people and uses indigenous African techniques like mime and dance. This was immediately obvious in his first play, *A Dance of the Forests*, which won the drama competition during the Nigerian independence activities in 1960 and was a major part of the celebrations. Soyinka went on to write over 30 plays dealing with all aspects of African society, but mainly the clash between the traditional and the modern and the depredations of modern African leaders as in *Kongi's Harvest* and *Madmen and Specialists*. He has also done African versions of celebrated Greek plays. Soyinka is also in the front rank of world poets, demonstrating his mastery of both Western and traditional African techniques, as in *Idanre and Other Poems*. His novels *The Interpreters* and *Season of Anomy* are amongst the best of their kind. The first is a brilliant exposé of the decadence that characterizes modern Nigerian life, making use of techniques such as flashbacks and very powerful symbolism drawn from Yoruba mythology. The second is a compelling presentation of the horrors of the Nigerian Civil War and must be regarded as one of the first war novels.

The Francophones and modern African novel

Let us look at what was happening in the Francophone territories in the meantime. The Francophone writers were also intent on denouncing those who for one reason or other wished to disseminate an unfavorable picture of Africa or impose alien values and practices on the African continent. We have already seen the impact of Negritude in so far as poetry was concerned. To a certain extent the Negritude concept and drive influenced the Francophone novel as well. Oyono and Beti, for instance, ridiculed the French imperialist attempt to impose French values on black African peoples and exposed its futility. However, it was probably the Guinean novelist Camara Laye who was most effective in the glorification of traditional African life and the assertion of its validity. The glorification is certainly obvious in his first work, *The Black Child* (*L'Enfant Noir*), sometimes translated as "The African Child." This is an autobiographical work in which he shows the child growing up in the midst of a secure, supportive, dignified, and confident African environment. But Laye's masterpiece is the compelling *The Radiance of the King* (*La Radiance du Ro*). This is a densely textured work with layers of meaning and, according to some, suggestions of the influence of Kafka. In the novel a white man, Clarence, who has lost all his possessions through gambling, finds that the only way in which he could salvage his reputation and his financial and social position is to enter the service of the black African king. He discovers, however, that the process is not so easy and he must divest himself not only of his Eurocentric arrogance and feelings of superiority, but of all the cultural assumptions and baggage he had had before he found himself in the African country. Clarence is bewildered by this African environment which is quite overpowering. Laye presents the reverse of the usual situation where the white man imposes his values on the African or assimilates the African into a "superior" Western culture. It is the white man Clarence who ends up being worn down and assimilated into African culture, and the authenticity, superiority, and validity of that culture are asserted.

Presentation of the anti-imperialist struggle

African literature not only celebrated the clash of authentic African values and the alien values of imperialism, it also presented the strenuous struggle for liberation. This was particularly true of the literature emanating from the so-called "settler territories"; that is, the territories where the European colonizers settled and had no intention of ever leaving. These countries included Algeria, Kenya, Southern Rhodesia, and South Africa. In these countries the struggle for independence resulted in actual warfare, guerilla warfare in some cases, in which thousands of Africans lost their lives. The Kenyan novelist Ngũgĩ wa Thiong'o is particularly compelling in his presentation of the liberation struggle in his novels. Although in a novel like *The River Between* he presents the clash between indigenous African culture and the new Christian civilization that the missionaries wish to impose, his main concern is the presentation of the brutality, the cruelty, and the evils of the colonialists. He does this very impressively in novels like *Weep Not, Child* and *A Grain of Wheat*. He displays the heroism of the freedom fighters, but he also reflects the dilemma of some people who find it difficult to choose between joining the patriotic struggle and providing a secure future for themselves. He is aware of the contributions made by the missionaries, but also of the cruelty and depravity of some of the British administrators.

Ngugi is pivotal to the drive to assert an authentic African identity quite independent of any Western influences. One of his most famous works is the non-fiction *The Decolonization of the Mind*. In this work he shows that he is aware of the ways in which colonialism has sought to brainwash the African into accepting Western values and parameters for judgment and to turn his back on African ones. Ngũgĩ actually started writing under the name James Ngũgĩ since he had been given the Christian name James. However, he soon changed his name to the completely African Ngũgĩ wa Thiong'o. Inevitably, also, Ngũgĩ has played a leading role in the debate about the language in which African literature should be written. He could not see how Africans could use the language of the former imperialists. He himself had started his writing career by writing in English because that was the only way he could find publishers and reach a wide audience, even a wide African audience. But as his consciousness altered, he came to the conclusion that African literature should only be written in African languages. Therefore, his authorial practice now is to write in his native Gikuyu and then have his works translated into English.

Southern Africa

The struggle against oppression was much worse in Southern Africa, particularly in South Africa where apartheid had been institutionalized, and the situation of the African writer was deplorable. A good number of writers had to go into exile and those who remained were subject to censorship. This had a stultifying effect on literature. Nevertheless, the anti-apartheid drive helped to produce literature of a very high-quality by writers both outside and within South Africa. Particularly notable was the poetry of Dennis Brutus and Arthur Nortje and the novels of Alan Paton. But numerous other writers bravely strove to condemn the atrocities of the South African government and its philosophy of apartheid. These include Alex La Guma, Sipho Sepamla, Nadine Gordimer, J. M. Coetzee, and Ezekiel Mphahlele. It must be noted that although Gordimer and Coetzee were white and therefore not subject to the same restrictions as other writers, they too took up a courageous stance against the government and its apartheid policy. Dennis Brutus was particularly active in persuading Western nations to join the struggle against the South African government by imposing sanctions. Apartheid is now over, and literature is flourishing in South Africa. It is not surprising that two South Africans, Gordimer and Coetzee, have won Nobel Prizes for Literature.

Literature of social comment

It can be seen that African writers played an important role in the drive towards independence and autonomy and the struggle for liberation. As we have seen, independence did not bring the millennium that had been promised. In most of Africa the story was of economic collapse, abandonment of democracy, the rise of one-party regimes and brutal dictatorships, and the installation of military regimes. The lot of the common people, in particular, was most deplorable. Where did the African writer stand in this, the African writer who had been regarded as a sage, or as the conscience of the nation? African writers lived up to their expected role and took on the responsibility of acting as the conscience of the nation, lamenting, like Old Testament prophets, the corruption, incompetence, brutality, dishonesty, and fraud of the powers that be. They now presented us with what can only be called literature of social comment, literature presenting all aspects of a very grim reality. The African writers were saying, in fact, that the previous emphasis on the evils of European imperialism, on the clash between the traditional African and the new values of Western culture, and the resistance to imperialism and oppression had been done very effectively. Independence had been achieved. Some countries had been independent for 20 years and more and that was time enough for the leaders to have made a marked contribution to turning things around. The need now was to present the evils in contemporary African society. Africans should stop blaming the imperialists for all of the continent's evils and turn the spotlight on the shortcomings of Africa's present leaders.

Actually, the process had started as early as 1965 when Achebe published his *A Man of the People* and Soyinka published *The Interpreters*. *A Man of the People* is a hugely comic novel in which Achebe mercilessly exposes the corruption, incompetence, depravity, and decadence of the Nigerian ruling elite. With its publication, Achebe must have felt he had said all he wanted to say in the novel form, and he did not write another novel for more than 20 years. In the interval, however, much that was deplorable had happened in Africa. Economies had collapsed, democracy had been whittled down, and military dictatorships had sprung up all over the continent. Since Achebe was regarded as a sage, as the grand old man of African letters, people wanted to hear what he had to say about the new situation, so in 1987 he obliged with the publication of his fifth and last novel, *Anthills of the Savannah*. That too, is a satirical novel in which Achebe presents Nigeria under a brutal military dictatorship and examines the responsibilities of writers and intellectuals in the midst of a deteriorating situation. This shows that the social comment phase of African literature continued well beyond the mid-1960s and Achebe was central to this continuing concern.

Soyinka's seminal novel *The Interpreters* was published at about the same time as Achebe's *A Man of the People*. Here the satirical exposure goes beyond the arena of politics to include virtually every segment of society. It also includes such issues as the moral bankruptcy of the university academics, the stupidity of apparently successful businessmen, the refusal of some of the educated elite to accept their position and nature as Africans and their mindless aping of Western mannerisms and culture, and the intellectuals' lack of awareness of the role they have to play in bridging the gap between the worlds of the traditional and the modern. However, it is probably the Ghanaian Ayi Kwei Armah's *The Beautyful Ones Are Not Yet Born* (1969) that really set the tone for the African novel of social comment. It will be noted that in the title the word is "beautyful," spelt with a "y," not "beautiful." The title is taken from an inscription on a so-called "tro-tro," as those methods of transportation in Accra are called. The painter who did the inscription did not, apparently, know how to spell "beautiful." The title itself is therefore a comment on education in Ghana and the societal disparities and inequities that exist. Like Soyinka's *The Interpreters*, *The Beautyful Ones Are Not Yet Born* is a scathing denunciation of almost every aspect of Ghanaian society in the post-independence era.

The Francophone writers were generally not as involved with social comment as the Anglophones, but some of them still showed concern about the direction in which Africa in general was moving. Two of these were Aminata Sow Fall and Ousmane Sembène, both from Senegal. In the fascinating novel *The Beggars' Strike*, Fall shows her concern with the plight of the lowest in society. This is a masterly novel from a woman writer who is one of the most prolific of the Francophone writers. Ousmane Sembène is even more concerned with the plight of the ordinary people. Some regard him as the most impressive of the Francophone novelists. In an earlier novel, *God's Bits of Wood*, which some would regard as his masterpiece, he had presented the mobilization of the people into political consciousness just before the achievement of independence. He showed that he did not share the complacency with which some of the Francophone leaders approached the issue of liberation. His main point was that the masses in general were much more politically aware than their leaders. One can thus see that from the earliest stages of his career his emphasis was on the masses, and he shows this very powerfully later in novels like *White Genesis, The Money Order*, and *Xala*. In *The Money Order* he uses the framework of the penurious Ibrahim Deng's attempt to cash a money order to expose the backward bureaucracy, dishonesty, and fraud characteristic of society. Ousmane Sembène had been a trade union leader and had studied cinema in Russia. Both his background and his concern for the masses seemed to move him gradually in the direction of a Marxist reorganization of society. He also wanted to reach the ordinary people through his art, but realized that he could not do this through literature. He thus turned his attention to making movies and thus succeeded in having a tremendous impact. Most of his movies were made out of his novels, and he is generally regarded as the most impressive of the African movie-makers.

The Kenyan writer Ngũgĩ wa Thiong'o also turned his attention to social comment and, as is the case with Ousmane Sembène, there is evidence that he, too, started leaning towards a Marxist reorganization of society. He spent some time in Russia, and the result was the massive novel *Petals of Blood* which also shows concern for the plight of the ordinary people. These were the people who gave their blood for liberation and independence. However, they now see that the members of society who are prospering are those who made no sacrifices or were even collaborators with the oppressors. Society in general, in Ngũgĩ's view, is heavily organized against the ordinary man and woman.

The tendency towards social comment during this period is massively reflected in poetry, particularly in the poetry of writers like Jack Mapanje and Frank Chipasula from Malawi, Kofi Anyidoho from Ghana, Niyi Osundare from Nigeria, and Syl Cheney-Coker from Sierra Leone. It is also reflected in the drama. Indeed, one of the most important developments in post- independence African literature is the rise of vernacular drama; that is, drama in the indigenous languages. Just as Ousmane Sembène used the cinema to reach the audience of ordinary people, so some writers realized that in order to reach the masses they must use a medium other than the written word. The spoken word or the vernacular could be used very readily in the field of drama. Moreover, drama had a direct impact on the people and could, indeed, reach all classes of people, literate and illiterate, and have a direct and universal appeal. It could therefore be used very effectively in the area of social comment. In Sierra Leone, in particular, a whole new breed of writers like Dele Charley and John Kolosa Kargbo arose, making use of Krio and other indigenous languages to comment on all aspects of society's life, and the people responded as they had never done before to any literary genre. The downside of this trend was that governments became nervous because of its direct impact on the people and imposed censorship of various kinds that had a deleterious effect on the growth of literature.

The rise of the women writers

The most important literary development in Africa during the last quarter of the twentieth century was the rise of an impressive number of women writers. Up to this point in Africa, women had lagged behind men in literary creativity. There were a few female voices like Flora Nwapa from Nigeria, Ama Ata Aidoo from Ghana, Grace Ogot from Kenya, and Gladys Casely-Hayford from Sierra Leone, but otherwise the presentation in literature of the African experience was left almost entirely to men. However, these male writers were accused by women of failing to present the totality of the African woman's experience in their writings. They confined themselves, so the claim goes, to presenting stereotypes: the woman as mother, good-time girl or prostitute, and goddess figure. Even the Negritude writers fell into this trap because they presented an over-idealized picture of the African woman. Chinua Achebe and Wole Soyinka came in for special criticism for denying women their voices and failing to present the female perspective. Critics like Florence Stratton, for instance, suggested that the female presence in *Things Fall Apart* is almost completely muted. There was a need, therefore, for a more comprehensive and fuller presentation of the woman's voice and experience in African literature, and it would be up to women writers to do it. As from the seventies, therefore, the women writers rose to the occasion.

Tribute must be paid to Flora Nwapa who can be regarded as the first African female novelist. Her *Efuru* is a delightful novel which begins the process of setting forth the woman's point of view, especially with regard to attitudes towards badly behaving African men. Some would claim, however, that Nwapa was much too conservative. The new women writers adopt a completely different stance. Quite a few of them have no hesitation in exposing the evils of polygamy, which had been accepted for generations as one of the bulwarks of the African social system. They deplore the fact that male relatives, especially fathers, have the right to decide whom daughters and sisters will marry, even if this leads to disastrous consequences. They expose the irresponsibility of men who feel that their only familial responsibility is to father the children and that the provision for and upbringing of the children should be left almost entirely to the mother. They also present all kinds of women in their works: harassed working women like Emecheta's Nnu Ego who grows old prematurely looking after her family because her feckless husband is not up to the task; self-confident prostitutes like Saadawi's Firdaus who sees herself as being every bit as worthy as the middle-class men and women who secretly despise her; women who allow their fathers to walk all over them and lack the guts to resist like Adichie's Kambili; and women who are openly rebellious and resist the males' attempts to keep them in cages like Dangarembga's Nyasha.

The best known and the most effective new female writers include Buchi Emecheta of Nigeria, Nawal El Saadawi of Egypt, Tsitsi Dangarembga of Zimbabwe, Mariama Ba of Senegal, Bessie Head of Botswana, Chimamanda Adichie of Nigeria, and Yema Lucilda Hunter and Aminata Forna of Sierra Leone. In the novels of Emecheta the evils of polygamy are blatantly displayed. She also clearly demonstrates in *The Joys of Motherhood* that there are no joys in motherhood. In her other novels Emecheta skillfully uses the imagery of slavery to present the plight of women in African society past and present. One of her novels is actually entitled *The Slave Girl*, and in *The Joys of Motherhood* a female slave is actually killed and thrown into her mistress's grave because the mistress will not have a decent burial unless one of her slaves is killed and sent to the other world with her. Buchi Emecheta was also distinguished by the fact that she became an entrepreneur who set up her own publishing company and published her own books when she found out that her Western publishers were not willing to give her a good deal. We also see the irresponsibility of the polygamous husband in Ba's *So Long a Letter* when the protagonist's husband of 30 years decides to take a second wife who is about the same age as their eldest daughter. In Nawal El Saadawi's *Woman at Point Zero* we see men's brutality and irresponsibility compounded by the gender inequities of an Islamic state. Adichie's *Purple Hibiscus* presents the consequences on his wife and children of a despotic and fanatical father, while Dangaremgba exposes the stupidity and unfairness of the view that the brother should always be given privileges while the sister should only be prepared for marriage; that novel also shows what a male-dominated society can do to a rebellious woman. In her own novels, Bessie Head, for her part, presents the intersection between the politics of race and the politics of gender.

It should be clear that these African women writers are engaged with what can only be called feminist concerns. Yet most of them resent being referred to as feminists. The reason is that feminism is a dirty word in Africa. Many Africans see it as a movement of white middle-class American women who are out to secure power. African women cannot see themselves as being allies with white women against men. For one thing, the white women were themselves allied with white men as oppressors during the days of slavery and colonialism. African women fought with their men against white men and women during the days of oppression. The white woman was, in a sense, an enemy also. White women were also not very concerned with the plight of the rural black woman in Africa, or the underprivileged black woman. Moreover, unlike some white feminists, African women cannot turn their backs on childbearing and marriage. Children are sacred in African society and motherhood completes African women. African women cannot turn their backs on those aspects of their femininity. They have therefore evolved their brand of feminism which, while stressing the need for empowerment, freedom to choose their own husbands, equality of opportunity, equality of rewards, and liberation from traumas such as female circumcision, allows them the freedom also to choose to marry and to have children.

War literature

Given the number of civil wars in Africa during the latter years of the twentieth century it was inevitable that a war literature should develop, involving both the novel and poetry. This is also one of the most important literary developments in Africa during that period. We can see this, for instance, in Wole Soyinka's memorable poem "Massacre, October '66." We can also see it in some of the poems of the Sierra Leonean Syl Cheney-Coker, particularly in the volume *Stone Child and Other Poems*. It is in the novel form, however, that we see the most extensive treatment of war in Africa, and we can meaningfully talk of the African war novel. The African war novel seems to have three main purposes. Firstly, it seeks to make its own contribution to the history of the times. Years later, when historians seek to compile the historical record, they might consult, and are in fact consulting, novels which, even if fictional, make use of historical material and are excellent in the presentation of the background, atmosphere, and emotions that historical records cannot do by themselves. Secondly, the novelists wish to analyze the issues in order to get explanations and answers to questions such as how normal human beings could degenerate so badly that they behave worse than animals. Thirdly, the novelists wish to present the horrendous suffering endured by ordinary men, women, and children who, in some cases, did not even understand what the fighting was all about.

The earliest civil wars in Africa go back to the 1960s, and some of the war novels, therefore, go almost as far back. Chukuemeka Ike's *Sunset at Dawn*, which examines the Nigerian Civil War, is one of the earliest and is noteworthy for its objective analysis, which can also be seen in other novels on the Nigerian Civil War such as Elechi Amadi's *Sunset in Biafra*, Chimamanda Adichie's *Half of a Yellow Sun*, Wole Soyinka's *Season of Anomy*, and Isidore Okpewho's *The Last Duty*. Yema Lucilda Hunter's *Redemption Song*, one of the most poignant of the war novels, is admirable in its presentation of the suffering of ordinary families that are completely destroyed during the Sierra Leone Civil War. Delia Jarrett-Macauley and Aminata Forna, both from Sierra Leone, are also admirable in their presentation, not just of the suffering, but also of the process of recovery in *Moses Citizen and Me* and *The Memory of Love*.

Stylistic and thematic innovations

Contemporary African writers seem to have been liberated from the need to do certain things or follow certain trends. Each is following his or her own inclination. One of the most successful is the Nigerian Ben Okri, a winner of the Booker Prize. In his magnificent novel *The Famished Road*, he goes back to the African tradition and the world of spirits and fortune-telling to present a magical realist work that is, nevertheless, very relevant to the contemporary situation. Another Sierra Leonean, Aminata Forna, has, among other things, written a compelling novel, *Happiness*, that deals with the need to preserve the environment and advocates for human beings to come to terms and learn to co-exist with the other elements of the creation. Perhaps the most intriguing is the Ghanaian writer Benjamin Kwakye. His first novel, *The Clothes of Nakedness*, won the 1999 Commonwealth Writers' Prize for Best First Book, Africa Region. His second novel *The Sun by Night* is a gripping presentation of several trends in contemporary Ghanaian life, but it is also unique for its subtle use of the second-person narrative form, something that is quite rare in literature. His *Three Books of Shama* is one of those rare African works presenting the fortunes of Africans living in the United States. His other novels include *Legacy of Phantoms* and *The Other Crucifix*. Kwakje has also published at least two books of poetry. His *Scrolls of the Living Dead* is a masterly epic in verse form in which the poet demonstrates unrivalled technical virtuosity, leaving the impression of fluidity but also of tautness and discipline.

Four African writers have won the Nobel Prize for Literature: Wole Soyinka of Nigeria, Nadine Gordimer of South Africa, J. M. Coetzee of South Africa, and Naguib Mahfouz of Egypt. African writers have also won prestigious world prizes like the Booker Prize and the Commonwealth Writers' Prize. This suggests that there is every justification for placing African literature on the same pedestal as other world literatures such as English literature, American literature, and European literature.

References and suggestions for further reading

Allen, R. 1982. *The Arabic Novel: An Historical and Critical Introduction.* Syracuse, NY: Syracuse University Press.
Banham, M., E. Hill, and G. Woodyard (eds.). 1994. *The Cambridge Guide to African and Caribbean Theater.* London: Cambridge University Press.
Bascom, W. 1969. *Ifa Divination: Communication between Gods and Men in West Africa.* Bloomington, IN: Indiana University Press.
Beier, U. 1967. *An Introduction to African Literature: An Anthology of Critical Writing.* Evanston, IL: Northwestern University Press.
Blair, D. S. 1976. *African Literature in French: A History of Creative Writing in French from West and Equatorial Africa.* Cambridge: Cambridge University Press.
Brench, A. C. 1987. *The Novelists' Inheritance in French Africa.* London: Oxford University Press.
Collins, H. 1969. *Amos Tutuola.* New York: Twayne Publishers.
Fagunwa, D. O., and W. Soyinka. 1968. *The Forest of a Thousand Demons: A Hunter's Saga.* Camden, NJ: Thomas Nelson & Sons.

Finnegan, R. 1970. *Oral Literature in Africa*. Oxford: Clarendon Press.

Gakwandi, A. S. 1977. *The Novel and Contemporary Experience in Africa*. London: Heinemann.

Gikandi, S. 1987. *Reading the African Novel*. London: James Currey.

Heywood, C. (ed.). 1971. *Perspectives on African Literature*. New York: Africana Publishing.

Irele, A. 1990. *The African Experience in Literature and Ideology*. Bloomington, IN: Indiana University Press.

Jablow, A. 1961. *Yes and No! The Intimate Folk-Lore of Africa*. New York: Horizon Press.

Jahn, J. 1966. *A History of Neo-African Literature*. London: Faber.

Jahn, J. 1961. *Muntu: An Outline of the New African Culture*. New York: Grove Press.

Jones, E. 1973. *The Writings of Wole Soyinka*. London: Heinemann.

King, B. (ed.). 1972. *Introduction to Nigerian Literature*. New York: Africana Publishing.

Laurence, M. 1968. *Long Drums and Cannons*. London: Macmillan.

Lindfors, B. 1969. *Amos Tutuola and His Critics*. Los Angeles: UCLA, African Studies Center.

Lindfors, B. 1994. *Comparative Approaches to African Literatures*. Amsterdam: Rodopi.

Moore, G. 1970. *Seven African Writers*. London: Oxford University Press.

Moore, G. (ed.). 1998. *The Penguin Book of Modern African Poetry*. Harmondsworth: Penguin.

Ngara, E. 1982. *Art and Ideology in the African Novel: A Study of the Influence of Marxism on African Writing*. London: Heinemann.

Ngũgĩ's, wa Thiong'o. 1981. *Decolonizing the Mind: The Politics of Language in African Literature*. Portsmouth, NH: Heinemann.

Obiechina, E. 1975. *Culture, Tradition and Society in the West African Novel*. Cambridge: Cambridge University Press.

Okpewho, I. 1992. *African Oral Literature: Backgrounds, Characters and Continuity*. Bloomington, IN: Indiana University Press.

Owomoyela, O. 1979. *African Literature: An Introduction*. Waltham, MA: Crossroads Press.

Palmer, E. 1973. *An Introduction to the African Novel*. London: Heinemann.

Palmer, E. 1979. *The Growth of the African Novel*. London: Heinemann.

Palmer, E. 2008. *Of War and Women, Oppression and Optimism: New Essays on the African Novel*. Trenton, NJ: Africa World Press.

Roscoe, A. 1971. *Mother Is Gold*. London: Cambridge University Press.

Soyinka, W. 1976. *Myth, Literature and the African World*. Cambridge: Cambridge University Press.

Wanjala, C. (ed.). 1973. *Standpoints in African Literature*. Nairobi: East African Literature Bureau.

Wauthier, C. 1966. *The Literature and Thought of Modern Africa*. London: Pall Mall Press.

Conclusion

What are the prospects for Africa in the twenty-first century? What progress will the continent make towards sustained development, the eradication of poverty, and political stability? Many commentators suggest that the prospects are good although there will be many challenges. This optimism is largely fueled by the progress that many African countries have made during the last two decades. Quite a few African countries have been listed among the top ten or so fastest growing economies, and the gross domestic product (GDP) of most African countries has improved during the period. Africa still has an abundance of untapped natural resources that is attracting the attention of local as well as foreign investors. Progress has been made in important fields such as education, agriculture, and health. Most importantly, almost the entire African continent has moved back to some form of democracy and political pluralism as well as economic liberalization. The World Bank itself has asserted that Africa will be able to claim the twenty-first century (World Bank, x).

The prospects are therefore quite good, but there will, of course, still be many challenges. In spite of the progress that has been made poverty is still rampant in many African countries where hordes of people still live on less than a dollar a day; have no access to adequate health care, water supply and electricity, and housing; cannot afford a proper education for their children; and can only look forward to a comparatively low life expectancy. Although the GDP of most African countries has improved since the turn of the century, it has still not reached the level required for the elimination of poverty. To combat these will require vision, determination, and a sense of purpose, proper exploitation and use of resources, adequate planning, and willingness to become engaged in the world economic order.

The elimination of poverty will require several measures, some not very palatable. In the first place, it will require determined income redistribution. There is wealth in many African countries, but it resides in very few hands, in some cases, and the gap between the rich and the poor, who constitute the vast majority of the population in most cases, is extremely wide. There are many African billionaires, some of them among the wealthiest people in the world. Some of them could single-handedly make a significant contribution towards the repayment of their countries' debts. One recognizes that some of them achieved success through the astute utilization of their talents, but many gained their wealth through manipulation of the system. Without resorting to Marxist methods which have failed in the past, the tax structure, which is now quite ineffective in some countries, could be used to redistribute income and generate revenue that could then be devoted to development that all could benefit from. There will also have to be a determined effort at job creation. The rate of unemployment is too high in most African

DOI: 10.4324/9781003111733-16

countries. South Africa, which is supposed to have one of the best economies on the continent, still has an extremely high rate of unemployment, particularly among young black men, and this is a potential source of conflict. Job creation will also mean encouraging foreign investment, which means the conditions within these countries will have to be favorable to such investment. In this respect, African countries will have to walk a very tight line. They will have to provide favorable conditions for foreign investors, but they will also have to arrive at agreements to prevent the kind of foreign economic imperialism that used to obtain in the past. The Chinese are showing tremendous interest in participating in the African economy, particularly in the field of agriculture, but African countries cannot afford to replace Western imperialist dominance of their economies by the Chinese.

Loans and aid will still have a part to play. Recently, there has been hostility to the idea of aid because, as some argue, it undermines the concept of self-reliance. African countries have now accepted that, in order to promote sustainable development, they must rely on their own efforts to a large extent. However, there will still be room for aid, if only because the resources necessary for development will not always be available in every African country. Besides, the continent has been subjected to centuries of exploitation by European powers through the slave trade and imperialism, and it is only fair that these European powers give something back. Loans mean debt, and, from past experience, African countries have to be wary about increasing the debt burden. It will probably be impossible to avoid loans altogether, but African authorities as well as the donors will have to ensure that the loans are used for the intended purposes and they eventually generate returns that enable the debt to be repaid. At least the interest must be serviced in such a way that it does not jeopardize development. With regard to the existing debt, progress has been made towards forgiveness or reduction, and efforts in this direction must be intensified.

A determined effort must also be made to eliminate corruption, which is one of the leading obstacles to sustainable development. Corruption is still rampant in most African countries and many of the wealthiest people achieved their wealth through this route. It results in the bleeding of resources that could have gone towards development. The elimination of corruption will mean that such resources will be available, but it will also encourage both local and foreign investment. Some countries have established so-called "anti-corruption commissions," but these have been largely ineffective because they have not always had total government support. All African countries have to realize that sustainable development is not possible unless there is a brake on corruption.

African countries will also have to come to terms with the fact of a globalized economy and become adept at participating in it. This will involve heightened awareness of the importance of technology, particularly the use of information technology. Fortunately, there are signs that this is progressing satisfactorily all over the continent. Participation in a globalized economy will mean attracting investment by multinational companies, gaining access to the markets of former imperialist powers, and, most importantly, reaching out to the emerging markets in places like Asia and Latin America. Fortunately, all this is being done.

The unrelenting execution of recent programs and agreements like the Millennium Development Goals, the African Free Trade Area, the new Eco Zone, and Agenda 2063 is of the utmost importance. In the past, ambitious programs were drawn and goals set, but most of the countries failed to live up to them. If Africa is to claim the twenty-first century, she will have to achieve the goals set in these programs.

There are several other areas in which progress has been made but where there is still room for further development. Most African countries have made great progress in education since independence, but universal free primary education has not been achieved by all, there is still a shortage of qualified teachers, teachers are badly paid, and there is still great gender inequity in gaining access to education, particularly at the primary and secondary levels. This has to be rectified. Although the condition of women in Africa has improved considerably in recent years, much still has to be done. Much more attention has to be paid to women's health, to the laws regulating property ownership and, of course, to the vexed issue of female circumcision (or female genital mutilation). Progress has also been made in the area of healthcare, but there are still many areas with inadequately equipped hospitals and few doctors, and healthcare is extremely expensive. More attention also needs to be given to the incorporation of traditional medicine into national healthcare systems. And, of course, African countries need to get involved with the international community for the preservation of the environment and dealing with the implications of climate change.

Sustainable development and the eradication of poverty cannot be achieved without political stability, and it is to this area that Africa has to devote most attention. With the reaction against dictatorial regimes and one-party systems and the move towards democracy and political pluralism that happened largely in the nineties, people in some quarters thought that Africa had at last found an adequate political recipe. This optimism has not been fulfilled. It is true that seemingly democratic elections have been held in most countries, but in many cases the results have been contested, there have been allegations of rigging, and defeated governments have refused to hand over power. Countries in which there has been post-election turbulence include, Côte d'Ivoire, Mali, Kenya, Zimbabwe, Guinea, the Gambia, and Tanzania. Of course, there have been successes in places like Liberia, Sierra Leone, Botswana, and Ghana where there was a peaceful transfer of power from one party to another. This bodes well for the future, but the failures are there, nonetheless. The problem is the perennial one of groups not wishing to be away from the corridors of power and from the decision-making process indefinitely. The "winner takes all" concept does not seem to be working satisfactorily. Africa still has to devise a political structure that is democratic; that is, one that enshrines the one person, one vote concept and ensures that anyone who is qualified and wants to stand for election can do so, but also makes it possible for all of the crucial segments of the population to be represented in the decision-making process. The emphasis should be on inclusion, not exclusion. Until such a system is devised there will be problems with African elections leading to political instability, which will have a deleterious impact on progress and development. Africa is poised for success in the twenty-first century, but there are several issues that will have to be confronted.

Reference

World Bank. 2000. World Bank Africa Data Base 2000. African Development Indicators. CD-ROM. Washington, DC: World Bank.

Index

Page numbers in **bold** refer to figures, page numbers in *italic* refer to tables.

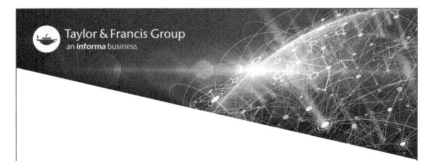

Made in the USA
Las Vegas, NV
11 August 2021